INSTITUTE OF ECONOMICS
AND STATISTICS
P OXFORD LA 3L
WITHDRAWN
Q 180.55
KU-548-500

Scientific productivity

Scientific productivity

The effectiveness of research groups in six countries

Frank M. Andrews, editor
Institute for Social Research, University of Michigan

Contributing Authors:

George Aichholzer
Frank M. Andrews
Joseph Bonmariage
Gerald A. Cole
Csaba Fajszi
Arpad Halász
Agnes Haraszthy
Y. de Hemptinne
Peter Hunya
Karin D. Knorr
Salomea Kowalewska
Edmond Legros
Roland Mittermeir
Rikard Stankiewicz
Veronica Stolte-Heiskanen
Lajos Szántó
Michel Vessière
Nicole Visart
George Waller

Cambridge University Press
Cambridge
London New York Melbourne

Unesco
Paris

Published by the Syndics of the Cambridge University Press
The Pitt Building, Trumpington Street, Cambridge CB2 1RP
Bentley House, 200 Euston Road, London NW1 2DB
32 East 57th Street, New York, NY 10022, USA
296 Beaconsfield Parade, Middle Park, Melbourne 3206, Australia

and by the United Nations Educational, Scientific and Cultural Organization
Place de Fontenoy, 75700 Paris, France

First published 1979

Printed in the United States of America
Typeset by Huron Valley Graphics, Ann Arbor, Michigan
Printed and bound by Vail-Ballou Press, Inc., Binghamton, New York

Library of Congress Cataloging in Publication Data

Main entry under title:

Scientific productivity, the effectiveness of
research groups in six countries.

Includes bibliographies.

1. Research. 2. Research – Methodology.
3. Performance. 4. Research – Europe.
I. Andrews, Frank M.
Q180.A1S35 507'.2 78-21978
Cambridge University Press ISBN: 0 521 22586 0
Unesco ISBN: 92 3 101599 0

Contents

Part 2: Organizational factors and scientific performance

Part 3: Methodological reports

Exhibits

Foreword by Unesco

The complexity of modern society and the sweeping changes that have occurred in everyday life over the past thirty years have placed new responsibilities on governments. The variety of concerns with which they are involved has increased enormously. Governmental programs exist today that were unknown even a decade ago. Other programs have expanded their responsibilities to take account of modern social wants and needs. Thus, the competition for resources has intensified greatly.

At the same time, citizens in many countries are asking for more public accountability. They want to know the use to which their resources are put, and they demand that the programs that receive support be both efficient and effective. In many countries, these concerns have been raised with particular reference to support of scientific and technological research. As a consequence, the importance of improving the productivity and the effectiveness of scientific research has been recognized.

More important perhaps, is that the gap between those countries with abundant financial and technological resources and those with fewer such resources will widen if some intervention is not undertaken. This has been obvious for many years, even prior to the initiation of the project reported in this book. The formal recognition of this situation occurred when the Declaration on the Establishement of a New International Economic Order was adopted by the General Assembly of the United Nations in 1974. An implication of the declaration is the need to make available to developing countries the methods and achievements of modern science and technology. Elucidating the means of engaging in effective scientific and technological research activities represents one of Unesco's contributions to this goal.

Meeting in 1976 in Nairobi at its nineteenth session, the Unesco General Conference, through Programme Resolution 2.01, reaffirmed "Unesco's front-ranking role and responsibility . . . for . . . the promotion . . . of scientific and technological progress (and) the encouragement of the application of scientific and technological advances to development," and authorized the Director-General "to place special emphasis on programmes in the field of science and technology aimed at . . . the building up and strengthening of institutional infrastructures." The work reported in this volume is thus part of Unesco's activities described in the foregoing resolution and in similar resolutions passed at earlier sessions of the General Conference.

In building a research team composed of people from a variety of national and institutional settings to undertake this work, Unesco consciously sought not only to encourage cross-national cooperation and fertilization of ideas, but to produce a work that, because of its origins, would be useful in many national and institutional settings.

The number of people and organizations that have made vital contributions to this International Study is very large. Clearly, the study could not have proceeded without the cooperation of the thousands of respondents who participted as members of the research units being studied, or without the dedicated work of the scores of people who collected and processed the data, or without the financial and institutional support of the sponsoring organizations in each of the participating countries. For this international cooperation and particularly for the valuable contribution of Dr. Frank M. Andrews, the scientific editor and one of the authors of this volume, Unesco wishes to express its gratitude. The members of the International Research Team that has been responsible for carrying out the study, all of whom are authors of chapters in this volume, are profoundly grateful for the many kinds of support that have been provided. It is the team's strong hope that the uses of the data and results – for both applied and theoretical purposes – will constitute a compelling justification of the resources and efforts that have been invested. Finally, it is appropriate to acknowledge the contributions of Dr. Michael Pesci, who for several years devoted his professional efforts to furthering this International Study.

The authors contributing to this volume have done so as individual professionals; neither Unesco nor the authors' employing institutions are responsible for the views and opinions expressed herein.

Preface

The nature of this book

This book reports results from The International Comparative Study on the Organization and Performance of Research Units. (For this study, a *research unit* is a cluster of scientists and technical support personnel working under single leadership, sometimes as a team, on a specific research or experimental development project.) Results from Round 1 of the study, involving data collected from over 11,000 participants in approximately 1,200 research units in six European nations, are presented here.

The study has had two broad purposes. One is goal oriented: to find ways to enhance the performance effectiveness of research units and of their members. The second is methodological: to develop and test methods for assessing the organization and performance of research units. Results relevant to both these purposes are described in this book.

Unesco initiated this study, under its Program of Science and Technology Policies, and has been responsible for its coordination. The design and implementation of Round 1 were carried out by a small international team of social scientists, natural scientists, and managers of research and experimental development (R & D). These are the individuals who wrote the chapters that follow.

As readers of this volume will quickly perceive, the interests of the authors are broad and varied. (There is a corresponding breadth to the International Study.) Each chapter is an independent presentation, the product of its own authors' interests, preferred analytic approaches, and professional judgments. With the exception of Chapters 1 and 2, which constitute the introduction to the book, there is no necessary or logical order among the chapters (indeed, within Parts 2 and 3 the sequence is alphabetical by the authors' national or international affiliation). However, although the chapters are independent presentations, they are not unrelated to one another: They share a common conceptual framework; they report analyses of a common set of empirical data; and they draw upon and refer to one another for complementary results and descriptive information.

Although each chapter will appeal to some readers, it is not expected that every chapter will interest every reader. Hence, to help readers find their way among the many topics discussed in this book, the following section describes the organization of the book and comments briefly on each of the chapters. The reader should also note that each chapter (except the first) concludes with a short summary or discussion of many of the key ideas, which can be used to help locate material of particular interest.

An overview of the chapters

The book is organized into three main parts. Part 1 consists of two chapters that introduce the background and purposes of the International Study and that describe the methods by which the Round 1 data were collected and analyzed. These chapters provide essential information that readers will need in order to fully understand the later chapters. Part 2 is made up of eight chapters that focus on relationships between various organizational factors and the performance effectiveness of research units and/or their members. Most chapters in this section begin by reviewing results obtained in previous investigations in scientific or other types of organizations and then proceed to extend this previous work through statistical analysis of the rich data from the International Study. Part 3 consists of four chapters with strong methodological orientations. These chapters focus primarily on issues of measurement quality, meaning, and procedures in the International Study, and link these issues to relevant prior research.

In Chapter 1, de Hemptinne and Andrews describe the considerations that led Unesco, within its program on Science and Technology Policies, to initiate the study; note some of the major design features of the project and ways it differs from previous research on R & D; summarize some of the broad trends of the statistical results that are reported in greater detail later in the book; and warn the reader about possible misinterpretations of the data.

Chapter 2 continues the introductory material by providing details about the design of the International Study. Described here are the sources of the data and the measurement procedures. In addition to laying the foundations for the analyses reported later in the book, Chapter 2 provides a brief but reasonably comprehensive description of a methodology that has proven helpful for studying the effectiveness of research units and that is now available for further development in future applications.

Chapter 3, by Knorr, Mittermeir, Aichholzer, and Waller, the first chapter in Part 2, selects one particular indicator of scientific performance – published written products (primarily articles) – and explores its relationships with a wide range of factors that might account for differences in individual and group productivity in academic and industrial research units. The social position of an individual within the social hierarchy of a research unit proves to be one important correlate of differences in performance at the individual level, and the size, age, and scientific exchanges of the research unit are additional factors that relate to group productivity.

Chapter 4, also by Knorr, Mittermeir, Aichholzer, and Waller, takes a different indicator of performance – ratings of a research unit's R & D effectiveness – and examines how this indicator of performance relates to selected organizational characteristics. A major conclusion is that the results from academic research units seem to be in accord with the "human relations thesis," that is, with the idea that good leadership leads to high group morale, and that high morale leads to increased productivity by group members. This chapter includes a brief discussion of how its results link to those presented in the preceding chapter.

Chapter 5, by Stolte-Heiskanen, examines the relationships between the levels of externally determined resources of research units (material resources, human resources, and information resources) and the rated performance of those units. Contrary to what some people would expect, the results show that satisfaction with resources, rather than objective resource levels, had the higher relationship to performance, and that of the several types of resources considered, human resources stood out as most significant.

Chapter 6, by Haraszthy and Szántó, is addressed to problems of research planning, with a particular emphasis on science policy planning in Hungary. Comparisons between Hungary and other countries participating in Round 1 of the International Study are presented for a number of variables relevant to the selection and completion of R & D projects by research units.

Chapter 7, by Kowalewska, was stimulated by some previous studies that suggest that the effectiveness of an organization may partly depend on the amount of influence different members have over decision making. Chapter 7 reports that results similar to those found in previous research emerge in the Round 1 data for the kinds of R & D performance more relevant in academic units, but that different results emerge for more applied aspects of performance.

Chapter 8, by Stankiewicz, explores relationships among the size, age, and effectiveness of research units. Drawing from previous studies of R & D, several competing hypotheses about these relationships are proposed and then tested in the Swedish data of the International Study. It is found that the hypotheses' applicability depends on several factors, including levels of group cohesiveness and characteristics of the group leaders. Although the chapter focuses exclusively on Swedish academic units, the key results have been replicated in the International Study's data from Austrian and Belgian academic units (according to a personal communication from Stankiewicz).

Chapter 9, by Visart, addresses the relationship between research-unit effectiveness and levels of communication within and between research units. The results show that higher levels of effectiveness tend to occur where there is more communication. The chapter details the particular indicators of effectiveness and communication for which this trend appeared, and other indicators where it did not appear, and explores numerous other characteristics of units that also relate to communication and effectiveness.

Chapter 10, by Andrews, investigates how the performance of research units relates to the motivation of their members and to the presence of "diversity" in the working environment of the unit. In accord with the results of previous research on R & D, a pervasive trend is found in the data of the International Study showing that higher-performing units tended to have more dedicated professional members with more diverse working roles and intellectual resources.

Chapter 11, by Bonmariage, Legros, and Vessière, the first chapter in Part 3, describes a methodological exploration of the ratings of research-unit effectiveness. With substantial reliance on the statistical technique of factor analysis, this chapter examines the extent to which the "meaning" and relevance of different performance measures varies across different types of research-unit settings and different types of raters.

Chapter 12, by Hunya, Halász, and Fajszi, describes a hierarchically oriented analysis strategy used by the authors in exploring the whole range of data collected in Round 1 of the International Study. Although the analysis procedure is rather different from that employed by other authors, in general it corroborates the results reported elsewhere in the book. One of the analyses that is unique to this chapter, however, is an examination of the relationships between R & D facilities and research-unit performance using data aggregated up to the country level.

Chapter 13, by Cole, details the theoretical and empirical considerations that led to the development of a scheme by which the research units of Round 1 could be classified into one of a small number of distinct types. This "typology" is based on distinctive patterns of research-unit performance (as identified through a multidimensional scaling technique) and proved strongly related to different patterns in the distribution of influence over the work of the unit. The typology plays an important role in the analyses performed by many of the other authors contributing to this volume.

Chapter 14, by Andrews, develops estimates of the quality of the rated-effectiveness measures using a structural modeling technique. Numerical estimates are presented for the portion of each measure's variation that is valid (i.e., estimated to reflect "true" differences), that is attributable to correlated errors, and that is attributable to random error. The chapter also discusses the implications of these estimated quality levels for the observed relationships reported in other analyses in this book.

Authors' addresses

Because the authors contributing to this volume are independently responsible for their respective chapters (within broad limits overseen by the editor), because some readers may wish to contact particular authors, and because the authors are widely scattered across eight countries, it seems desirable to list here the mailing addresses (as of early 1978) for those whose names appear first on each chapter.

Frank M. Andrews, Institute for Social Research, University of Michigan, Ann Arbor, Michigan 48109, U.S.A.

Joseph Bonmariage, Belgian Archives for the Social Sciences, Batiment SH2, B–1348 Louvain-la-Neuve, Belgium
Gerald A. Cole, Institute of Public Policy Studies, University of Michigan, Ann Arbor, Michigan 48109, U.S.A.
Agnes Haraszthy, Group for Science Organization, Hungarian Academy of Sciences, V Munich Ferenc u. 18, Budapest 19, Hungary
Y. de Hemptinne, Division of Science and Technology Policies, Unesco, 75700 Paris, France
Peter Hunya, Jate Laboratory of Cybernetics, Jozsef Attila University, Aradi Vertanuk tere 1, 6722 Szeged, Hungary
Karin D. Knorr, Institute for Advanced Studies, Stumpergasse 56, A–1060 Vienna, Austria
Salomea Kowalewska, Institute of Philosophy and Sociology, Polish Academy of Sciences, ul Nowy Swiat 72, 00–330 Warsaw, Poland
Rikard Stankiewicz, Research Policy Programme, Lund University 8, 22–362 Lund, Sweden
Veronica Stolte-Heiskanen, Institute of Sociology, University of Helsinki, Franzeninkatu 13, SF–00500 Helsinki 50, Finland
Nicole Visart, Division of Science and Technology Policies, Unesco, 75700 Paris, France

Acknowledgments

A general acknowledgment of the many kinds of support that have contributed to this International Study appears in the concluding portion of the Foreward. In addition, many of the individual chapters of this book include acknowledgments to persons and organizations that made particular contributions to work reported in that chapter. Here, however, it is appropriate to acknowledge contributions to the actual processing of the manuscript for this book that have been made by Gregory A. Marks and Verna Yarrington: Their advice and skills have been of great help to the editor.

Frank M. Andrews, editor

Part 1. Introduction

1 The International Comparative Study on the Organization and Performance of Research Units: an overview

Y. de Hemptinne
Division of Science and Technology Policies, Unesco, Paris
Frank M. Andrews
Institute for Social Research, University of Michigan, Ann Arbor

1. Research on research and development

The need for an international and cross-cultural study of the performance-effectiveness of scientific research and experimental development (R & D) arose during the early 1960s out of Unesco's program of assistance in the field of science policymaking and research organization. Although the industrialized nations witnessed an exponential growth of R & D outlays during that period, and did not worry too much about the effectiveness of their ongoing research activities, nations that had barely reached the stage of political independence increasingly turned to Unesco for advice on how to reap maximum developmental benefits from the limited scientific and technological research capabilities that many of them had inherited from colonial times. Increasing their expenditures for R & D often was economically unfeasible, or exceeded the absorptive capacity of their available scientists and technologists.

So, the idea of taking a hard look at the performance-effectiveness of national R & D systems naturally came to the fore.

Since 1971, an International Research Team (IRT) of natural scientists, social scientists, and research managers has worked together with Unesco program specialists and outside consultants in order to: (1) delineate the problem and its possible approaches, (2) develop a well-defined methodology of work, (3) test this methodology in several countries with well-developed national R & D systems (six volunteer countries of Europe), and (4) propose modifications of the methodology based on results of these tests.

Although Unesco's initial motivation arose from the practical need of enhancing the performance of R & D through the improvement of its managerial environment and organizational setting, the International Research Team soon made the decision to go far beyond a mere testing of the traditional "rules of thumb" that have until now governed the planning, management, and logistics of scientific and technological research. The group committed itself to the ambitious hope of significantly extending a new field of research: the scientific management of R & D.

The methodological path chosen by the International Research Team was based on the procedures of modern empirical social science, and included hypothesis formulation, construction of measuring instruments, collection of data in standardized ways from large and heterogeneous populations of R & D personnel, and subsequent multivariate analysis of these data. This approach was well suited to the two major goals of the undertaking: description and prescription. With respect to *description,* it seemed important to develop a methodology that could broadly and accurately describe the current state of a complex R & D system. With respect to *prescription,* it was intended that the methodology, when suitably applied, would yield new knowledge of basic scientific relationships that could help guide science policymakers and R & D managers toward more effective and efficient ways of organizing research and development activities.

The purpose of this collective book is to present the international readership interested in the management of R & D with some of the scientific and methodological results that have emerged in the recent work of the International Research Team. The book is based on the analysis and interpretation of data collected in Round 1 of the International Study – the first major application of the methodology in six European countries.

In presenting the first results of the study in this book, the International Research Team is fully conscious of the fact that the new field of "research on research" is at an early stage of development. Fortunately, the way in which the International Study was designed permits an open-ended deployment of further effort, both by Unesco and by the international scientific community.

A separate methodological guidebook, describing in detail the recommended procedures for subsequent applications of the methodology developed by the International Research Team, is also being published by Unesco.[1] This guidebook is addressed to science policymaking bodies and research institutions of those countries that may wish to launch–or to repeat–such a study on the performance of research units either on the whole of its national R & D system, or on a subset of research units selected therefrom.[2]

An attractive possibility for such future surveys is to design them right from the start to be fully compatible with the methodology that has been adopted by Unesco.[3] This permits the gradual building up of international, accessible, and cumulative archives, the raison d'être of which lies in the possibility of making international comparative analyses on the performance-effectiveness of research units as related to the organization of R & D and to the managerial practices adopted by different countries. It may also lead to the development of new theoretical concepts and approaches concerning the performance of research, the validity of which could be tested by reference to the archived data.

2. Some distinctive features of the International Study

Distinctive, and in some ways original, features of this Unesco-coordinated International Comparative Study on the Organization and Performance of Research Units include the following:

1. In harmony with the line of thought that evolved in the early 1940s and culminated in new conceptual approaches to human activity (such as control, communication, and cybernetics), it was decided to recognize purposeful *systems* as the new organizing concept of science-in-the-make, that is, of R & D.

2. Goal-seeking systems were defined as a set of interrelated elements that can display choice of either objectives or resources (or both). For the purpose of this study, Unesco selected–for a variety of reasons that later turned out to be generally valid–the lowest formal organizational grouping of research scientists and technicians–that is, the *research unit*–as the basic structural element of R & D systems. It was also decided that the R & D systems would be artificially limited, because of purely policy-making and managerial considerations arising from the principle of national sovereignty, to the set of research units belonging to a given nation, that is, the focus would be on the *national R & D system* (or a selected subset therefrom). This, of course, does not deny the essentially international character of modern science–and in some respects of technology also–whose basic characteristic of universality remains firmly founded on evidence arising out of verifiable experiment and observation.

3. The boundaries of the system – short of a worldwide managerial utopia – have thus been chosen to coincide geographically with sovereign nation-states, not so much from the point of view of the objectives of the system, as from that of its resources in manpower, finances, information, and material base, which together form its manageable input.

4. As a consequence, Unesco contracted the appropriate science and technology policymaking organizations of the six European countries that volunteered to participate in the International Comparative Study. The contractual agreements included five basic conditions:

(a) that the contracting organization would select and finance the work of a national research team responsible for the scientific aspects of the study; and that the national team leaders of the six countries, together with the responsible program officers of Unesco and the international consultants, would form the International Research Team (IRT) entrusted with the design and management of the study;

(b) that a sample of approximately 200 research units per country (roughly 1,000 research scientists and technicians per country) would be approached by the interviewers of the national research teams in order to collect their answers to the international survey questionnaire, which was prepared under the aegis of Unesco with the assistance of front-ranking specialists in modern survey research, of scientific researchers, and of research managers;

(c) that the replies collected from individual scientists and technicians would be treated in complete confidentiality, in particular with respect to the hierarchy of the institutions to which they belonged and to the sponsoring science and technology policymaking organization of the country concerned;

(d) that the members of the International Research Team would adopt a common methodological approach for data management, statistical calculations, and multivariate analyses to be performed on the collected data; and

(e) that a complete set of *anonymized* data (cleaned to prevent the identification of individual respondents and single research units) would be made generally available through Unesco by depositing them, after an embargo period of two years, in archiving centers that volunteered for the task and were agreed upon by the International Research Team.[4]

5. The two-year embargo period on the survey data allowed the members of the International Research Team to analyze their own national data and to compare them with those of the other

participating countries. This book, based on these explorations, is thus a collection of selective and mutually complementary analyses prepared by the members of the International Research Team.

6. The publicly archived survey data will allow further research on the performance-effectiveness of R & D by sociologists of science and R & D management specialists throughout the world. Moreover, national research teams belonging to countries that subsequently join the International Comparative Study under contractual association with Unesco will have at their disposal a set of baseline data permitting immediate national and international comparisons; they, in turn, will contribute their national data to the growing international archives of the study.

7. Given the rather modest scale of previous empirical research on R & D, Round 1 of the International Study is distinctive for both the magnitude of its data base and the breadth of its international perspective. With information from approximately 10,000 respondents regarding characteristics of over 1,200 research units in six nations, the study considerably extends the scope of empirical research on the organization and performance of R & D systems.

8. Moreover, the structure of the data (and of the data files) is such that *multilevel* analyses are both useful and feasible. Because the data were collected from several members of the same organizational entity – the research unit – and because many of the specific pieces of information concern that entity, it is logical to consider the data at both the respondent level and the unit level. Although much of the previous research on R & D processes and on R & D management has focused on individual scientists and engineers, sometimes within a laboratory setting, the conceptualization of R & D as the *collective* activity of a particular group has been much less common.

3. Theoretical and practical foundations of the study

The theoretical and practical foundations of the approach adopted for the International Comparative Study derive from several sources. These include: (1) the theoretical perspectives of cybernetic modeling and systems analysis; (2) the concepts and findings from previous research in the fields of organizational psychology, sociology of science, sociology of organizations, creativity, and research on R & D; and (3) the experience gained from the continuing efforts of Unesco's Division of Science and Technology Policies to respond to the needs of national policymaking, planning, and program budgeting in the field of science and technology.

The study seeks to identify and assess the importance of numerous organizational, environmental, and other input factors that influence the performance-effectiveness of research units. Furthermore, critical to the effectiveness of national R & D systems as a whole are such questions as the following, which the study also seeks to address: (1) How do the basic structural elements of national R & D systems, that is, the research units, interact and work together, both within and across the boundaries of these systems? (2) What is the role and influence on the performance of research units of the higher organizational echelons within national R & D systems – such as the institutions and organizations to which the research units belong, and the national policymaking bodies concerned with science and technology? (3) What are the significant elements in human behavior and perception of situations that affect or reflect creativity and efficiency in the performance of R & D? (4) How do research units respond to the goals and purposes they are supposed to serve, or to the functions they are expected to perform?

Much preparatory work went into sharpening up the concepts underlying the performance and effectiveness of research units. Policymakers and planners dealing with R & D at all levels of government or private enterprise are naturally interested in maximizing output for given levels of input. But this cannot be reduced to simple economic cost–benefit analysis, as has been clearly shown during the past decades. Other factors nowadays increasingly come to the foreground when evaluating the performance of research units, such as product quality and originality, the applicability and social impact of R & D results, and – last, but not least in the minds of research scientists – the professional recognition and prestige accruing from breakthroughs in science or technology. Taken together, these perspectives have suggested a broader assessment of research-unit performance, and hence the study has explored total performance-effectiveness from a broad range of qualitative as well as quantitative reference points.

As is described in greater detail in Chapter 2, the dimensions of the criteria of effectiveness include recognition, extent of applications, social utility, general contribution to scientific or technological knowledge, plus effectiveness measures concerning R & D proper, training, and the management of the research work itself. Actual counts of such R & D products as books, articles, patents, and prototype devices are also available.

The social and organizational factors assessed by the study that might influence or relate to the performance of research units can be grouped into the following broad categories: R & D activities; research methods; scientific exchanges and contacts with other units; evaluation methods; planning of the work and choice of research themes; availability of resources; amounts and patterns of influence; supervision; remuneration and career advancement; working climate; and numerous demographic variables such as age, experience, staff size, staff turnover, institutional setting, and scientific discipline. The analytic possibilities posed by this rich array of information are vast, and the analysis-oriented chapters of this book, which provide a first exploration of the material, certainly do not exhaust its potential.

4. Some general findings from the study

Although this is not the place to present detailed summaries of statistical results, it may be useful to briefly sketch some of the general trends in the analyses that have been conducted to date. The kinds of trends we wish now to emphasize are those that emerge when one synthesizes the results of many individual specific analyses. These specific analyses are described in subsequent chapters of this book or in other studies for which examples will be cited.

One of the most important general findings of this International Study is that the R & D process seems to be responsive to *similar* psychological, social, organizational, and structural factors whatever the particular national setting (among these six countries) in which research units happen to be located. Although significant differences appeared in the survey data between the participating countries as regards R & D management practices, organizational settings, and climate of work, the *relations* that emerged between these factors and the performance of research units tend to show the same directional patterns. Furthermore, the major relationships observed in the present data from European countries tend to be consistent with findings from previous research on R & D, most of which has been conducted within the United States of America.[5] This cross-national replicability of major trends is, we believe, of major significance in that it opens the way for the development of a basic science of research-on-research that can be widely and generally applied for science policy purposes and the management of R & D.

A second general finding has to do with the criteria of R & D performance. The study confirms the International Research Team's expectation that the performance-effectiveness of research units is a multidimensional concept, encompassing a variety of distinct aspects. Although it is tempting to think of research units as falling somewhere along a simple good–bad or effective–ineffective dimension, the data show that this is a much too simplistic conception. On the contrary, units that "look good" by some criteria may–or may not–rate highly on other criteria.[6] Furthermore, the factors that predict to high levels of certain kinds of effectiveness are frequently different from the factors that predict to high levels of other aspects of effectiveness. Of course, this is not to say that all research units "average out" to be equally effective. Rather, it leads to the conclusion that if one wants to understand and/or enhance the performance of R & D units, one has to be clear about the particular aspects of performance that are of primary concern.

A third general finding has to do with the kinds of factors that showed notable relationships to various aspects of effectiveness. These include sociological characteristics (e.g., a person's position in the social system of the research unit), organizational characteristics (e.g., the size of a research group), social-psychological characteristics (e.g., communication between research scientists or between research units), psychological characteristics (e.g., scientists' morale, motivation, and satisfaction with supervision and with resources), and various characteristics of the way the technical work itself is planned, configured, and conducted.[7] Whereas the demonstration of a relationship between factors such as these and certain aspects of performance does not prove that a causal connection exists, the identification of such relationships opens up numerous possibilities for ways in which research-unit effectiveness, *might* be enhanced through improved management techniques.

A fourth general finding, related to what has just been described, is the rather consistent and somewhat surprising *absence* of notable relationships between indicators of economic or physical resources and the effectiveness of research units. The reasons for this lack of relationship are not completely understood, but it seems quite clear that once the resource base is sufficient to keep a research unit viable (and hence eligible for inclusion in a study such as this one), there is no necessary linkage between material endowment and quality of research performance. In short, a unit can be poor but make great contributions–or be rich but ineffective. Although no one expected a tight linkage between resources and quality, the apparent absence of any linkage, if this continues to appear in further analyses, holds great import for science policy.[8]

A fifth general finding is of a more methodological kind. Although many notable relationships have already been identified in the data from the International Study, almost without exception they tend to be of rather modest strength. Several considerations converge to suggest that one should *not expect* massively strong relationships (and should be highly suspicious of any that appear) between any single characteristic of research units and performance: (1) The effectiveness of research units is almost certainly determined by *many* factors; hence, no one factor by itself will account for a large part of the variation between units in effectiveness. (2) The actual data about research-unit characteristics and performance provide only imperfect indications of the true characteristics and performance levels. There is no reason to believe that the quality of measurement in the International Study is unusually poor – on the contrary, the use of standardized instruments and data-collection procedures, and of broadly based performance indices (described in Chapter 2), almost certainly enhanced the quality of the measures. Nevertheless, it would be naive to assume that the data are totally without error or bias.[9] (3) The performance measures developed by the International Research Team probably depend only *partially* on the organizational, managerial, and psycho-sociological variables that have been assessed in the present study. Some members of the International Research Team gradually developed the feeling that independent variables, differing in kind from those tested during the Round 1 surveys, played a significant part in the performance-effectiveness of research units. These factors are probably linked with the cognitive structure of modern scientific thought and are usually somewhat loosely referred to under the concept of intuition. In any event, such a line of research seems worthy of further exploration, with appropriate and distinct methodological tools.

5. Possible misinterpretations

Readers and those who analyze these data in the future should be cautioned regarding possible misinterpretations of statistical results. The modest size of the important relationships, just discussed, combined with several subtle aspects of the structure of the data, require considerable sophistication when dealing with this material. The following points should be borne in mind:

1. The finding of a statistical relationship between X and Y (e.g., morale and performance) does not prove that X causes Y. Although this might be the case, it is also possible that Y causes X, or that both X and Y are influenced by other factors.

2. In the data of the International Study, one important set of *other factors* that has consistently emerged is the institutional setting and disciplinary orientation of the research unit (which have been jointly taken into account in the typology of research units described in Chapter 13 and used in many of the other chapters). For many analyses it has proved inappropriate and misleading to combine units of different types without first taking account of the typological differences between them.

3. A second other factor is Country.[10] Whereas the economic, cultural, and social differences between countries may in part account for the relationships that Country shows to many other variables in the study, another part of the apparent "Country effect" is nothing but a methodological artifact. This artifact results from differences among countries in the types of research units that are represented in the study. (Chapter 2 provides further details.)

4. A third other factor is the type of respondent. As expected, heads of research units, staff scientists, and technical support personnel all tended to report somewhat different experiences. In recognition of this, the answers from these groups have been kept separate. This separation, however, leads to a more subtle effect: Because the answers of each person responding to a questionnaire are somewhat influenced by that person's particular perceptual style and biases, and because the answers from different types of respondents have been kept separate, the data of the International Study tend to show greater relationships between answers from the *same* type of respondent than between answers from *different* types of respondents. Such effects are clearly visible in many of the analyses reported in this book (e.g., Chapters 5, 7, 9, 10, 11, and 14), and should be recognized–as some authors do–as being at least partly artifactual.

6. Concluding comments

A number of remarks ought also to be made at this stage concerning the evaluation and prediction of R & D performance-effectiveness in general, and about the future development of the study methodology in particular.

With regard to the need for maximizing the output from national investment in R & D, it is certainly rewarding to the humanist that one of the major conclusions that emerges from the study points to the primary importance, for the performance-effectiveness of research units, of the competence and personality of the unit head, *together* with the satisfaction of the unit members vis-à-vis the quality and sufficiency of its human resources. Financial resources are not to be reckoned as number one in the national investments in R & D.

Hence, crude cost–benefit analysis applied as a tool to evaluate the performance-effectiveness of research units also appears – from this point of view – both simplistic and inadequate. The main reason for the inadequacy of cost–benefit analysis probably lies in the nature of R & D itself, whose effectiveness is not a continuous and linear function of capital input. Indeed, the action of R & D on the progress of science and technology has a more random and catalytic nature: Sudden breakthroughs occur at unforeseen intervals, and these may in some ways be compared to genetic mutations. The output of such processes – when they occur – is a hundred- or thousandfold out of proportion to the input. In short, one cannot utilize classical cost–benefit analysis techniques to evaluate the performance-effectiveness of research units (or research projects), except perhaps if applied at a macroscale involving large numbers of units, in which case aggregative probabalistic approaches might be warranted.

The way of attacking the evaluation and prediction of performance-effectiveness of research units presented in this study does not rely on cost–benefit analysis or other input–output techniques, but rather involves determining the optimum organizational, managerial, and psycho-sociological conditions for successful R & D, and therefore appears more rewarding and closer to reality. Above all, this approach gives policymakers and research managers a whole set of indications concerning how to act on important variables that relate to R & D performance. This subtler and more flexible approach is in our view more appropriate for dealing with intellectual work, and more respectful of human dignity.

True enough, the merits of this new approach go together with a restriction that may be a cause of concern to some research managers: The strict confidentiality of the replies made by the research scientists, engineers, and technicians of the research units surveyed by the present method does not permit *direct* evaluation of a given unit's performance-effectiveness. Quite to the contrary, the method relies on *indirect* evaluation of a unit's performance by comparing the existing conditions and situational parameters of the unit concerned with the profile of similar units that perform best. Corrective action can then be taken by people at all levels of the organizational hierarchy, including by individual scientists and technicians interested in raising their own performance-effectiveness and, as a consequence, that of the unit to which they belong.

The present method of performance evaluation is thus fundamentally based on the *confidence,* by those occupying leading positions in R & D management, that self-corrective action will be exerted by the heads of research units and by bench researchers in order to improve their performance-effectiveness as a team. This brings to the fore the paramount importance of the *feedback procedures* by which the results of a survey of research-unit performance are disseminated. In addition to making the results available to the top management of research institutions and to those in charge of national science policy, it is important that the results be fed back to the heads and members of the research units that participated in the study. Such feedback procedures may usefully include a series of seminars and informal meetings organized by, and including as participants, those specialists who carried out the survey and analyzed its results.

Looking ahead, beyond the immediate and practical needs of assessing the performance and effectiveness of research units, one cannot avoid reflecting on the crucial problem of mankind's future, whose doomsday through civilization collapse has been adumbrated by many a futurologist working on the basis of present-day (and constant) knowledge in the field of science and technology. Pioneering research and experimental development, by increasing mankind's power to control and decisively influence the course of events, may radically change mankind's present predicament. Nothing, then, seems so urgent as making this possible, in particular by encouraging worldwide support of scientific and technological research, and by searching for ways and means of making this quest for knowledge as productive and effective as possible. Faith in mankind's future is inseparable from the sense of hope that must be nurtured in the minds of the upcoming generations. But this hope must not be just a passive hope; as the French saying goes, "Aide-toi, et le Ciel t'aidera."

References

Cheng, J. L., 1977, *Organizational Coordination, Integration, Interdependence and Their Relevance to Research Unit Effectiveness: A Comparative Study,* Ph.D. dissertation, University of Michigan, Ann Arbor.

Pelz, D. C., and Andrews, F. M., 1966, *Scientists in Organizations: Productive Climates for Research and Development,* New York, Wiley.

Pelz, D. C., and Andrews, F. M., 1976, *Scientists in Organizations: Productive Climates for Research and Development* (revised ed.), Ann Arbor, Institute for Social Research, University of Michigan.

Notes

1. This monograph, tentatively titled *Survey Research Techniques as Applied to the International Comparative Study on the Organization and Performance of Research Units,* and scheduled for release by Unesco during 1979 in the series "Science Policy Studies and Documents," provides detailed recommendations on procedures for sampling, data collection, computer file construction, and the like. Inquiries should be addressed to The Director, Division of Science and Technology Policies, Unesco, 75700 Paris, France.

2. Such subsets may be delineated in any of several ways: e.g., geographically, or according to a sector of the national economy such as industry, agriculture, health, education, etc., or according to the type of institution to which the research units belong–universities, academies of science and research councils, government research laboratories, etc.

3. At the time this was written, such studies were being conducted in India and Poland.

4. At the request of the scientific directors of the six national research teams that took part in Round 1, the data collected during Round 1 have been archived by the Unesco Secretariat at the Belgian Archives for the Social Sciences (BASS), Batiment J. Leclercq, Place Montesquieu 1, Louvain-la-Neuve, B-1348 Belgium, under BASS study number 7511. Under the archiving contract signed between Unesco and BASS in 1975, BASS has the responsibility for distribution of the data and subcontracting with other archives. One such distribution contract is being developed with the Interuniversity Consortium for Political and Social Research (P.O. Box 1248, Ann Arbor, Michigan 48106, U.S.A.)

5. For an extensive example see Pelz and Andrews (1966, 1976).

6. Chapters 2 and 11 are particularly relevant to this observation.

7. In addition to analyses in this book that address these topics (all the chapters in Part 2), an investigation by Cheng (1977), conducted on the archived data from Round 1 of the International Study, is also relevant.

8. One of the original goals of the International Study was to find factors that might explain differences between research units with respect to their *efficiency*–i.e., factors that would account for differences in effectiveness *after* taking into account the material resources that had been invested in the unit. The general lack or relationships between material resources and effectiveness required that this particular goal of the study be abandoned and cast real doubt on the usefulness of applying an "efficiency" criterion to R & D units. Details on the lack of relationship between objective material resources and performance appear in Chapters 5 and 12.

9. Chapter 14 provides some empirical estimates of measurement validity.

10. Throughout this book, when a word or phrase refers to the name of a specific variable, the initial letter is capitalized.

2 The International Study: its data sources and measurement procedures

Frank M. Andrews
Institute for Social Research
University of Michigan, Ann Arbor

1. Introduction

This chapter describes the data sources and measurement procedures of the International Comparative Study on the Organization and Performance of Research Units. The chapter provides methodological information that is basic for all of the chapters that follow. Furthermore, in describing the procedures developed for the study, the chapter contributes to one of the central goals of the undertaking: Summarized here are many of the key aspects of a methodology that has proved both feasible and helpful for studying the effectiveness of research units and that is now available for use and further development in future applications.

In addition to this brief introduction and a concluding summary section, the chapter includes four other main sections. Section 2 describes the nature and sources of the extensive body of empirical data that were collected during Round 1 of the International Study and on which this book is based. Section 3 details the procedures of data collection. Information on the sampling of research units, and on data collection and processing, appear here. Section 4 describes the construction of certain measures that play central roles in later analyses. This section briefly describes the development of a typology used to classify research

Although this chapter was written by the editor, and he alone is responsible for its content, the procedures and methods it reports reflect the collective work and decisions of the entire International Research Team. I am grateful to my fellow team members for their comments on a draft of this chapter.

units into five distinct groups. This section also presents basic information about the performance measures, that is, the measures of research-unit effectiveness that are used as dependent variables in many of the later chapters.

2. Nature and sources of the data

The six countries

Data of Round 1 of the International Study come from six countries: Austria, Belgium, Finland, Hungary, Poland, and Sweden.

A number of considerations influenced which countries participated in Round 1. The relatively *well-developed state of the scientific establishment* in each of these countries was one factor. A methodology that was intended to tap the functioning of research units and of national R & D systems needed to be developed and tested in countries where such systems were well established. A second consideration was that the *medium size* of these countries made the pursuit of this task at a national level somewhat easier than would have been the case in countries with larger or more elaborate scientific systems, such as the USA or the USSR. Third, the socio-political systems and scientific traditions of these countries, when considered together, are very *heterogeneous* and thus permit an unusually broad test of the general applicability of any statistical results that emerge. A fourth consideration was *geographic proximity:* Because the process of developing a new methodology required frequent and significant collaboration among those conducting the study, facilitation of travel and communication was important. Fifth, these were countries with the *necessary resources* for active participation, that is, a group competent to perform the research, financial resources to support it, and a willingness to be involved. Finally, the *interest* of the countries themselves in participating in the project was a prerequisite. The fact that the project involved the cooperative, international development of a general methodology for conducting research on R & D was only one of a number of factors that led these countries to be interested in the project. Another important outcome for most countries was the descriptive information the study generated about selected portions of that country's own scientific establishment.

The two levels: research units and respondents

By basic design, the International Study is oriented primarily toward assessing the organization and performance of *research units.*

However, because much of the data about research units comes from their individual members, many analyses can also be conducted on the respondents as *individual scientists or technicians.*

The term *research unit* designates any of a number of different forms of collective entities that produce research or experimental development. In many cases, the entity is a cohesive research *team,* but in other cases it might be a more loosely federated cluster of individuals.

The fundamental observation that led to a focus on research units was that significant modern R & D is generally (but not always) conducted by *groups* of individuals. Furthermore, most modern R & D is supported and administered through some form of organization that focuses on clusters of people, not on single individuals. Given that most R & D output is the joint product of several minds, and of complementary skills and efforts, it seemed reasonable to examine directly the entity that is the actual producer of research and/or development. Although there have been several major studies on the performance, productivity, or creativity of scientists considered as individuals, there are no previous major studies of research units.

Criteria for identifying research units. For a group of individuals to be regarded as a research unit, it had to meet the following criteria: (1) The group had to have at least one recognized leader who was significantly involved in its work. (2) The group had to include a total of at least three people (including the leader) who were significantly involved in its work, and each of these people had to have been a member of the group for at least half a year. (3) The group had to have an expected life span of at least one year. The notion of *significant involvement* (in criteria 1 and 2 above) was operationalized through the definition of a *core member:* one who devotes at least eight hours per week to the work of the unit and who has communication (direct or indirect) with the unit leader(s) at least once each month. Thus for a group to be considered a research unit, it had to have at least three core members – a leader and at least two other people.

It may be noted that these criteria require the presence of a recognized and active leader, and impose certain minima on size, involvement, and duration. It was recognized that these criteria would exclude very small and/or very short-lived R & D undertakings from the study, and this was intentional: The social and organizational factors on which the study primarily focuses have only marginal relevance for very small or short-lived undertakings. However, in line with the observations sketched above, it was expected that most of the more significant R & D activities carried out within the modern world would be conducted by groups of individuals who met the criteria for a research unit, and who would thus fall within the purview of the International Study.

In an elaboration of the research unit concept, it was noted that the boundaries of a research unit might not match those of a formal entity within the R & D organization.[1] Whereas the group of individuals who constituted a research unit *might* appear as a separate unit on a formal organizational chart, several alternatives were also suggested.[2] One was that several distinct research units might be contained within a single formal group. Another was that the research unit might be composed of individuals from several different formal groups within a single organization. Still another possibility was that the research unit might consist of individuals from two or more different organizations.

The definition of a research unit adopted for the study permits inclusion of some quite small clusters of individuals. For example, one professional with two part-time technical support people could qualify. However, in most cases the research units actually present in the data were somewhat larger than this, with typical units consisting of four to seven professionals and several technical support individuals.[3] The definition, however, does not exclude large units (so long as they are not themselves composed of smaller units)[4] and a few units included as many as 30 to 40 individuals.

Round 1 of the International Study obtained data from 1,222 research units, approximately 200 in each of the six countries.

The five types of respondents

Data about research units in Round 1 were provided by five different types of respondents, each of whom answered a questionnaire designed especially for individuals in his or her particular role. These five respondent types were: unit heads (the questionnaire sent to them was designated SA), other professional members of the unit (i.e., staff scientists) (SB), technical support personnel in the unit (TS), unit administrators (RU), and external evaluators (EV). (The questionnaire codes for the respondents appear at various places in this volume and in the documentation of the data.)

Over 11,000 questionnaires were completed for Round 1 of the International Study. As described in more detail below, in general for each research unit there are one SA and one RU questionnaire, and several SB, several TS, and several EV questionnaires. On the average, there are about 9.3 questionnaires for each research unit in the study.

Several considerations led to the decision to seek information about the research unit from multiple sources: (1) Of course, some types of information can be better supplied by a person in one role than by someone in another role. For example, the unit head was expected to have the best knowledge about the factors that influenced the choice of the research projects being pursued by the unit. Conversely, staff scientists and technical support personnel were the most appropriate for answering questions about perceptions of supervisory behavior. (2) Beyond the sheer matter of who has the needed information was the consideration that research units, like most social groups, are multifaceted entities and as such may have different appearances even to people in the same role. As a consequence, it seemed important to obtain information from *several* staff scientists and/or technical support people (if the composition of the unit made this possible). It is entirely possible that two staff scientists (or two technical support persons) might give different but equally valid answers because their experiences within the research unit were different. The same can be argued for evaluations of performance: Individuals might disagree with regard to a unit's effectiveness because they were acquainted with different aspects of its work. (3) Finally, even where several individuals describe exactly the same phenomenon, there is an advantage in obtaining separate, independent assessments from different individuals because this permits "averaging out" some of the personal biases, differences in frames of references or expectations, and other sources of potential discrepancies, and thereby yields somewhat more dependable measurements.

Unit heads. Because all units, by definition, must have at least one recognized leader, every unit should have data from at least one SA questionnaire. (Because an early assessment suggested that very few units had more than one head, it was decided not to try to obtain data from the "second" head if such existed. Later analysis supported the wisdom of this decision as only about 10% of units had more than a single leader.)

Staff scientists. Data from one or more staff scientist (SB) questionnaires may or may not exist, depending on whether staff scientists were present in the unit. If one, two, or three staff scientists meeting the definition of a core member (given above) were part of the unit, separate questionnaires were to be answered by each one individually; if more than three were affiliated with the unit, data were to be obtained from *at least* three.[5]

A total of 2,835 staff scientists contributed data to Round 1 of the International Study, an average of 2.3 per research unit. Of the 1,222 research units included in Round 1, less than 5% have no data from any staff scientist, about one-quarter have data from 1 staff scientist, another quarter have data from 2 staff scientists, somewhat more than one-third have data from 3 staff scientists, and roughly 10% have data from 4 or more staff scientists.

Technical support persons. The same selection procedures just described for staff scientists were also followed for technical support personnel, that is, data were collected from all such persons (who met the criteria of being core members) up through three, and from *at least* a randomly sampled three if the unit included more than three.

A total of 2,257 technical support personnel responded to Round 1 questionnaires (an average of 1.8 per research unit). About 15% of the 1,222 research units have no data from any technical support person, about one-quarter have data from 1 such person, another quarter have data from 2 such people, still another quarter have data from 3 such people, and the remainder (about 10%) have data from 4 or more.

Research administrator data. Every unit was to be described by data from one (and only one) RU questionnaire. This questionnaire was completed by the unit's administrative person if such a person were part of the group; if there was no administrator, the RU questionnaire was completed by the head of the unit.

External evaluators. The external evaluators were professional scientists or engineers, or persons in senior administrative or policy positions, who were familiar with the work of the unit. Names and addresses for external evaluators were gleaned from a number of different sources, including lists provided by unit members themselves.[6] The external evaluators were invited to participate in the study by the national research team that was conducting the International Study in that particular country, and they were assured that their evaluations would be kept confidential.

Each external evaluator received a copy of the EV questionnaire and assessed the work of one or more research units on a set of standard scales (described in Section 4 of this chapter). The external evaluators reported general familiarity with the work of the unit before being asked to make assessments, and the option of answering "unable to reply" or "not applicable" was available for each of the specific quality dimensions.

Ratings from 3,885 external evaluators are included in the Round 1 data, an average of 3.2 per research unit. These are distributed across the units as follows: About 10% of the units have data from no external evaluators, approximately 12% have data from 1 evaluator, about 17% have data from 2 evaluators, about 33% have data from 3 evaluators, about 12% have data from 4 evaluators, and the rest (approximately 15%) have data from 5 or more (ranging up to 15) evaluators.

Because the external evaluators were recruited from many diverse sources, it cannot be said that they represent any particular population. Nevertheless, they do constitute a heterogeneous set of observers, external to the research unit itself, whose evaluation of the effectiveness of the unit promised to be of some interest.[7]

3. Sampling of research units and data-collection procedures

Selection of research units

The selection of research units to participate in the International Study was made by sampling from all units in certain predetermined subpopulations. In technical terms, the units constitute a multistage, stratified, probability sample that, within each separate country, is expected to be representative of certain subpopulations of units. However, because it was decided not to sample from all subpopulations, the units are *not* representative of all units in any given country, nor in all six countries together.

Definition of subpopulations. Subpopulations of research units, from which later sampling occurred, were defined on the basis of the following three characteristics of the units: Country, Type of organization, and Scientific field. We describe each in turn.

1 *Country:* This includes the six countries that participated in the study.
2 *Type of organization:* This refers to the nature of the organization in which the research unit was located and includes the following major categories:
   (a) academic organizations and those closely affiliated with academic organizations;
   (b) national research organizations, for example, academies of science;
   (c) cooperative research organizations serving a sector of production, industry, or public service;

(d) research laboratories of productive enterprises;
(e) contract research institutes and all others.

3 *Scientific field:* This refers to the field of science in which the unit was active and is based on the proposed *International Standard Nomenclature for Fields of Science or Technology,*[8] which classifies scientific fields into a hierarchical system. Examples at a global level include: mathematics, chemistry, agricultural sciences, medical sciences, psychology. Examples at a more specific level (falling within the more global categories just mentioned) include: algebra, analytical chemistry, forestry, pharmacology, social psychology. At this more specific level, the nomenclature lists several hundred scientific disciplines.

Selection of subpopulations. The sample design, as finally implemented, involved a mixture of collaborative and independent decision making among the six participating countries. There was an understanding that each national research team would survey approximately 200 research units in its country. Furthermore, it was agreed that within each participating country subpopulations of research units would be defined on the basis of jointly considering the units' Type of organization and Scientific field, and that the research units to be surveyed would be selected by representative probability sampling from certain of these subpopulations. Decisions about the particular subpopulations within which sampling was to occur, however, were made by each national team, taking into account the kinds of units that existed in the country, national interests, and the opportunities for cross-national comparisons.

The first of these factors, existence of units, needs little explanation: Some potential subpopulations (e.g., forestry units in academic organizations) might not exist in every country, and the kinds of research units that existed had to be considered.

Consideration of the second factor, the interests of the authorities that sponsored the study within a given country, helped to ensure that the results, when finally obtained, would be of interest to those within the country and that financial support to complete the study would be forthcoming. Interests of sponsoring authorities varied considerably from country to country. In one country there was a strong interest in data from research units associated with private industry (i.e., from productive enterprises); in another, the primary interest was in academic units; in still others, the interests ran along disciplinary lines (e.g., in units doing research in biochemistry).

The third factor, potentials for cross-national comparisons, represented a collaborative attempt to effect at least a partial knitting together of what otherwise might have been very disparate choices of subpopulations of research units. The constraints imposed by the first two factors still left some choice of subpopulations, and where possible each national research team agreed to choose subpopulations that matched those chosen in other countries. An attempt was made to ensure that if units of a particular scientific discipline were to be studied in one country, then units active in that same discipline would be studied in at least one other country.[9]

Sampling of research units. Once subpopulations had been selected within each country, the process of sampling units could begin. In every instance an attempt was made to achieve a representative sample of the given subpopulation, but the sampling procedures necessarily varied from country to country and depended on what information was available. In some instances reasonably complete and up-to-date lists of all research units had been compiled for other purposes and could be used to draw a systematic probability sample. In other instances no lists of units existed, but the needed lists could be assembled through consultation with appropriate national and local authorities. In still other instances a two-stage sampling procedure was used: A list of *institutions* was assembled and sampled, then lists of *research units* were constructed in consultation with the leaders of the selected institutions, and finally units were selected by sampling from these institution-specific lists.

Given the diverse ways in which research units were sampled, and the substantial variation in the sizes of the subpopulations from which sampling occurred, it is not possible in a short space to provide full information regarding sampling or response rates.[10]

What the research units represent. Although the representative aspects of the units included in the International Study may be of considerable concern to those interested in descriptive information for particular countries, this is not a primary concern of most of the analyses reported in this book. The authors of the chapters that follow have chosen to regard the 1,222 units included in the Round 1 data simply as a *set of heterogeneous units drawn from a variety of national, disciplinary, and organizational settings.* The diverse nature of these settings is explicitly recognized in many of the analyses by the use of one or more control variables that tap differences that can be attributed to Type of organization, Scientific field, and/or Country. What the authors have *not* done, and what several explorations have suggested is not needed (so long as the above sources of differences are controlled), is to be greatly concerned with precise representations of the specific subpopulations from which research units were originally sampled.[11]

Even when the data are viewed simply as a heterogeneous set of research units, rather than as precisely representing some larger population of units, it is of considerable interest to know the nature of the units that are present. Exhibit 2.1 shows how the units are distributed on the three major variables that guided the original selection of units. One can see that each of the six participating countries is represented by roughly one-sixth of the units, slightly more (20%) for Austria, and slightly less (12%) for Sweden. With respect to the types of organizations from which units were selected, slightly more than half the units (57%) were in academic organizations, roughly one-fifth were in cooperative institutes, and another one-fifth were in productive enterprises (mainly private industries); national research institutes, such as academies of science, and private research institutes contributed relatively few units to the Round 1 data. The units are distributed broadly across scientific fields with the larger concentrations being in the technological sciences (28%),[12] chemistry (20%), the life sciences (18%), and the agricultural sciences (10%); mathematics, astronomy, physics, the earth and space sciences, and the social sciences are also present in smaller proportions.

Relationships among Country, Type of institution, and Scientific field. Given the way research units were selected, there are some substantial relationships within the data among Country, Type of institution, and Scientific field. Examples include: (1) the scientific fields of units from productive enterprises are heavily concentrated in the technological sciences; and (2) the Swedish units are all from academic institutions. These relationships, and many others that could be cited, result from a mixture of two effects – the actual characteristics of research units in the six countries that participated in the study, and the particular choices made by national teams regarding the subpopulations of units to be sampled (choices which, as described above, varied from country to country). Separating these two effects in the Round 1 data would not be a simple matter and has not been attempted in the analyses reported in this book.

What has been done (as described later in this chapter) is to develop a five-category typology of research units that is able to represent many of the statistical effects attributable to Type of institution and Scientific field. In many of the succeeding chapters, the authors have replicated their analyses within the sepa-

Exhibit 2.1. Distribution of the Round 1 research units by Country, by Type of organization, and by Scientific field

Countries	N	%	Type of organization[a]	N	%	Scientific field	N	%
Austria	244	20	Academic organizations	694	57	Mathematics	13	1
Belgium	193	16	Academies, etc.	45	3	Astronomy	6	—
Finland	219	18	Cooperative organizations	257	21	Physics	77	6
Hungary	222	18	Productive enterprises	217	18	Chemistry	240	20
Poland	192	16	Private institutions, etc.	9	1	Life sciences	215	18
Sweden	152	12				Earth, space sciences	69	6
			Totals	1,222	100	Agricultural sciences	125	10
Totals	1,222	100				Medical sciences	57	5
						Technological sciences	345	28
						Social sciences	75	6
						Totals	1,222	100

[a]See text for more complete descriptions of categories.

rate categories of this typology and/or have used an adjusted version of the performance measures (also described later in this chapter) in order to eliminate the possibility that spurious effects attributable to Type of unit might influence their results. Similarly, many authors have replicated their analyses separately within each country in order to check for cross-national comparabilities. Although these kinds of procedures meet the needs of most of the analyses presented in this book, it must be recognized that there are some research questions for which the Round 1 data cannot provide answers because of the way the selection of research-unit subpopulations has affected the overlaps among Country, Type of institution, and Scientific field.

Data collection and processing

As described in Section 2 of this chapter, the information about the 1,222 research units surveyed in Round 1 of the International Study came from questionnaires completed by five types of respondents. Each type of respondent received a different questionnaire, but these different questionnaires included overlapping portions. Organizational and individual characteristics assessed in the questionnaires included the following: remuneration and advancement, R & D activities, research methods, scientific exchanges and contacts with other units, evaluation methods, choice of research themes and planning of the work, working climate, availability of resources, patterns of influence, supervision, plus various demographic characteristics of the unit itself and of its individual members. (All the major questions included in any of the questionnaires, and an indication of what questions were included in which questionnaires, appear in the Appendix to this volume.)

The development of the questionnaires required approximately two and a half years, during which time two substantial pilot tests were conducted and final questionnaires were produced in nine languages (English, Finnish, Flemish, French, German, Hungarian, Polish, Spanish, and Swedish).

The first of the two pilot tests took place in Belgium, Austria, Spain, and Sweden, and involved administration of questionnaires to approximately 100 respondents in 20 research units (5 units per country). The second pretest was more extensive, involving more than 1,500 respondents in about 160 research units (about 40 each in Austria, Belgium, Spain, and Sweden). A quota system was used in selecting research units to participate in this second pretest to ensure that the test would be applied to a widely heterogeneous set of units.[13] These pretests provided important information regarding the feasibility of the general approach, the effectiveness of particular question wordings, the time requirements of each of the questionnaires, and numerous other matters that enhanced the effectiveness of the Round 1 data collection.

The data of Round 1 of the International Study were collected during the first part of 1974 in the six countries and from the five types of respondents described in Section 2 of this chapter. Standard field procedures called for a preliminary visit by one or more members of a national research team to each institution that was to participate in the study. At this time, the cooperation of the institutional leaders was solicited and arrangements were made for data collection. Subsequently, members of the national research team returned to the institution to administer questionnaires and, in some cases, to conduct personal interviews. Data were collected from heads of units and from administrative officers (if any) using either a personal interview or a self-administered questionnaire approach, depending on local circumstances. Staff scientists and technical support personnel usually received self-administered questionnaires, often preceded by a meeting in which an interviewer introduced the study and answered general questions. Even when questionnaires were self-administered, arrangements were made to have an interviewer available to answer whatever specific questions might come up. In most cases, external evaluators received and returned their questionnaires through the mail. Guarantees were made to *all* respondents that the information they provided would be kept confidential.

Prior to collecting the Round 1 data, interviewers received training in appropriate field procedures for this particular study, and a core guide for interviewers was available to guide this training and subsequent activities during the actual data collection.

Once collected, the data were checked (edited) for completeness and legibility, punched onto cards, and built into a series of files. These files were then further checked for wild codes and consistencies, and then matched, merged, and aggregated to derive unit-level data.[14]

Because the unit-level data include certain aggregations of the information collected from individual respondents, it will be helpful to consider briefly the exact nature of the information that describes each research unit. Each unit-level information record contains approximately 1,200 basic variables, plus at least 70 additional derived indices. The roughly 1,200 basic variables come from the following sources:

1 identification variables (Country, Type of institution, etc.): 5 variables.
2 data about the unit obtained from questions in the RU questionnaire (addressed to the unit's administrative officer): about 90 variables.
3 data about the unit obtained from questions in the SA questionnaire (addressed to the head of the unit): about 230 variables.
4 data about the unit derived by aggregating answers provided by one or more staff scientists (i.e., from SB questionnaires). Most questions in the questionnaire addressed to staff scientists yielded four types of information after the aggregation process: (a) the *number* of staff scientists who had answered a given item, (b) the arithmetic *sum* of their answers to the item, (c) the *average* (mean) value of their answers to the item, and (d) the *variation* among their answers to the item (assessed by the standard deviation).[15] There are about 670 such variables derived from staff scientists' questionnaire responses.
5 data about the unit derived by aggregating answers provided by one or more technical support members of the unit. The same four types of data described above for the staff scientist (i.e., counts, sums, means, and dispersions) were also derived by aggregating answers to the TS questionnaires. There are about 190 such variables.
6 data about various aspects of the unit's performance derived by aggregating answers from the several external evaluators who assessed that unit. The same four types of data described above for the staff scientists were also derived by aggregating answers to the EV questionnaires. There are about 50 such variables.

The 70-plus indices associated with each research unit include different versions and combinations of the performance measures, which are described in Section 4 of this chapter.

Of course, the data-management procedures required to check and assemble this very substantial amount of information were themselves rather complex and cannot be fully documented here. Details regarding the procedures are described in a methodological monograph intended for future implementors of the International Study (Unesco, forthcoming).

4. Assessment of unit types and of unit performance

A typology of research units

Because research units located in different types of institutions and/or active in different fields of science operate in very different ways, it was necessary to find ways to cluster units into relatively homogeneous groups. Chapter 13 describes the detailed analyses that led to the construction of a five-category typology of research units (henceforth designated simply the Typology). However, because the Typology has played a fundamental role in the analysis of much of the data, and because it was used to produce an adjusted form of the measures of research-unit performance (described below in this section), it seems wise to provide a brief description of the Typology here.

The Typology classifies units into one of five categories based on the unit's Type of institution and Scientific field (both of which have been discussed in Section 3 of this chapter). After considerable exploratory analysis, the five categories of the Typology were defined as follows:

1 units located in academic institutions and pursuing research in the natural and exact sciences;
2 units located in academic institutions and pursuing research in the medical or social sciences;
3 units located in academic institutions and pursuing research in the applied or technological sciences;
4 units located in cooperative R & D institutions that serve a sector of production, industry, or public service; and
5 units located in research laboratories of productive enterprises and pursuing research in the applied or technological sciences.

The analysis that led to this particular definition of the Typology was an examination of patterns of research-unit performance. For example, units in academic settings tended to be rated substantially higher with regard to Training effectiveness than units in industrial labs; but the latter tended to rank higher on Applications effectiveness. Similarly, units pursuing research in the medical or social sciences tended to score relatively high in their output of published documents, whereas units pursuing research in the technological sciences tended to outperform others with regard to production of patents and prototype devices. Of course, differences such as these were not surprising, and they merely reflect expected differences in the purposes for which the research units were formed, and well-known precedents and traditions that characterize different scientific disciplines. Nevertheless, if allowed to persist in the data, these differences could have seriously influenced the statistical results; hence, it seemed desirable to find a means by which they could be controlled.

The actual formation of the Typology proceeded as follows: (1) Based on each unit's institutional setting and scientific field, it was assigned to one of 35 possible institution/field combinations. (2) Mean performance profiles (i.e., average scores for each of 10 different performance measures) were computed for each of the 35 institution/field combinations. (3) The similarities among the average performance profiles were examined, and it was found that 5 reasonably distinct and conceptually meaningful clusters could be identified. (4) These 5 clusters became the categories of the Typology. Thus the Typology groups together certain institution/field combinations that showed similar *patterns* of performance.

For many purposes, the 5-category Typology is much simpler to use than the full set of 35 combinations from which it was derived, yet various analyses have shown that for many variables the five categories of the Typology have nearly as much explanatory power as the more extensive set of 35. Furthermore, it has been found that this Typology, derived on the basis of patterns of *performance,* is strongly related to patterns of *influence and decision making* within research units. This latter result suggests that the Typology reflects similarities and differences among units that are of much wider functional significance than might be guessed merely from its pattern-of-performance origins.

The reader is referred to Chapter 13 for further details on these analyses.

Exhibit 2.2 presents some basic descriptive data about the distribution of the 1,222 research units in the Round 1 data on this Typology and indicates how the Typology relates to Country. From the exhibit one may see that the Belgian and Swedish units are, relative to other units in the Round 1 data, disproportionately from academic settings (note that the Swedish units come *only* from academic settings); that the Finnish, Hungarian, and Polish units are more likely than those in other countries to have been located in cooperative organizations; and that the Austrian and Finnish samples include relatively heavy concentrations of units from productive enterprises. A closer look at the first three categories of the Typology, all of which involve units from academic organizations, shows that applied science academic units are present in roughly similar proportions from each country; but that the medical and social science academic units occur only among the Belgian, Hungarian, and Polish units; and that exact and natural science academic units, although present in data from each country, are disproportionately present among the Swedish units. As noted in Section 3 of this chapter, these disproportionalities in part reflect the particular subpopulations that each country chose to study.

Measurement of research-unit performance

Basic considerations. Because the performance – that is, the effectiveness – of research units is one of the matters of fundamental interest in the International Study, considerable efforts have gone into measuring this concept. Several different types of mea-

Exhibit 2.2. Distribution (percent) of Round 1 research units by Typology and Country

Typology	Austria	Belgium	Finland	Hungary	Poland	Sweden	Total
1. Academic organizations, exact and natural science	38	46	18	42	24	80	39
2. Academic organizations, medical and social sciences	0	27	0	10	20	0	9
3. Academic organizations, applied sciences	14	11	14	8	16	20	14
4. Cooperative organizations, various sciences	11	5	34	26	40	0	20
5. Productive enterprises, applied sciences	37	11	34	14	0	0	18
Total	100	100	100	100	100	100	100
Number of units	(244)	(193)	(219)	(222)	(192)	(152)	(1,222)

sures have been constructed, and within each type there are measures of several different aspects of performance, and (where it seemed reasonable to do so) these are based on information collected from several independent sources.

The construction of performance measures proceeded from the assumption, amply confirmed in subsequent analyses, that research-unit performance is a multidimensional concept. In other words, it was presumed that there are different, and somewhat independent, aspects to be considered when assessing the effectiveness of a research unit. Although a few research units might be strong with respect to many aspects of performance, and a few might be generally weak, much more common would be units that were strong in some respects and weak in others.

A second fundamental assumption was that it was important to include both quantitative information about a unit's performance, such as counts of various types of outputs, and also more qualitative ratings by informed individuals regarding its effectiveness. The fact that the two types of assessments provide different information about performance has been extensively documented in the past (e.g., Pelz and Andrews, 1966). Furthermore, many observers have noted that some "good" units may not be prolific producers, and that the copious work of some other units may be of only moderate or low quality. These past statistical results and observations were also confirmed in the data of the International Study.

A third assumption, also supported by the data, was that even those people who reported being well informed about a unit's work might disagree to some extent about its quality, and that, hence, it was important to obtain performance ratings from a number of different individuals and from individuals who could be expected to view the work of the unit from a number of different perspectives.

These considerations led the International Study to seek performance information of two types (quantitative and qualitative), from three sources (unit heads, staff scientists, external evaluators), regarding about 30 different criteria. Exhibit 2.3 portrays the original data–56 measures in all–that were subsequently combined and aggregated to produce a final set of 10 basic performance indicators.

The sections that follow briefly describe the analytical steps that led to the 10 basic performance measures that have been most heavily used by members of the International Research Team.[16] It should be stressed that the analyses were performed over a period of years by various members of the team, that a

Exhibit 2.3. Sources of original information about research-unit performance

Counts of outputs by the unit		Ratings of performance by the unit			
			Rated by		
Product[a]	Reported by unit head	Quality[c]	unit head	staff sci.	ext. eval.
Books	x[b]	Productiveness	x	x	x
Original articles published within unit's country	x	Innovativeness	x	x	x
Original articles published outside unit's country	x	R & D effectiveness	x	x	x
Patents or patent applications within unit's country	x	Training effectiveness	x	x	x
Patents or patent applications outside unit's country	x	Effectiveness for non-R & D objectives	x	x	x
Algorithms, blueprints, flow-charts, drawings, etc.	x	International reputation	x	x	—
Published reviews, bibliographies	x	Demand for publications	x	x	—
Internal reports on original R & D work	x	Social value of work	x	x	x
Routine internal reports	x	Usefulness	x	x	x
Other written products	x	Success in meeting quality requirements	x	x	x
Experimental prototypes of devices, instruments, etc.	x	Success in meeting schedules	x	x	x
Experimental materials such as fibers, plastics, etc.	x	Success in staying within budget	x	x	x
Prototype computer program	x	General contribution to science and technology	x	x	x
Audiovisual materials	x	Application of research results	x	x	—
Other undocumented products	x	Use made of development activities	x	x	—

[a]See question R in the Appendix to this volume for exact wording of each item.
[b]An "x" indicates that data were obtained from source given at head of column.
[c]See questions S and T in the Appendix to this volume for exact wording of each item.

series of intermediate and exploratory measures were constructed that are not described here, and that this chapter does not attempt to comprehensively document all the development work that has taken place. Although the measures described below constitute a set that has proved useful for the intended purpose, these measures are not the only ones that might be constructed from the rich information that is available. (Chapters 11 and 14 describe two methodologically oriented analyses relevant to the meaning and quality of the performance evaluations.)

Composite output measures. Three composite measures of the research unit's output were constructed from information provided by the unit head regarding the number of various types of products produced by the unit during the previous three years. The three composite output measures are: Published written products, Patents and prototypes, and Reports and algorithms. The original variables from which these measures were constructed appear in the lefthand portion of Exhibit 2.3.

It was no surprise to find that nearly all the original output variables showed highly skewed distributions. There were many research units that had produced none or just a few of a particular type of output, and relatively few units that had produced many of that product. The skewed form of the distributions reflected both the fact that some products were of low relevance for some of the units (a result of the intentional heterogeneity of the sample), and the well-known phenomenon that even where a product is relevant for a set of units there tend to be more low producers than high producers.[17] Although the skewed distributions were expected, they would have complicated later analyses. Accordingly, the original variables were transformed by a bracketing procedure to reduce skews.[18] The transformed output variables still reflect most of the original information regarding the ranking of units with respect to production of a particular output, but the actual number of outputs is not retained.

The next step in the derivation of the output measures was to examine the cluster structure of the transformed original variables. A series of analyses were performed using factor analysis and several techniques for nonmetric multidimensional scaling, and using (as input to these techniques) various statistics that made alternative assumptions about the data. The results suggested that 3 reasonably distinctive types of products were represented among the answers to the original 15 output questions. These were:

1 Published written output, represented by:
    number of books published in the country
    number of articles published abroad
    number of articles published within the country
    number of published reviews and bibliographies
2 Patents and prototypes, represented by:
    number of patents abroad
    number of patents within the country
    number of prototype devices, instruments, etc.
    number of experimental materials

3 Reports and algorithms, represented by:
  number of internal reports on original R & D work
  number of algorithms
  number of routine reports

On the basis of these results, it was decided to construct three composite output measures by combining a research unit's three-year production of the products indicated above. (This left four of the original output questions unused – because the type of output being assessed was too rare or too nonspecific: prototype computer programs, audiovisual materials, other written products and other undocumented products.)[19]

Because it was felt that the products within each of the clusters were of unequal scientific importance, it was necessary to determine a set of weights to use in the combination process. (For example, it was felt that a unit ought to receive more credit for publishing one book than for publishing one article.) After considering seven different possible methods for determining appropriate weights, and actually implementing two that seemed to be feasible and theoretically reasonable, a simple ordinal scheme based on judgments of the relative importance of products within each cluster was adopted.

Members of the International Research Team, a group of investigators with considerable knowledge regarding the functioning of scientists and scientific organizations, acted as judges and independently allocated a predetermined number of points among the various types of outputs in each cluster. These values were then averaged across the judges and the means were ranked. The resulting order of importance is shown by the sequence in which products are listed within each cluster in the list above. Thus in the above listing of the components of Published written output, Books appears first (and received a weight of 4) Articles published abroad appears next (3), Articles within the country appears next (2), and Reviews and bibliographies appears last (1). A similar scheme was followed in constructing the Patents and prototypes cluster, again resulting in weights of 4, 3, 2, and 1. It happened that in the third cluster equal mean weights were assigned by the judges to Internal reports on original R & D work and to Algorithms, and hence these two components each received weights of 2.5, whereas Routine reports was assigned a weight of 1.

Thus construction of the composites involved a weighted additive combination of the (transformed) original variables.[20] The result was a set of three composite output measures, each of which taps a distinctively different type of product, and each of which is in a form convenient for subsequent analysis. Because of the various transformations, weightings, and summings, the composite measures do not immediately indicate a numerical quantity for a given product, but rather serve to rank-order research units according to their relative total three-year production of various products falling within that general type, after taking account of the judged scientific importance of the component products.[21]

Composite measures of rated effectiveness. The composite measures of the qualitative aspects of a research unit's effectiveness are based on ratings made by the unit head, by the staff scientists, and by the external evaluators. The measures assess the following qualities: General contribution, Recognition, R & D effectiveness, Social effectiveness, Training effectiveness, Applications effectiveness, and Administrative effectiveness. The original information from which these composites were constructed are the 41 variables shown in the righthand portion of Exhibit 2.3.

The 41 original variables were submitted to an extensive series of analyses that led to the following conclusions. (1) All items were suitable for use as performance ratings except two: Success in meeting quality requirements and Effectiveness for non–R & D objectives (on both of which judges showed relatively high rates of nonresponse and low rates of agreement, probably because of the lack of specificity in the quality being assessed). (2) For all the remaining items there was: (a) at least modest agreement among raters in different roles (i.e., among unit heads, staff scientists, and external evaluators) regarding the relative performance of the research units, and (b) fulfillment of the basic requirement that there be greater agreement among ratings of the *same* unit than among ratings of *different* units. (3) Structural analyses suggested the items could be clustered into approximately seven discriminably different qualitative aspects of research-unit effectiveness. (4) The cluster structure among the items was essentially the same regardless of whether the items had been answered by unit heads, staff scientists, or external evaluators. (5) The interrelationships among the seven clusters were reasonably stable across different types of institutions, fields of science, and national settings. (6) The relationships among the items and among the clusters were essentially linear and proved not to be dependent upon the levels of other effectiveness items or clusters. (7) Combining information from unit heads and staff scientists promised to produce a more reliable indicator of a unit's performance than using only data from one source, and adding in the data from external evaluators offered further (but slight) enhancement of the quality of the measure.[22]

The structural analyses of the effectiveness ratings, as has been briefly alluded to above, led to the identification of seven discriminably different (but not totally unrelated) qualitative aspects of a research unit's effectiveness. A performance measure was constructed for each of these seven aspects by using the following items.

1 General contribution of the unit:
   general contribution to science and technology
2 Recognition accorded to the unit:
   international reputation of the unit
   demand for the unit's publications
3 Social effectiveness of the unit:
   social value of the unit's work
   usefulness of the unit's work
4 Training effectiveness of the unit:
   training effectiveness
5 Administrative effectiveness of the unit:
   success in meeting schedules
   success in staying within budgets
6 R & D effectiveness of the unit:
   productiveness
   innovativeness
   R & D effectiveness
7 Applications effectiveness of the unit[23]:
   application of research results
   use made of development activities

Although these seven rated-effectiveness measures are the basic set that has been used most extensively by the International Research Team, a number of variations have also been used. One that merits particular mention and that appears in exhibits below resulted from the observation that ratings on General contribution were substantially related to ratings on the three items that were subsequently combined to form the R & D effectiveness measure. Accordingly, a measure called General R & D effectiveness was constructed by combining these four items. General R & D effectiveness has been treated as a one-measure alternative to the two composites General contribution and R & D effectiveness.

Each of the composite rated-effectiveness measures is based on a series of aggregations and transformations. First, individual judgments of staff scientists who were members of the same unit were averaged to produce a single unit-level score for each unit (as has been described above in Section 3 of this chapter). A parallel aggregation occurred for the data from external evaluators. Next, using the unit-level data, answers to the questionnaire items indicated above were combined by simple averaging to produce scores on each of the seven measures.[24] At this point there were separate scores for each of the three types of respondents. Third, data were aggregated across the three types of respondents, again by simple averaging, to produce a single joint rating combining the evaluations of all respondents who had answered the relevant items. Thus most of the rated-effectiveness measures combine data from unit heads, staff scientists, and external evaluators; however, because the external evaluators were not asked to answer the items used for constructing the Recognition and Applications effectiveness measures, these two are based on ratings from unit heads and staff scientists only. Finally, the composite scores were made more convenient for analysis by reversing them (so high scores would indicate high levels of performance) and by transforming them (to produce an eight-category scale with an approximately rectangular distribution).

Comments on the performance measures. Although the methodological analyses for which conclusions are summarized above provided substantial support for the International Research Team's decision to construct a small number of substantially aggregated rated-effectiveness measures, one must note that answers to single questionnaire items showed more evidence of imprecision and/or lack of agreement than would have been optimal. Presumably, this is attributable to the inherently difficult nature of assessing the quality of a research unit's performance, to the intentionally heterogeneous array of raters who were asked to make these judgments, to the wide range of different research-unit types that were being assessed, to imprecisions of translation from one language to another, and to the limitations of any assessment based on a single short questionnaire item.

One of the important reasons for constructing *composite* measures of research-unit performance is that some of the invalidities and biases in answers to single questionnaire items can be made to cancel out. The result, more fully described in Chapter 14, is that the composite measures, after incorporating data from different items and also from different raters, have estimated internal validities reaching quite acceptable levels (in the range .7–.8). In short, although the rated-effectiveness measures are not ideal, statistical results suggest that they offer considerable potential for use in other analyses, and their present form reflects the refinements from a substantial amount of development work.

From a more fundamental perspective, however, one may ask

about the *meaning* of all the performance measures. Should one believe that they provide useful indications of the level of performance of a research unit? This question has been of much interest to the International Research Team, and has inspired much speculation and analysis. At this point, comments on two subquestions may be of interest, the first having to do with data sources, the second having to do with data relevance.

With respect to data sources, one may legitimately ask about the appropriateness of giving substantial weight, when constructing a measure of research-unit effectiveness, to ratings made by people who are members of the unit being assessed. In an ideal world in which pure scientific elegance were feasibly obtainable, one would probably not do this. However, faced with the practical necessity of making some, even imperfect, assessments of effectiveness, no more useful approach has been identified. Assessing scientific performance is an inherently difficult task because of the highly specialized and fractionated nature of the research process and product. Although it is not the only criterion, one prerequisite for R & D performance is that a unit's efforts extend the frontiers of knowledge or application. By definition, the unit members – if they are doing first-rate work – are *the* experts in their subspeciality. It follows that finding other people who are well qualified to judge the unit's work may be somewhat difficult, and this in fact proved to be the case when attempts were made to identify external evaluators.

But can members of a research unit be expected to know how good their work is? And if they do, can they be expected to accurately report its quality? The International Study provides at least a tentative "yes" to both these questions. First, the wordings of the items that asked for ratings of effectiveness were sufficiently explicit so that nearly all respondents did answer them (with the two exceptions, subsequently omitted from later analyses, noted above). Furthermore, nearly all respondents provided ratings even after having been explicitly invited to indicate "unable to reply," if that was their situation, or "not applicable," if that was their view of the quality being assessed. Thus there is strong evidence that respondents felt they could make the requested judgments.

Next, there is evidence that the judgments they made were not random ones. As noted above, there was at least modest agreement (not as high as would have been ideal, but of very great statistical significance) among different raters about the qualitative performance of a unit. Although it is entirely conceivable that the agreement among raters from within the unit itself might be caused by some factor other than the true level of the unit's performance, it is not easy to account for the agreement among the external judges, or the agreement between external judges and unit members, on the basis of some factor other than performance. The parsimonious way to account for these agreements is to believe that scientists have at least a general idea about how good their work is, and that when faced with a serious questionnaire for which strong pledges of confidentiality have been made they will report their perceptions with substantial accuracy.

Finally, and of very considerable importance, results from the study show that unit members tended to be *more critical* of their own unit's work than did the external evaluators. Thus although there may well be certain individuals who upwardly biased their evaluations because they were rating their own unit, this was not a general phenomenon. The external evaluators tended to give more positive ratings to a unit than did its members.

The second subquestion that deserves attention concerns the relevance of the data. There can be no doubt that some of the composite performance measures have greater or lesser relevance depending on the type of unit. For example, many academic units are not in the business of producing patents; similarly, some units in private enterprise labs do not seek to provide training. In such cases, one may legitimately ask whether criteria assessing goals not sought should be applied to the unit. (The answer is not an unambiguous "no," because it could be argued, for example, that even if patents are not the business of a unit, its effectiveness would be higher if it did do work that resulted in one.) The International Study has left resolution of this issue to the individual data analysts, and they have adopted two major strategies. One is to perform separate analyses for different types of units, and choose performance measures for their relevance to the particular type of unit being analyzed. A second strategy is to perform analyses with different types of units combined, but use performance measures that have been adjusted so that the effect is to compare a unit's performance on a given dimension only with what might be expected for other units of its own type. The first of these strategies is the topic of the immediately following paragraph and is more extensively addressed in Chapter 11; the second strategy involves a discussion of the adjustment of performance measures, which is the topic of the following subsection in this chapter.

The immediate relevance of some of the 11 measures of performance to units in different categories of the typology can be readily inferred from a general knowledge of how science operates. As has been observed above, the measures of Training effectiveness and Output of published written products are of direct relevance primarily in academic settings (categories 1–3 of the Typology). Applications effectiveness is of primary relevance to labs in cooperative institutes and private enterprise laboratories (categories 4 and 5 of the Typology), though it is also of some concern to units in academic settings if they deal in the applied, medical, or social sciences. Output of patents and prototype devices is primarily relevant to units in private enterprise labs (though it is also of some direct concern to units in cooperative institutes and in applied science academic settings). All these inferences have been supported by empirical analyses conducted on data from the International Study (see Unesco, 1976, for one example). These analyses also suggest some relevancies that the casual observer might not have expected in advance: There is evidence that the Social effectiveness measure is of most concern in medical or social science academic units and in cooperative institutes (categories 2 and 4 of the Typology), and that the Reports and algorithms measure shows up primarily in more applied settings – applied science academic units, cooperative institutes, and private enterprise labs (categories 3–5 of the Typology). Finally, there are a few performance measures that may have relevance in all five types of units: General contribution, R & D effectiveness, General R & D effectiveness, and Administrative effectiveness.[25] The implication of these differential relevancies is that one appropriate strategy for analysis is to subdivide the units according to Type, and then for any given type to consider only those performance measures that are of most direct relevance.

An alternative strategy is to examine units of different types within a single analysis but to first express their performance relative to that which might be expected for units of their type. This strategy offers the advantages of making more efficient use of the data and having greater conceptual simplicity, but yields fully appropriate results only when the phenomenon being analyzed operates in similar ways for each type of unit (an assumption that can, of course, be checked). The following section of this chapter describes how the adjustments to the performance measures that are necessary for this second strategy were implemented.

Adjustment of performance measures for Type of unit

When research units were grouped into different types, there proved to be some systematic differences in the levels of certain performance measures. This was entirely expected and, in fact, is part of the evidence that supports the validity of these measures. For example, units in academic settings tended to have higher scores on Published written output, Recognition, and Training effectiveness than did units in cooperative institutes or laboratories of private enterprises; but these latter units tended to outrank academic units with respect to Patents and algorithms and Applications effectiveness. Somewhat similar differences occurred for units working in different scientific fields.

The actual magnitude of these relationships (percent of variance explained) ranged from 0% to about 25%. Performance measures that were only very weakly related to Type of institution or to Scientific field included General contribution, R & D effectiveness, General R & D effectiveness, and Administrative effectiveness; no relationships involving these measures exceeded 2%. On the other hand, relatively strong relationships appeared for Training effectiveness, Applications effectiveness, Patents and prototypes, and Published written output, in each of which at least 20% of the variance could be explained by the combined effects of Type of institution and Scientific field. The remaining performance measures showed relationships of intermediate strength.[26]

Although of undoubted reality, these kinds of systematic differences could result in spurious relationships in subsequent analyses if different types of research units were treated together. One solution to this problem is to remove from the performance measures any differences that could be associated with the institutional setting or scientific field of the research unit. Technically, this involves producing adjusted (i.e., "residualized") measures from which all variation that might be attributed Type of institution or Scientific field has been removed.

As has been noted above in this chapter, a five-category typology of research units was contructed with the specific intention of being sensitive to difference in patterns of performance. Because this simple five-category Typology was just about as effective in reflecting performance differences as the more elaborate Type of organization and Scientific field variables,[27] the Typology variable was used as the basis for adjusting each of the 11 performance measures described above. Thus 11 new adjusted performance measures were produced by adding or subtracting appropriate values to the original scores of each unit so that the mean scores on each performance measure became the same for units in each of the five categories of the Typology.

The net effect is that the adjusted performance measures reflect the performance of a unit *relative to the best available estimate of what might be expected for units of its type.* The operation is analogous to expressing the athletic prowess of swimmers and runners in terms of their relative standing within their respective groups, rather than by recording the absolute number of minutes they require to cover a distance such as 1,500 meters.

Although these adjusted performance measures will often provide more refined indications of the potential effect that a particular organizational or social factor may have on the performance levels of a research unit, in the data of the International Study the major *trends* of the results are rarely influenced by whether the analyst has used adjusted or unadjusted performance measures. This is because the two are very substantially correlated with one another. Among the three output measures, these relationships are all very close to .9 (ranging from .87 for Reports to .92 for Publications). Among the rated-effectiveness measures, R & D effectiveness, General R & D effectiveness, and Administrative effectiveness all showed correlations exceeding .99, whereas the relationships for the rest were approximately .90. In short, the adjustment for Typology produced an important refinement in the performance measures, but did not result in widespread and fundamental shifts.

Interrelationships among performance measures

Having described the derivation and adjustment of the three output measures, of the seven basic rated-effectiveness measures, and of one alternative rated-effectiveness measure, it is of considerable interest to examine the interrelationships among these assessments of research-unit performance. Exhibit 2.4 presents these data for both the unadjusted and adjusted measures.

The upper left portion of the exhibit shows the correlations among the three output measures. Prior to adjustment, Published output was almost completely independent of the two other output indicators, and there was a mildly positive relationship ($r = .34$) between Patents and prototypes and Reports and algorithms. After adjustment, these relationships continued to be mild but all became slightly positive. It is clear that even after adjustment these measures, as intended, tap distinctly different aspects of research-unit output.

In the lower right portion of Exhibit 2.4 appear the interrelationships among the eight rated-effectiveness measures. With a few notable exceptions, here also the relationships tend to be rather low, again supporting the distinctiveness of the various

Exhibit 2.4. Relationships among performance measures[a]

	A	B	C	D	E	F	G	H	I	J
A. Published output										
B. Patents & prototypes	−.02[b] .16									
C. Reports & algorithms	−.06 .16	.34 .21								
D. General contribution	.30 .29	.08 .17	.02 .09							
E. Recognition	.51 .45	−.04 .11	−.11 .08	.55 .56						
F. Social effectiveness	.10 .14	.05 .07	.14 .12	.32 .35	.09 .16					
G. Training effectiveness	.26 .14	−.10 .05	−.16 .04	.30 .31	.35 .24	.09 .19				
H. Administrative effectiveness	.07 .06	−.05 −.02	−.06 −.05	.25 .24	.15 .15	.19 .17	.12 .13			
I. R & D effectiveness	.17 .21	.22 .22	.10 .10	.67 .68	.44 .48	.29 .33	.33 .40	.21 .21		
J. Applications effectiveness	−.18 −.03	.17 .06	.23 .08	.13 .17	−.04 .10	.26 .24	−.08 .10	.08 .09	.32 .33	
K. General R & D effectiveness	.22 .25	.20 .22	.09 .10	.82 .82	.51 .54	.32 .36	.35 .41	.24 .24	.97 .97	.29 .31

[a] All measures in the exhibit are composites, as described in the text; measures D–K combine information from unit heads, staff scientists, and external evaluators (where applicable).

[b] Figures show Pearson *r*s. Upper figure is based on unadjusted measures; lower figure, on measures adjusted to remove effects attributable to type of unit.

assessments. (The two cells with the highest correlations–.97 and .82, both involving General R & D effectiveness–should be disregarded as artifactual: Recall that this measure is an alternative to General contribution and to R & D effectiveness and involves the same original items. Beyond this, only a few relationships exceed .40, and most of these involve combinations of General contribution, Recognition, and R & D effectiveness.) Comparing the pairs of correlations in each cell of this portion of the exhibit shows that the adjustment process did not alter the basic pattern of relationships among the rated-effectiveness measures, though a couple of mildly negative original relationships became instead mildly positive (an effect of the adjustment that has some intuitive appeal).

Finally, the lower left portion of Exhibit 2.4 shows how the output measures relate to the rated-effectiveness measures. Here again, nearly all relationships are low, and (after adjustment) all but three are positive. Ratings of effectiveness are thus seen to provide information that is distinctly different from assessments based on quantitative output. The only really marked exception is the entirely reasonable correlation of approximately +.5 between the Number of published written outputs and ratings of Recognition. As in other portions of the exhibit, one can see that the adjustment process did not change the basic pattern of relationships, though here one can see instances where combining different types of research units affected the original relationships and how the adjusted measures correct for this. For example, note that the .26 relationship between Training effectiveness and Publications (both of which are heavily emphasized by academic units) receded to .14 after adjustment for type of unit, and that a similar recession is evident for the relationship of Applications effectiveness and Output of reports (both of which are heavily emphasized by units in private enterprise). Conversely, the originally negative relationship of −.16 between Training effectiveness and Reports and algorithms (which are primary concerns in different kinds of units) *rose* to +.04 after adjustment. Several other examples of such very reasonable and understandable, but modest, refinements in the relationships as a result of the adjustment process are also evident in this portion of the exhibit.

5. Summary

The first major section of the chapter describes the nature and sources of the data of the International Study. The data come from six countries: Austria, Belgium, Finland, Hungary, Poland, and Sweden. Although it was individual people who answered the study's questionnaires and interviews, and although the data can be analyzed at the level of the individual person, the study is basically designed to investigate research units, that is, the (usually small) groups of people who organize themselves to actually carry out research or development activities. The formal criteria for defining a research unit are described in the chapter. Five types of respondents, chosen because of their different roles in the research units that participated in the study, individually filled out separate questionnaires with partially overlapping content. The five types of respondents were: unit heads, staff scientists, technical support persons, administrators, and external evaluators. More than 11,000 questionnaires were completed during Round 1 of the International Study, and these describe 1,222 research units.

The second major section of the chapter describes how research units were selected to participate in the International Study and the procedures by which data were collected and processed. Subpopulations of research units were defined on the basis of their country, type of institution (academic, private enterprise, etc.), and scientific field. Certain subpopulations were chosen for study in each country according to particular national interests, and then a probability sample of units was selected from all units within the designated subpopulations. Although the units in Round 1 of the study represent their respective subpopulations, they do not represent all units in any one country or in all six countries combined; rather, they are regarded by most authors contributing to this book simply as a set of heterogeneous units drawn from a variety of national, disciplinary, and institutional settings. Because of the way units were selected, there are certain interrelationships between the factors of Country, Type of institution, and Scientific field that must be considered when interpreting later analyses.

Data were collected in 1974, using standardized questionnaires and interview instruments that had been developed for Round 1 of the International Study through a series of extensive pretests. Data on a wide range of organizational and individual characteristics were assessed. Topics included: staff remuneration and advancement, R & D activities of research personnel, research methods used, scientific exchanges and contact with other units, evaluation methods, factors affecting choice of research themes and planning of the work, working climate, availability of resources, patterns of influence, supervision, individual and research-unit products, ratings of research-unit effectiveness, and various demographic characteristics of the unit itself and of its individual members. After aggregating the data from certain types of respondents, each research unit in Round 1 of the study was described by more than 1,200 variables. (The chapter describes the aggregations and the general nature of the variables.)

The third major section of the chapter focuses on the development of certain measures that are important in many subsequent chapters. One of these is a powerful and efficient five-category typology of research units. The derivation of the Typology, which is based on differences in patterns of performance, is briefly described in the chapter, and more fully elaborated in Chapter 13.

This section of the chapter also describes the development of the performance assessments, that is, the measurements of research-unit effectiveness. The approach started from the assumptions (later found to be supported in the data) that research performance was a multidimensional phenomenon, that both quantitative and qualitative aspects were worth consideration, and that a range of different perspectives should be tapped. A series of methodological analyses led to the eventual construction of 11 composite measures of performance, derived from an original set of 56 variables. These 11 include 3 assessments based on quantitative data (Published written output, Patents and prototypes, and Reports and algorithms), and 8 based on qualitative ratings (General contribution, Recognition, R & D effectiveness, General R & D effectiveness, Social effectiveness, Training effectiveness, Applications effectiveness, and Administrative effectiveness). The analyses and procedures that led to the construction of these measures are briefly described, references are given to sources of more complete documentation, and some comments about the meaning and about appropriate ways of using these measures are presented.

Finally, this section of the chapter describes how the 11 composite performance measures were adjusted to remove differences that could be attributed to Type of unit, which is necessary if one is to avoid spurious effects when different types of units are combined in the same analysis, and presents the interrelationships among the 11 composites, both before and after adjustment.

References

Labovitz, S., 1970, The Assignment of Numbers to Rank Order Categories, *American Sociological Review,* 35: 515–525.

Pelz, D. C., and Andrews, F. M., 1966, *Scientists in Organizations: Productive Climates for Research and Development,* New York, Wiley.

Unesco, 1975a, *Identification of RU Output Clusters: A Preliminary Analysis Report* (document STP/524), Paris.

Unesco, 1975b, *Construction and Testing of RU Output Composite Measures: A Preliminary Analysis Report* (document STP/1713), Paris.

Unesco, 1975c, *Summary of the December 1974 Workshop on Data Analysis and the Construction of Performance Measures for the First Round* (document STP/2250), Paris.

Unesco, 1975d, *Summary Report of Analysis Findings on Trial Performance Measures Created During the Louvain Workshop* (document STP/136), Paris.

Unesco, 1976, *Assessing the First Round Performance Measures for Their Potential Use Within Categories of the Unesco Typology Variable: An Application of the MNA Program* (document STP/836), Paris.

Unesco, forthcoming, *A Summary Methodology for Assessing the Organization and Performance of Research Units,* Paris.

Notes

1. An R & D *organization* was defined as "the body containing the unit and whose activity (total or partial) can be considered as scientific or technological; it constitutes a legal person under the applicable national legislation."

2. Page 2 of the RU questionnaire, which is reproduced in the Appendix to this volume, provides a graphic portrayal of various ways in which a research unit might be related to an R & D organization.

3. The 1,222 research units included in Round 1 of the International Study contained the following number of scientists and engineers: 12% had 1 or 2 professional-level members, 18% had 3, 16% had 4, 12% had 5, 15% had 6 or 7, 14% had 8 to 10, and 13% had 11 or more. The average (median) number of professional-level members was 4.9. The distribution of units according to the number of technical support personnel was as follows: 16% of the units had no technical support person, 21% had 1 such person, 16% had 2, 13% had 3, 15% had 4 or 5, and 19% had 6 or more. The median number of technical support persons was 2.3.

4. The noninclusion of smaller units is implicit in the definition and explicit in one of the diagrams that accompanied the definition (see page 2 of the RU questionnaire, reproduced in the Appendix to this volume).

5. Because the amount of new information about a research unit provided by each respondent was expected to decrease as the number of respondents of the same type increased, the study advocated that staff scientists be randomly *sampled* when their number exceeded three in order to economize on data-collection costs. This procedure was followed in some countries, but in others it seemed desirable to collect data from *all* core-member staff scientists within a single unit, even when their number exceeded three.

6. Unit heads and staff scientists were asked in their respective questionnaires: "Please list below names of up to five people who work in your specialty, or in the closest possible specialities to your own, either in your country or abroad." (A following instruction asked for addresses.) The questionnaire included no indication as to why this information was being sought; however, if respondents asked and were not satisfied with an initial vague answer, then a direct explanation was provided.

7. Chapter 14 includes an assessment of the quality of the data obtained from the external evaluators.

8. At the time sampling for Round 1 of the International Study was being planned, the *International Standard Nomenclature for Fields of Science or Technology* was under development by Unesco, and the 1973 draft version was used.

9. In many cases, but not always, this matching of scientific disciplines also resulted in a cross-national matching of units active in the same discipline *and* existing within the same type of organization.

10. Further information on sampling as well as other aspects of the data is available from the Belgian Archives for the Social Sciences, B-1348 Louvain-la-Neuve, Belgium. Although a detailed response rate analysis has not been performed, preliminary estimates indicate that the average response rate (i.e., the proportion of all units selected by the sampling process in which data were actually collected) varied between .70 and .85, depending on the country and the scientific field, and no indication of serious response bias by rank of respondent, Field, or Type of organization has been found.

11. One way to ensure precise representation would be through use of appropriate sampling and response-rate weights. Although these have been computed and are available for each unit, the computational costs of including them in the analyses, and the observation that their inclusion had little effect on the statistical results in some test analyses, led to the decision to analyze the data in an unweighted form.

12. "Technological sciences" include what people in some parts of the world call "engineering" specialities.

13. Each country surveyed about 25 units active in the field of biochemistry and about 25 active in metallurgy, with each of these disciplinary categories subdivided into halves according to unit size. In addition, an attempt was made to choose units from different types of institutional settings.

14. The Osiris software system was used for processing most of the Round 1 data. Osiris is being developed and distributed by the Institute for Social Research and the Inter-university Consortium for Political and Social Research, both of which are headquartered at the University of Michigan, Ann Arbor, Mich., USA.

15. Sums, means, and standard deviations were computed during the aggregation process when the original answers were on an ordinal, interval, or ratio response scale, as was the case for most answers. (Although it was recognized that the application of these statistics to ordinal scales involved some special assumptions, substantial experience with such operations – such as that reported by Labovitz (1970) – suggests that these assumptions tend to hold for most data of the kind considered here.) When the original response scales were nominal (i.e., unordered categories), different aggregation procedures were used; these are individually described as required in later chapters.

16. An eleventh measure, examined by some members of the International Research Team, can be regarded as a combination of 2 of the 10 basic measures and is discussed with them, below.

17. In a number of previous studies, the outputs of scientific products have been found to show a *log-normal* distribution; see, for example, Pelz and Andrews (1966:273).

18. Details on the transformations appear in Table 2 and Annex 1 of Unesco, 1975a.

19. A further check on the clustering of different types of R & D outputs was obtained by performing a series of analyses, parallel to those described here for output of a research unit, on data describing the *personal* output of both unit heads and staff scientists. (See question A3 in the questionnaire in the Appen-

dix to this volume.) The cluster structure for both types of individuals closely replicated that just described for research units, thereby supporting the generality of the structure just described. Full details on these analyses appear in Unesco (1975a and 1975b).

20. In addition to the transformation to reduce skew, discussed above, an additional adjustment was made to approximately equalize the range of scores (and hence–in this case–the variance) of the variables before they were weighted and summed; details appear in Unesco (1975b: Annex 1).

21. Some readers may wonder why the simple ordinal weights (applied to the original variables doubly transformed to reduce skew and equalize ranges) were used in preference to the more "obvious" approach of applying a set of absolute weights to the untransformed original output data. The brief answer is that both approaches were fully implemented and compared; that the differences between the two approaches proved to be only modest (the two approaches yielded measures that correlated in the .7 to .8 range, depending on the particular type of output); but that when tested against a series of methodological criteria, the measures derived using the ordinal weights proved superior. These criteria included relationships to selected predictor and control variables, stability of distributional characteristics across subgroups, skews, and explorations involving criterion and construct validity. Full details appear in Unesco (1975b).

22. A very substantial amount of analysis lies back of the conclusions summarized here, and the complete documentation of these analyses would require a large monograph by itself. A partial summary appears in three unpublished working papers developed by the study (Unesco, 1975c, 1975d, and 1976), and important further results appear in Chapters 11 and 14.

23. An alternative name for this measure is "extent of application."

24. This simple averaging of item scores produced approximately equal weights for the items in the resulting composite because all items used to form any one composite were answered on the same response scale and had approximately equal variances.

25. Unfortunately, the comparative analyses done to date have not been able to distinguish between measures relevant in *all* types of units and measures relevant in *none* of the types. However, the substantive analyses reported below in this book make this latter possibility a realistic alternative only for the measure of Administrative effectiveness.

26. Exhibit 13.3 presents the exact magnitudes of these relationships and further details on how these analyses were performed.

27. Chapter 13 presents this comparison.

Part 2. Organizational factors and scientific performance

3 Individual publication productivity as a social position effect in academic and industrial research units

Karin D. Knorr, Roland Mittermeir, Georg Aichholzer, and Georg Waller
Institute for Advanced Studies, Vienna

1. Productivity and stratification in science

Throughout the development of the sociology of science, the study of normal scientific activity has focused on the general stratification and communication system in science. This seems to affect all scientific fields and manifests itself most clearly in the skewed distributions of productivity and rewards. There have been productivity studies on scientists of a variety of disciplines, including, among others, physiologists (Meltzer, 1956), psychologists (Clark, 1957), sociologists (Meltzer, 1949; Axelson, 1959; Babchuk and Bates, 1962; Clemente, 1974), medical researchers (Ben-David, 1960), biologists and political scientists (Crane, 1965), psychometricians (Thomasson and Stanley, 1966), physicists (Cole and Cole, 1967, 1968; Gaston, 1969; Cole, 1970; Zuckerman and Merton, 1971) and chemists (Hagstrom, 1971; Blume and Sinclair, 1973a, b). Other studies, like that of Pelz and Andrews (1966), covered a wide variety of scientists from different specialities and disciplines.

We are grateful to S. S. Blume, G. Cole, D. Crane, and E. van Hove for their valuable comments and critical remarks on an earlier version of this paper. We thank R. Kofler, R. Matuschek, and W. Raidl for their help in preparing the manuscript. A previous version of this chapter was presented at the PAREX–IAS colloquium on "The role of research organizations in orienting scientific activities," Vienna, 5–6 July 1976. This research was supported by the Austrian Industrial Research Promotion Fund.

Although many of the findings reported in this body of literature are, as Kaplan (1964: 967) has noted, ambiguous and often contradictory, there seems to be an emergent consensus that scientific activities are highly stratified and elitist in nature. For example, as has been known since Lotka (1926), only a small and select minority of scientists produce the bulk of scientific papers published in the literature. Price (1963) suggested that the square root of the population of scientists produces 50% of scientific discoveries. Merton (1968) proposed the *Matthew effect,* which asserts that those who are well known receive more credit for their work than those who are less well known ("unto everyone that has shall be given" according to the Gospel of Saint Matthew, Chapter 25, Verse 29).

Various aspects of social stratification in the scientific community have recently been examined by Cole and Cole, using citation counts as a measure of the quality of scientific output. Their findings suggest that scientists located in the top stratum of academic science predominantly cite the discoveries produced by other members of the same elite stratum, and furthermore that even members of the lowest stratum disproportionately cite the work produced by distinguished scientists, although to a lesser extent than those who are themselves members of the scientific elite (Cole, 1970). Additionally, according to Cole and Cole (1968), quality of work, as measured by citations received and rank of department, accounts for most of the variance in the "visibility" or reputation of a scientist.

Those results, as well as some of the earlier ones by Crane (1965) as to the high correlation between academic setting and both productivity and recognition, seemingly lend themselves to the interpretation that greater ease of publication and hence higher visibility and reputation stem from having high levels of individual or academic status. Rewards received not so much as a consequence of the individual's general contribution to science but rather as the result of the preferential citing of the eminent or of the appointment of the eminent must, as noted by Blume and Sinclair (1973a: 134), truly be called unmerited. However, Zuckerman and Merton (1971) found that the formal control mechanisms of science, such as reviewing and publication processes, are *not* affected by status differentials of the authors or papers submitted. The findings of Hargens and Hagstrom (1967) and Hagstrom (1971) support those conclusions: Hargens and Hagstrom showed that status does not relate to productivity on the individual level, although it does on the aggregate. In addition, Hagstrom (1971) claimed that no sociological variables either singularly or in combination account for much of the differences in productivity.

If status does not confer easier access to publication and if ascriptive factors are not primarily relevant for the recognition accorded the like contributions of two unlike scientists, this raises the question as to how the large publication differentials between higher- and lower-rank scientists can be explained. The above studies provide no simple explanation for this differential productivity. Zuckerman (1970) showed that age is associated with rank and hence with productivity, and Pelz and Andrews (1966) report a continuing increase of productivity with age up to the early or late 40s (varied for different types of laboratories and education), with a renascence of productivity manifesting itself in a second peak of the age curves about 10 to 15 years later. These findings, in addition to standing in distinct contrast to data presented by Lehmann (1953, 1958, 1960) as to a continuing decline of major scientific contributions from the late 30s onward, also do not lend themselves to an easier understanding of productivity differentials. If age and professional experience are important explanatory variables, how does it come about that the average productivity in a unit of time (as measured by the number of written products within the last 3 or 5 years and hence adjusted for the accumulating effects of age) rises so steadily not only during the first years of a professional career – where initial lack of research experience alone might provide an adequate explanation – but rather for 15 to 20 years after graduation?

This chapter attempts to supply some further details as to how productivity differences associated with rank or age can be understood by extending the above research to include intraorganizational variables as a source of explanation. As noted by Whitley (1976), scientists may be affected more by organizational settings and structures than is usually emphasized in stratification studies. If one were to take the idea of science as a highly stratified system one step further and apply it to the system of a single organization, this would lead one to expect scientific productivity to be associated with the status or position a scientist holds in the formal or informal scientific hierarchy of the organization. The question as to why higher position should confer greater productivity can then be answered by pointing to the differential resources and task structures associated with different levels. It is our contention that higher positions – except for the extreme case where the scientist moves out of science altogether – provide better opportunities for publication, for the simple reason that a scientist's publication capacity is multiplied by the task force he or she supervises and by the project (and other) money to which he or she gains access (compare Mullins, 1975).

More explicitly, one could reason that status in general might not confer greater ease of publication in the simple sense of intriguing referees and publishing companies toward publication of whatever is submitted by a high-status scientist, but rather that status may confer greater ease of production by opening up channels or resources not accessible to those in low positions. The relationship between age and productivity found in previous studies would then have to be discussed in the light of the association between a scientist's age and the position he or she has attained in his organizational environment. Because age and the level of supervisory position are presumably highly correlated in bureaucratic organizations (like universities or academies of science), it may well be position and the resources and task structure associated with it – and not so much mere chronological age or professional experience – that account for most of the variance in productivity.

At this point, sufficient research has been done in the present study to outline the contours of a model that uses the intraorganizational position of a scientist as a key element associated with productivity. Because productivity differences are linked to social mechanisms, the model can be interpreted in terms of the *accumulative advantage* hypothesis (e.g., Allison and Stewart, 1974).

Before describing the model mentioned above (which will be represented within a structural equation approach), this chapter proceeds to examine the relationship between age and productivity, and to explore whether age can be considered a proxy for the position a scientist has attained in a research organization. Furthermore, the relationship between years spent in research and productivity, and the nature of task structures that may be conducive to a high quantity of output, will be analyzed. Finally, the social-position model of individual publication productivity will be supplemented by some details as to how group productivity is related to individual productivity and what additional factors have to be taken into account when group output is examined.

2. Data

The data presented in this chapter are drawn from the International Comparative Study on the Organization and Performance of Research Units. The analyses focus on the professional-level members (unit heads and staff scientists) in three types of units:

units working in the natural sciences and located in academic organizations, units working in the technological sciences[1] and located in academic organizations, and units working in the technological sciences and located in industrial organizations. These three types of units were chosen as relevant subgroups for which all analyses were conducted separately. This decision was based on a typological analysis of quantitative and qualitative performance measures in different disciplines and types of institutions in the present data set (Cole, 1978; Chapter 13 of this volume), which showed that performance patterns differed markedly among the above settings but that no significant gain was made by looking at single disciplines separately, for example, at academic chemistry. Most of the analyses in this chapter examine data from individual respondents; however, near the end of the chapter some unit-level results are presented. All analyses use data that have been aggregated across the six countries that participated in the study.

3. Measurement of productivity

In order to examine scientific productivity in relation to stratification or organizational variables, a variety of approaches to the construction of operational indicators of performance have been used in the literature. As noted by Blume and Sinclair (1973a), the only valid assessment of a contribution to science must come from within the respective speciality, for only members of a speciality are sufficiently competent to judge the significance of a scientific contribution to their field. Despite the fact that most social scientists working on scientific productivity have agreed on the ideal of such a measurement of scientific quality, in practice many have gone on to use a simple counting of published papers as the most viable way of dealing with the problem (e.g., Coler, 1963; Price, 1963; Crane, 1965; Gaston, 1969). Meltzer and Salter (1962; 354) note some of the objections that might be raised against such a productivity measure: a co-author is given the same amount of credit as a full author, a short paper is counted the same as a long one, no distinction is made between poor and excellent products, no difference can be distinguished between highly original work and the repetition of old ideas, and the benefits of having written the product may be attributed to those who only exploited the ideas or research work of others.

Despite the plausibility of those arguments, fairly consistent evidence has come up in the literature for a high or moderate correlation between the sheer volume of a scientist's published papers and the quality of his or her work, as measured by ratings of competence by peers or citation counts (see Meltzer, 1949, 1956; Dennis, 1954; Clark, 1957; Pelz and Andrews, 1966; Thomasson and Stanley, 1966; Cole and Cole, 1967, 1971; and Blume and Sinclair, 1973a,b).[2] The conclusion seems to be that where citation counts are not readily available – as in the case of a study including countries not adequately or not at all represented in the science citation index – publication counts are roughly adequate indicators of the significance of a scientist's work (cf. Cole and Cole, 1971: 26).

Although our data allow for the assessment of the rated quality[3] of the scientific work of our respondents in addition to its quantity, they do not include a measure of citation counts for the reason mentioned above. In the present examination, we shall rely almost exclusively on the quantitative measurement of research productivity. This will enable us to relate our results to findings in the existing literature more directly than would be the case if results were based on the rated performance measures.

Following a frequent procedure (e.g., Pelz and Andrews, 1966; Hagstrom, 1967; Gaston, 1969), we took as our indicator of "publication productivity" the self-reported number of papers a respondent had published in scientific journals in connection with his or her work in the research unit. In order to eliminate the cumulative effect of sheer professional age, respondents were to list only the papers published during the last three years. Where the Lisrel technique has been used (below in this chapter), the number of scientific books published in the same time period has been included in the analysis as a second indicator of publication productivity, justified by a sufficiently high correlation between both kinds of output.[4]

4. Age, professional experience, and productivity

Earlier work to which we have referred above suggested a somewhat curvilinear relationship between a scientist's age and his or her scientific productivity. Whereas Lehmann's results show a continuous decline of productivity after achievement peaks around the late 30s (depending on discipline), Pelz and Andrews generally report the peak at a later age, in the 40s, followed by a 10 to 15 years sag with a comeback in the 50s. Our data offer a partial verification of those results: Exhibit 3.1 shows the mean production of papers by scientists in different fields and settings for different age categories, and Exhibit 3.2 gives the equivalent productivity curves for what we have called professional experi-

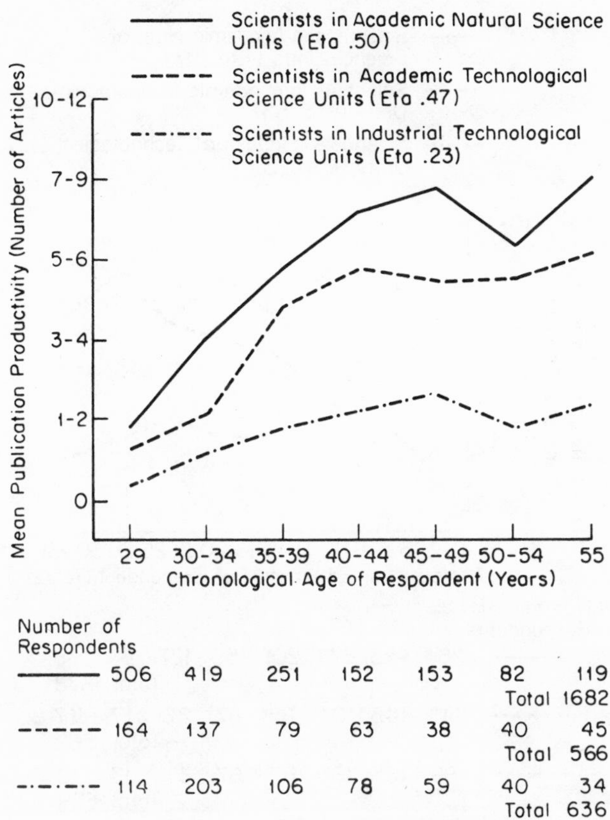

Exhibit 3.1. Mean publication productivity by chronological age for scientists in academic natural and technological sciences and in industrial units.

ence, that is, a scientist's number of years of R & D experience. The latter concept has been introduced in addition to chronological age in order to adjust for the differential disadvantages of those scientists who for various reasons were not continuously involved in scientific work or who started their careers at a somewhat later age. As age and professional experience were highly correlated,[5] productivity curves turned out to have a similar shape for both measures.

When comparing these exhibits, the most interesting difference lies in the fact that the two-peak form of the curve for chronological age, which nicely verifies the results of Pelz and Andrews, tends to change when professional experience is considered. In academic natural science settings, a peak after 15 to 20 years of steadily rising productivity is followed by a period of

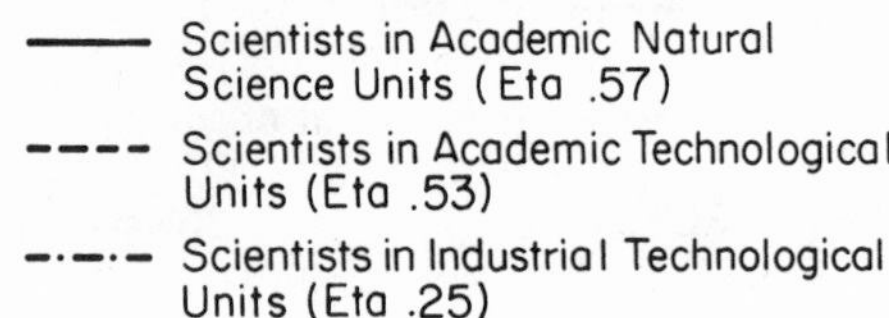

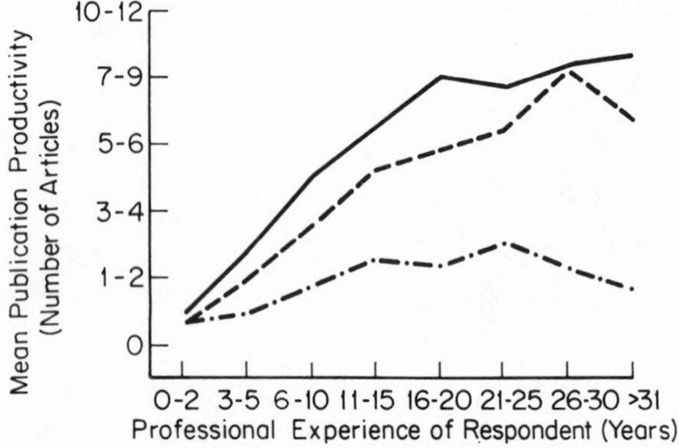

Number of Respondents	0-2	3-5	6-10	11-15	16-20	21-25	26-30	>31	Total
———	264	423	374	201	155	127	66	68	1678
- - - - -	111	145	104	65	67	36	17	17	562
-·-·-·	88	165	160	87	67	37	13	12	629

Exhibit 3.2. Mean publication productivity by professional age for scientists in academic natural and technological sciences and in industrial units.

stagnation or a very slow rise in the second part of a scientist's career. Scientists working in the technological sciences show a decline in productivity toward the end of their careers, with a very late peak after nearly 30 years of professional work in academic settings and an earlier one after nearly 25 years in industrial research laboratories. In the latter case, the curve is remarkably flatter than in academic settings, implying that age is less related to this kind of productivity in industry. The late peaking of productivity with professional experience of technological scientists in academic settings is mirrored by an early peak when chronological age is considered, suggesting that perhaps a professional career starts earlier in those fields.

Stagnation or decline after a certain period of rising productivity, as more or less confirmed in the present data, has met with different attempts at explanation in the literature. The most popular interpretation points to the possibility that the more productive scientists may be drawn off into teaching, administration, and other work not productive of scientific output. This is supported in our data, for example, by a positive correlation between age and the number of years the scientist has been head of the research unit, a negative correlation between age and the percent of time spent on research, and a positive correlation between age and the percent of time spent on administration.[6] However, upon closer examination of the age curves for percent of time spent in research and administration, one finds a more or less steady decrease (with research) and steady increase (with administration) of the curves from the very beginning of a professional career almost to the end of it. As an example, Exhibit 3.3 shows the decreasing involvement in research activities with age in all three institutional settings studied in this chapter.

Phrased differently, the results presented so far indicate that publication productivity is *rising* (sharply in academic settings and moderately in industrial settings) for about the first 20 years of a professional career, in spite of the fact that nonresearch tasks are increasing steadily and time in research is *decreasing* continuously during the same time. The most interesting question – somewhat ignored in the literature – is how we explain this more or less steady and continuous rise of productivity for such a long time period, given that (1) scientists are drawn off in work not directly productive of scientific output from the very beginnings of their careers, and (2) it should take only a few years of professional work for a scientist to establish the scientific knowledge and technical competence necessary for scientific publication.

5. Age as a proxy for position in the research laboratory

The fact that scientists are drawn off from research and drawn into administrative and other tasks from the very beginnings of their careers suggests that age – in accordance with our initial thesis – might be considered a proxy for the degree to which scientists occupy various informal and formal supervisory positions.[7] A simple check of such an assumption can be made by asking whether there is any significant direct effect of age and professional experience on productivity, over and above the effect that runs through the position a scientist attains in the research unit. If there were such a direct effect, it could mean that increasing age is accompanied by rising technical knowledge and competence, and that these could account for the increase in

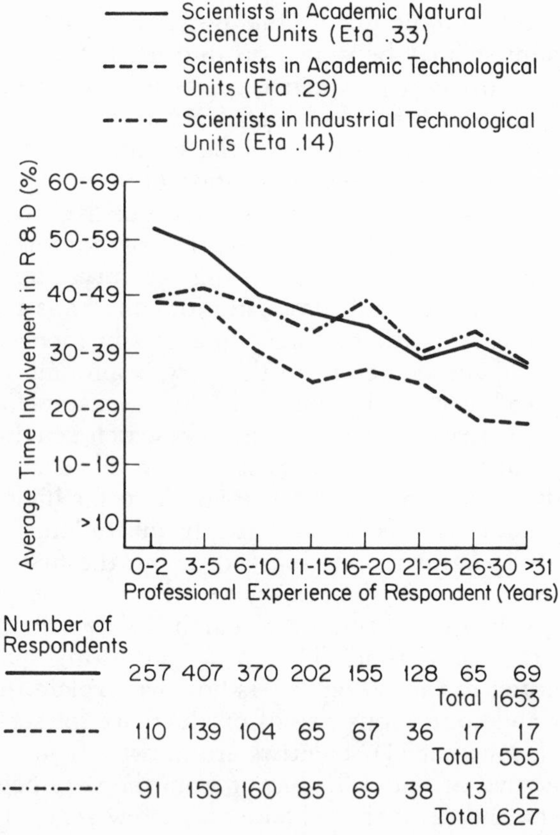

Exhibit 3.3. Mean percentage of time in research by professional experience for scientists in academic natural and technological science units and in industrial units.

productivity, regardless of the position a scientist holds and the task structure and resources that position provides.

By looking at the correlations between age or professional experience and productivity separately for formally acknowledged supervisors like unit heads (which we could differentiate in our data set) and other scientific members of a research unit, including scientists of various supervisory positions below unit heads and nonsupervisory researchers (whom we could not differentiate), the primary importance of position as opposed to sheer age or experience was underlined. For clearly identified supervisory scientists (unit heads), where position was controlled for, the correlation between age/experience and productivity went down and became insignificant, whereas for other scientific

Exhibit 3.4. Pearson *r*s between age/experience and publication productivity for different subgroups of academic scientists

	Pearson *r*s between productivity and:	
	Chronological age	Professional experience
Unit heads		
natural scientists	.05	.13
technological scientists	.00	.13
Unit members		
natural scientists	.34[a]	.43[a]
technological scientists	.32[a]	.44[a]
Academic natural scientists (all)	.46[a]	.51[a]
Academic technological scientists	.43[a]	.50[a]

[a]$p \leq .001$.

members (position not controlled for) it remained significant. This implies that position and not age accounts for productivity differences (see Exhibit 3.4).

Another more indirect check of the theoretical priority attributed to position, for which age stands as a proxy in this analysis, can be made by pointing to the following relationship: If position rather than age were to explain publication differentials, then there should be a positive relationship between a supervisory scientist's access to manpower resources and his or her productivity, for the simple reason that the number of scientists and support staff supervised should act as a multiplying factor as far as the supervisor's quantity of output is concerned. If, however, it were age or professional experience and the presumed rise in personal scientific competence to which increasing numbers of publications per unit of time should be attributed, then there should be no such correlation between a supervisor's manpower resources and his or her productivity.

Again the argument can be checked very simply by looking at the publication productivity of the subgroup of formally acknowledged supervisors, that is, unit heads, for whom the information as to how many scientists, engineers, technicians, etc., they supervised during the last three years (the period of the publication counts) is available. Exhibit 3.5 shows how publication productivity in this subgroup rises with the size of scientific

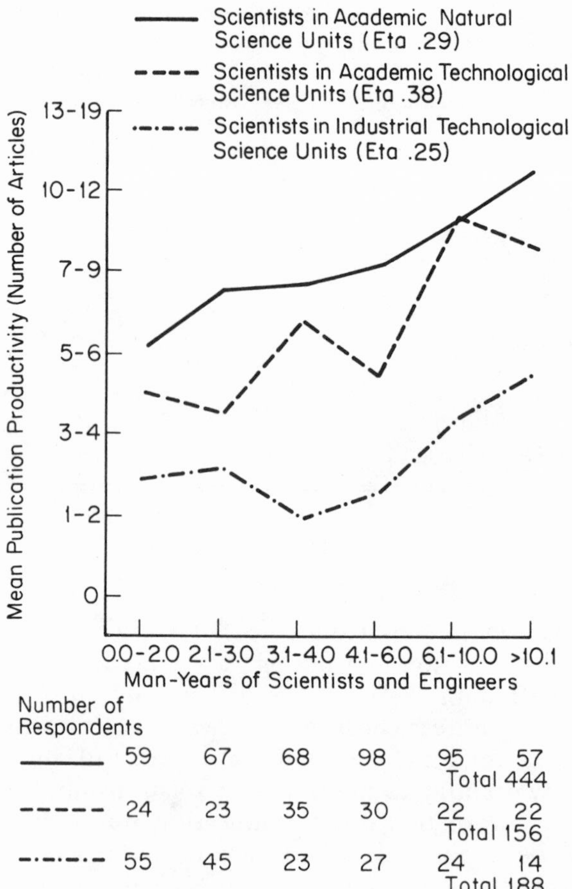

Exhibit 3.5. Mean publication productivity for different manpower resources (scientists and engineers) for supervisory scientists in academic natural and technological science units and in industrial settings.

manpower resources. Exhibit 3.6 documents the equivalent relationship for the size of the technical and service staff supervised.[8]

One can see in Exhibit 3.5 that, as resources in highly qualified manpower increase, there is an almost linear increase in a supervisory scientist's publications in the natural sciences, a two-peaked increase in the technological sciences, and a somewhat less pronounced relationship in industrial settings. Similarly, in both fields and in both kinds of institutions there is a more or less continuous growth of productivity as the size of the technical and service staff supervised by the scientist increases (Exhibit 3.6). Because availability of and access to scientific and technical manpower resources depends on the position a scientist holds in his or her

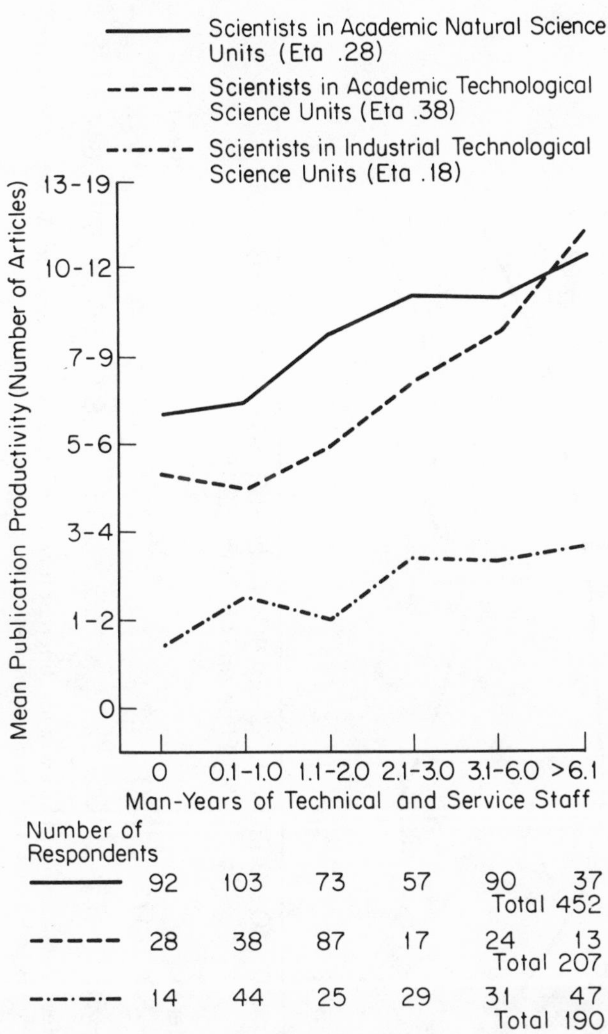

Exhibit 3.6. Mean publication productivity for different manpower resources (technical and service staff) for supervisory scientists in academic natural and technological science units and in industrial settings.

laboratory, we conclude that the existence of the above significant positive relationship supports our general thesis.

6. Age, task structure, and productivity

If age acts as a proxy for position in the present data, then age should also be related to certain characteristics of the task struc-

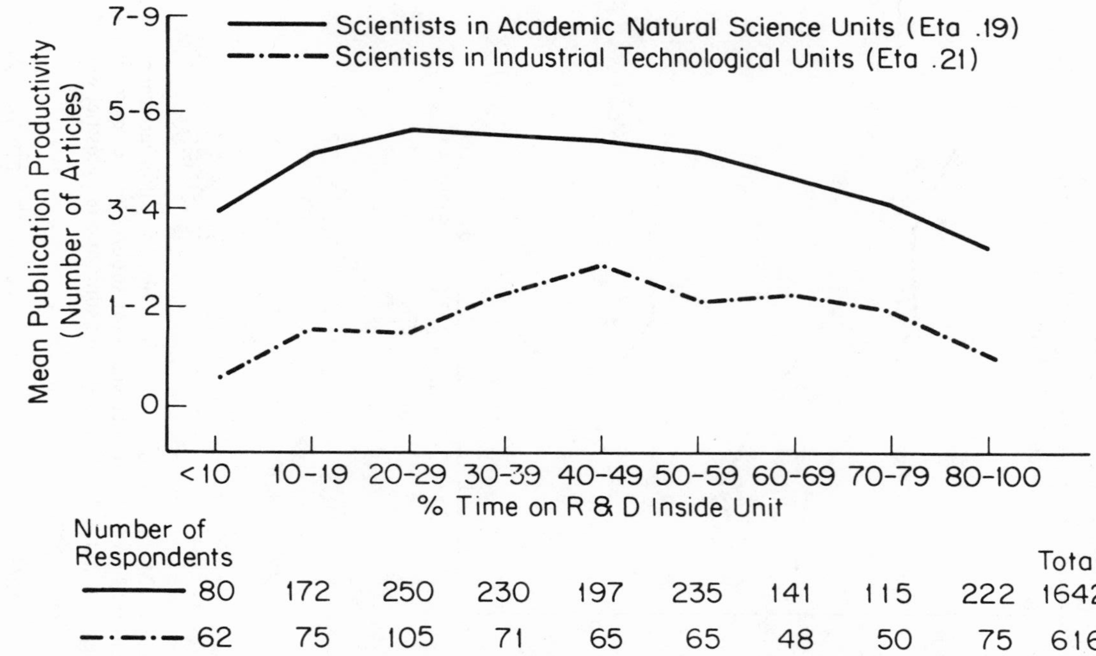

Exhibit 3.7. Mean publication productivity for different time involvements in research for scientists in academic natural science units and in industrial technological science units.

ture associated with supervisory positions. We have already shown that the amount of time in research decreases with age from the very beginning of a career and that involvement in administrative tasks increases steadily. Because productivity also rises continuously, we might suspect that scientists' written productivity does not profit much from sheer time spent in research. Because this seemed somewhat counterintuitive, productivity curves were plotted for different time involvements, controlling as usual for academic field and type of institution. Exhibit 3.7 shows the results for scientists in academic natural science settings and in industrial laboratories involved with technological research. In both cases, the shape of the curve is slightly curvilinear, replicating nicely some of the results in the literature (cf. Pelz and Andrews, 1966): Time involvements lower than 10% *and* around 80% or more are associated with less achievement. In academic settings, publication productivity peaks when about one-third of a scientist's time is spent in research, and it peaks at a somewhat greater time involvement (between 40% and 50%) in industrial units. In sum, however, relationships do not look impressive, as indicated by eta-square coefficients of .04 in both cases.

In order to more specifically address the question of supervisory task structure and its relation to productivity, we controlled for a scientist's position in the unit, assuming that time spent on research might play a more pronounced role in the case of the staff scientists of the unit as compared to unit heads (who in academic settings are often university professors). Exhibit 3.8 shows the resulting productivity curves for both kinds of scientists in academic natural science units. Somewhat unexpectedly, relationships were particularly weak for the staff scientists: Except for the well-known negative effect of extremely little or extremely much research, productivity seemed to be more or less independent of the percent of time spent on development activities within the unit. If it pays for one to be *more* involved with research, then it is the supervisor in the highest position or the head of a unit who reaches a higher level of productivity by spending at least 30% of his or her time on research activities.

If sheer time spent in research does not relate significantly to the publication productivity of a scientist, then it may be the change in the *nature* of involvement in research that is associated with attainment of supervisory positions that accounts for the productivity difference. Devoting relatively small amounts of time to many projects at the early (research conceptualization) and late (report and paper writing) stages clearly offers better

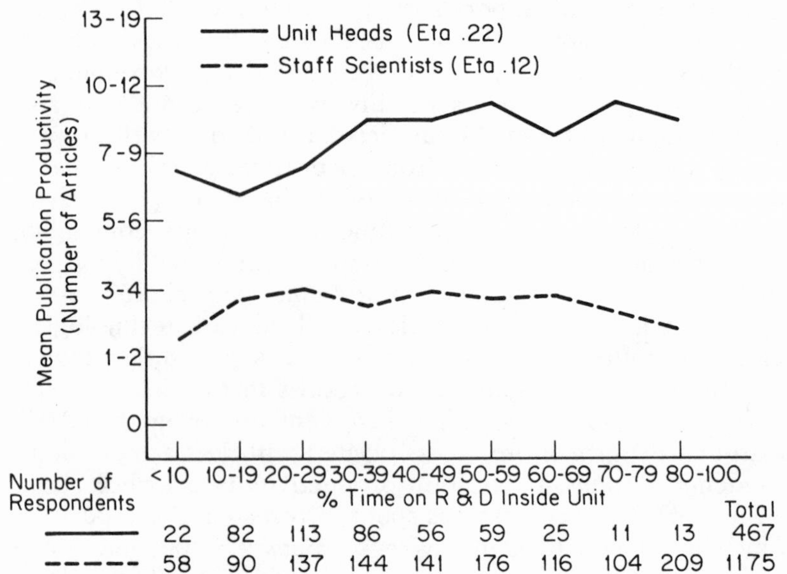

Exhibit 3.8. Mean publication productivity for different time involvements in research for unit heads and staff scientists in academic natural science settings.

opportunities for authorship or co-authorship than devoting large amounts of time to actually doing all the tedious work of one research task. Consequently, if the negative relationship between age or experience and time spent in research, and the lack of a significant correlation between time spent in research and productivity (except for extreme time involvements), can be supplemented by a positive relationship between age/experience and the degree to which the scientist is charged with goal setting rather than executing functions (and if the goal-setting functions are positively related to productivity), this would support our argument that it is the differential advantages associated with supervisory positions that account for much of the productivity differences in research organizations.

To check our argument the following three dimensions have been chosen to represent – to various degrees – a task structure oriented toward goal setting: (1) the diversity of functions of a scientist, an index based on a simple count of every incidence of a greater than 0% time involvement of the scientist in (a) research, (b) teaching, (c) administration, and (d) other scientific activities (like consulting work, scientific documentation, etc.);[9] (2) the degree to which the scientist was involved in setting research goals for execution by others (like "perception and identification of an area of interest" for the unit) as opposed to genuinely executing the tasks her- or himself (like "collection and production of data" or "literature review");[10] (3) the total number of projects in which a scientist was involved, as an indicator of his or her ability to attract resources in connection with his or her work in the unit.

All three dimensions were thought to mirror the position a scientist held in the unit. The higher the scientist in the hierarchy of the research laboratory, the more he or she would be confronted with a variety of scientific and nonscientific functions in addition to research, the more the nature of his or her involvement would change toward goal setting rather than executing activities, and the more he or she would be able to attract project money and consequently be involved in more projects (as a supervisor or just formally) within and outside the unit.

As can be seen in Exhibit 3.9, which shows correlation coefficients between the above dimensions of task structure, position (as approximated by "professional" age), and productivity, the data substantiate these expectations.

7. A social-position model of publication productivity

We have shown so far that age and professional experience can be used as a kind of proxy for the degree to which a scientist holds a supervisory position,[11] and that the manpower resources and task structure associated with this position relate positively to a scientist's publication productivity. As a final check on our general thesis, we now present a path-analytic model of the presumed structure of relationships as implied so far, ignoring for a moment manpower resources, which were only measured for the unit heads. The fit of the path-analytic model representing this structure has been tested with the help of the Lisrel technique (cf. Joreskog and Van Thillo, 1972; Joreskog, 1974).

The Lisrel technique is a computer program for estimating general linear-structural equation models with the special advantage of allowing for unmeasured hypothetical constructs or latent variables, each of which may be measured by several indicators. The method allows for a differentiation between errors in equations (disturbances) and errors in the observed variables (measurement errors) and yields estimates for both. To check the measurement characteristics that are assumed by Lisrel, a test of linearity of bivariate relationships was made; it showed no significant nonlinearities in the data. All parameters reported in the

Exhibit 3.9. Pearson *r*s between various dimensions of the research task structure of a scientist, publication productivity, and professional experience, for scientists in academic settings

	Academic natural scientists		Academic technological scientists	
Dimensions of task structure	Years of prof. experience	Publication productivity	Years of prof. experience	Publication productivity
Diversity of functions	.34[a]	.28	.32	.24
Degree of involvement in setting research goals	.40	.42	.38	.34
Number of research projects	.42	.47	.44	.39

[a] For all Pearson *r*s, $p \leq .001$.

models pertain to standardized variables. Linkages between latent dimensions (circles) represent true relationships[12] and are reported as path coefficients; those between observed (rectangles) and unobserved dimensions represent the construct validity of the measures and are reported as regression coefficients. Other arrows pointing to observed[13] variables indicate the amount of measurement error, whereas those pointing to latent dimensions indicate disturbances or residuals.

As in previous analyses, we chose scientists in academic natural science and technological science units as well as scientists in industrial units as relevant subgroups for replicating the model. Results for academic natural sciences are shown in Exhibit 3.10; for technological sciences in industry, in Exhibit 3.11. The model for academic technological science settings is not included, because results are the same as for natural sciences, with an even higher amount of variance explained.[14]

The ability of Lisrel to reproduce the input correlations among observed variables was generally good: The mean deviation of the estimated correlations from the observed correlations in the model of Exhibit 3.10 was .025, and in Exhibit 3.11, .024; the highest discrepancies were .134 and .161, respectively.

The good fit of the model supports the presumed structure of relationships: A scientist's age (used as a proxy for the degree to which he or she holds a supervisory position) is related to his or her task structure in the research laboratory, and this in turn is related to his or her publication productivity.

Because the Lisrel method allows for multiple indicators (shown by the rectangles in Exhibits 3.10 and 3.11) of each concept (shown by the circles), age is assessed by both chronological age and professional experience. Similarly, supervisory task structure, as described above is represented by three dimensions: the diversity of functions, the volume of goal-setting research functions, and the number of projects in which the scientist was involved.[15]

When screening the data to detect other potential organizational effects upon individual publication productivity, no further variables were significantly related to an individual scientist's output in academic settings. It is important to note that the five-variable pattern of relationships that identifies supervisory position as the major explanatory concept relating to intraorganizational productivity differences seemingly dominates all other bivariate relationships between organizational variables and publication productivity as emerging from correlation analyses.[16]

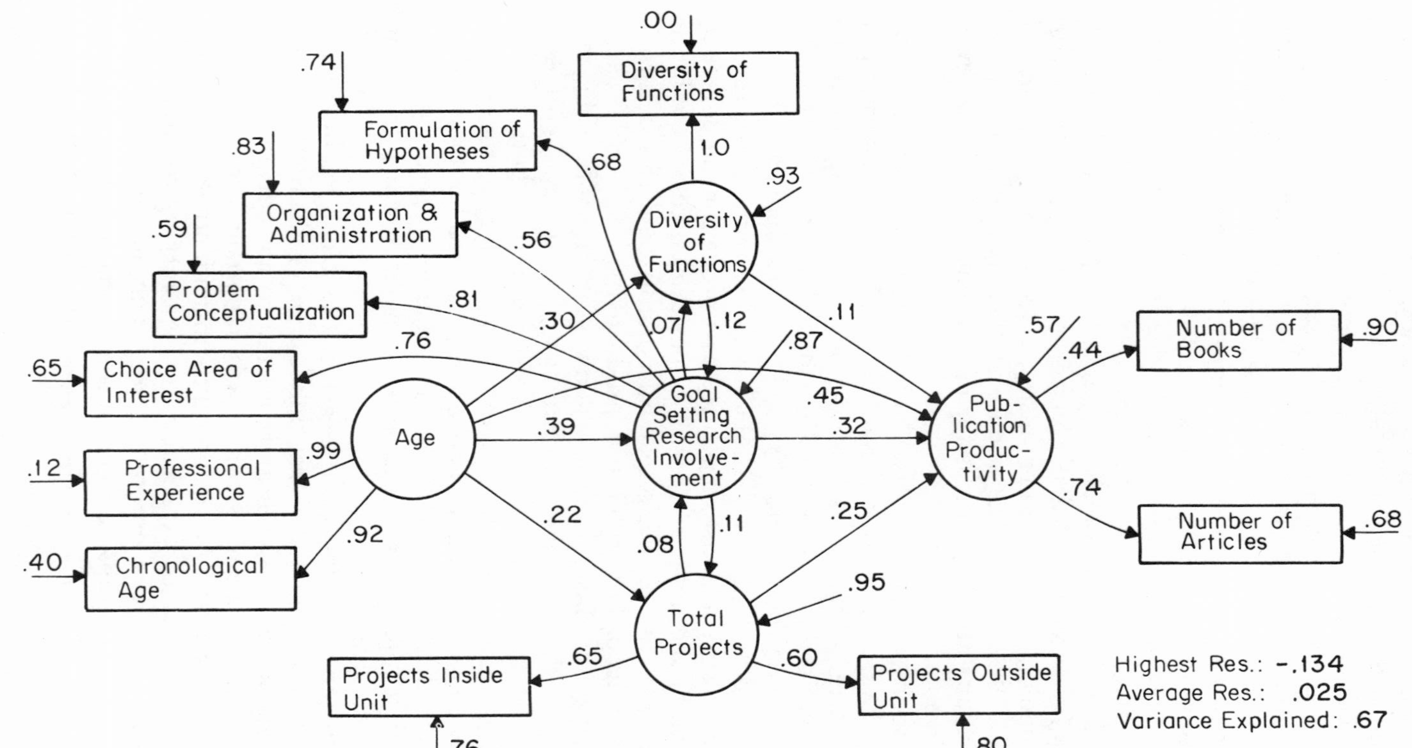

Exhibit 3.10. Lisrel model of individual publication productivity for scientists in academic natural science settings.

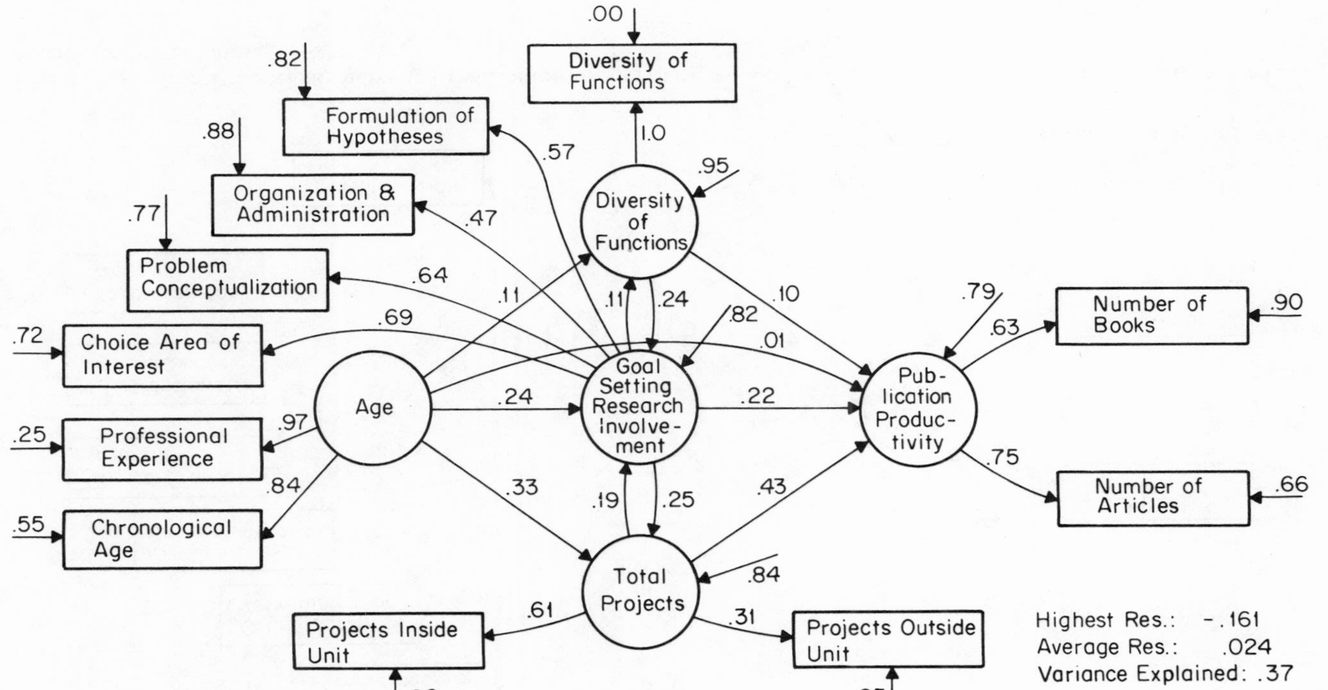

Exhibit 3.11. Lisrel model of individual publication productivity for technological scientists in industry.

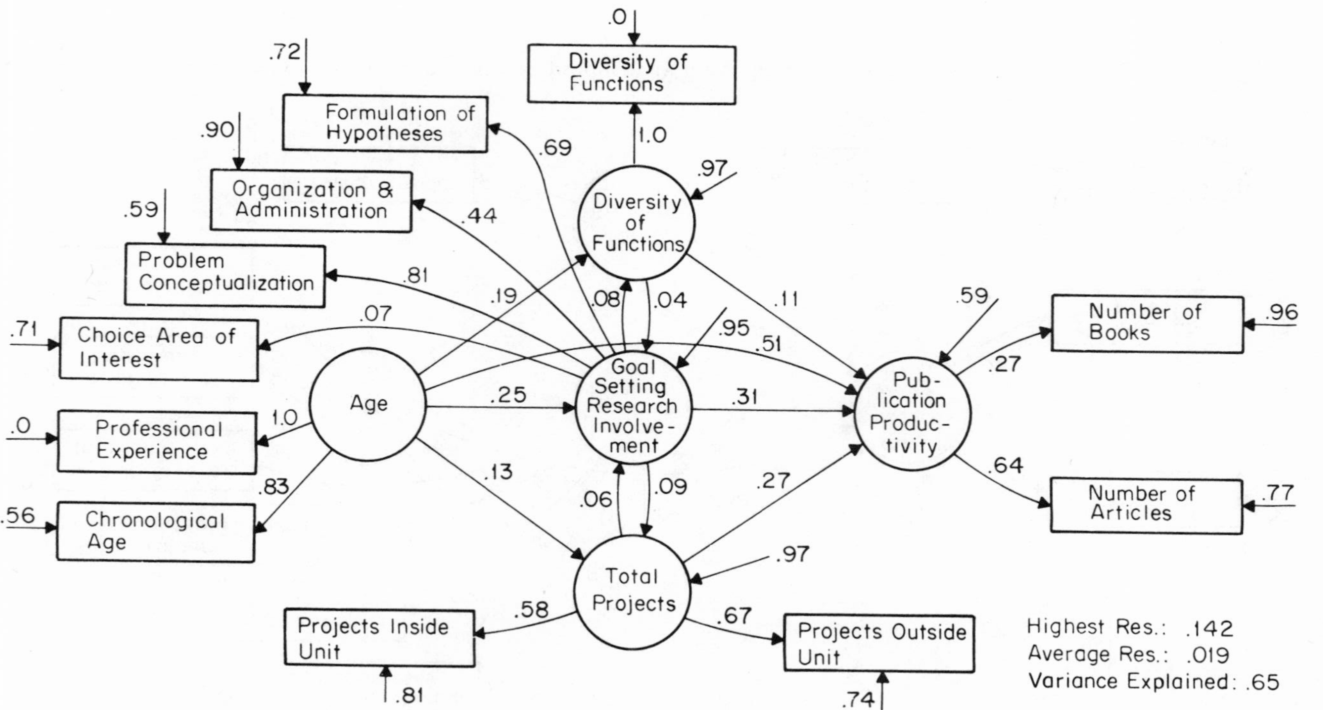

Exhibit 3.12. Lisrel model of individual publication productivity for staff scientists (i.e., excluding unit heads) in academic natural science settings.

8. Control for a scientist's position

As can be seen from an inspection of the models presented so far, there remains a relatively high direct effect of age and professional experience on publication productivity in academic settings.[17] We have already shown that the relationship between age/experience and productivity tends to disappear when a scientist's supervisory position is controlled for (see our discussion of Exhibit 3.4). In order to check the validity of our previous argument in the case of the multivariate relationships we are now confronted with, we estimated the social-position model of individual publication productivity in academic natural science settings separately for supervisory scientists (unit heads) and unit members. In accordance with what we have said so far, the model would be expected to replicate nicely for unit members (because this subgroup includes various kinds of supervisory positions below unit heads), but should, being a social-position model, change significantly when unit heads are looked at exclusively.

Exhibits 3.12 and 3.13 substantiate these expectations: In the case of scientific members of a unit (Exhibit 3.12), the model maintains its significance, with only slight changes in the parameters linking concepts, and an explained variance in productivity of 65% (as compared to an original 67%). In the case of unit heads (Exhibit 3.13), the variable "quantity of manpower resources at the head's disposal" (which was not measured for unit members) was included in the model. This latter variable yields the highest path coefficient, followed by the variable "number of projects" (the supervisor is involved in). This suggests that once a supervisory position is attained, *manpower resources* and *project tasks* account for much of the variance in *further* productivity differences. In accordance with this, the direct relationship between age/experience and productivity is reduced to .03 (from .45 in the global model!), clearly indicating that there is no remaining effect of age once position and what it stands for are taken into account.

9. Technological scientists in industrial research units

From an inspection of Exhibits 3.10 and 3.11, it can be seen that both models in general show good fit, as assessed by highest and average residuals, yet the amount of variance explained in individual productivity varies greatly between the two types of institutions involved: There is a decrease of 30 percentage points between the variance explained with the model for scientists in

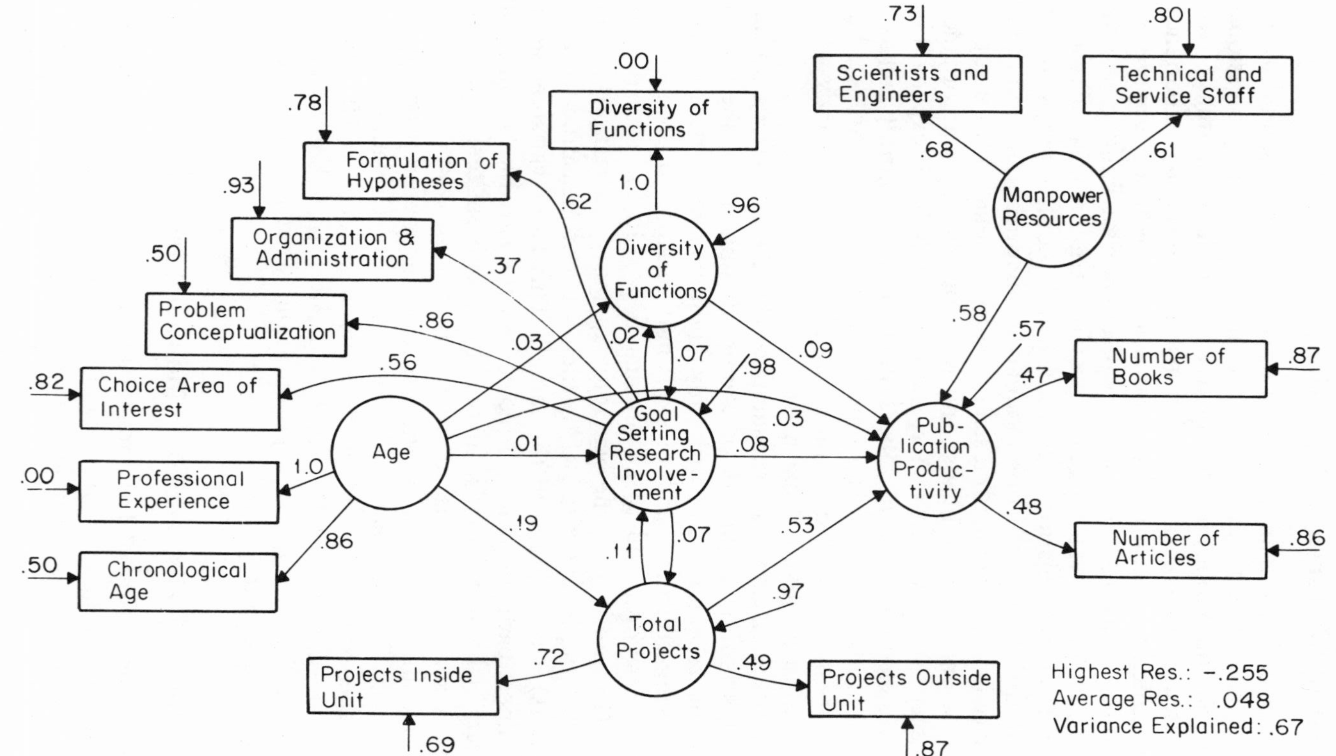

Exhibit 3.13. Lisrel model of individual publication productivity for supervisory scientists (unit heads) in academic natural science settings.

academic natural science settings (67%) and for scientists in industrial firms (37%).[18]

The smaller amount of variance explained in industrial settings by the social-position model of publication productivity suggests that there might be other factors specific to industry that should be taken into account. Exhibit 3.14 presents a model that includes two principal other sources of explanation, one referring to influences on the *choice of the research theme* of an industrial laboratory, the other referring to the amount of *external communication*[19] the unit maintains.

The first source subdivides into two different factors relevant to enhancing productivity: the degree to which scientific significance is taken into account when the research tasks of a laboratory are being determined, and the degree to which science policymaking bodies determine the choice of research tasks (as in socialized industry). Whereas the first factor seemingly points to an industrial research unit's orientation toward basic research, which is itself linked to external communication and to more emphasis on publications, the second factor could imply a certain policy of legitimizing public (governmental) money spent on research by pressure toward publishing all the results obtained. Both factors refer to characteristics of the organizational context in which a scientist is working. It is plausible to assume that this context is especially important for enhancing or restricting publication productivity in industry because: (1) Scientists in industry are generally operating under more organizational constraints than in academic settings; and (2) publications are not a typical form of industrial research output and hence will flourish only under special conditions.

The expanded model is shown in Exhibit 3.14. Reproduction of observed correlations by parameters produced by the Lisrel program was good again: The average discrepancy between observed and fitted correlations was .033; the highest discrepancy was .161. The model now accounts for somewhat more than half the variance in individual publication productivity in this setting (53%). A gain of 16 percentage points resulted from adding organizational context variables to the individual position effects of the former model in Exhibit 3.11.

10. Group productivity and its correlates

Having outlined the position of a scientist and the manpower resources and supervisory task structure associated with it as the major explanatory factor in accounting for the productivity dif-

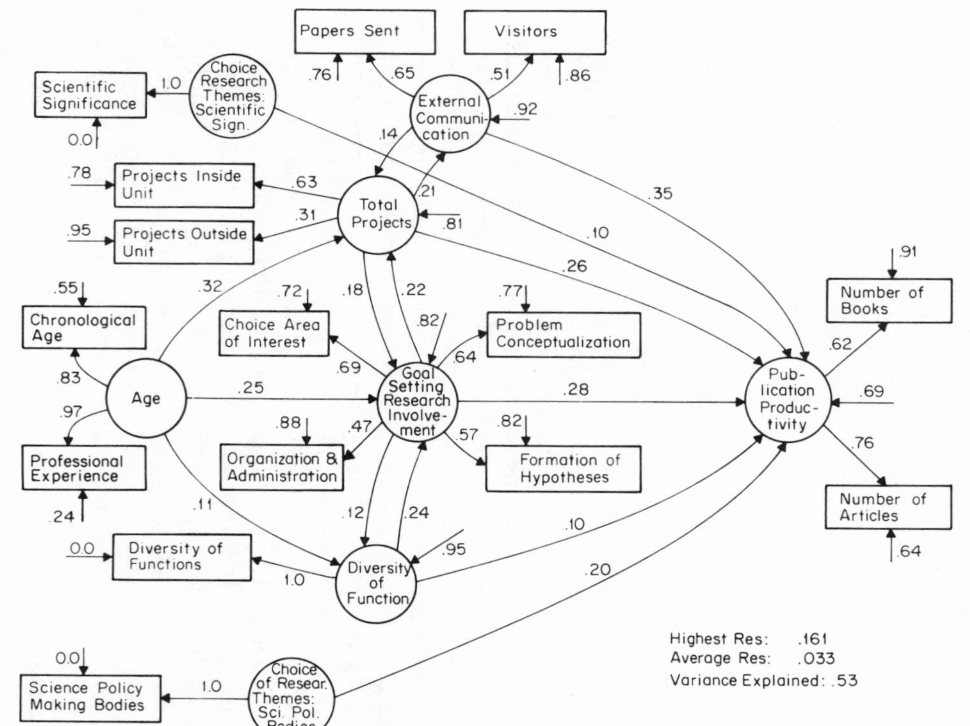

Exhibit 3.14. Lisrel model of individual publication productivity including choice of research themes, for technological scientists in industry.

ferences of scientists, we were interested to explore whether group publication productivity can be explained by individual members' productivity or whether the analysis would have to incorporate additional factors.

Group publication productivity can be introduced here as a measure of the quantity of papers published in scientific journals by the members of a research unit during the last three years in connection with the work of the unit (we shall also consider the publication of books). Group productivity defined this way is not identical with the sum of publications reported by group members during that period, nor with mean productivity as defined by the sum divided by the number of persons in the group. The quantity of group publications differs from the sum of individual members' publications in that (1) the effect of multi-authorship has been eliminated,[20] and (2) the aggregate character of the concept assures that individual productivity differentials are wiped out in the group measure.

Seen this way, the quantity of publications should be a more valid indicator of the group's overall contribution to science than the sum of individual publication productivities (because it is the number of actual products that is counted). Furthermore, group productivity scores might allow for a better exploration of context (organizational) effects than would individual productivities (and their possibly more personality-linked origins).

Before attempting to account for group productivity, let us show how productivity scores of supervisory scientists (unit heads) and scientific members of the unit relate to group productivity. Because many of the results in the literature refer to departmental prestige in relation to quantitative productivity, Exhibit 3.15 includes a measure of the recognition[21] received by the research unit in order to check for its association with quantitative output.

In accordance with the analysis presented so far, there is a dominant relationship of supervisory productivity over group productivity. Exhibit 3.15 shows that, on the average, supervisory productivity accounts for three to five times more variance in group productivity than does the output of the research members of the group in academic settings. In industrial settings, this ratio is somewhat lower, but there are still pronounced effects of the supervisor, especially as far as articles abroad and books are concerned. The same holds for departmental prestige as measured by the recognition the unit receives by the scientific community: Here too the correlations are higher for supervisory scientists than for scientific members of the unit.

Exhibit 3.15. Pearson *r*s between publication productivity scores of individual scientists of a unit and group productivity scores of the unit for different measures of productivity

	Group productivity measure							
	Articles publ. in country		Articles publ. abroad		Articles and books		Recognition of unit	
Publication productivity of:	r	r^2	r	r^2	r	r^2	r	r^2
Academic natural scientists:								
unit heads	.39	.15	.48	.23	.62	.38	.44	.19
unit members	.26	.07	.19	.04	.29	.08	.26	.07
Academic technological scientists:								
unit heads	.61	.40	.43	.18	.68	.46	.39	.15
unit members	.39	.15	.18	.03	.34	.12	.19	.03
Industrial technological scientists:								
unit heads	.60	.36	.36	.13	.68	.46	.44	.19
unit members	.50	.25	.23	.05	.38	.14	.32	.10

Exhibit 3.16. Predictive power of several variables in explaining group publication productivity

Predictor variable	Academic natural science groups (N = 450) Beta	Eta²	Academic tech. science groups (N = 154) Beta	Eta²	Industrial tech. science groups (N = 180) Beta	Eta²
Group head's publication productivity	.47	.38	.49	.46	.52	.40
Staff scientists' publ. productivity	.23	.19	.24	.23	.17	.16
Size of research unit	.22	.17	.29	.26	.31	.15
Scientific exchanges of group	.14	.15	.24	.22	.15	.13
Age of research unit	.12	.08	.14	.11	.16	.03
Multiple R^2 unadjusted	.54		.64		.54	
Multiple R^2 adjusted	.50		.59		.44	

Note: Results are from multiple classification analysis.

The existence and size of the above correlations already suggest that individual publication productivity accounts for a substantial amount of variance (varying according to individual position) in group productivity. When exploring different *organizational* characteristics by means of multiple classification analysis[22] in a further attempt to explain group productivity, we found that the following three variables – in addition to individual productivity – seemed to influence the published output of a group: the *size* of the research units, as measured by the average number of man-years of scientists and engineers working in the group during the last three years; the *age* of the unit, as measured by the number of years the unit has existed formally under its present name and goal structure; and the *scientific exchange* maintained by the unit by exchanging publications with other groups or individual scientists working in the field. Exhibit 3.16 lists the beta and eta-square parameters[23] as well as the multiple correlation coefficients for this set of predictors for academic groups in natural and technological sciences and for industrial groups in technological sciences.[24]

Exhibit 3.16 confirms that the supervisors' productivity can account for most of the variance in group productivity in all subgroups, followed by either group members' productivity or unit size. Scientific exchanges and age contribute less to overall explanatory power. The relationships of head's and members' productivity, of size, and of scientific exchanges to group productivity are all positive and tend to be monotonic.

Generally, one could say that although the variables listed above account for a reasonable amount of variance in the dependent measure, they do not contribute significantly to our understanding of mechanisms associated with group productivity. That the size of a research team should be related to the number of articles it produces comes as no surprise, and it would have been a serious blow to our confidence in the results if individual productivity had not come up as a major contributor to group productivity. The same holds true for the scientific exchanges of a group: High publication productivity in most cases will be associated with more activities in sending out and receiving papers, and this may be a result much more than a cause of the quantity of output of a group. The least clearcut and least easily predicted relationship is that with unit age; however, unit age seems to contribute only marginally to explaining group productivity.

In order to check the above results and to improve our understanding, it seemed essential to adjust the number of group publications for the average size of the group during the last three years[25] and then to try and predict the resulting per capita publication productivity of the group using the same and other variables. Although relationships between per capita productivity and the variables above were maintained but did change in size and form, it is interesting to note that no other variables were identified as substantially contributing to the explanation of group productivity when bivariate relationships were examined.

Exhibit 3.17 presents the results of the multiple classification analysis on the above input variables when per capita productivity measures are used as the dependent variable.

By comparing the beta and eta-square coefficients of Exhibit 3.17 with those of Exhibit 3.16, it can be seen that the contributions of the head's and members' productivity to group productivity remain about the same in academic units and tend to be somewhat higher in industrial settings;[26] similarly, the relationship between scientific exchanges and group productivity remains positive and is sometimes more pronounced than with total productivity scores. Additionally, unit age again contributes only marginally to the overall variance explained.[27] The most interesting result clearly pertains to the relationship between *group size* and adjusted productivity scores. Exhibit 3.18 presents the raw and adjusted[28] means of per capita publications for groups of different sizes in academic and industrial settings; it shows that size is *negatively* related to per capita productivity in natural sci-

Exhibit 3.17. Predictive power of several variables in explaining per capita group publication productivity

Predictor variable	Academic natural science groups (N = 456)		Academic tech. science groups (N = 157)		Industrial tech. science groups (N = 175)	
	Beta	Eta^2	Beta	Eta^2	Beta	Eta^2
Group head's publication productivity	.45	.23	.46	.33	.59	.49
Staff scientists' publ. productivity	.27	.16	.26	.16	.28	.24
Size of research unit	.46	.16	.36	.14	.15	.09
Scientific exchanges of group	.17	.10	.22	.14	.22	.18
Age of research unit	.11	.02	.16	.09	.19	.05
Multiple R^2 unadjusted	.55		.54		.65	
Multiple R^2 adjusted	.51		.42		.57	

Note: Results are from multiple classification analysis.

Exhibit 3.18. Raw and adjusted means of per capita group productivity (number of articles) by group size in natural and technological sciences

Group size (average scientific man-years)	Academic natural science groups (N = 456)		Academic technological science groups (N = 157)		Technological science groups in industry (N = 175)	
	raw	adjusted	raw	adjusted	raw	adjusted
0 – 2.0	3.8	4.3	2.6	3.3	1.6	1.8
2.1– 3.0	3.9	4.3	3.0	3.7	1.7	1.7
3.1– 4.0	4.0	4.2	3.4	3.3	1.3	1.4
4.1– 6.0	3.5	3.5	2.6	2.7	1.8	1.7
6.1–10.0	3.8	3.4	3.8	2.9	1.7	1.2
>10.0	3.2	2.7	3.0	2.5	2.3	2.5
Eta	.40		.37		.29	
Eta^2	.16		.14		.09	

Note: Results are from multiple classification analysis.

ence groups, and that the raw relationships, which tend to be positive in technological sciences, become negative when the effects of other variables are controlled and one looks at adjusted means.

A number of studies have appeared on the effect of organizational size, with inconsistent findings. Whereas Meltzer and Salter (1962), for instance, report that size remained totally insignificant in explaining the productivity of physiologists, Wallmark and associates (Wallmark and Sellerberg, 1966; Wallmark et al., 1973) claim that the efficiency of research teams increases exponentially with the size of the team. However, both authors use definitions of the "team" or "unit" that are not comparable to our case.[29] Hagstrom (1971) presents an argument in favor of a positive effect of size by saying that size permits breadth to be combined with that specialization that is necessary for rapidly developing research fronts. Furthermore, one could argue that if innovations occur randomly in a speciality field, then the likelihood of this phenomenon would be greater in larger units. Similarly, if productivity depends on the availability of substantial resources and is linked to high-status scientists (cf. Mullins, 1975), then again larger groups should provide more chances of fulfilling this requirement. On the other hand, according to Worthy's (1950) well-known theory, larger size is accompanied by a proliferation of hierarchical levels and institutionalized relationships that prevent the exploration of an individual's full capability and lead to low morale and output. We might add that scientific field and the associated technology requirements could play a key role in determining optimal group size, as suggested by the far less pronounced negative effect of size in technological science research units and especially in industry in our data. Blume and Sinclair (1973a,b), for instance, found that the relationship between size and productivity varies considerably between areas of a single discipline (chemistry). They speculate on the multiplicity of skills required for some types of research and on the degree of "mechanization" and typification of the research procedure as influencing this relationship. Whereas considerations such as these might be relevant for explaining the differential importance of size in natural and technological science disciplines, the results are not directly applicable to the present analysis because measures of individual publication productivity are considered. Finally, we should point to results by Stankiewicz (1976) on the present data set, which show that the relationship between group size and productivity in academic settings varies in different countries, suggesting that differing organizational structures of the university system (e.g., is size associated with a flat type of structure or highly correlated with the number of levels in the organization?) will have to be taken onto account when analyzing the problem.[30]

Summarizing our results on group productivity, we might say that there are two major results worth noting: (1) Individual publication productivity emerges as the major explanatory variable of group per capita output (which means that we are referred back to our individual publication models); and (2) the size of the group tends to relate negatively to per capita productivity (varying in degree according to field and institution) in the six-country data set.

11. Discussion

Some of the limitations of the preceding analysis can be made apparent by pointing to two different interpretations that can be associated with what we have documented: that individual productivity when analyzed in terms of organizational variables is mainly accounted for by the social position the scientist holds in the scientific hierarchy of his organization. One interpretation (put forward by us so far) would attribute differences in publication rates to the operation of the stratification system inside organizations. Advancement on the (formal or informal) hierarchy is associated with differential access to resources and with differences in functions and involvement in research, which in turn leads to a higher probability of authorship or co-authorship for the scientist. This hypothesis suggests that the status of a scientist significantly affects the quantity of publications he or she can claim, irrespective of his or her personal innovativeness and productivity. The second interpretation would describe differential productivity associated with position as an outcome of the differential capability and technical competence of a scientist, deriving the higher productivity of higher-position scientists from a movement of more capable and higher-performing researchers into supervisory positions.

The two interpretations do not necessarily contradict each other. If early publication productivity based on personal capacity and dynamic orientation[31] leads to promotion into supervisory status, then resources and functions conducive to producing output might replace or strongly reinforce original capacities. The last-mentioned effects are verified in the present data by the significant increase of supervisory productivity obtained with an increase in the size of the scientific and technical staff supervised: It will be remembered that staff size and volume of projects together account for almost all the variance of the unit head's publications in the Lisrel model.

The present data do not permit a check of original productivity capacities. They do, however, call into question the argument that a scientist's productivity suffers as he or she takes on supervisory duties that involve higher percentages of nonresearch tasks and hence keep him or her from pursuing research work. Except for the rare cases where a scientist leaves the scientific hierarchy, he or she seems to be not drawn off, but rather drawn *into* publication productiveness by advancement in the hierarchy, whatever his or her original production capacities may have been.

These results can be used to shed new light on the meaning of productivity as measured by publication counts and on some of the earlier findings relating to it.[32] If what is measured is authorship rather than talent for creating research results, and if–as pointed out by Crane[33]–the norms in some fields allow supervisors to claim authorship for the work of students or staff scientists whereas the norms of other fields do not permit this, then it may be more appropriate to attribute productivity to the privileges of higher rank and to supervisory efficiency in productively organizing the task force than to seek explanations in terms of factors enhancing individual production capacities. Consequently, switching the attention from the notion of (publication) productivity as used in the literature to the notion of authorship as emerging from the present analysis may pave the way for a better understanding of science as a highly stratified and elitist system and of the impact this has on the development of scientific knowledge.

12. Summary

Studies of stratification in science have increasingly accepted the idea that science is a highly stratified and elitist system with skewed distributions of productivity and rewards. Attempts to explain the higher productivity of higher-status scientists by pointing to the greater ease with which their work might be accepted by journals and publishers were not supported by the data in some recent studies. If status in general does not confer greater ease of publication, this chapter argues that position within a research organization does confer greater ease of author- or co-authorship, and that this is the major explanatory variable accounting for productivity differences within research laboratories as far as quantity of articles (and books) is concerned. Upward moves in a laboratory's formal or informal hierarchy are associated with a change in a scientist's research involvement from goal-executing to goal-setting functions as well as with an increase in access to scientific manpower and project money. Having goal-setting tasks permits a significant reduction in the time expenditures in research necessary to assure that the scientist is identified with the research results and, hence, permits involvement in more research tasks than originally. Equivalently, resources in scientific manpower and project money act as multiplying elements as far as quantity of output is concerned. When group productivity is considered, individual publication productivity and especially supervisory productivity retain a major significance. Additionally, the size of the research unit seemingly plays a key role: In the present data set, size tends to be negatively related to per capita group productivity, with the most pronounced relationships occurring in academic natural science units.

References

Allison, P. D., and Stewart, J. A., 1974, Productivity Differences among Scientists: Evidence for Accumulative Advantage, *American Sociological Review,* 39: 596–606.

Andrews, F. M., et al., 1973, *Multiple Classification Analysis* (2d ed.), Ann Arbor, Institute for Social Research, University of Michigan.

Axelson, L. J., 1959, Differences in Productivity of Doctorates in Sociology, *Journal of Educational Sociology,* 33: 49–55.

Babchuk, N., and Bates, A., 1962, Professor or Producer: The Two Faces of Academic Man, *Social Forces,* 40: 341–344.

Ben-David, J., 1960, Scientific Productivity and Academic Organization in Nineteenth Century Medicine, *American Sociological Review,* 25: 828–843.

Blume, S. S., and Sinclair, R., 1973a, Chemists in British Universities: A Study of the Reward System in Science, *American Sociological Review,* 38: 126–138.

Blume, S. S., and Sinclair, R., 1973b, *Research Environment and Performance in British University Chemistry,* London, Her Majesty's Stationery Office, Science Policy Studies No. 6.

Clark, K., 1957, *America's Psychologists,* Washington, D.C., American Psychological Association.

Clemente, F., 1974, Early Career Determinants of Research Productivity, *American Journal of Sociology,* 79(2): 409–419.

Cole, G., 1978, *Development of a Performance Typology of Research Units in the First Round Data: A Preliminary Analysis Report,* Unesco, Paris, Science Policy Division.

Cole, J. R., 1970, Patterns of Intellectual Influence in Scientific Research, *Sociology of Education,* 43: 377–403.

Cole, S., and Cole, J. R., 1967, Scientific Output and Recognition: A Study in the Reward System in Science, *American Sociological Review,* 32: 377–390.

Cole, S., and Cole, J. R., 1968, Visibility and the Structural Bases of Awareness of Scientific Research, *American Sociological Review,* 33: 397–413.

Cole, S., and Cole, J. R., 1971, Measuring the Quality of Sociological Research: Problems in the Use of the Science Citation Index, *American Sociologist,* 6: 23–29.

Coler, M. B. (ed.), 1963, *Essays on Creativity in the Sciences,* New York, New York University Press.

Crane, D., 1965, Scientists at Major and Minor Universities: A Study of Productivity and Recognition, *American Sociological Review,* 30: 699–714.

Dennis, W., 1954, The Bibliographies of Eminent Scientists, *Scientific Monthly,* 79: 180–183.

Gaston, J. C., 1969, Big Science in Britain: A Sociological Study of the High Energy Physics Community, New Haven, Conn., Yale University, Ph.D. thesis.

Goodman, L. A., 1972a, A Modified Multiple Regression Approach to the Analysis of Dichotomous Variables, *American Sociological Review,* 37: 28–46.

Goodman, L. A., 1972b, A General Model for the Analysis of Surveys, *American Journal of Sociology,* 77: 1035–1086.

Goodman, L. A., 1973, Causal Analysis of Data from Panel Studies and other Kinds of Surveys, *American Journal of Sociology,* 78: 1135–1191.

Hagstrom, W. O., 1967, Competition and Teamwork in Science, Madison, Department of Sociology, University of Wisconsin, mimeographed.

Hagstrom, W. O., 1971, Inputs, Outputs and the Prestige of University Science Departments, *Sociology of Education,* 44: 375–397.

Hargens, L. L., and Hagstrom, W. O., 1967, Sponsored and Contest Mobility of American Academic Scientists, *Sociology of Education,* 40: 24–38.

Joreskog, K. G., 1974, Analyzing Psychological Data by Structural Analysis of Covariance Matrices. *In* Krantz, D. H.; Luce, R. D.; Atkinson, R. C.; and Suppe, P. (eds.); *Contemporary Developments in Mathematical Psychology,* vol. 2, San Francisco, Freeman.

Joreskog, K. G., and Van Thillo, M., 1972, Lisrel: A General Computer Program for Estimating a Linear Structural Equation System Involving Multiple Indicators of Unmeasured Variables, Princeton, N.J., Educational Testing Service, unpublished research bulletin RB-R-26.

Kaplan, N., 1964, The Sociology of Science. *In* Faris, R. L. (ed.); *Handbook of Modern Sociology,* Chicago, Rand McNally.

Knorr, K.; Mittermeir, R.; Aichholzer, G.; and Waller, G.; 1976, Published Written Output: Unit Versus Individual Productivity, Vienna, Institute for Advanced Studies, paper presented at the 13th workshop of the International Comparative Study on the Organization and Performance of Research Units.

Lehmann, H. C., 1953, *Age and Achievement,* Princeton, N.J., Princeton University Press.

Lehmann, H. C., 1958, The Chemist's Most Creative Years, *Science,* 127: 1213–1222.

Lehmann, H. C., 1960, The Age Decrement in Scientific Creativity, *American Psychologist,* 15: 128–134.

Lotka, A. Y., 1926, The Frequency Distribution of Scientific Productivity, *Journal of the Washington Academy of Sciences,* 16: 317–323.

Meltzer, B. M., 1949, The Productivity of Social Scientists, *American Journal of Sociology,* 55: 25–29.

Meltzer, L., 1956, Scientific Productivity in Organizational Settings, *Journal of Social Issues,* 12: 32–40.

Meltzer, L., and Salter, J., 1962, Organizational Structure and the Performance and Job Satisfaction of Physiologists, *American Sociological Review,* 27(3): 351–362.

Merton, R. K., 1968, The Matthew Effect in Science, *Science,* 59: 56–63.

Mullins, N. C., 1975, A Sociological Theory of Scientific Revolution. *In* Knorr, K.; Strasser, H.; Zilian, H. G. (eds.); *Determinants and Controls of Scientific Development,* Dordrecht, Holland, D. Reidel.

Pelz, D. C., and Andrews, F. M., 1966, *Scientists in Organizations: Productive Climates for Research and Development,* New York, Wiley.

Price, D. J. de Solla, 1963, *Little Science, Big Science,* New York, Columbia University Press.

Stankiewicz, R., 1976, Research Groups and the Academic Research Organization, paper presented at the 13th workshop of the International Comparative Study on the Organization and Performance of Research Units, Vienna, Institute for Advanced Studies.

Thomasson, P., and Stanley, J., 1966, Exploratory Study of Productivity and "Creativity" of Prominent Psychometricians, Madison, University of Wisconsin, unpublished manuscript.

Waller, G., 1976, Individuelle Produktivitaet in Akademischen Forschungsorganisationen: Eine Goodman Analyse, Vienna, Institute for Advanced Studies.

Wallmark, J. T., and Sellerberg, B., 1966, Efficiency vs. Size of Research Teams, *IEEE Transactions on Engineering Management,* EM-13: 137–142.

Wallmark, J. T., et al., 1973, The Increase in Efficiency with Size of Research Teams, *IEEE Transactions on Engineering Management,* 20(3): 80–86.

Whitley, R., 1976, Types of Science, Organizational Strategies and Patterns of Work in Research Laboratories in Different Scientific Fields, Vienna, Institute for Advanced Studies, paper presented at the PAREX–IAS, Colloquium.

Worthy, J. C., 1950, Organizational Structure and Employee Morale, *American Sociological Review,* 15: 169–179.

Zuckerman, H. A., 1970, Stratification in American Science, *Sociological Inquiry,* 40: 235–257.

Zuckerman, H., and Merton, R. K., 1971, Patterns of Evaluation in Science: Institutionalization, Structure and Functions of the Referee System, *Minerva,* 9: 66–100.

Notes

1. The technological sciences as defined by the Unesco nomenclature basically comprise all applied branches of natural science disciplines (such as chemical technology and engineering or nuclear technology), in addition to such inherently technological fields as motor vehicle technology or materials technology.

2. To cite but a few examples, Blume and Sinclair obtained a Goodman-Kruskal correlation coefficient of .63 between peer group assessment of the work of a scientist and number of published papers; Cole (1967) found a Pearson correlation of .60 between citation and paper count and a correlation of .72 between number of papers and number of citations to the three most frequently cited contributions of the scientist (a measure that cannot be an artifact of the quantity of publications); and Pelz and Andrews (1966) report a

Pearson correlation coefficient near .40 between ratings of a scientist's contribution to technical or scientific knowledge in the field by members of the same laboratory and number of papers published in professional journals within the past five years.

3. The quality of scientific work of a researcher was measured by peer and supervisory ratings of his group from within and outside the unit on several dimensions. See Chapter 2.

4. The average correlation between output of papers and of books for unit heads and staff scientists in academic science and industrial research units is .25. As expected, publication measures were highly skewed in that only a small number of scientists proved to be highly productive, whereas most scientists either had not produced at all or reported only very few papers; accordingly, publication measures were grouped before further use to reduce skewness.

5. The Pearson *r*s between age and professional experience for academic natural scientists, and for technological scientists in academic settings and in industrial settings, are .85, .83, and .76, respectively.

6. The correlations (Pearson *r*s) are, respectively, .47, −.36, and .44 in academic natural science settings; .36, −.34, and .37 in academic technological science settings; and .39, −.14, and .26 in industrial technological science settings.

7. Examples of such positions might be supervising the work of technicians and graduate students, directing–instead of participating in–projects, and heading a laboratory.

8. Manpower resources in both cases are measured in terms of the average number of man years of (1) scientists and engineers (Exhibit 3.5), and (2) technical and support staff (Exhibit 3.6) in the unit supervised by the scientist during the last three years.

9. The range of the index accordingly varies from 1 to 4; the index is based on a general question as to how much of the total work time of the scientist this year was devoted to the above categories, additionally including "routine and control analyses," "design and engineering studies," and "other professional functions" under category (d) above.

10. Indicators used to measure the volume of goal-setting functions are the following: degree of involvement in "perception and identification of an area of interest," in "problem precision: conceptualization, formulation, analysis," in "time-table, administration, organization and economic considerations," and in "formulation and statement of hypotheses"; all items were measured on five-point Likert scales.

11. More specifically, one should say that age and experience act as a proxy for position in relation to publication productivity because there seems to be no direct effect of age over and above what is explained by a scientist's supervisory position. However, that age should be associated with position to such a degree in academic settings is in itself interesting, and points to the fact that advancement in academic bureaucracies is based upon the principle of seniority.

12. To ensure the identifiability of the model, the parameters associated with the symmetric linkages between the unobserved dimensions of functions and tasks performed by the scientist were constrained to be equal.

13. When there was only one observed indicator for a latent dimension (e.g., diversity of functions), the linkage between the two was fixed at 1.0 and the measurement error in the observed indicator was assumed to be zero.

14. The highest residual in this case is .191, the average residual .032, and the amount of variance explained is 81%.

15. Positive relationships between these dimensions and the voluntary overtime a scientist devotes to his or her work and his or her attachment to the research unit can be shown (for example, Pearson *r*s between the age of a scientist and his or her attachment to the unit are .36 for academic natural scientists and .24 for scientists in industry), but were left out of the model because they contributed practically nil to explaining publication productivity when other concepts were included.

16. The final version of the model has been checked with the help of the Goodman technique (Goodman, 1972a, 1972b, 1973), which has the advantages of not requiring any of the assumptions of linear regression to be met by the data and of allowing for an explicit inclusion of interaction effects. Results confirmed that there are no significant interactions or nonlinearities in the variables; furthermore, the model showed an excellent fit, in accordance with what we would expect from the Lisrel results (see Waller, 1976).

The model for scientists in academic natural science units has further been replicated for all six countries individually. The fundamental relationship between age and publication productivity held in all instances. The major discrepancies were that the diversity of functions related negatively to publication productivity for Finland and that the amount of variance transmitted via the number of projects differed. In Belgium, a high correlation between age and projects was found, whereas Austria was on the other side of the spectrum, showing a high direct correlation between age and publication productivity but only a small one between age and projects.

17. This is indicated by a parameter of .45 in the Lisrel model of academic natural scientists (see Exhibit 3.10) and by a parameter of .36 for academic technological scientists (model not included). It is worthwhile noting that this direct effect disappears in industrial settings and hence the linkage has been eliminated in the final model (see Exhibits 3.11 and 3.14).

18. Parameter estimates differ between the models most markedly with respect to the total number of projects (which seems more important in the technological sciences than in the natural sciences) and with respect to the direct linkage between age and publication productivity (which practically disappears in industrial research units).

19. Two indicators have been chosen as measures of external scientific communication: the number of visiting scientists from the country who had visited the unit during the past year, and the number of publications of the unit sent to other individuals or organizations in the field. Several other indicators could also be used here, e.g., the number of scientists from abroad or the number of publications received by the unit (cf. Knorr et al., 1976). It must be noted, however, that the number of publications sent to other groups might be a result rather than a cause of publication productivity; the same holds – to a less obvious degree – for all indicators of external contacts. This points to the hypothetical character of the causal links specified, which should be kept in mind when interpreting the models.

20. With group publications, it is the number of papers that is counted and not the number of authors, as would be the case if publications reported by group members were added together.

21. Recognition has been measured by aggregating responses of unit members as to the degree to which the unit has a high international reputation and the degree to which publications of the unit are in high demand and often cited in the literature. The index was built by combining the scores of the unit heads and mean scores of staff scientists. (Chapter 2 provides further details.)

22. Multiple classification analysis is a multivariate technique for examining the raw, adjusted, and multiple effects of several predictor variables on a dependent variable based on an additive model. Unlike traditional regression analysis, the technique can handle predictors with no better than nominal measurement and with nonlinear interrelationships, but cannot handle (directly) interaction effects (see Andrews et al., 1973).

23. Betas are analogous to standardized regression coefficients; see Andrews et al. (1973: 47 ff.) for full discussion. "Eta-square" is the correlation ratio and indicates the proportion of the total variance in the dependent variable that is explainable by the predictor.

24. These and the following analyses refer to the *research unit* as the unit of analysis to which the variables size, age, and scientific exchange pertain; group members' publication productivity is calculated as the average of the productivities of the unit's staff scientists; the unit head's publication productivity was scored separately.

25. This was done by dividing the number of articles in the unit during the last three years by the average number of man-years of scientists and engineers in the same period.

26. The result that the multiple classification analysis explains only about half the variance of per capita group publication productivity, in spite of the inclusion of individual group members' publication productivity among the predictor variables, is related to the fact that the group measure refers to the number of products *in the group,* whereas the measure of individual publication productivity refers to total authorships.

27. It should be noted, however, that the form of the relationship in industrial settings changes from a negative to a curvilinear relationship.

28. The adjusted means control for the effects of individual publication productivity (heads' and members' productivity), unit age, and scientific exchanges.

29. Additionally, Wallmark et al.'s definition of team size as the number of authors from a given organization seems to be correlated with their productivity measure.

30. See also Chapter 8.

31. Meltzer (1949) showed a negative association between age at first publication and career productivity and points to the general proposition that the best predictor of an activity is a specimen of past performance in the activity.

32. The results of Blume and Sinclair (1973b), which show that higher-ranking scientists are more productive in larger groups and that the relationship between group size and individual productivity varies between specialities, can for instance be reinterpreted as showing the advantages higher-rank scientists gain from staff size. Equivalently, the results can be held to confirm the relevance of norms specific to single fields in establishing higher-rank privileges.

33. Comment on this chapter.

4 Leadership and group performance: a positive relationship in academic research units

Karin D. Knorr, Roland Mittermeir, Georg Aichholzer, and Georg Waller
Institute for Advanced Studies, Vienna

In a recent paper (Knorr et al., 1976b, and Chapter 3 of this volume), we have shown that supervisory status within a research laboratory is associated with higher productivity in terms of the quantity of published articles and books; in fact, position seems to be the major explanatory variable accounting for productivity differences in academic research settings. Although that analysis showed the differential advantages in terms of productivity associated with supervisory status for the supervisors, the present analysis addresses the somewhat complementary question as to how–and in which respects–supervisory scientists matter for those who are supervised by them. Switching the attention from the gain supervisors experience from their status to the gain scientists supervised experience from their supervisor implies that we no longer focus on individual data, but on group data, and that we have to introduce quality ratings of supervisory behavior in order to differentiate leadership effects. Leadership differences, as measured by the subordinates' satisfaction, will be analyzed in terms of the impact they have on work organization, working climate, and group productivity, and will be discussed in the light of the controversial evidence on the meaning of the results.

Richard Kofler, Rudolf Matuschek, and Waltraud Raidl assisted in the preparation of this chapter. This research was supported by the Austrian Industrial Research Promotion Fund. We are grateful to Arnold Tannenbaum for his comments and suggestions.

1. Previous research

The literature on leadership in organizations is large and dominated by what came to be called the *human relations* approach. Whereas purely sociological theories of organizations have tended to ignore the question of leadership,[1] human relations theory, which is mostly psychological in orientation, takes as its general focus the thesis that good leadership should lead to high morale, that high morale should lead to increased effort, and that increased effort should result in higher productivity by the members of an organization.

Most of the studies presented so far constitute variations or elaborations of the two-factor theory of leadership style. They differentiate between "initiating structure" and "consideration," a result of the Ohio State studies (Fleishman, 1953a, 1953b; Fleishman, Harris, and Burtt, 1955; Stogdill and Coons, 1957), or they differentiate between Likert's principle of "supportive leadership" and "instrumental" or "task-oriented" leadership styles (Katz, Maccoby, and Morse, 1950; Likert, 1961; Bowers and Seashore, 1966). Newer studies have been characterized by introducing progressively more complexities: Herzberg (1966) suggested that factors contributing to satisfaction and those contributing to dissatisfaction are independent, and House and Wigdor (1967) found considerable evidence that job satisfaction and climate depend on the alternatives perceived and accessible to the individual as well as on the individual's sex, age, education, culture, professional status, etc. Etzioni (1965), partly substantiated by Rossel (1970), related the level of commitment an organization requires of its constituent groups to the kind of leadership that will be effective, proposing that the higher the required labor commitment the more the formal leadership roles tend to be expressive.[2] Fiedler's "contingency" theory of leadership (1967) demonstrated that the climate of a group had a considerable influence upon the effectiveness of leadership styles; his theory gave rise to a series of attempts to specify those moderating variables upon which the effect of leadership behavior is contingent (e.g., Hollander and Julian, 1969; Lawrence and Lorsch, 1969; House, 1971; Wofford, 1971).

If the history of research in this area is one of introducing progressively more complexities in terms of the contingencies and conditions that have to be taken into account, it is also one of "progressive disenchantment" (Perrow) with the possibility of any simple and easy understanding of the relationship between supervisory behavior, climate, and productivity.[3] Consequently, the human relations approach has increasingly come under criticism in the past decade, with two objections standing out particularly. The first says that "the literature is large but the findings are few" (Meyer, 1976: 516), referring to inconsistent empirical evidence or to the fact that emerging relationships tended to be very low (cf. Vroom, 1964; Korman, 1966; Hulin and Blood, 1968; Campbell and Dunnette, 1968). The second objection centers around the underestimation of the conflict of interest between organizational goals and individual objectives linked to the assumption that organizations are moral[4] and cooperative in nature (cf. Silverman, 1970: 76; Perrow, 1972: 145). The critique implies that the relevance of leadership for climate and productivity should be determined theoretically, considering structural and environmental characteristics of a specific organizational setting and the significance they have for leadership roles. As noted by Hollander (1971: 1), the effect of leader characteristics and style as emphasized by industrial psychology must be gauged in the light of two sources of influence: (1) the attributes and the perceptions of the led, which should bring into play cognitive psychology; and (2) the structure and setting within which the leader and followers interact, as addressed by purely sociological approaches to organization.

2. The leadership role in academic research units

Although there is some empirical evidence and a series of theoretical discussions referring to the special problems of managing the scientist in organizations (e.g., Pelz, 1956, 1957; Marcson, 1960; Burns and Stalker, 1961; Kornhauser, 1962; Pelz and Andrews, 1966; Scott, 1966; Merton, 1968), most of this literature addresses the situation of scientists in nonacademic and particularly industrial settings. Organizational theory has not until recently attempted to systematically consider different types of organizations (e.g., Parsons, 1960; Etzioni, 1961; Blau and Scott, 1962; Perrow, 1968); nevertheless, it is clear that universities differ markedly both in terms of structure and goals from industrial or government institutions.[5] When attempting to summarize these differences, three points emerge as being of major significance:

1. In contrast to industry, the legal organizational entity of the university must be considered an organizational umbrella hosting a variety of institutes or departments that in themselves constitute more or less independent *small-scale organizations.* Generally, in most Western European countries most of the potential

structural power and authority of universities (in terms of budget, goal setting, resource allocation, and control) are held by the units formed by a single university professor and the assistant and service staff associated with his or her chair.

2. In contrast to industry, there is less *structural* conflict of interest between organizational goals and individual objectives: Presumably, the goals of the academic organization are satisfied best if the individual scientist is given the autonomy to realize the aspirations that have been imparted to him or her by academic socialization.[6] In accordance with this, academic organizations have far more "slack" than industrial organizations, that is, an excess of time and ideas that remain at the exclusive disposal of the individual scientific members.

3. Finally, the *office* (to borrow from Weber) *of the supervisors* or heads of the above-mentioned units is equipped with far more formal and factual power and adorned with far more symbolic insignia of power than any supervisory office at a comparable level in nonacademic institutions. As already implied by what we have said under point 1, the role of the university professor is hence much more similar in structural terms to the role of top management than to the role of a laboratory or department head in an industrial firm.

In sum, academic units can be characterized as "truncated" organizations in which there is a combination of highest-level supervisory roles and traditional low-level subordinate positions, and where the research goals of the organizational umbrella (the university) are fulfilled if members follow their professional values and interests. Seen this way, academic organizations exemplify the cooperative and moral nature of organizations postulated by the human relations approach for industrial firms (and correctly rejected there by the critique that has come up): Academic organizations are *cooperative,* because there is no necessary structural conflict of interest between the organization and its members, and they are *moral,* in Barnard's sense, because they rely upon intrinsic motivation[7] and because they fulfill nonprofit goals of service to the society.

The general thesis underlying the present analysis of academic units can consequently be summarized: In the light of the structure and goals of academic organizations, and in the light of the power and authority granted to the leadership role, the basic assumption of the human relations approach of positive relationships between supervisory behavior, group climate, and group productivity should be verified.

We will test an approximation of this thesis by relying on

measures of satisfaction linked to supervisory quality as experienced by subordinates. The analysis proceeds by first establishing the relationship between the latter and a measure of group climate. Second, the associations between group climate and several components of group performance – productiveness, innovativeness, and usefulness – are examined, and the multivariate relationship between the predictor variables found most significant in the present data and performance is analyzed. Because it is not clear whether perceived organizational climate and perceived leadership quality are attributes of the individuals or of the organizations (cf. Guion, 1973; Johnston, 1976), and because there is evidence that the causal relationships between supervisory behavior, climate, and productiveness might well be reversed (see below), there is no effort to definitely specify causal dependencies. We do, however, attempt to estimate the bias or halo effects that arise from our use of perceptual rating scales, and to derive specific estimates for different hierarchial levels. In doing so, we venture to specify a hypothetical structural equation model.

3. Data

The data presented in this chapter are drawn from the International Comparative Study on the Organization and Performance of Research Units. For this chapter's analysis, measures derived exclusively from answers of staff scientists of the units have been used, with the exception of the index of group performance (described below). Furthermore, scores of individual unit members were combined into average group scores and employed on the aggregate level, because the concepts and questionnaire items relevant here characterize organizational entities (the research unit or group) rather than individual scientists. Finally, all analyses were conducted separately for academic natural and technological sciences; results for industrial technological science groups are available as a check and will be referred to in notes where appropriate. The decision to look at natural and technological sciences separately is based upon considerations of the potentially different technologies in both fields and upon a typological analysis of quantitative and qualitative performance measures in different disciplines and types of institutions in the present data. Chapter 13 shows that performance patterns differ markedly in the above settings, but that no significant gain is made by looking at single disciplines separately, for example, at academic chemistry.

4. Measures employed

The following measures[8] were used to capture the basic dimensions of supervisory quality, group climate, and group performance:

1. an index of *supervisory quality,* which included the degree of satisfaction with the supervisor's technical competence, with his or her knowledge of the field, with his or her personality and character, with his or her leadership qualities, with the amount of work he or she does, and with his or her supportiveness for the researcher's work;[9] a final item asked for the degree to which contacts with the supervisor had beneficial effects upon the scientific or technical performance of the respondent.[10]

2. an index of *group climate,* where group climate was measured by seven items referring to the spirit of innovation in the unit, the degree of dedication to work, the degree to which new ideas in technical and nontechnical matters are given adequate consideration, the degree to which ideas from junior staff members are accepted, the degree of cooperation, and the frequency of staff meetings. With the items mentioned, the index basically comprises the dimensions of spirit-of-innovation, communication, cooperation, and dedication.

3. an index of *group performance.* Although our data include various assessments of the quantity and quality of research-unit performance, this chapter's analysis focuses mainly on "R & D effectiveness" as the most general measure of a group's contribution to research and development.[11] The construction of this performance measure is described in Chapter 2. As noted there, the index is based upon qualitative ratings of the group's *productivity* (in the sense of adding knowledge or inventions to its field), of its *innovativeness* (in terms of generating new ideas, approaches, methods, inventions, or applications in its field), and of the *usefulness* of the group in helping the organization to which it belongs to carry out its responsibilities with regard to R & D.[12]

5. Perception of the supervisor and what it relates to

Before systematically exploring the relationships between supervisory ratings, group climate, and performance, an attempt was made to identify those variables that account for most of the variance in supervisor's quality as perceived by those supervised in academic settings. Basically, four dimensions were found to yield significant associations:

1. measures associated with the *planning and coordinating func-*

tions of the supervisor, that is, the rated quality of the research program,[13] satisfaction with personnel policy, and satisfaction with the administrative and technical services at the disposal of the group.

2. measures linked to the *integrative functions* of the supervisor, that is, the rated group climate,[14] the attachment to the unit on the part of group members, and their degree of information on the research activities and research planning of the unit.

3. a measure related to the *career-promoting function* the supervisor has for the scientists working with him or her.

4. a measure of the supervisor's *overall status* and standing, as given by the total amount of influence he or she was perceived to have on various decisions.

Exhibit 4.1 presents the results of a multiple classification analysis[15] of perceived supervisory quality using the above measures as predictors. This exhibit and those that follow list the beta and eta-square parameters[16] as well as multiple correlation coefficients for both types of academic organizations.

The beta coefficients show that measures related to the supervisor's planning function seem to be most important in academic natural science settings, whereas variables linked to his or her total influence, to group climate (integrative function), and to his or her career-promoting function predominate in academic technological sciences. This set of variables explains about half of the variance in perception of supervisors in academic natural science units and somewhat more than one-third of the variance in academic technological sciences.

6. Perception of the supervisor and organizational climate

When examining the bivariate relationship between supervisory quality as perceived by those supervised and group climate in the research units, a moderately strong, significant, and almost linear association appeared in academic units.[17] Exhibit 4.2 presents these results. As indicated by eta-square coefficients of .29 in natural science groups and .30 in technological sciences, supervisory quality, if considered alone, accounts for nearly one-third of the variance in perceptions of organizational climate.

In order to validate this bivariate relationship, a series of structural and functional variables characterizing organizational units (such as the size of the unit, fluctuation in manpower, relative equipment lack, average time in research and administration) were examined for their bivariate and multivariate associations with group climate. None of the structural or functional

Exhibit 4.1. Multiple classification analysis of perceived supervisor's quality in academic natural and technological science units

Predictor variables relating to:	Academic natural science units (N = 467)		Academic technological science units (N = 159)	
	Beta	Eta^2	Beta	Eta^2
Supervisory planning functions:				
Quality of research program	.33	.36	.20	.21
Personnel policy	.25	.33	.18	.13
Administrative and technical services	.07	.05	.18	.01
Supervisory integrative functions				
Group climate	.15	.27	.34	.28
Attachment of scientist to unit	.12	.15	.19	.16
Information on research planning and activities	.08	.11	.15	.12
Supervisory career-promoting function				
Satisfaction with career opportunities	.12	.13	.28	.12
Supervisor's standing				
Total influence of head of unit	.18	.14	.37	.09
Multiple R^2 unadjusted	.55		.52	
Multiple R^2 adjusted	.50		.36	

variables examined showed a relationship as great as $r = .20$ with group climate;[18] nor did variables characterizing individual scientists, rather than the units, markedly improve the predictive power. Rather, in the relatively small and independent organizational units we are confronted with in academic settings, group climate apparently is best understood by looking at perceptions of supervisors and the rated quality of the planning and integrative functions performed by the supervisor. These predictors seem to account for most of the variance in group climate that can be explained in the present data. Exhibit 4.3 presents the results.

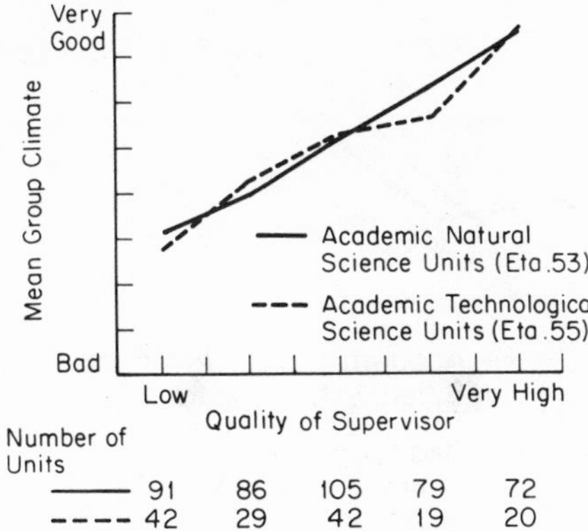

Exhibit 4.2. Perceived supervisory quality and mean group climate in academic natural and technological science units.

Exhibit 4.3. Multiple classification analysis of group climate in academic natural and technological science units

	Academic natural science groups (N = 437)		Academic technological science groups (N = 155)	
Predictor variable	Beta	Eta²	Beta	Eta²
Information on research planning and activities	.31	.27	.22	.24
Quality of research program	.26	.35	.29	.33
Personnel policy	.21	.28	.23	.19
Quality of supervisor	.19	.29	.28	.30
Multiple R^2 unadjusted	.51		.51	
Multiple R^2 adjusted	.49		.45	

7. Supervisory perception, group climate, and performance

When the variables used so far were explored for their bivariate and multivariate association, with R & D effectiveness as our main performance measure, the most pronounced relationships in all organizational settings involved the group climate experienced, the rated quality of the research program, and the perceived quality of the supervisor. Exhibit 4.4 gives an example of the strength of the association between climate and performance. As indicated by the eta coefficients, group climate explains between 10–20% of the variance in R & D effectiveness.

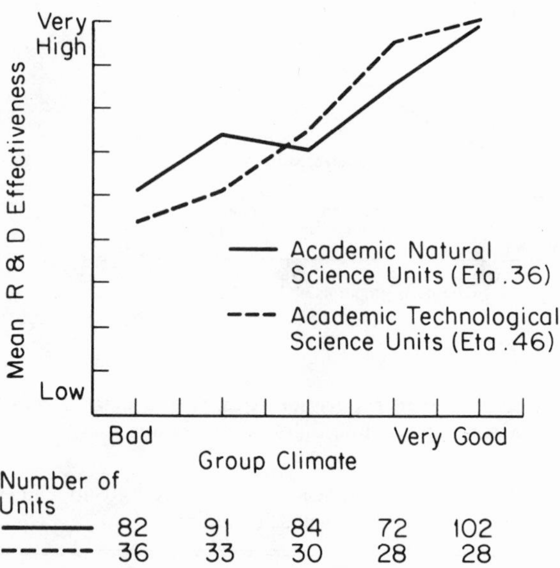

Exhibit 4.4. Group climate and mean R & D effectiveness in academic natural and technological science units.

Exhibit 4.5. Multiple classification analysis of R & D effectiveness in academic natural and technological science units

Predictor variable	Academic natural science units (N = 473) Beta	Eta²	Academic technological science units (N = 164) Beta	Eta²
Group climate experienced	.28	.12	.30	.19
Quality of supervisor	.19	.10	.22	.14
Quality of research program	.17	.09	.50	.25
Personnel policy	.15	.05	.15	.11
Information on research planning and activities	.11	.02	.21	.23
Multiple R^2 unadjusted	.19		.41	
Multiple R^2 adjusted	.15		.30	

When the full set of variables employed above is introduced, this percentage rises moderately, to 15–30%. See Exhibit 4.5.

Among the interesting results in this exhibit are (1) that there is at least a moderate association between R & D effectiveness (rated productivity, innovativeness, and usefulness) on the one hand and supervisory behavior and group climate on the other hand, in accordance with assumptions of the human relations approach (but contrary to the axiomatic theory of organizations as proposed by Hage, 1965); and (2) that the size of this association varies considerably between the two organizational settings, with the more pronounced relationships occurring in the academic technological science units. The latter result can perhaps best be understood in the light of Woodward's finding (1965) that more integrated production technologies tend to have better interpersonal relationships. Presumably, the degree of variability and uncertainty (Perrow, 1968) is lower in technological than in natural sciences; consequently, "technologies" in technological science institutes should be more integrated and productivity more dependent upon interpersonal relations and group climate than is to be expected in natural science organizations.[19]

8. A model including measurement error

When evaluating the moderate association found between rated supervisory quality, group climate, and research planning on the one hand, and R & D effectiveness on the other hand, one should recall that the performance measure combines equally weighted ratings from three different sources (the supervisor, the staff scientists, and external evaluators), whereas all predictor variables are based on ratings by staff scientists only. If a multivariate analysis with the above predictor variables is used to account for R & D effectiveness as judged solely by staff scientists, the amount of explained variance in R & D effectiveness rises to 27% in academic natural sciences and to 42% in academic technological sciences. Although such a procedure could be rejected on the ground that the increase in explained variance may be due to an increase in measurement/halo effects because of the use of the same kind of subjective rating scales for the same kind of subjects on all variables, it could also be argued that perceptual ratings always depend on the respondents' positions and their relationships to what is being rated, and cannot be attributed to measurement error induced by the instrument used.[20] If this is true, we cannot argue in favor of a measure combining the ratings of different groups at different levels without giving a theo-

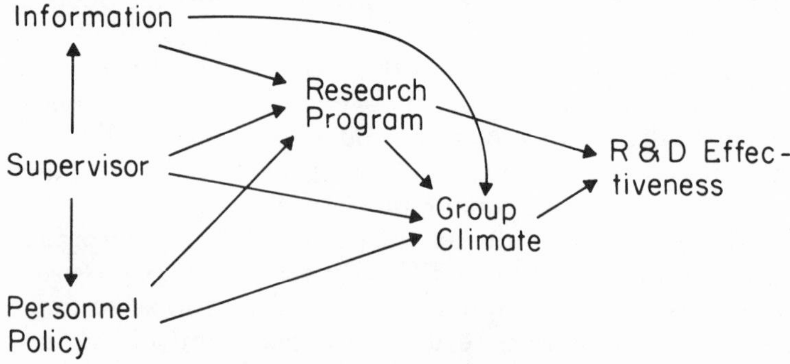

Exhibit 4.6. Presumed causal dependencies in academic settings.

retical justification for the assumption that group- or level-specific perception differences do wipe each other out when scores are aggregated. Because there is no theory of the social perception of reality specific enough for the present purpose currently available, no decision can be made as to the desirability of one or the other measurement approach.

In the present data, an attempt was made to estimate the amount of response bias for different groups of respondents (i.e., supervisors or unit heads and staff scientists), where response bias can be understood as measurement error induced by the use of the same rating scales or as a social perception effect presumably identical for respondents of the same hierarchical level. To accomplish this, we ventured to specify a minimum of causal relationships between the predictor variables so far identified as most important, restricting our attention to one indicator of supervisory planning functions (quality of research program, neglecting personnel policy). With respect to supervisory power and authority in academic settings, the causal dependencies among the above variable set can be presumed to be as shown in Exhibit 4.6.[21]

However, it should also be noted that results such as those by Fiedler (1967) and Lawler and Porter (1967) would put into question the causal flow suggested in Exhibit 4.6: Fiedler showed that the climate of a group had a substantial impact upon the effectiveness of leadership styles, and Lawler and Porter–after examining over 30 studies of performance–reached the conclusion that satisfaction and climate might *result* from high performance rather than being a cause of it.[22] Both studies imply that the main causal sequence might well be reversed in Exhibit 4.6.

In view of this, the following Lisrel[23] model of the relationships between the quality of the supervisor, his or her planning

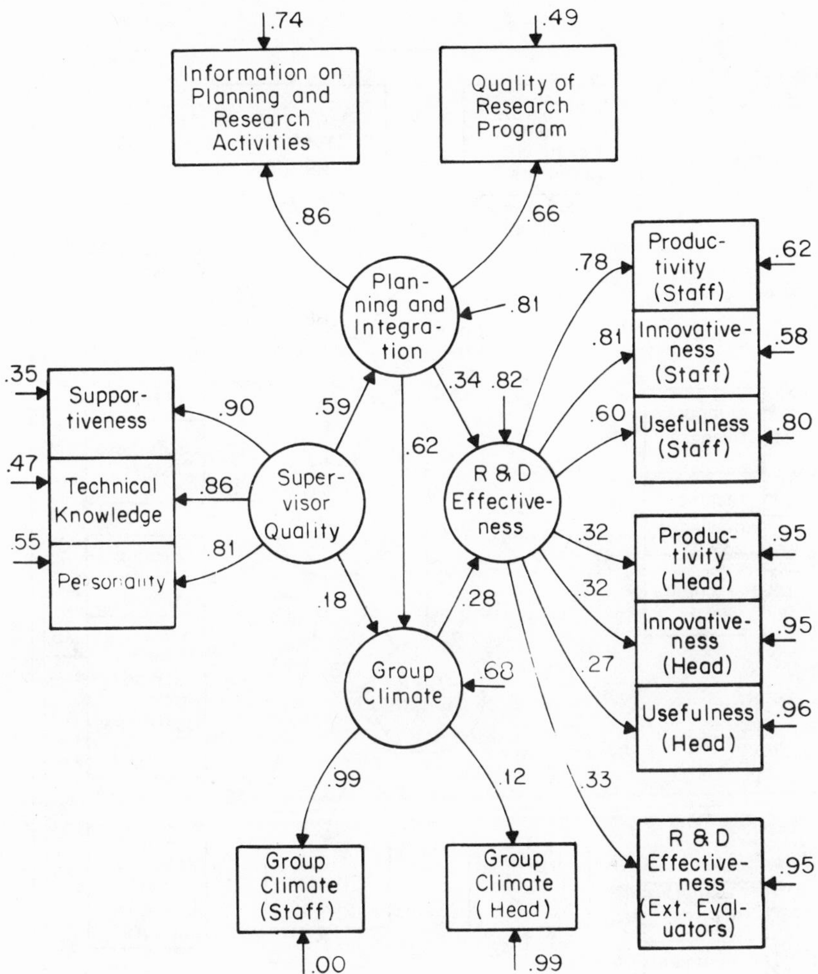

Exhibit 4.7. Lisrel model of R & D effectiveness (without response bias) for academic natural science units.

and integrating functions, group climate, and R & D effectiveness should primarily be evaluated for the information it provides about the amount of response bias in the data. Exhibit 4.7 presents parameters showing the strength of linkages among the above concepts when no bias estimation was attempted.[24] The

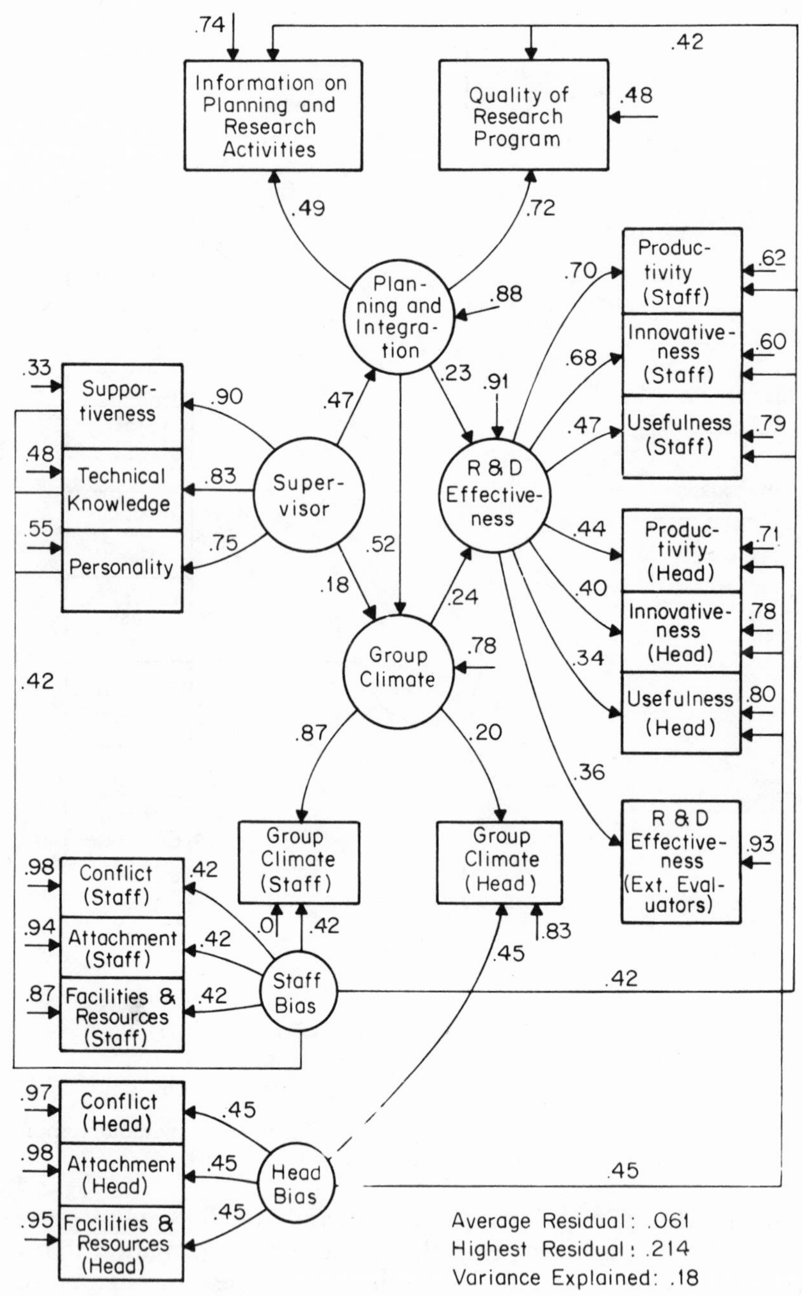

Exhibit 4.8. Lisrel model of R & D effectiveness (response bias included) for academic natural science units.

model in Exhibit 4.8 adds three measures covering different sections of the questionnaire in order to provide for estimating bias effects.

Introducing bias variables into a model that contains only concepts that are quite strongly related to each other poses a methodological problem in that one has to ensure that only the common variance due to perceptual "bias" is taken into account by the bias variables, whereas common variance giving substance to the model is left for explanation by the substantive concepts. The solution adopted here is to provide for a broader basis of variables from which the bias factors can be estimated. Hence, the inclusion of three additional dimensions from the questionnaire, which, being measured in the same way as the concepts used so far, should be subject to the same response bias. The dimensions used are those of the degree of "attachment of scientists to the unit" (described in the Annex to this chapter), an indicator of the amount of nontechnical conflict in the unit, and an index of the overall evaluation of the "facilities and services" at the disposal of the group, composed of items such as the degree to which the unit is well equipped scientifically, the satisfaction with the administrative and secretarial assistance and with the technical assistance and services, and the adequacy of the current budget of the unit for completion of the group's research and/or scientific tasks. The penalty for this kind of solution is that relatively high residuals (e.g., around .4) between these additional variables, which are only linked to the bias variables, remains. (No attention is given to their interrelationship or to their being related to other dimensions in the model.)

The model in Exhibit 4.7 is characterized by a relatively high relationship between supervisory quality and the quality of planning and degree of information in the unit, and an equivalently high relationship between the latter and perceived group climate. The model explains 33% of the variance in R & D effectiveness;[25] additionally, supervisory quality and the quality of planning and integrating account for more than half the variance in group climate. Although most residuals are satisfactorily low (average residual = .070, as shown in Exhibit 4.7), this model produces a few high residuals,[26] indicating a less-than-optional fit.

In contrast to Exhibit 4.7, the model in Exhibit 4.8 includes two bias variables, linked to supervisory ratings and staff ratings in the respective observed indicators. Allowing the bias factors to be different for supervisors and staff scientists results in a much better fit of the model: The highest residual relating to indicators

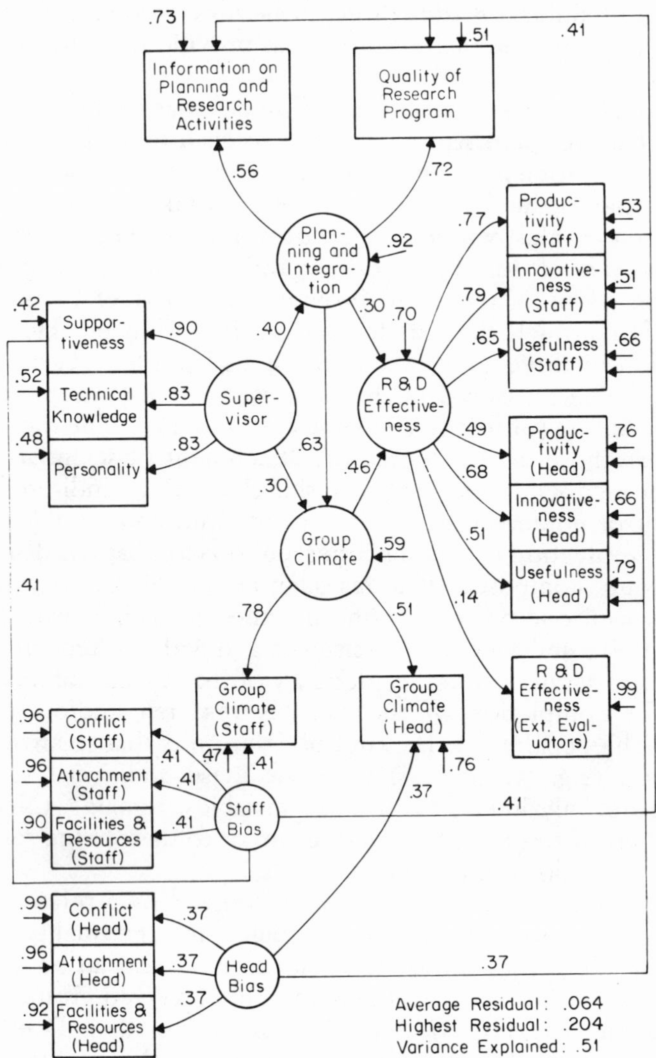

Exhibit 4.9. Lisrel model of R & D effectiveness (response bias included) for academic technological science units.

of the four main concepts of the model is now .214, the average residual is .061.[27] A further comparison of the parameter estimates of Exhibits 4.7 and 4.8 also shows a moderate reduction of all the direct effects in the model and a reduction in explained variance in R & D effectiveness due to the common perceptual bias in the original variables having been removed; only the link between the quality of supervision and group climate seems unaffected by bias factors. Finally, the perceptual bias effects are estimated at .45 for supervisors and at .42 for staff scientists. These figures closely replicate bias estimates of .43 and .41, respectively, that were developed as part of a large attempt to estimate the construct validity of the rated-performance measures used in the International Study (cf. Chapter 14).

As would be expected from the previous multiple classification analyses, applying the model to academic technological sciences results in a much higher explanatory power than obtained in the natural science models described so far. According to Exhibit 4.9, 51% of the variance in R & D effectiveness is accounted for by supervisory quality, planning and information, and group climate, whereas bias effects are only slightly reduced (to .37 for unit heads and to .41 for staff scientists).

Again, the effect of the quality of planning and information shows a predominant influence on group climate; yet the direct effect of group climate on performance turns out nearly twice as high as in the case of natural sciences. Both the relatively high amount of variance explained in the performance measure and the significantly higher contribution of group climate presumably substantiate the assumptions that work in technological science involves more integrated production technologies and is associated with a lower degree of variability and uncertainty than does research in natural science. Consequently, in technological science groups performance will be more directly dependent upon the factors specified in the model (especially group climate) than in natural science units.

9. Discussion

The main interest of this chapter's analysis, which confirms the positive association between supervisory behavior, group climate, and productivity postulated by the human relations approach, derives from the fact that the study was not designed to investigate this particular relationship. In other words, the predominant importance of the above variables for explaining group performance was the result of close investigations of a large variety of organizational variables and their relationship to group performance rather than the inevitable side effect of a continuing research focus on the above relationship.

In connection with this, it may be worthwhile to point once more to other organizational variables, in addition to the main concepts just mentioned, that also related to R & D effectiveness. In order of importance they were: the quality of the research program, information on research planning and activities, and personnel policy. Assuming that the flow of causality is as specified in the Lisrel models, these three variables confirm the importance of the planning and integrating functions (through information) of the supervisor in research laboratories.

The results of this chapter can be contrasted with the results of the preceding one: There it was shown that supervisory status and a series of intervening concepts linked to it account for most of the variance in productivity as measured by *quantity* of publications, here it is shown that supervisory quality and a series of intervening factors linked to it account for most of the variance in rated *quality* of performance. Both analyses imply that supervisors (unit heads) are of preeminent importance in academic settings as far as productivity in general is concerned. The relation between these two kinds of performance is presumably mediated by the recognition a research unit receives in the scientific community. The question, however, as to how this relationship manifests itself must await further research.

10. Summary

The literature on leadership in organizations is dominated by the human relations thesis that good leadership should lead to high morale and that high morale should lead to increased productivity of group members. Although the moral and cooperative nature of organizations presupposed by this thesis might be rejected for industrial settings, university organizations may warrant a description in those terms because of their special structural characteristics. In this chapter, it is shown that the above relationships, if measured by satisfaction with supervisory quality and perception of group climate, do indeed hold for academic institutions; additionally, planning and integrating functions of the supervisor emerge as important intervening variables. As compared with the natural sciences, the relationship is significantly stronger in the technological science groups, pointing to the fact that more integrated production technologies may be more dependent upon leadership functions and group morale than technologies associated with a higher degree of uncertainty and variability, as in the natural sciences. Finally, with the help of the Lisrel technique, an attempt is made to estimate the amount of response bias in the perceptual rating scales. Although the adjustment for bias results in a reduction of the variance explained in performance, the main substantive variables remain of substantial explanatory value.

Annex

This annex lists the components of various indices used in the analysis.

The indices that were related to perceptions of supervisory quality, as described in Section 5, titled "Perception of the supervisor and what it relates to," and used in Exhibit 4.1, include the following:

The index *quality of the research program* includes the items: quality of the conception of the research program, interest of the research activities, and the degree of coherence of the research program.

The index of satisfaction with *personnel policy* includes two items: the degree of satisfaction with the manpower recruitment system of the unit, and the degree of satisfaction with training and career development facilities available to group members.

The measure of satisfaction with *administrative and technical services* includes the items: satisfaction with administrative secretarial assistance received by the unit, and satisfaction with technical assistance and services.

The measure of *attachment to the unit* on the part of group members is based on the items: degree of feeling of high job security, degree to which leaving the unit is considered or would be done if there were a suitable opportunity, and degree to which the work the researcher was doing was interesting.

The index *information on research planning and activities* includes the components: degree to which the group members are kept informed about all aspects of the research carried out by the unit, degree of information on all aspects of the research planning, and degree of participation (at every stage) in the planning of the research.

The measure of *career opportunities* is based upon the items: degree to which advancement opportunities seem to be essentially dependent upon the performance of the researcher, and degree of satisfaction with advancement opportunities in relation to those of others with comparable qualifications, training, and experience.

The index *total amount of influence of the head of the unit* is based upon ratings of the head's influence over the following matters: choice of specific research tasks, choice of methods used, publication and circulation of research results, allocation of work within the unit, coordination and/or cooperation with other units, use of training and career development facilities, hiring personnel for a definite period, termination of employment of personnel, and hiring or buying low-cost equipment.

The latent dimensions (concepts) in Exhibit 4.7 were measured as follows:

The latent dimension *quality of supervisor* is measured by three indicators referring to the supervisor's supportiveness, his or her technical knowledge, and his or her personality; the three indicators cover exactly the same items as listed for the overall supervisor's quality index (as described in Section 4, titled "Measures employed") but leave out the question on his or her workload for conceptual reasons. The latent dimension *planning and integration* uses the two indices *quality of research program* and *information on research planning and activities* employed in previous analyses as observed indicators of the fulfillment of planning and integrating functions. The dimensions *group climate* and *R & D effectiveness* are based upon indicators stemming from different groups: indices of the supervisor's and staff's ratings in the case of group climate, both in terms of items identical to the index used prior to Exhibit 4.7, and supervisor's and staff's ratings on the items productiveness, innovativeness, and usefulness in the case of R & D effectiveness in addition to an overall measure of R & D effectiveness based upon external evaluator ratings.

References

Aichholzer, G., 1976, Uber die Effektivitaet Naturwissenschaftlicher Forschungseinheiten im Hochschulsektor, Vienna, Institute for Advanced Studies.

Andrews, F., et al., 1973, *Multiple Classification Analysis* (2d ed.), Ann Arbor, Institute for Social Research, University of Michigan.

Blau, P. M., and Scott, W. R., 1962, *Formal Organizations,* San Francisco, Chandler.

Blume, S. S., and Sinclair, R., 1973, Chemists in British Universities: A Study of the Reward System in Science, *American Sociological Review,* 38: 126–138.

Bourdieu, P., 1976, The Specificity of the Scientific Field and the Social Conditions of the Progress of Reason, *Social Science Information,* 14(6): 19–47.

Bowers, D. G., and Seashore, S. E., 1966, Predicting Organizational Effectiveness with a Four-Factor Theory of Leadership, *Administrative Science Quarterly,* 11(2): 138–163.

Burns, T., and Stalker, G. M., 1961, *The Management of Innovation,* London, Tavistock.

Campbell, J. P., and Dunnette, M. D., 1968, Effectiveness of T-Group Experiences in Managerial Training and Development, *Psychological Bulletin,* 70(2): 73–104.

Clark, K., 1957, *America's Psychologists,* Washington, D.C., American Psychological Association.

Cole, S., and Cole, J. R., 1967, Scientific Output and Recognition: A Study in the Reward System in Science, *American Sociological Review,* 32: 377–390.

Cole, S., and Cole, J. R., 1971, Measuring the Quality of Sociological Research: Problems in the Use of the Science Citation Index, *American Sociologist,* 6: 23–29.

Dennis, W., 1954, The Bibliographies of Eminent Scientists, *Scientific Monthly,* 79: 180–183.

Etzioni, A., 1961, *A Comparative Analysis of Complex Organizations,* New York, Free Press.

Etzioni, A., 1965, Dual Leadership in Complex Organizations, *American Sociological Review,* 30: 692–698.

Fiedler, F., 1967, *A Theory of Leadership Effectiveness,* New York, McGraw-Hill.

Fleishman, E. A., 1953a, The Description of Supervisory Behavior, *Journal of Applied Psychology,* 37: 1–6.

Fleishman, E. A., 1953b, The Measurement of Leadership Attitudes in Industry, *Journal of Applied Psychology,* 37: 153–158.

Fleishman, E. A., Harris, E. F., and Burtt, E. E., 1955, *Leadership and Supervision in Industry,* Columbus, Ohio, Bureau of Educational Research.

Guion, R., 1973, A Note on Organizational Climate, *Organizational Behavior and Human Performance,* 9: 120–125.

Hage, G., 1965, An Axiomatic Theory of Organizations, *Administrative Science Quarterly,* 10: 289–320.

Herzberg, F., 1966, *Work and the Nature of Man,* New York, Collins-World.

Hollander, E. P., 1971, Style, Structure and Setting in Organizational Leadership, *Administrative Science Quarterly,* 16(1): 1–9.

Hollander, E. P., and Julian, J. W., 1969, Contemporary Trends in the Analysis of Leadership Processes, *Psychological Bulletin,* 71: 387–397.

House, R. J., 1971, A Path Goal Theory of Leader Effectiveness, *Administrative Science Quarterly,* 16: 321–338.

House, R. J., and Wigdor, L. A., 1967, Herzberg's Dual-Factor Theory of Job Satisfaction and Motivation: A Review of the Evidence and a Criticism, *Personnel Psychology,* 20: 369–389.

Hulin, L., and Blood, M. R., 1968, Job Enlargement, Individual Differences and Worker Responses, *Psychological Bulletin,* 69(1): 41–55.

Johnston, H. R., 1976, A New Conceptualization of Source of Organizational Climate, *Administrative Science Quarterly,* 21: 95–104.

Joreskog, K. G., and Van Thillo, M., 1972, Lisrel: A General Computer Program for Estimating a Linear Structural Equation System Involving Multiple Indicators of Unmeasured Variables, unpublished research bulletin, RB-R-26, Princeton, N.J., Educational Testing Service.

Katz, D., Maccoby, N., and Morse, N. C., 1950, *Productivity, Supervision and Morale in an Office Situation,* Detroit, Darel Press.

Knorr, K. D., Mittermeir, R., Aichholzer, G., and Waller, G., 1976a, Towards a Core Model of Academic Unit Performance: Preliminary Results, paper presented at the 13th workshop of the International Comparative Study of the Organization of Research Units, 26–30 April 1976, Vienna, Institute for Advanced Studies.

Knorr, K. D., Mittermeir, R., Aichholzer, G., and Waller, G., 1976b, Individual Publication Productivity as a Social Position Effect in Academic and Industrial Research Units (revised version), paper presented at the PAREX–IAS Colloquium on the Role of Research Organizations in Orienting Scientific Activities, 5–6 July 1976, Vienna, Institute for Advanced Studies.

Korman, A. K., 1966, Consideration, "Initiating Structure" and Organizational Criteria: A Review, *Personnel Psychology,* 19(4): 349–361.

Kornhauser, W., 1962, *Scientists in Industry: Conflict and Accommodation,* Berkeley and Los Angeles, University of California Press.

Lawler, E. E., and Porter, L. W., 1967, The Effect of Performance on Job Satisfaction, *Industrial Relations,* 7(1): 20–28.

Lawrence, P. R., and Lorsch, J. W., 1969, *Organization and Environment,* Homewood, Ill., Irwin.

Lieberson, S., and O'Connor, J. F., 1972, Leadership and Organizational Performance: A Study of Large Corporations, *American Sociological Review,* 37(2): 117–136.

Likert, R., 1961, *New Patterns of Management,* New York, McGraw-Hill.

Likert, R., 1967, *The Human Organization,* New York, McGraw-Hill.

Marcson, S., 1960, *The Scientist in American Industry,* New York, Harper & Row.

Meltzer, B. M., 1949, The Productivity of Social Scientists, *American Journal of Sociology,* 55: 25–29.

Meltzer, L., 1956, Scientific Productivity in Organizational Settings, *Journal of Social Issues,* 12: 32–40.

Merton, R. K., 1968, The Role of the Intellectual in Public Bureaucracies, *In* Merton, R. K., *Social Theory and Social Structure* (enlarged ed.), New York, Free Press.

Meyer, 1976, Leadership and Organizational Structure, *American Journal of Sociology,* 81(3): 514–542.

Parsons, T., 1960, *Structure and Process in Modern Societies,* New York, Free Press.

Payne, R. L., and Mansfield, R., 1973, Relationships of Perceptions of Organizational Climate to Organizational Structure, Context and Hierarchical Position, *Administrative Science Quarterly,* 18: 515–526.

Pelz, D. C., 1956, Some Social Factors Related to Performance in a Research Organization, *Administrative Science Quarterly,* 1(13): 310–325.

Pelz, D. C., 1957, Motivation of the Engineering and Research Specialist, *Improving Managerial Performance,* General Management Series, no. 186, New York, American Management Association.

Pelz, D. C., and Andrews, F. M., 1966, *Scientists in Organizations: Productive Climates for Research and Development,* New York, Wiley.

Perrow, C., 1967, A Framework for Comparative Organizational Analysis, *American Sociological Review,* 32(2): 194–208.

Perrow, C., 1968, The Effect of Technological Change on the Structure of Business Firms. *In* Roberts, B. C. (ed.), *Industrial Relations: Contemporary Issues,* London, Macmillan.

Perrow, C., 1972, *Complex Organizations: A Critical Essay,* Glenview, Ill., Scott, Foresman.

Pritchard, R., and Karasick, B., 1973, The Effects of Organizational Climate on Managerial Job Performance and Job Satisfaction, *Organizational Behavior and Human Performance,* 9: 126–146.

Pugh, D. S., et al., 1968, Dimensions of Organization Structure, *Administrative Science Quarterly,* 13: 65–105.

Rossel, R. D., 1970, Instrumental and Expressive Leadership in Complex Organizations, *Administrative Science Quarterly,* 15(3): 306–316.

Scott, W. G., 1962, *Human Relations in Management,* Homewood, Ill., Irwin.

Scott, W. G., 1966, Professionals in Bureaucracies – Areas of Conflict. *In* Vollmer, H. M., and Mills, D. L. (eds.), *Professionalization,* Englewood Cliffs, N.J., Prentice-Hall.

Silverman, D., 1970, *The Theory of Organizations,* London, Heinemann.

Stogdill, R. M., and Coons, A. E., 1957 (eds.), *Leadership Behavior: Its Description and Measurement,* Columbus, Ohio, Bureau of Business Research.

Thomasson, P., and Stanley, J., 1966, Exploratory Study of Productivity and "Creativity" of Prominent Psychometricians, unpublished manuscript, Madison, University of Wisconsin.

Thompson, J., 1967, *Organizations in Action,* New York, McGraw-Hill.

Vroom, V. H., 1964, *Work and Motivation,* New York, Wiley.

Wofford, J. C., 1971, Managerial Behavior, Situational Factors, and Productivity and Morale, *Administrative Science Quarterly,* 16(1): 11–17.

Woodward, J., 1965, *Industrial Organization: Theory and Practice,* London, Oxford University Press.

Woodward, J., 1970 (ed.), *Industrial Organization: Behavior and Control,* London, Oxford University Press.

Worthy, J. C., 1950, Organizational Structure and Employee Morale, *American Sociological Review,* 15: 169–179.

Notes

1. Meyer (1976: 517) derives this tendency from the nature of the organizational theories available: Whereas Weberian theory overlooks leadership on the grounds that organizations that are rational (bureaucratic) are efficient and stable because of their structure, which overpowers the single official's action potential, contemporary organizational theory overlooks leadership because rational organizations have to be responsive to environmental uncertainties, which can only partly be handled by (and attributed to) a single leader.

2. Etzioni's propositions are based upon his earlier (1961: 89–126) differentiation between an organization's primary goals and the bases of compliance. Examples of organizations requiring little commitment or compliance are prisons or mental hospitals; moderate commitment, according to Etzioni, is necessary in production and service organizations; high commitment is required in religious socializing organizations. Taking into account different kinds and origins of compliance, in addition to organizational goals, remedies some of the critical objections raised against goal-approach organizational theories (compare Silverman, 1970; Perrow, 1972).

3. Some might even want to go so far as to reject the concept of leadership altogether, deriving the popular emphasis on leadership from the feeling of indirect control generated through the belief in a leader's ability, and from the scapegoat function served by the possibility of locating guilt and responsibility in a specific role (compare Lieberson and O'Connor, 1972).

4. "Moral" as used by Barnard refers to the assumption that the common purpose of organizations is the purpose of all. Organizations are legitimized here by their very definition (cf. Perrow, 1972: 93).

5. They may also differ in terms of what has come to be called technology (cf. Woodward, 1965, 1970), i.e., in terms of the kinds of tasks that are performed, which presumably affect the structure and to some extent organizational goals.

6. The term *structural* is crucial here: It refers to the definition of roles and to compliance, i.e., to the fact that participant involvement in universities should as a rule be neither alienated nor calculative (as in industry, where members calculate whether the wages are worth it), to use Etzioni's distinction (1961). Running a university institute in order to make a reputation should be in accordance with the no-conflict-of-interest thesis; running it in order to make private money (e.g., money not used for investments in equipment, etc.) clearly would not be in accordance. Teaching goals, if they become predominant as in the case of many German universities at present, may become the origin of structural conflict. Consequently, the thesis should hold on the aggregate and with respect to the formal structure of university organizations; it may not hold in single cases.

7. The validity of the distinction between extrinsic and intrinsic interests has been questioned recently by Bourdieu (1976), who points to the fact that

investments are always organized by reference to conscious or unconscious anticipation of average chances of profit (which may be symbolic, as in the case of scientists striving for recognition and prestige). Although this is true, the *analytic* distinction between degrees of intrinsic motivation may still be warranted but should perhaps be couched in terms of the concept of alienation from work.

8. All measures were additive combinations of items measured on five-point Likert ratings. The items to be combined were identified by multidimensional scalings and correlation analyses. Because we were working with aggregate data, original scores were group mean values, the direction of which was reversed as compared to the questionnaire before index construction.

9. The question asked for a rating of the immediate supervisor; consequently, in the case of a very large unit the head (usually a university professor) and the supervisor who was rated might not be identical. However, because the largest units proved not to comprise more than six scientists, the problem can be ignored.

10. The question included one more item, which asked for the frequency of contacts with the supervisor, but this was not included in the index because it did not correlate sufficiently with the other items (see item SB:M1a in the questionnaire in the Appendix).

11. The other rated quality measures developed in the International Study capture somewhat different dimensions: "social" effectiveness, "training" effectiveness, "administrative" effectiveness, and "recognition." The latter dimension, albeit potentially suited for the present purpose, refers more to the feedback of the (international) scientific community on the work of the unit because this dimension was assessed by the degree to which the unit has a high international reputation and the degree to which the publications of the unit are in high demand and often cited in the literature.

12. In using quality ratings of competence by peers, we follow a frequent procedure that presumably constitutes the most valid assessment of a contribution of science despite its increasing replacement by the more convenient use of citation counts as a quality measure (see Meltzer, 1949, 1956; Dennis, 1954; Clark, 1957; Pelz and Andrews, 1966; Thomasson and Stanley, 1966; J. Cole and S. Cole, 1967, 1971; Blume and Sinclair, 1973). Because the present study includes countries that are not adequately or not at all represented in the Science Citation Index, and because citation counts refer to individual rather than to group productivity, the use of the index was not feasible.

13. All measures were constructed as described in the previous section. The Annex to this chapter identifies the components from which each of the following indices were composed.

14. For the measure of perceived "group climate," see the previous section.

15. Multiple classification analysis is a multivariate technique for examining the raw, adjusted, and multiple effects of several predictor variables on a dependent variable based on an additive model. In contrast to traditional regression analysis, the technique can handle predictors with no better than nominal measurement and with nonlinear interrelationships, but cannot handle directly interaction effects. See Andrews et al. (1973) for a full discussion of the technique.

16. "Betas" are analogous to standardized regression coefficients; see Andrews et al. (1973: 47 ff.) for a full discussion. "Eta-square" is the correlation ratio and indicates the proportion of the total variance in the dependent variable that is explainable by the predictor.

17. In industrial units, the relationship is less pronounced, as indicated by an eta-square of .19.

18. This is especially noteworthy in the case of size of the unit and size of the organization, because according to a well-known theory and some empirical evidence, size should be negatively related to the climate and atmosphere in an organization (e.g., Worthy, 1950; Pugh et al., 1968; Payne and Mansfield, 1973). In general, the argument runs that larger size leads to increased bureaucratization, which in turn enhances a climate where interpersonal aggression, emotional control, and leaders' psychological distance, as well as the number of rules and concern with following rules, are all higher. It should be noted, however, that the sign of the relationship depends on the aspects of "climate" measured. Although the correlation between size and the above-mentioned dimensions should come out negative, large size has been assumed to be positively related to scientific and intellectual diversity, readiness to innovate, and concern for the involvement of employees in the above-mentioned studies. Because the index of group climate used in this chapter is somewhat biased toward measuring innovative orientation (as thought appropriate for a measure developed for research organizations), we might as well have expected a positive correlation between group climate and size in the present data. This possibility has been checked by using a subindex including only those items of our general climate index that refer to innovation-orientation; again, no substantially significant correlations were obtained.

19. Degree of "variability" and "uncertainty" point to the distinction between basic and applied research, and this may be a distinction between the natural and technological sciences. If the technological sciences more or less coincide with applied sciences, routinization of tasks and hence needs of integration and cooperation will be higher than in natural sciences.

20. As mentioned above, there is some evidence that climate perceptions depend on position in the organizational hierarchy, as recently suggested by Payne and Mansfield (1973: 525) and explained by Thompson (1967). Johnston (1976: 101) expects that climate varies with the level of uncertainty absorbed at different organizational levels, and Pritchard and Karasick (1973) found that climate in regional offices of an organization is a function of overall organizational climate and the demands of local environments. Theoretically most interesting, Bourdieu has recently made a point in showing that "judgments on a student's or a researcher's scientific capacities are *always contaminated* at all stages of academic life by knowledge of the position he occupies in the instituted hierarchies" (1976: 20).

21. This model has also been examined using path analysis and the Goodman technique (cf. Knorr et al., 1976a; Aichholzer, 1976).

22. According to Lawler and Porter (1967), this would be the case if the employee was rewarded for high performance.

23. Lisrel is a computer program for estimating general linear structural equation models with the specific advantage of allowing for unmeasured hypothetical constructs or latent variables, each of which may be measured by several observed indicators. The method allows for differentiation between errors in equations (disturbances), and errors in the observed variables (measurement errors) and yields estimates for both (Joreskog and Van Thillo, 1972; Joreskog, 1974).

24. In order to estimate level-specific response bias, the model includes, where possible (i.e., where the respective questions had been asked in the questionnaire), measures based upon data from the unit heads in addition to the

measures based upon data from staff scientists. The Annex to this chapter lists the indicators used to measure various concepts included in Exhibit 4.7.

25. The increase in variance explained as compared to the results of multiple classification analysis (see Exhibit 4.5) is due to the fact that here we estimate errors in equations only (attributing measurement error to the special error terms for observed indicators), whereas traditional techniques yield one estimator combining both kinds of errors.

26. The high residuals originate from discrepancies between ratings by unit heads and ratings by staff scientists. This is in accordance with the assumed dependence of perception and experience on hierarchical level.

27. These figures exclude residuals originating from variables introduced solely for the purpose of bias estimation.

5 Externally determined resources and the effectiveness of research units

Veronica Stolte-Heiskanen
University of Helsinki, Helsinki

1. Introduction

In the bygone days of the Republic of Science when research was an inexpensive vocation done mainly by professors in universities, there was little call for either support of or interest in research by the various socio-economic and political institutions of society. With the rapid development in science and its growing societal importance, scientific activity has become more and more dependent on resources that are determined and allocated by decision makers outside the actual research groups or even the scientific community. This is reflected in the emergence of the institution of *national science policy*.

Obviously a central factor in any national science policy is the scarcity of resources. This in turn imposes the notion of priority. Not only is there competition with other societal institutions, but also within science itself the setting of priorities in the allocation of inputs is influenced by a variety of factors. Decisions are based, among other things, on the national importance of the development of research, on the relative importance of the various branches of science for the achievement of national goals, on what should be done to foster various kinds of research activity, and on which organizational settings should be promoted. As one observer has noted, the assumption underlying "the various 'ra-

The assistance of Erkki Lehtovuori in the data processing for this chapter is gratefully acknowledged.

tional' techniques is that resources for scientific research can be arranged in an optimal set of priorities, which when administered through central authorities would guarantee the full development of science" (Gibbons, 1972: 188).

In recent decades, considerable efforts have been spent on macrolevel cost-effect estimates and forecasts, but the actual effect of inputs on the contribution of science to national development in general, or on the productivity of research in particular, has not been concretely demonstrated. As one surveyor of the current situation concludes, "the discrepancy between the present high stage of scientific-technological development and the empirical intuitive organization through which many spiritual and material resources are used in the development of science and technology is very startling" (Dobrow, 1969: 301).

This chapter focuses on those resources of research units that are largely determined by factors independent of the research units themselves. The role these resources play in scientific productivity is examined on the concrete level of performance of research units. (The analysis is conducted on the full set of units (N = 1,222) from the six countries that participated in Round 1 of the International Comparative Study on the Organization and Performance of Research Units.)

Although it is obvious that certain resources are a necessary precondition for any scientific activity, it is also true that even an unlimited supply of funds, equipment, or personnel alone cannot explain creativity. Like any other individual activity, scientific productivity may be influenced by a variety of subjective factors, such as the perception and interpretation of objective realities. For example, Andrews (1975) has shown scientific creativity to be related to several subjective factors, including individual commitment and motivation.

This chapter also examines the ways research-unit members themselves interpret and judge the adequacy of their resources. The relationship between the actual resources and the subjective perceptions of resources is then shown, and their separate and joint relationships to the performance of research units is discussed.

Organization of the chapter

This chapter consists of four main sections after the Introduction. In Section 2, the conceptual relationship between actual resources and the perception of these resources by members of the research units is examined, and the notion of congruency is introduced. The ways the various resources were measured and the empirical relationships between objective and subjective resources are described. In Section 3, variations in patterns of congruency among the countries included in the sample are analyzed. Section 4 focuses on the relationship between effectiveness and resources. First the relative importance of objective versus subjective measures of resources is analyzed, then the relationship between patterns of congruency and measures of effectiveness is described, and lastly the relative predictive power of these two types of measures is discussed. This section ends with the major conclusions of the analysis. Section 5 consists of a summary and some general conclusions of the study.

2. Available resources and their subjective perceptions: the notion of congruency

The idea that subjective perceptions do not always correspond to objective reality is well known to students of sociology and psychology. Equally well documented is the importance of *subjective reality* for determining individual or group behavior. Such classical concepts as W. I. Thomas's "definition of the situation," L. Festinger's "cognitive dissonance," Merton's "relative deprivation," and the more recent works of the so-called phenomenological sociologists (e.g., Berger), all deal with some aspects of this phenomenon. Evidence about the importance of subjective factors for various aspects of scientific activity also comes from a variety of studies of scientists (e.g., see Pelz and Andrews, 1966).

Although – as far as is known – the relationship between actual resources of research units and perceptions of resources by unit members has not been studied, it can be reasonably assumed that subjective perceptions do not always correspond to objective reality. Some research units with good resources may find them unsatisfactory, whereas other units may express high satisfaction with the same resource level. Scientists in rich industrial laboratories working on nationally recognized, important projects may have different conceptions of adequacy than a research group working on some esoteric project in some small, remote university. Absence of congruency may exist for a variety of psychological or social-psychological reasons, which undoubtedly would deserve more detailed examination. The main interest here, however, is not to explore the reasons for congruency as such, beyond the possible influence of a few global factors. Rather, the present problem is to examine the relationship between the presence or absence of different types of congruency and the effectiveness of research units. For example, if both objective conditions and subjective states relate to effectiveness, is their combined influence on performance greater than their simple additive effects?

In order to explore the relative importance of objective resources, subjective perceptions, and the agreement between them, a set of pattern variables, which will be here referred to as *congruency variables,* was constructed for various types of resources in such a way that different types of congruency or incongruency can be distinguished. The relationship of these variables to effectiveness is then examined in Section 3.

Measurement of objective and subjective resources

The questionnaire used in the International Study includes a variety of items concerning the various resources available to research units. Members' satisfaction with these resources will be referred to as subjective resources. Resources that are largely dependent on circumstances outside the influence of the units themselves will be defined as *objective resources.* Both objective and subjective resources may be conceptually divided into three different types: material resources, human resources, and information resources.

From a large number of items measuring objective and subjective resources selected from the separate questionnaires administered to unit heads, other scientists, and technical support staff, a set of indices was constructed on the basis of various correlational techniques.[1]

Material resources. Although the questionnaires did not include any direct questions regarding the amount of funds available to the unit, information on the amount of work space, on the amount of equipment, and on the extent of delays in obtaining equipment gives a fair reflection of the material resources of the units. Indices of these objective material resources were constructed from the following items. The number of square meters of premises the unit has for its use (RU:2.1a) was divided by the total size of the research unit to form the index of *work space.*[2] From questions measuring the need for and availability of equipment, the number of low-cost ($2,000–$5,000) equipment items available (RU:2.2a) divided by the total size of the research unit was taken as the index of *low-cost equipment resources.* From questions concerning delays in satisfaction of various needs, items measuring the approximate length of delay in weeks "between initiation of request and approval decision in the organization" in "hiring or buying low-cost equipment," and in "hiring or buying expensive equipment" (RU:5bi,ii) were combined into an index called *delays in decisions for equipment.* Analogously, the delays in "approval decision and satisfaction of need for hiring and buying low-cost and expensive equipment" were combined to create the index of *delays in obtaining equipment.*

Corresponding indices of subjective material resources were constructed as follows. Respondents were asked to express their satisfaction with a variety of resources by picking one of five categories along a scale ranging from "X" to "Y". The combined responses of the unit head and other scientists[3] to the X and Y statements: (X) "The space required for the work of the unit is highly adequate"; (Y) "The space . . . is highly inadequate" (SA,SB:Ka), is called the index of *satisfaction with space.* The responses of both unit head and other scientists to the two statements: (X) "The unit is well equipped scientifically"; (Y) "The unit is poorly equipped . . ." (SA,SB:Kb), and (X) "The unit has excellent office equipment"; (Y) "The unit has very poor. . ." (SA,SB:Kc) are combined into an index of scientists' *satisfaction with equipment.* The response of the technical support staff to the statement: (X) "I am very satisfied with the equipment available for my work"; (Y) "I am very dissatisfied. . ." (TS:J3n) is taken as a separate index of *technicians' satisfaction with equipment.*

Human resources. The manpower resources of the unit, the training and experience of scientists and technicians, and the contact possibilities with other scientific bodies were selected as indicators of the units' externally determined human resources. Indices of objective human resources were constructed as follows.

The total size of the unit divided by the number of research projects conducted by the unit at the present time (SA:E2) was defined as the index of *capacity of the unit.*

The combined "number of years of full-time equivalent education/training," and "the number of year(s) of R & D experience" of the unit head (SA:A2c,d) constitutes the index of *competence of unit head.* Analogously, an index was constructed for other scientists, defined as *competence of unit scientists* (SB:A2c,d). The "number of years of full-time education" of the technical support staff is used as the index of *technician's competence* (TS:A2c).

The possibilities for interaction with other scientists are measured by a number of different items. First, unit heads indicated the number of research units "belonging to your organization, within easy access and active in the same or similar fields" (SA:Q1a,b). Secondly, both unit heads and other scientists indicated the "number of research units outside your organization within easy access and active in the same or similar fields" (SA, SB:Q1c). Thirdly, both unit heads and other scientists answered (on a six-point scale ranging from "very rarely" to "daily") the questions: "How often do you discuss your work with members of other research units within your organization" (SA,SB:Q2a), and "How often do you visit (or are visited by) colleagues from other organizations working the same field either in your own country or abroad" (SA,SB:Q2b). The seven items combined form the index of *contacts of the unit.*

As in the case of material resources, corresponding indices of subjective human resources were constructed. Responses of the unit head, other scientists, and technical support staff to the statement: (X) "I am very satisfied with the manpower recruitment system of the unit"; (Y) "I am very dissatisfied. . ." (SA:J2h; SB,TS:J2m) combined with the unit scientists' responses to the statement: (X) "I am satisfied with the human resources available to the unit, as compared with its current research project(s) and/or scientific task(s)"; (Y) "I am very dissatisfied. . ." (SB:Kk) constitutes the index of *satisfaction with human resources.* The combined responses of the unit head and other scientists to the statements: (X) "The administration and secretarial assistance the unit receives is very satisfactory"; (Y) "The administrative . . . is very unsatisfactory" (SA,SB:Ke), and (X) "The technical assistance and services the unit receives are very satisfactory"; (Y) "The technical . . . are very unsatisfactory" (SA,SB:Kf), form the index of *satisfaction with technical and administrative assistance.* Responses of unit scientists (on a five-point scale ranging from "very satisfied" to to "very dissatisfied") to the questions: "How satisfied are you with the opportunities you have to discuss your work with members of other research units within your organization" (SB:Q3a), and "How satisfied are you with the opportunities you have to visit colleagues in other organizations working the same field" (SB:Q3b) are taken together as the index of *satisfaction with contacts.*

Information resources. Although it may be argued that the exchange of scientific information increasingly takes place via informal contacts among an "invisible college" of scientists (Crane, 1972; Gaston, 1972), there is equally strong evidence for the growing need for efficient information technology (Richta, 1969). Hence, the units' access to institutionalized information services is considered here as a distinct resource category.

Objective information resources were measured by two indices based on questions answered by the unit head: "Is there an internal library service available to your unit" (RU:2a), and "Does your unit enjoy the services of a science information officer" (RU:2b). The former is here referred to as the index of *internal library service;* the latter as the index of *science information service.*

Correspondingly, a subjective information-resource index was built from the combined responses of unit scientists to the following two statements: (X) "The library facilities available to the unit are highly satisfactory"; (Y) "The library . . . are highly unsatisfactory" (SB:Kg), and (X) "The information services available to the unit are very satisfactory"; (Y) "The information . . . are very unsatisfactory" (SB:Kh). This index is called *satisfaction with information.*

Construction of congruency indices

The notion of congruency between various types of objective and subjective resources implies a ranking of the objective resources along some quantitative high–low, much–little, etc., dimension, on the one hand, and the categorization of subjective perceptions into various degrees of satisfaction, on the other. For the subjective resource items this presents no special problem for–as already indicated–they were originally measured on five-point satisfaction scales. The objective resources, however, were measured in terms of actual quantities. Yet, the objective resource requirements of units obviously vary in different scientific disciplines, and possibly in different types of organizational settings.

For example, the equipment requirements of a research project in solid-state physics may be quite different from that for animal husbandry. The number of highly skilled technicians in electronics research differs from that in sociology. Hence, it was decided that instead of an absolute ranking along the different quantitative continua, the "amount" of objective resources would be categorized separately for different types of research units. This was done by dividing the total sample of research units into five subgroups.[4] In order to take into account possible systematic differences in subjective responses, these resource items were also subjected to this procedure.

The expected variations in resources by types of units were confirmed by the results of a one-way analysis of variance. Variations in resources *between* the types of units were generally significantly greater than *within* the groups of units (F values for most variables were statistically significant beyond the .01 level–data not shown). On the whole, research units in industrial applied science and cooperative institutions had considerably higher material resources, whereas academic medical–social science units ranked systematically lowest on all objective material-resource indices. However, there was no corresponding pattern for satisfaction. For example, the comparatively more generously supplied units of cooperative institutions were on the average less satisfied with their resources than the relatively poorer academic natural science units.

It is interesting that the overall pattern was almost reversed for human resources, with the exception of contacts of the unit. Compared with others, industrial applied science units tended to have the lowest human resources, whereas there was great variation among the other types of units according to different indices. On this very superficial aggregate level of examination, these results are in accord with the often-voiced belief that research units of industrial laboratories are "rich," but that they do not attract especially competent scientific manpower.

On the basis of these results, each resource index was transformed into a qualitative *high–medium–low* variable, separately within the five types of units, by using as cutting points the values within which the lowest, middle, and highest 33% of the subgroup units fell. Thus, for example, low delays in equipment decisions in academic natural science units (which ranged from 27 to 192 weeks) does not mean the same in an absolute sense as in industrial applied science units (which ranged from 12 to 112 weeks). Lowness is thus to be interpreted to mean that a unit ranks low on a given resource item relative to other units of the same type.

After trichotomizing each index, the bivariate relationships between the objective and corresponding subjective variables were examined. The magnitude of the relationships between the relevant pairs of variables, measured by the *tau* statistic, suggests that there is very little agreement between the actual level of a resource and its corresponding subjective perception by members of the units (see Exhibit 5.1). The fact that subjective perceptions seem to be relatively independent of objective reality confirms the relevance of exploring the effect of the congruency between actual resource levels and satisfaction with those levels on the effectiveness of research units.

For each resource, a new pattern variable was constructed using various combinations of the objective and subjective indices. (These also appear in Exhibit 5.1.) The nine logically possible patterns of congruency were used in recoding to make both the presence or absence of congruency and the level of the objective

Exhibit 5.1. Components of the congruency-pattern variables and relationships between the components

Congruency-pattern variables	Components		Relationship between components (*tau*)
	Objective resource index	Subjective resource index	
Material resources			
Work space	Work space	Satisfaction with space	.140
Equipment I	Low cost equipment	Scientists' satisfaction with equip.	.016
Equipment II	Low cost equipment	Technicians' satisfaction with equip.	.040
Decision delays I	Delays in decision re. equip.	Scientists' satisfaction with equip.	.135
Decision delays II	Delays in decision re. equip.	Technicians' satisfaction with equip.	.041
Supply delays I	Delays in obtaining equip.	Scientists' satisfaction with equip.	.188
Supply delays II	Delays in obtaining equip.	Technicians' satisfaction with equip.	.096
Human resources			
Unit manpower I	Capacity of unit	Satisfaction with human resources	.028
Unit manpower II	Capacity of unit	Satisfaction with tech. & adm. personnel	.053
Unit head competence	Competence of unit leader	Satisfaction with human resources	.036
Scientific staff competence	Competence of unit scientist	Satisfaction with human resources	.020
Support staff competence I	Technicians' competence	Satisfaction with human resources	.017
Support staff competence II	Technicians' competence	Satisfaction with tech. & adm. personnel	.014
Unit contacts	Contacts of unit	Satisfaction with contacts	.142
Information resources			
Library service	Internal library service	Satisfaction with information	.119
Information service	Science information service	Satisfaction with information	.026

and subjective resource identifiable, as shown in the accompanying table.

Objective resource	Satisfaction with resource: *High*	*Medium*	*Low*
High	Congruent: high objective & subjective resource	Intermediate (2)	Incongruent: high objective & low subjective resource
Medium	Intermediate (4)	Congruent: medium objective & subjective resource	Intermediate (6)
Low	Incongruent: low objective & high subjective resource	Intermediate (8)	Congruent: low objective & subjective resources

As will be recalled, the information-resource indices are constructed from dichotomous measures. These two indices were therefore recoded into the four possible patterns of congruency as the next table shows.

Information resource	Satisfaction with resource: *High*	*Low*
Yes	Congruent: high objective & subjective resource	Incongruent: high objective & low subjective resource
No	Incongruent: low objective & high subjective resource	Congruent: low objective & subjective resource

3. Congruency patterns in different types of research units

Although the focus of this chapter is on the relationship between external resources and performance of research units, the effect of at least one crucial factor, country, on the variations in patterns of congruency is of substantive interest in itself. The types of external resources considered in this chapter are presumably influenced or determined by the broader societal setting in which research units function. The goals, ideologies, and implementation of science policies; the financial, organizational, and scientific manpower resources; and even the "scientific culture" may vary from one country to another. Intercountry variations in congruency patterns for different types of resources are therefore examined in this section.

In recoding the objective and subjective indices into trichotomies within separate types of research units, the effects of type of organization and of scientific field have already largely been taken into account. However, in order to explore the remaining separate effects of Field and Type of organization these variables were also included in the following analysis.[5]

The joint and separate effects of Country, Scientific field, and Type of organization on congruency regarding different resources was examined by means of multivariate nominal scale analysis (MNA) (Andrews and Messenger, 1973). This multivariate analysis technique is well suited to the data and problem here explored. The technique is designed to handle problems where (1) the dependent variable is a set of mutually exclusive categories, as are the nominal-scale congruency pattern variables, and (2) the independent variables are measured at the nominal level of measurement, as are Country, Field, and Organization; an additive model is assumed; and any form of relationship may exist between any independent variable and the dependent variable, and between any pair of independent variables (Andrews and Messenger, 1973: 5).

Congruency patterns of material resources

The results of the multivariate nominal scale analysis for the seven pattern variables measuring congruency of material resources showed that Country, Scientific field, and Type of organization together explained from 3% to 10% of the variance in the patterns of congruency. As expected, Country related more strongly to different resource items than Field or Organization (generalized eta-squares ranged from .01 to .07).

Comparison of the distributions of the congruency patterns across the different countries showed that, in general, the highest proportion of congruent units at the high or medium level of objective and subjective resources were in the Swedish and Finnish samples, and that the highest proportion of congruent units at the low level of objective and subjective resources were in the Polish sample. Moreover, the Swedish sample contained the smallest proportion of units with high objective resources and low satisfaction and the most units where satisfaction was high even when objective resources were low. In contrast, the reverse tended to hold for the Polish sample: A high proportion of units fell into the category where resources were high but satisfaction was low, and few units were characterized by a low level of resources but a high level of satisfaction. Thus, with respect to material resources, these results suggest a kind of *halo effect:* When resources are in general relatively high and are generally perceived as such, then there tends to be also high evaluation of resources even when they are in fact low. This is the pattern that emerges in the Swedish sample, and the reverse is seen in the case of Poland.

The magnitude of the independent effect of Country on type of congruency pattern when Field and Organization were held constant tended to be greatest for two congruent categories: where both objective and subjective resources were high and where they were both low. There were, however, some interesting differences in this respect between the six countries. In *Austria,* there tended to be a relatively high proportion of units in the categories where satisfaction with resources was high and objective resources were either high or low. However, on the whole, the distribution of the congruency patterns of the Austrian units did not greatly differ from the average of the total sample. In the *Belgian* sample, the largest proportions of units tended to be in the two congruent categories where both objective and subjective resources were at high or medium levels, and fewest in the congruent category where both objective and subjective resources were low. Similar to the Belgian sample, the *Finnish* sample, too, tended to be characterized by high proportions of research units in the congruent categories where both objective and subjective resources were on high or medium levels, and fewest in the congruent category where both resources were low. In contrast, the highest proportions of units in the *Hungarian* sample tended to be in the congruent category where both objective and subjective resources were low, and there were relatively few in the incongruent category where objective resources were high but satisfaction was low. As already noted, the distribution of the congruency patterns in the *Polish* sample differed considerably from that of the other countries. With respect to all the resource items considered here, there were notably higher proportions of Polish units in the congruent category where both objective and subjective resources were low than in any other category. Correspondingly, there were few units in the category where both objective and subjective resources were high. The distribution of the congruency patterns in the *Swedish* sample showed the highest proportion of research units in the congruent categories where both objective and subjective resources were at the high or medium levels.

Congruency patterns of human resources

An analysis parallel to that just described for material resources was performed for the seven human-resource congruency items.

On the whole, the predictive power of Country, Scientific field, and Type of organization was consistently lower than for material resources. The variance explained ranged from 3% to 5%. There was no one particular type of congruency pattern that was best predicted by the three independent variables for all human-resource items. The specific association between Country and the different human-resource items was generally around .02, and in contrast to the material resources, Scientific field tended to play a somewhat greater independent role than did Type of organization.

Comparison of the relative percentage of units in different categories across the countries showed that the highest proportion of units in the congruent category where the level of both objective and subjective resources was high was in the Polish sample for Unit head competence and Scientific staff competence, whereas the same held for the Swedish sample for Unit manpower and Support staff competence. On the other hand, in the case of these latter two resource items, the Polish sample contained the highest proportion of units in the congruent category where both the level of objective resource and satisfaction was low, and in the incongruent category where the objective resource was high but satisfaction was low. Almost without exception, the highest proportions of units in the incongruent category where the objective resource was low but satisfaction was high were in the Swedish sample.

The distributions of the units according to congruency-pattern categories varied from one resource item to another in the *Austrian* sample. However, the Austrian units did not deviate in any notable way from the overall average. The same can be said of the *Belgian, Hungarian,* and *Finnish* units. (The one exception is that in both the Belgian and Hungarian samples there tended to be fewest units in the incongruent category where the level of objective resource was low but satisfaction was high, whereas the opposite was true of the Finnish sample. In the *Polish* sample, two different patterns of distribution emerged. With respect to Unit manpower and Support staff competence, Polish units were less likely than average to fall into the high-objective/high-subjective resource or low-objective/high-subjective resource categories. The opposite was true with respect to the two items measuring scientific staff resources (Unit head competence and Scientific staff competence): Here the highest proportion of units was in the congruent category at high levels of objective and subjective resources. In the *Swedish* sample, the halo effect, noted for material resources, was also apparent for human resources: The highest proportions of units were in the categories that were congruent at a high level of objective and subjective resources, or where the level of objective resource was low but satisfaction was high.

Unlike the case of material resources, there was no distinct type of congruency that was consistently predicted by the three independent variables across all the different items measuring human resources. Two separate clusters of human-resource items seemed to be distinguishable: one measuring the scientific manpower of the unit (Unit head competence and Scientific staff competence), and one the more general manpower resources (Unit manpower II and Technical support staff II). Despite the fact that the general pattern that emerged with respect to human resources was not as consistent as in the case of material resources, the Polish and Swedish samples again stood out as being different–each in its own way–from the overall average. The halo effect described above was seen for most of the resource items in the Swedish sample, but not in other countries.

Congruency patterns of information resources

The two information-resource items represent somewhat different measures than those discussed so far. As described in Section 2, the other congruency-pattern variables were based on a trichotomization of continuous variables. Library service and Information service, however, are measured in terms of simple presence or absence. Thus although the information measures do not capture more subtle quantitative differences in the amount or quality of the resource, they do give a more exact measure of the concept of congruency. The absence of the cumbersome "intermediate" categories make interpretation clearer from a statistical point of view. The lack of congruency becomes more obvious, for example, in the case of a unit that has no internal library service but still is "very satisfied" with library and information facilities.

As before, a multivariate nominal scale analysis was performed using Country, Field, and Type of organization to predict the congruency categories. The total proportion of variance explained by the three independent variables was considerably higher for both items than for either the material or human-resources measures. (The variance explained was 10% for Library service and 12% for Information service.) Part of this greater explanatory power may be due to the more exact nature and fewer categories of the congruency variables. Country, Scientific field, and Organization together best predicted the category where information service was low (i.e., absent) but satisfaction was high, and the category where the library-service resource was high (i.e., exists) and corresponding satisfaction was also high. Although Country was the major source of variation, a large residual independent contribution by Type of organization was evident in the case of Information service.

The two information-resource items suggest different patterns of congruency. In the case of Library service, variations by country were particularly due to differences in the proportions in the congruent category where both objective and subjective resource levels were high. Although the location of the variation was different in the case of Information service, here, too, the Swedish units were the major source of variation by country.

Regardless of country, more units on the whole have library services than information services, yet unit members were often dissatisfied with the former but satisfied with the latter, irrespective of the actual presence of these resources. The most striking example of this was the Swedish sample, where almost 100% of the units had library service but about 20% were dissatisfied with it, whereas about 80% of the units had no information service but more than two-thirds were satisfied. One explanation for this may be that scientists may have learned to have high expectations with respect to a traditionally institutionalized internal library, and within this frame of reference are more likely to express dissatisfaction when such a service exists, whereas an information service is such a new scientific commodity that even when there is little of it satisfaction tends to be high.

General conclusions concerning variations in congruency

The foregoing paragraphs consider to what extent there is agreement between the level of different resources of research units and the perception by unit members of the adequacy of these resources. The results lead to the conclusion that, as could be expected, scientists' evaluations of objective states are not necessarily rational. Irrespective of the type of resource item considered, units were distributed among all the nine (or four) logically possible congruency types.

On the whole, the three independent variables, Country, Scientific field, and Type of organization, together accounted for a rather small proportion of the total variance in congruency patterns.[6] More important, however, is that consistent differences emerged both between countries and between the types of resources considered.

The variations in congruency patterns in the different countries are of substantive interest as such. More significant, however, is the finding that the congruency patterns of units from two countries, Poland and Sweden, rather consistently deviated from others. Polish units, with the exception of the two items measuring scientific manpower, were on the whole characterized by a comparatively larger proportion of units with low levels of resources and expressed congruently low levels of satisfaction with them. The outstanding characteristic of Swedish units was their generally high level of satisfaction, irrespective of the level of objective resources, which, however, on the whole also tended to be comparatively high. These two consistent deviations from the overall sample in patterns of congruency point to the need for further analyses by country to investigate the extent to which these countries may also be unique in other respects.[7] One can here only speculate on the possible influence of such external factors as national science policy, resources, or broader scientific or cultural traditions on levels of satisfaction that might together or separately "explain" the distinctions noted in the patterns. Obviously a further exploration of the sources of these variations is not only of substantive interest, but also has a methodological relevance for future cross-cultural studies of this type in another set of societies.

Secondly, not only are differences observed among countries, as such, but congruency patterns tend to vary according to different types of resources. Although scientists may not be exceptionally rational, that is, congruent, neither are they entirely irrational. With respect to *material* resources, given a relatively high level of objective resources in a country, there is a tendency to express high satisfaction even when a particular objective resource level is low. The same pattern was also noted in the case of one of the more general dimensions of *human* resources, the items related primarily to the technical and administrative support staff of the units as well as with science information services. As a possible explanation, the concept of a halo effect was introduced. Very generally, one can speculate that for such resources as material resources, technical personnel, or science information, which are relatively new paraphernalia of research activity and for which no universal known high standards exist within the scientific community, scientists tend to evaluate the adequacy of these resources within the context of the general environment: If the levels of these resources are generally relatively high, scientists "learn" to perceive their own resources as satisfactory even when in specific instances they may be actually low (or nonexistent). Considering the patterns of congruency regarding resources in general in the Swedish sample, one can almost say that here the halo effect gets confirmation on the national level. On the other hand, a different pattern of congruency characterizes what has been here called scientific manpower resources and library service. Here we find relatively high proportions of units that were congruent at high levels of both objective and subjective resources, and at the same time many units that were dissatisfied even when their objective resource level was high. One possible interpretation for this pattern is that it reflects some type of relative deprivation. Presumably, there exist universal high standards within the scientific community regarding well-established concerns such as scientists' competence and scientific libraries. Many scientists may use these ideal norms as their reference group and thus be overcritical of their scientific manpower or library resources even when, comparatively speaking, they are objectively relatively high.

Both these interpretations imply some type of structural and contextual effects that suggest that there may be some consistent socially determined patterns underlying the relationship between objective resources and their subjective perceptions. The results suggest that the patterns of congruency are not random; therefore, the exploration of the factors that produce different congruency patterns and their possible consequences for the functioning of research units seems one relevant direction for further analyses. Here, however, we limit ourselves to the exploration of the relationship of different patterns of congruency to the performance of research units.[8]

4. Resources, satisfaction, and the effectiveness of research units

After having looked at the relationships between objective and subjective resources in some detail, we now turn to the analysis of their relationships with effectiveness. First, the separate relationships with performance are examined. Next, variations in the levels of performance by different patterns of congruency are discussed for different resource items. Lastly, the extent to which congruency measures can account for variations in performance levels over and above objective and subjective indices as such is compared and discussed.

Six rated-performance measures that reflect different dimensions of scientific productivity are used as measures of research-unit effectiveness. These are Recognition, General contribution,

R & D effectiveness, Training effectiveness, Administrative effectiveness, and Social effectiveness.[9] All performance measures have been adjusted to remove differences attributable to type of unit (as described in Chapter 2).

Objective resources, subjective satisfaction, and effectivenss

The relationship of objective and corresponding subjective indices to the different effectiveness measures was examined separately for each resource item. The results are summarized in Exhibit 5.2. Because the focus of interest here is on the effect of each objective resource and satisfaction item by itself on different dimensions of effectiveness, the exhibit shows the percentage of variance explained by each item (eta-square, adjusted).

As could be expected, on the whole, the magnitude of the effect of a given item on any specific performance measure is small. Satisfaction with the human resources of the unit explains the highest percentage of variance (about 5%), and this is for Administrative effectiveness.

There is no indication of any systematically greater predictive power of either the objective or the subjective resource items. The magnitude of the effect of a given satisfaction item is greater than that of the objective resource item in just about as many pairwise comparisons as the other way around. (The pairings are shown in Exhibit 5.1.) Moreover, the relative strength of the relationship varies from one performance measure to another for any given resource pair.

An analysis of the results in Exhibit 5.2 suggests some general conclusions regarding the effect of resources on various dimensions of effectiveness. *Material* resources of the unit seem to play a very insignificant role in the effectiveness of research units. On the whole, the relationships of objective material resources to various performance measures are either almost nonexistent or negative. Only Delays in obtaining equipment show some positive effect on General contribution and Social effectiveness. The independent effects of either objective or subjective *information* resources are also very small and inconsistent. On the other hand, the actual contacts of the units apparently have a greater effect on all dimensions of effectiveness than satisfaction with contacts.

Of all the various objective and subjective resource items, Satisfaction with human resources seems to have the most important single effect on performance. Both relative to the corresponding objective resources and in terms of its consistent recur-

Exhibit 5.2. Predicting research-unit performance on the basis of objective and subjective resources (figures show percent variance explained)

Resources	Performance measures					
	Recog.	Gen. cont.	Train. eff.	R & D eff.	Adm. eff.	Soc. eff.
Objective						
Work space	—	—	—	—	—	1.8(−)
Low-cost equipment	—	—	—	—	0.5(−)	1.1(−)
Delays in decisions re. equip.	0.2	—	—	—	—	—
Delays in obtaining equip.	—	2.4	—	—	—	3.2
Capacity of unit	—	—	0.3	—	0.6	1.3
Competence of unit leader	2.3	0.9	—	—	0.3	1.4
Competence of unit scientists	0.7	—	—	—	0.7	—
Technicians' competence	—	—	—	—	—	—
Contacts of unit	1.7	0.2	1.8	1.3	—	1.2
Internal library service	0.1	—	—	—	—	—
Science information service	—	—	—	—	0.6	0.3
Subjective						
Satisfaction with space	—	—	—	—	—	0.8(−)
Scientists' satisfaction with equip.	0.1	—	—	—	1.9	1.0(−)
Technicians' satisfaction with equip.	—	—	—	—	—	—
Satisfaction with human resources	—	—	1.3	2.1	5.1	—
Satisfaction with tech. & adm. personnel	—	—	—	—	0.3	1.0(−)
Satisfaction with contacts	1.0	0.8	0.2	1.0	—	0.5
Satisfaction with information	0.2	—	0.3	—	0.5	—

Notes: Figures are based on eta-squares, adjusted for degrees of freedom.

Where no figure is shown, the variance explained is $< 0.1\%$.

All relationships are positive (i.e., higher performance was associated with higher resources) except where a "−" is shown.

All performance measures have been adjusted to remove differences attributable to type of unit.

rence with different performance measures, the relationship of this item with effectiveness is comparatively high. The strongest indication of this is in the case of Administrative effectiveness.

Interestingly, the relationships to Social effectiveness differ from other dimensions of effectiveness. Irrespective of the item in question, satisfaction is either unrelated or negatively related to Social effectiveness. The same negative effect can also be seen in the case of Work space and Low-cost equipment. On the other hand, many of the other objective resource items show positive effects with Social effectiveness.

Thus, roughly speaking, it seems that Satisfaction with human resources, Delays in obtaining equipment, and Contacts of the unit are the three factors that show the strongest relationship to the effectiveness of research units. From the point of view of the different performance measures, these three resources most consistently explain variations in levels of Administrative effectiveness and Social effectiveness.

Patterns of congruency and effectiveness

The relationship between the congruency patterns of different resources and the performance measures were examined by means of one-way analysis of variance. Exhibit 5.3 shows the *F* values for each congruency-pattern variable for each dimension of effectiveness. The general impression from Exhibit 5.3 is that the congruency-pattern variables show statistically significant relationships to the performance measures in a substantial number of cases. Thus it is clear that there tend to be differences in performance among research units that have different congruency patterns.

A detailed examination of the nature of these differences has been made, and Exhibit 5.4 presents one sample of the results. Shown there are the mean performance scores on Administrative effectiveness when units are classified according to congruency pattern with respect to Scientific staff competence. This example is chosen because it has the highest *F* value in Exhibit 5.3 and because it illustrates the general trend of results that underlies nearly all the other *F* values as well.

The nine means shown in Exhibit 5.4 indicate the average ratings of Administrative effectiveness for units that fall in each of the nine congruency categories of Scientific staff competence. It is obvious that the means do vary, and this is what accounts for the substantial *F* value in Exhibit 5.3. Furthermore, because Exhibit 5.4 makes it convenient to link the nine categories of the

Exhibit 5.3. Predicting research-unit performance on the basis of the congruency-pattern variables (figures show F values)

Congruency-pattern variables	Performance measures					
	Recog.	Gen. cont.	Train. eff.	R & D eff.	Adm eff.	Soc. eff.
Work space	—	—	—	—	—	4.4
Equipment I	—	—	—	—	4.7	3.9
Equipment II	—	2.0	—	—	2.2	2.8
Decision delays I	2.1	—	—	—	3.5	—
Decision delays II	—	—	—	—	—	—
Supply delays I	—	3.7	—	2.0	3.7	3.9
Supply delays II	2.0	3.2	—	—	—	3.8
Unit manpower I	—	—	3.2	2.7	7.2	2.1
Unit manpower II	—	—	—	—	2.5	4.5
Unit head competence	3.8	2.5	—	4.0	7.9	2.3
Scientific staff competence	3.0	—	2.7	—	8.0	—
Support staff competence I	—	—	2.3	—	6.4	—
Support staff competence II	—	—	—	—	—	—
Unit contacts	4.3	2.4	3.6	3.9	—	2.8
Library service	3.7	—	4.3	—	3.4	—
Information service	2.8	—	—	—	5.9	2.8

Notes: *F*s ⩾ 2.5 are statistically significant at the .01 level; other *F*s shown here are statistically significant at the .05 level; where no *F* is shown, the differences between the means were not statistically significant.

All performance measures have been adjusted to remove differences attributable to type of unit.

gories of the congruency variable to the objective and subjective resource variables that define the categories, one can readily see the general trend of the differences: Administrative effectiveness tends to increase (means decrease) as either or both resource measures increase. Of course, this is perfectly consistent with the separate positive relationships shown in Exhibit 5.2 between Administrative effectiveness and Competence of unit scientists, and between Administrative effectiveness and Satisfaction with human resources. Given the way the congruency-pattern variables were constructed, this had to occur; what is important is to see whether any effects *beyond* the separate effects attributable to the two components of the congruency-pattern variable are present. Such effects, formally known as

Exhibit 5.4. Mean ratings of Administrative effectiveness by congruency with respect to Scientific staff competence

Competence of unit scientists	Satisfaction with human resources		
	High	Medium	Low
High	2.15	2.29	2.52
Medium	2.15	2.40	2.50
Low	2.34	2.45	2.63

Notes: Low numerical values on Administrative effectiveness imply high levels of performance. Differences attributable to type of unit have been removed.

Congruency with respect to Scientific staff competence involves joint consideration of both objective resource Competence of unit scientists, and subjective resource Satisfaction with human resources; see Exhibit 5.1.

statistical interactions, would appear if some combination of levels of objective and subjective resources were *particularly* good – or bad – for performance. As a matter of fact, examination of Exhibit 5.4 suggests that there is no marked interaction (with minor exceptions, the shift in the means from column to column, or from row to row, is fairly regular), and – as will be detailed in the next section – this proved to be the general pattern.

In short, the separate positive and negative trends identified in Exhibit 5.2 provide a good indication of how the congruency-pattern variables – which combine selected pairs of these trends – relate to effectiveness. As an example, for Recognition the lowest performance levels tend to be in a congruency category where the subjective resource is low, and generally the highest performance levels are in the categories where there is a high or medium level of satisfaction and a congruently high level of an objective resource.

The congruency variables are most consistently related to Administrative effectiveness. As was noted in the previous section, it is for this aspect of performance that the satisfaction items have a greater independent effect compared both with objective resources and with other performance measures. This is also reflected in the patterns of congruency. Generally, the highest and lowest performance levels are in the congruent categories at high and low objective and subjective resource levels, respectively. However, performance levels are always higher in those categories where satisfaction is high, irrespective of the objective resource level. In the case of Equipment – which, it may be recalled, is negatively related to performance – the same pattern holds, but in a reverse order.

A large number of congruency variables are also associated with Social effectiveness. Because practically all satisfaction items as well as two of the objective *material*-resource items are negatively related to performance, a unique pattern emerges for most of the material-resource items. Highest performance levels are in the congruent category where both objective and subjective resources are low, and lowest where both types of resource levels are congruently high. For *human* resources, however, generally high and low performance levels are in categories where objective resources are high and low, respectively, regardless of the level of satisfaction.

Comment. From the point of view of the different types of resources discussed, the relationships between the effectiveness measures and the congruency patterns of *human* resources are most consistent. Of the 21 significant associations between effectiveness measures and human-resource items, 14 of the lowest performance levels are in the congruent category at low levels of objective resource and satisfaction, and 12 of the highest performance levels are in the category where both resource and satisfaction are high.

On the whole, the relationship between patterns of congruency and effectiveness is not as conclusive as had been expected. There is, however, some indication that a high level of satisfaction and a corresponding high resource level has some reinforcing effect on performance, and the negative effect of both low objective resource and low levels of satisfaction is frequently notable. The major exception to this is the pattern for Social effectiveness, where there are negative associations between the level of most material resources and performance.

Alternative measures of resources and effectiveness

The foregoing sections have described the relationships of effectiveness to objective resources and corresponding satisfactions, on the one hand, and to the combined congruency pattern variables, on the other. It remains to compare the relative explanatory power of the two different approaches. Statistically, this implies the comparison of the amount of variance in performance explained by the two alternative ways of measuring resources.

Exhibit 5.5 provides this comparison for three performance

measures having the largest number of significant relationships to the congruency-pattern variables (as shown in Exhibit 5.3). The basic result evident in Exhibit 5.5 was also apparent for the three performance measures that are not shown there. The first of each pair of columns in the exhibit shows the percentages of variance in performance explained by the (additive) effects of a given objective resource and its matched satisfaction item; the second column in each pair shows the corresponding percentage of variance explained by the matching congruency-pattern variable. Both figures include adjustments for sample size and number of categories in the predictor variables.[10] The difference between the paired values shows the magnitude of the interaction effects, that is, whether the relationship between effectiveness and the congruency-pattern variable reflects anything beyond the simple additive effects of the two resource components. The significance of the magnitude of this difference was tested by the *F* ratio.[11]

As could be expected on the basis of the results presented above, the percentage of variance explained by any given pair of variables is very small. The differences in the magnitude of the additive effects of resources and satisfaction and that of the congruency-pattern variable are on the whole also very small and in some cases there is no interaction of any kind.

Slight gains in the variance explained by the congruency-pattern variable are most consistent in the case of Recognition and R & D effectiveness. Only for Equipment II, Unit head competence, and Library service is the magnitude of the strength of the relationship of the congruency-pattern variable consistently slightly higher than that of the additive effect. However, on the whole, the differences between the magnitudes of the strength of the relationship are so small that one must conclude that there are hardly any kind of interaction effects. A statistically significant interaction effect is found only in the cases of Scientific staff competence for Recognition ($F = 2.85$) and Equipment I for Administrative effectiveness ($F = 2.41$). In other words, the congruency-pattern variables as such do not predict performance any better than the simple additive effects of an objective resource and its matched satisfaction.

The absence of any interaction effects implies that *pure congruency*–that is, one particular kind of interaction consisting of *agreement* in the levels of an objective resource and a satisfaction, irrespective of what that level is–thus does not seem to have any influence on the effectiveness of research units.

Exhibit 5.5. Predicting research-unit performance on the basis of objective resources and satisfaction, and on the basis of congruency-pattern variables (figures show percent variance explained)

Congruency-pattern variables	Recognition		Administrative Effectiveness		Social Effectiveness	
	Obj. res. & sat.	Congru. pattern	Obj. res. & sat.	Congru. pattern	Obj. res. & sat.	Congru. pattern
Work space	—	—	—	—	2.5	2.6
Equipment I	—	—	2.6	3.2	2.7	2.7
Equipment II	—	—	0.7	1.2	1.4	1.8
Decision delays I	1.2	1.1	2.7	2.5	—	—
Decision delays II	—	—	—	—	—	—
Supply delays I	—	1.1	2.5	2.9	3.5	3.3
Supply delays II	0.6	—	—	—	3.8	3.4
Unit manpower I	—	—	6.0	5.9	1.3	1.1
Unit manpower II	—	—	1.4	1.2	2.6	2.8
Unit head competence	2.4	2.6	5.7	6.2	1.4	1.3
Scientific staff competence	0.9	1.8	6.4	6.3	—	—
Support staff competence I	—	—	5.1	4.9	—	—
Support staff competence II	—	—	—	—	—	—
Unit contacts	2.6	2.8	—	—	1.8	1.6
Library service	0.5	0.7	0.6	0.6	—	—
Information service	0.2	0.5	1.3	1.3	0.5	0.5

Notes: Figures are based on R-squares, adjusted for degrees of freedom (see text).
Where no figure is shown neither prediction approach explained a statistically significant fraction of the variance.
All performance measures have been adjusted to remove differences attributable to type of unit.

Comments. The finding that the congruency-pattern variables do not predict effectiveness any better than the simple additive effects of the available resources and level of satisfactions is contrary to our expectations and has important implications both for theoretical perspectives as well as for science policy.

First, it was assumed that the agreement between the level of an objective resource and satisfaction, that is, pure congruency as such, would have an impact, or cumulative effect, on performance. Secondly, it was also expected that both actual resources and satisfaction would influence performance in the same way, that is, that the more resources research units had, or the more satisfied they were with them, the higher their performance would be. On the basis of these assumptions, one would conclude that the most effective research units would be those that have congruently high levels of resources and are greatly satisfied with them; and the least effective, those that have congruently low objective resources and satisfaction. The results of the analysis of empirical data, however, suggest that this is not so. Empirically, the level of satisfaction more often than not does not correspond to the actual amount of resources available. For some aspects of performance, high resource levels and/or great satisfaction have a negative influence on effectiveness. And, the *agreement* between the objective resource level and corresponding satisfaction does not influence the likelihood of research units being more or less effective.

Before making final conclusions, however, some qualifying remarks are in order. First, it will be recalled that this chapter's analysis of resources, satisfaction, and effectiveness is based on combined six-nation data. On the other hand, intercountry variations in congruency patterns of different resources are also notable. In order to explore the possibility that the absence of interaction effects may be due to combining samples with different patterns of congruency, analyses of variance of the resource, satisfaction, and interaction variables were done for Administrative effectiveness and for General contribution separately for each country. Significant interactions are found only for Poland for Administrative effectivenss ($F = 2.86$) and for Sweden for General contribution ($F = 2.36$). Thus only in those cases where distinct types of congruency patterns consistently characterize units across many different resource items – as in the Swedish and Polish samples – did there appear interaction effects of some magnitude. Hence, whereas most of the findings reported here seem generalizable across country samples, further separate analyses for each country are in order.

Secondly, it should be pointed out that this chapter's analysis is concerned with specific dimensions of effectiveness that reflect aspects of the quality of research units' productivity from the point of view of different goals of research activity. This, of course, does not exclude the possibility that patterns of congruency regarding external resources may have important interaction effects on other aspects of research activity, or even other dimensions of effectiveness, for example, the concrete products (articles, patents, etc.) of the unit.

Finally, the analysis focuses on certain specific types of resources, that is, on those that have been here defined as "externally determined." Agreement between objective states and perceptions regarding some other aspects of scientific activity, for example, the degree of autonomy of the unit and the unit's satisfaction with the extent of external control, may prove to have significant effects on, among other things, the effectiveness of research units.

5. Summary and conclusions

In the foregoing pages, the relationship between externally determined resources and the effectiveness of research units was explored.

Empirical analysis of different types of resources showed the actual resources available to research units to be relatively unrelated to subjective perceptions of their adequacy. More often than not, the extent of satisfaction with different material, human, and information resources of research units does not correspond to the actual level of these resources. This finding in itself raises interesting theoretical and practical questions about why this should be so, what mechanisms explain the presence or absence of agreement in general, and what implications it has for various aspects of the functioning of research units. This is one area in which further research is needed.

The concept of pattern of congruency was introduced to define the *agreement* between different resource levels and degrees of satisfaction. Comparisons of the patterns of congruency with respect to different resources suggest that congruency patterns vary according to different types of resources.

For certain types of resources that are less traditionally associated with scientific activity (e.g., the presence of a science information officer, the adequacy of technical support staff, etc.), when research units are generally relatively well-off even those units that rate low in these resources tend to express high satisfaction. This was interpreted as a kind of halo effect. It implies that if there are no established objective criteria of adequacy, and if research units are on the average well provided with resources that are also defined as adequate by general opinion, then even units with comparatively low resources evaluate them like the better-off majority.

A tendency toward a different kind of structural effect is seen in the case of traditional scientific manpower resources, where units tend to express dissatisfaction even when their own resource level is relatively high.

Both these findings suggest that congruency patterns are not random, and there may be some socially determined factors that underly the relationship between objective resources and subjective perceptions of them.

Not only do congruency patterns vary according to resources, but also there are systematic variations among samples of different countries. For example, the congruency patterns of research units of the Polish and Swedish samples show consistent deviations from the others, the former being generally characterized by high frequencies of units with low levels of resources and congruently low satisfaction, the latter by generally a high level of satisfaction irrespective of the level of objective resources.

The differences noted among countries imply the need for further analyses of the sources of these variations both within the context of the present data as well as from the perspective of the unique policies, historical development, structure, and social function of science in each of the countries studied. The "deviant" samples noted above are not only of great interest from a substantive point of view, but also indicate the need to explore in future research whether and why they also represent distinct patterns in other respects.

Analysis of the relationships of objective resources and satisfaction with resources to six rated-effectiveness measures showed some unexpected results. The so-called externally determined resources of research units have only weak relationships to any of the dimensions of effectiveness here considered. The amount of variance in effectiveness explained by any given resource item, or by its matched satisfaction measure, is very small. Nor are all resource and corresponding satisfaction items related to all measures of effectiveness.

The relationships of objective *material* resources to effectiveness are generally minimal and in the case of some items even consistently negative. This result seems contrary to the generally held assumptions of many science policies and the scientific community, and needs to be interpreted with great caution. The result may partly be due to the type of resource items considered. More conventional measures of resources, such as the units' annual budgets, might show stronger relationships to effectiveness.[12] Also, for theoretical reasons, here the focus is on the influence of each resource item by itself on effectiveness. Presumably the combined, cumulative effect of a variety of resources would be greater.

Obviously, a certain minimum level of material resources is needed for the functioning of any research unit. However, these results suggest that not all types of material resources are equally crucial and that their contribution to effectiveness may be rather complex. This casts doubt on the utility of the assumptions of simple cost-effect estimates of R & D activity.

On the whole, *human* resources seem to play a more important role in the effectiveness of research units. Of these, the contacts of the unit and the competence of the unit head seem to be the most important objective resources. However, one of the most significant findings of this chapter's analysis is that satisfaction with human resources appears to make the most important single contribution to effectiveness. In view of this, such questions as why Satisfaction with human resources is significantly related to Administrative effectiveness but not to Social effectiveness obviously deserve further investigation.

Both in terms of the magnitude of the relationships as well as the number of resource measures that show relationships, external resources in general seem to be most relevant for Administrative and Social effectiveness. It is interesting that insofar as external resources have any relationship with the effectiveness of research units, they seem to contribute mainly to those dimensions that reflect more "extrascientific" goals of research, as compared to the conventional "scientific" criteria represented by the other effectiveness measures.

The relatively greater role of external resources in Administrative effectiveness is not very surprising. Such factors as staying within the budget or meeting schedules, which is what Administrative effectiveness taps, are rather concrete, technical aspects of effectiveness that can be expected to be dependent on resources to a larger extent. However, what is interesting is that irrespective of the type of resource, it is not the actual level of resources but satisfaction with them that seems to make the single greatest contribution to effectiveness. In fact, the strongest single relationship that emerged from this chapter's analysis is that between Satisfaction with human resources and Administrative effectiveness.

Social effectiveness is a relatively new concept in evaluating the results of scientific activity. As such, the fact that the observed relationships between resources and Social effectiveness differs from that of other effectiveness measures is of considerable importance. Not only do certain objective material resources have a negative relationship–as also noted for other effectiveness measures–but it is only with respect to Social effectiveness that satisfaction items are negatively related (or unrelated) to performance. One possible interpretation of this unique pattern is that a low level of satisfaction with external resources may reflect a more general dissatisfaction with broader environmental phenomena, which in turn may motivate units to orient their research activity toward social utility. The results show that high satisfaction tends to be associated with higher performance with respect to all other dimensions of effectiveness, but with lower performance for Social effectiveness. On an aggregate level, this suggests the possibility that units that are effective with respect to Social effectiveness are ineffective with respect to other criteria. Of course, because the relationships between satisfaction and various measures of performance are far from perfect, we cannot make this conclusion on the basis of this chapter's analysis. This would demand comparisons of the performance levels of different dimensions of effectiveness on the level of individual units. Because the social utility of scientific activity is of increasing concern to both the scientific community as well as to science policymakers, further investigation of the possibility that in practice, for whatever reasons, social effectiveness and other research goals may be mutually exclusive alternatives, seems of utmost significance.[13]

Finally, it is of considerable interest that research-unit effectiveness is independent of the correspondence between subjective perceptions regarding external resources and actual resource levels. Part of the reason for this may be that, depending on the particular resource, either the actual objective level or the degree of satisfaction plays such a dominant role that the less important of the two produces no change in effectiveness.

The rational allocation of scarce resources, the general well-being (satisfaction) of scientific workers, and R & D effectiveness are integral parts of science policy goals. This chapter's analysis suggests that the interrelationships among these factors are more complex than is often assumed by macrolevel models, and that they deserve much more attention on the microlevel of actual research units.

References

Andrews, F. M., 1975, Social and Psychological Factors which Influence the Creative Process. *In* Taylor, I. A., and Getzels, I. W. (eds.), *Perspectives in Creativity,* Chicago, Aldine, pp. 117–145.

Andrews, F. M., and Messenger, R. C., 1973, *Multivariate Nominal Scale Analysis: A report on a new analysis technique and a computer program,* Ann Arbor, Institute for Social Research, University of Michigan.

Andrews, F. M., Morgan, J. N., Sonquist, J. A., and Klem, L., 1973, *Multiple Classification Analysis: A Report on a computer program for multiple regression using categorical predictors,* Ann Arbor, Institute for Social Research, University of Michigan.

Crane, D., 1972, *Invisible Colleges,* Chicago, University of Chicago Press.

Dobrow, G. M., 1969, *Wissenschaftswissenschaft,* Berlin.

Gaston, J., 1972, Communication and the Reward System of Science: A Study of a National Invisible College. *In* Halmos, P. (ed.), The Sociology of Science, *Sociological Review Monograph,* 18: 25–41.

Gibbons, M., 1972, Some Aspects of Science Policy Research. *In* Halmos, P. (ed.), The Sociology of Science, *Sociological Review Monograph,* 18: 187–208.

Pelz, D. C., and Andrews, F. M., 1966, *Scientists in Organizations,* New York, Wiley.

Richta, R., 1969, *Civilization at the Crossroads,* White Plains, N.Y., International Arts and Sciences Press.

Stolte-Heiskanen, V., 1975, Suomalaisia Suurprojekteja [Finnish big science]. *In* Bruun, K., Eskola, K., and Viikari, M. (eds.), *Tiedepolitiikka ja Tutkijan Vastuu* [Science policy and the responsibility of scientists], Helsinki, Tammi, pp. 149–165.

Notes

1. Unless otherwise indicated, measurements are simple additive indices.

2. Here and in the rest of the chapter the location of the question is indicated in parentheses after the item (e.g., "RU:2.1a" refers to question number 2.1a in the RU questionnaire). Selected portions of the questionnaires are reproduced in the Appendix to this volume.

Total size of the research unit represents the sum of first-, second-, and third-level scientists, engineers, and technicians identified as core members and either administratively or nonadministratively attached at present to the unit (RU:4.1a,b).

3. The analysis is based on unit-level data, i.e., the responses of nonsupervisory scientists and technical support staff have been aggregated across all interviewed scientists and technical staff of the unit, respectively.

4. The five types of research units are: (1) units engaged in exact and natural sciences and located in academic organizations (Acad/Nat); (2) units engaged in medical and social sciences and located in academic organizations (Acad/Med-SS); (3) units engaged in applied sciences and located in academic organizations (Acad/Appl); (4) units located in cooperative R & D institutions (CoopIns); (5) units engaged in applied sciences and located in industrial organizations (Indust/Appl). For a description of the statistical explorations that led to this typology, see Chapter 13.

5. The types of organizations were: (1) universities and similar institutions

of higher education; (2) research institutes closely associated with (and often managed by) universities; (3) institutions attached to the academies of science and to national research organizations; (4) research institutes serving, wholly or partly, a sector of production, a branch of industry, or a public service; (5) research laboratories of productive enterprises; (6) contract research institutes; (7) other.

The scientific fields were grouped as follows: (1) Mathematics, Astronomy, and Astrophysics; (2) Physics; (3) Chemistry; (4) Life sciences; (5) Earth and space sciences; (6) Agricultural sciences; (7) Medical sciences; (8) Technological sciences; (9) Anthropology, Economic sciences, History, Juridical sciences and Law, Pedagogy, Political Science, Psychology, Sociology.

6. The low relationships with Field and Type of organization were to be expected, for most of the potential explanatory power of these variables was intentionally removed when the congruency variables were constructed, as described in Section 2.

7. As far as the Swedish sample is concerned, one might be tempted to say that the differences were due to the unique sampling design (see Chapter 2). However, the possible biasing effects of having units from one specific type of organization and from a limited set of scientific fields have been already taken into account in the construction of the congruency indices within separate typologies of research units. Nor have specific field or organization effects appeared in the multivariate analysis where field and organization were included as independent variables.

8. The effects of Scientific field and Type of organization need a brief comment. The facts that one specific field, the medical sciences, and that academic research institutes and national research organizations all rather consistently showed some residual independent effects even after the adjustment made in the process of index construction, may be due to their "misclassification" in the construction of the Typology of research units and points to the need for further investigation in future analyses.

9. For a description of these measures, developed by the Unesco Secretariat and the International Research Team, see Chapter 2.

10. The percent of variance was obtained by multiple classification analysis (MCA) (Andrews et al., 1973) when the additive effects of the objective and subjective resources were estimated, and by one-way analysis of variance (ANOVA) where congruency pattern was the predictor, as follows:

MCA: adjusted $R^2 = 1 - (1 - R^2)\,[(N - 1)/(N + P - C - 1)]$,
where N = number of cases
P = number of predictors
C = number of categories (summed across all predictors)

ANOVA: adjusted $R^2 = 1 - [(T - E)/(N - C)]/[T/(N - 1)]$
where T = total sum of squares
E = explained sum of squares
N = number of cases
C = number of categories in the pattern variable

11. $F = S_I^2/S_W^2$,
where $S_I^2 = (BSS - ESS)\,/\,df_1$ (= 9)
S_W^2 = within groups sum of squares / df_2 (= 900)
ESS = explained sum of squares (MCA)
BSS = between groups sum of squares (ANOVA)

12. It may be mentioned, however that the results of analyses of Finnish data, where a greater variety of material resources were considered, including the research unit's budget, tend to confirm the present findings (Stolte-Heiskanen, 1976).

13.. Certain analyses in this volume examine this matter; see Chapter 11 and the latter part of Chapter 14. The results suggest that although Social effectiveness is rather different from other effectiveness measures (i.e., statistically independent or only weakly related), there are no marked *negative* relationships [editor's note].

6 Some problems of research planning: data from Hungary compared to other Round 1 countries

Agnes Haraszthy and Lajos Szántó
Hungarian Academy of Sciences, Budapest

1. Introduction

Nowadays it is generally believed that the overproduction of information is characteristic of our age: Much more information is supplied than can be learned and absorbed. In reality, however, mankind has an eager desire for more information. In our age, the demand for fresh information about the objective world is significantly greater than the possibilities for satisfying it. Every country having a more or less developed social structure makes serious efforts to meet this demand. However, all societies have limited financial sources, and in each stage of the historical development of the society they are able to devote only limited resources to the development of science. In each social system, this process is controlled by the laws of distribution of the available wealth.

Certain scientific indicators, such as the funds spent for scientific activity, characterize the *consumer* function of scientific research. These measures indicate what science gets from the society, and they carry implications about the level of social development as well.

Besides the consumer function, science also has a *production* function. The production function of science is reflected in the expansion of the intellectual system of human knowledge about the objective world, and this is characterized by indices based to a great extent on intellectual values or payoffs, especially in the case of basic sciences. Accordingly, the production activity of a scientist can be evaluated using indices that show practical relationships to the scientific activities of scientists of the past.

When evaluating scientists and scientific research, the successful solution of science-management problems involving the efficient employment of scientists has been hampered by arbitrariness, which may restrain scientific and technical progress.

Studying and comparing the indices of the consumer and production functions of science (even if they are based on self-evaluation) provides both the management of scientific research organizations and the scientific public with the possibility of demonstrating the efficiency and effectiveness of the scientific activity of a certain scientific organization or research team.

The demand for adequate and reliable information on scientific activity continues to increase, and experts on science policy and research organization search more and more often for methods that provide possibilities for measuring the qualitative phenomena of scientific activity that may not lend themselves to quantitative measurement. Often these methods will involve certain modifications in the methodology of the exact sciences. The Unesco-coordinated International Comparative Study on the Organization and Performance of Research Units, in which Hungary has participated, constitutes such a methodological program.

An enormous volume of information has been made available by Round 1 of this Unesco program: Approximately 1.1 million answers from 1,200 research units and 10,000 respondents have been analyzed. This material, because of its volume, remains to be fully exploited; it is too early to talk about a reliable method for examining the efficiency and effectiveness of scientific research. We have concentrated our attention on just a few areas. On the basis of preliminary studies using mathematical-statistical methods, we have divided the enormous mass of variables into 22 groups. Each group contains a set of interdependent questions that concern the same subject.

The analyses to be reported here are based on variables concerning research planning (this is one of the 22 groups mentioned above). We shall consider three subjects related to research planning, as follows: (1) problems concerning the planning and organization of the activity of the research units; (2) information on the research themes and projects of the units: influences on the choice of research themes, the number of research projects, their distribution in various fields of science, their level of readiness, and their duration; and (3) data on the types of methods applied in the research work.

The data on research themes and projects are based on data from heads of research units; the data on research planning and research methods include opinions from both heads of research units and staff scientists. For the purpose of analysis, the following mathematical-statistical methods have been used: univariate statistical analysis, three types of cluster analysis, factorial analysis, nonmetric multidimensional scaling, correlation analysis, multiple regression analysis, and an exploratory search technique incorporated in the AID program.[1]

The choice of topics and variables that will be analyzed is supported by the following three considerations of science policy:

1 In the field of research planning, Hungarian research management has significant organizational experience, especially concerning long-range and medium-range planning at the national and institutional levels. Therefore, it will be particularly interesting to compare our planning routines with those in other countries.
2 We believe that the number of a unit's research projects, and the structures and durations of those projects, provide useful information about characteristics of the science policy and science management of a country.
3 The fact that researchers suitably apply a scientific methodology may justify the prior investment in R & D planning.

2. Analysis results

Planning and organization of research-unit activities

Our first topic is the planning and organization of the activity of research units. We shall examine data obtained from Section N of the questionnaire (which was answered by unit heads) and from Section P (answered by staff scientists).[2]

In accordance with expectations, there proved to be a substantial relationship ($r = .5$) between ratings of the extent of cooperation among unit members and the likelihood that unit heads reported that "The scientific or technical objectives of the . . . unit are closely related." However, these items were essentially unrelated to another item that asked about how the budget was established for the unit – whether it was established as a whole, or with allotments earmarked for each research worker. Thus the data of the study suggest that scientific activity based on close cooperation of team members does not necessarily require funding through a unified budget.

Unit heads also provided information about the frequency with which two broad types of methods were used in planning the research: "formal planning methods" (e.g., opportunity and constraint analysis, dynamic system modeling, risk analysis, etc.)

and "scheduling methods" (e.g., PPBS – Program Planning and Budget System, PERT – Program Evaluation and Review Technique, etc.). Neither of these two types of methods was used very frequently in any of the six countries that participated in Round 1 of the International Study (the "scheduling methods" were used even less frequently than the "formal methods"), and there was no relationship between the frequency of using one and the frequency of using the other.

Looking at the results obtained, it can be stated that the repertory of research planning – on the level of research units – does not contain abundant methodological knowledge. Therefore, in order to achieve a suitable application of the methodology of microlevel research planning, we believe it would be advisable to increase the requirements for drawing up research plans on the basis of some specific planning method.

Essentially, this same set of topics is approached from the staff scientists' point of view through the questions included in Section P of the questionnaire. Perceptions about the adequacy of research planning, the interest of the research work, and the coherence of the research program all proved to be closely correlated, as expected (*r*s ranged from .5 to .6). Furthermore, being well informed about the research planning and research program of the unit tended to accompany reports of having participated in the planning (*r*s ranged from .7 to .8).

We conclude that, within the six countries participating in the International Study, a favorable picture can be drawn of this field: Although specific research-planning methods tend to be used rather infrequently, the amount of research planning and the information about the plans approach levels that are deemed ideal by staff scientists and heads of research units.

Research themes and projects

Themes. Heads of research units were asked to indicate, in percentage terms, the relative influence of the following factors on the choice of research themes on which the unit worked:[3] (1) guidelines and/or instructions from national science policymaking bodies, (2) guidelines coming from the authority or industrial enterprise(s) controlling the organization to which the unit belonged, (3) guidelines from the governing organ(s) of the organization to which the unit belonged, (4) practical needs identified by the unit itself, (5) the scientific significance and promise of the research, and (6) other factors. Exhibit 6.1 shows the average percentage of influence assigned to each of these factors within each of the six participating countries.

As can be seen in Exhibit 6.1, the national science policymaking bodies have comparatively great influence in Hungary.

The Hungarian Academy of Sciences–as an institution adapted to the socialist circumstances and functioning in accordance with the directives of science policy–has a basic role in the management of science policy. It influences all scientific research and acts as an advisory body on principles and methodology as it takes part in the national management of scientific research and as it manages research carried out in its institutions. Its scope of activity covers the whole area of Hungarian scientific research, with special regard for basic research. Scientific research carried out in the independent scientific research institutes belonging to the academy is complemented by the R & D activities of universities and high schools, as well as institutes belonging to branch ministries and to research centers of enterprises, etc. The research institutes that constitute the main base for scientific research have been established by the Hungarian Academy of Sciences and by different ministries. The former is responsible for basic research, whereas the latter's responsibility is applied research and developmental research. A significant part of the financial burden is met from state resources.

The comparatively great influence of science policymaking bodies that is characteristic of socialist circumstances is also demonstrated by the data collected in Poland. Exhibit 6.1 shows that this source of influence also exceeds the average value in the case of Poland.

Scientific research activity as a whole is covered by a unified science policy of the state, and the required organizational structures and mechanisms are established accordingly. Within the whole national science organization, state and social management is coordinated. Planning is one of the basic elements of the management system for scientific research activity.

In Hungary, the most important scientific plan is called the National Perspective Plan for Scientific Research for 1971–1990 (subsidiary plans of different ranges are attached to it). This plan is a long-range document of the goverment's scientific-political strategy. Its directing effect is expressed through determination of the most important research tasks, and it uses indirect economic and scientific means of influence.

It is advisable to maintain direct contacts with the users of research results and those carrying out research when determining the majority of research tasks. However, sometimes it is

Exhibit 6.1. Influence of six factors on a unit's choice of research themes, by country (figures show mean percentages of total influence)

Influence factor	All	Countries					
		Austria	Belgium	Finland	Hungary	Poland	Sweden
National science policy making bodies	11	4	5	4	24	19	10
Authority or enterprise(s) controlling organization to which unit belonged	10	9	4	12	16	15	1
Organization to which unit belonged	14	13	6	22	12	13	15
Practical needs identified by unit itself	27	35	28	29	20	25	22
Scientific significance and promise of research	33	32	52	23	27	24	44
Other	5	7	5	10	1	4	8
Totals	100	100	100	100	100	100	100

necessary to determine research tasks for certain national organizations if these tasks are required for the complex development of some fields or branches of research or of the people's economy. The main directives at the national level determine the general trends of national research and scientific development. The national-level research projects serve directly for the purpose of material production, and they implement the central development programs included in the plan of the people's economy. The long-range perspective plans for scientific research promote the increase of the social effectiveness of science. Coordination is accomplished by the coordinating councils or centers that reconcile the medium-range plans for research institutes with the targets of the National Perspective Plan for Scientific Research.

The medium-range research plans are drawn up considering national interests, with suitable stimulation and persuasion for individual researchers. The research plans should not be rigid, and researchers should be provided with possibilities to deal with subjects initiated by themselves. According to the National Perspective plan for Scientific Research, only one-quarter of all research expenditures is to serve the purpose of central plans.

A research-planning system established in this way seems to be suitable, provided that it is guided by appropriate information on the planning of research activity.

Projects. Factors that influence the choice of research themes represent certain *external* characteristics of the structure of R & D activity. In contrast, the number of projects carried on by a research unit, and the structure and duration of such projects, indicate *internal* structural characteristics.[4]

As can be seen in Exhibit 6.2, the average number of research projects per research unit in Hungary is not far from the international six-country average.

It is interesting to compare the data on research projects included in the International Study with those of the official Hungarian research statistics. According to the Hungarian Central Office of Statistics (KSH, 1976), the number of projects per capita was 0.92 at the R & D organizations that participated in the International Study. (In the official Hungarian statistics, the projects are not calculated per researcher; however, using the exact definition of a research unit, this comparison is easily made and proves to be very close to 1.0 project per researcher.)

In 1974, more than half of all the research projects consisted of newly commenced ones, and this fact reflects the inadequacy

Exhibit 6.2. Mean number of projects conducted within research units, by country

Country	Projects
Austria	7.8
Belgium	5.2
Finland	5.9
Hungary	4.4
Poland	5.4
Sweden	4.5
All countries	5.7

Exhibit 6.3. Number of Hungarian research units included in the International Study that conducted designated numbers of research projects

Number of projects being conducted	Number of research units		Number of all projects	
	N	%	N	%
1	21	10	21	2
2	25	11	50	5
3	26	12	78	8
4	22	10	88	9
5	25	11	125	13
6 or more	102	46	612	63
Total	221	100	974	100

Note: 221 units × 4.4 projects per unit (see Exhibit 6.2) = 974 projects.

of research planning. A related statistic is the increase in the number of unsuccessfully finished projects (in 1974 it was 21% more than in the previous year). Although the number of projects per researcher in Hungary shows the negative sides of research management and research planning, it appears to be comparable to what obtains in other countries.

Exhibit 6.3 presents further details about the number of research projects being conducted by the Hungarian research units that participated in the International Study. Based on Exhibit 6.2, a research unit dealing with four to five projects can be regarded as an average one within Hungary. As shown in Exhibit 6.3, such units constituted 21% of all units and conducted 22% of all projects. About a third of all units dealt with less than four

Exhibit 6.4. Mean number of years projects have been going on, by country and by order in which projects were listed

Country	Project listed first	Project listed second	Project listed third	Project listed fourth	Project listed fifth	Project listed sixth
Austria	6.2	4.7	4.3	3.2	2.6	1.7
Belgium	8.8	6.5	4.5	3.5	2.2	2.2
Finland	6.5	2.6	1.7	1.0	0.6	0.2
Hungary	12.2	11.9	10.4	9.3	9.0	9.8
Poland	8.2	6.2	4.5	2.9	1.6	0.8
Sweden	9.5	5.4	3.6	2.4	1.4	0.8
All countries	8.5	5.9	4.6	3.1	2.2	1.5
% of units listing such a project	100	69	54	37	26	18

projects, and these accounted for 15% of all projects. The proportion of units that worked on six or more projects was substantial (46%) and they conducted 63% of all projects.

The ratio of about one researcher per research project, cited above, points to unfavorable factors. Teamwork and the breaking up of projects are generally contradictory ideas. Furthermore, conducting research on several projects at the same time means breaking up financing as well, and this – considering the limited financial sources available – might become a restraining factor for a unified research policy.

Because scientific research is always carried out as a function of time, important characteristics of the whole R & D structure can be explored by examining the duration of each research project. Exhibit 6.4 shows average project durations in each of the six countries participating in the International Study.

When one compares the duration of projects according to the order in which unit heads listed them in the questionnaire, Exhibit 6.4 shows that there was a clear tendency for longer-established projects to be listed in advance of newer ones. When the data are aggregated across all six countries, this trend is quite regular, with each subsequent project having been in operation, on the average, about two-thirds to three-quarters of the time of the immediately preceding one. (This trend is much weaker for Hungary.)

Of greater substantive interest, however, are the comparisons across countries. In Finland, Austria, and Sweden, the average

Exhibit 6.5. Degree of completion of research projects, by country and by order in which projects were listed (figures show percent of total time for a project that has already elapsed)

Country	Project listed first	Project listed second	Project listed third	Project listed fourth	Project listed fifth	Project listed sixth
Austria	61	40	58	53	54	53
Belgium	66	60	53	60	55	59
Finland	63	62	53	50	50	50
Hungary	57	47	51	52	53	56
Poland	60	42	55	62	56	50
Sweden	67	43	56	63	57	75
All countries	61	56	54	58	55	60

duration tended to be relatively short (2.5 to 4.0 years, when averaged across the total number of projects reported upon). Poland and Belgium did not differ much from these. In Hungary, however, the average time research projects had been underway was surprisingly long (9 to 12 years).

The relatively long duration of research projects in Hungary can be explained by some characteristics of the research structure and organization, which have both advantages and disadvantages. The stable, academy-centered research network and base provides possibilities for a longer duration of certain research projects than in Western countries, where a research team's activity is organized to carry out research tasks of shorter duration.

An analysis of the degree of completion of the projects provides further information about R & D structures. "Degree of completion" is here defined as the percentage of the total planned duration of a project that it has been underway. Exhibit 6.5 presents average values for degree of completion for each of the six participating countries.

Exhibit 6.5 shows that the average degree of completion of projects was between 50% and 60%. There was no significant difference either between countries or according to the order in which projects were listed. Hence, the research units in all the countries being studied have – on the average – progressed as far as the middle of their projects. In the case of Hungary, we believe this disproves the hypothesis that the increase in the number of projects active in 1974 is a result of the National Perspective Plan for Scientific Research, which started in 1972.

It is true that this plan should link the thematic structure of R & D activity to the most important requirements of the people's economy, and therefore the higher ratio of "changing projects" is natural. If, however, the Hungarian scientists had proceeded as far as the middle of their projects at the time data were collected for the International Study, and if the average duration of projects was 9 to 12 years, then the National Perspective Plan for Scientific Research has not much changed the quantity of research projects.

Methods used in research work

Both heads of units and staff scientists were asked to rate the significance of certain broad groups of research methods for their work.[5] Our analysis suggests that the way in which methods were grouped in the questionnaire was not very favorable, and we found during the survey that some of the scientists were unclear about some of the methods that were enumerated and about where some other methods belonged. Nevertheless, this does not explain away the unfavorable place of Hungary on the scale developed from the answers. In the case of Hungary, the inadequate application of methods for research design and analysis reveals the same negative characteristics that occur in the research-planning activities.

The questionnaire inquired about the following five types of methods: (1) use of hypotheses and verification methods; (2) formulation of axioms and postulates; (3) factorial analysis, multivariate analysis, probabilistic models, etc.; (4) operational models, morphological models, inductive models; and (5) brainstorming, forecasting, synectics, etc.

The analysis of the significance ratings of the above five methods for the units' research activity shows that the order of significance was the same for Hungarian units as for the international data as a whole, and that heads of units tended to assign the same relative significance levels as did staff scientists. Everywhere the verification methods were rated most significant, and the use of axioms and postulates least significant.

Further analysis showed, however, that Hungarian scientists (both heads of units and staff scientists) tended to report that all these methods were less significant for their work than did scientists in other participating countries. This raises a question regarding the methodological awareness of the Hungarian scientists compared with those elsewhere.

Perhaps the Hungarian scientists were not fully aware of the

Exhibit 6.6. Percentage of units using research methods, theories, or other specific elements developed in fields of science other than their own, by country and type of respondent

Country	Type of respondent	
	Unit heads	Staff scientists
Austria	43	25
Belgium	56	46
Finland	44	28
Hungary	86	77
Poland	67	53
Sweden	54	30
All countries	58	41

definition of the methods they used, or to which of the methodological groups specified in the questionnaire their methods belonged. The latter seems to be supported by answers to another question that asked about the application of methods developed in other fields of science, on which Hungarian research units scored unusually high.[6] Exhibit 6.6 shows these results.

In all fields of research work, the significance of carrying out interdisciplinary research is increasing. As shown in Exhibit 6.6, a substantial proportion of units, both in Hungary and elsewhere, turn to methods developed in other fields not normally used in their own research. It is interesting to note that it is the Hungarian (86%), Polish (76%), and Belgian (56%) heads of units who apply methods from other fields most frequently, and that it is the Austrian and Finnish heads of units who are least likely to do it (43–44%). The pattern for staff scientists is similar, but with lower absolute levels that probably reflect less general methodological awareness.

If these data on interdisciplinary borrowing are considered jointly with information on the duration of projects, the following interesting relationship can be obtained. The six participating countries may be divided into two groups: group A, consisting of Austria, Finland, and Sweden; and group B, Belgium, Hungary, and Poland. Countries belonging to group B typically deal with one research project for 6.4 years (as an average across six projects); countries in group A, for 3.3 years, that is, about half. The proportion of units that apply methods or theories developed in other fields of science is 69% (as reported by heads of units) and

58% (as reported by staff scientists) in countries belonging to group B, whereas it is 47% and 27%, respectively, for group A. Thus it seems that scientists working on one project for a longer time have better opportunities to use elements available in other fields and that the interdisciplinary-mindedness of these scientists can come to light.

3. Conclusion

The majority of researchers still seem to show some skepticism toward research planning. They feel their own freedom in research is hurt if sometimes they have to subject their conceptions to a planned research project. As a result of financial stimulation (which is not always sufficient, either) they put a different label on their own research plan. A main weakness of the research-planning system in Hungary is the establishment of unsuitable reporting practices, that is, the control carried out by the coordination councils is not sufficient, and consequently the number of research projects per researcher may be too high; in addition, certain themes may be dealt with separately and in parallel without any cooperation. This means that the researchers' individual interests and their ambitions for their own careers may come into conflict with the interests of the society and with those of the people's economy. The honor to be derived from collective teamwork is still not up to that from obtaining individual recognition and success. This explains the relatively long duration of research projects in Hungary as well: The researcher may not be deeply concerned about rapid completion of the work, and the research plan may not stimulate this either. Consequently, the basic elements of planning that might enhance the effectiveness and efficiency of research (such as: (1) researchers being free to look for projects and methods, (2) management being flexible, (3) research freedom being not absolute but instead research projects having to be adjusted to the research plan that serves the interests of the people's economy, and (4) the researchers being independent to a certain extent but responsible for their activity) do not yet predominate.

These insights have been obtained from the analysis conducted to date. Further analysis is required to relate the variables studied in the chapter to measures of the effectiveness of research units. We believe it would be worthwhile to carry out this analysis at a later date, because some variables used in our analysis show significant correlations with these performance measures.[7]

References

KSH [Central Office of Statistics] 1976, *Tudomanyos Kutatas, 1974* [Scientific research, 1974], Budapest, KSH.

Sonquist, J. A., Baker, E. L., and Morgan, J. N., 1974, *Searching for Structure,* Ann Arbor, Institute for Social Research, University of Michigan.

Notes

1. The AID program is described in Sonquist, Baker, and Morgan (1974).

2. These portions of the questionnaire appear in the Appendix to this volume.

3. For details, see question H1 in the Appendix.

4. Information about research projects is drawn from Section E of the questionnaire (see Appendix). The questionnaire defined a research project as follows: "A group of interrelated research and experimental development activities aimed at obtaining *original* results by creating new theories and methods, improving the understanding of nature, inventing and developing new products or processes, discovering new fields of investigation, etc. The progress achieved on a research project is usually reported upon *separately* as one whole to higher hierarchical levels or sponsoring authorities of the unit. The work performed may – or may not – be directed towards a specific practical aim."

5. See question D1 of the questionnaire in the Appendix.

6. This is question D2a; see Appendix.

7. The highest *r*s range from .4 to .5 and pertain to correlations between "general effectiveness" (as rated by staff scientists) and ratings by these same staff scientists of the adequacy of research planning, the interest of the research, and the coherence of the research program (see Exhibit 11.4). Certain other planning-related measures examined in this chapter also relate to one or another of the performance measures developed in Chapter 11, with *r*s in the .2 to .3 range (see Exhibits 11.4 and 11.6–11.10). The extent to which these relationships might be attributable to different types of research units being included within the same analysis has not been determined [editor's note].

7 Patterns of influence and the performance of research units

Salomea Kowalewska
Institute of Philosophy and Sociology, Polish Academy of Sciences, Warsaw

1. Introduction

The organization of scientific activities has become an object of discussion and evaluation for a number of different social groups. Science policy makers want to determine the distribution of resources used for R & D and wish to find a relationship between these inputs and the output. The managers of scientific institutes, being subjected to pressures from both within and without, seek to reconcile the expectations of the scientists inside their organizations with those of the financing bodies. Each actual need for support comes into conflict with traditional attitudes that defend against any strange mechanism of control or intervention that could threaten the autonomy of the scientist.

Finding an adequate type of organization for scientific activities – one that will stimulate creativity and promote the solution of cognitive tasks – is still an object of wishful hope and speculation rather than real fulfillment.

In looking for a more satisfactory organizational model, one can examine previous research on organizational effectiveness, and one can test the relationships between certain variables re-

The assistance of Marek Prussak, research associate in the Institute for Organization of Machine Industry (Warsaw), in performing some of the computer analyses; of Gerald A. Cole and Cinda Yates, Unesco staff members, in performing other computer analyses; and of Frank M. Andrews, editor of this volume, in revising the original draft of this chapter, are gratefully acknowledged. Arnold Tannenbaum has provided helpful suggestions.

cently discovered as important for organizational functioning and measures of scientific performance. This is the approach we have taken for exploring patterns of influence in research units.

In studies that have focused on the functioning of economic and political organizations, *influence* is treated as being almost synonymous with *control* or *power.* The relative difference in influence exercised by the leader in an organization and by the subordinates working under him is treated by authors of many organizational studies as an indicator of the extent of democracy and participation in management practice (Burns and Stalker, 1961; Likert, 1961).

We shall pursue the same topic to see whether scientists' participation in the power structure bears any relationship to their performance and achievements. Such a relationship has been found in studies of many industrial organizations, and in certain other kinds of organizations, such as voluntary ones, for example, labor unions (Tannenbaum and Kahn, 1957). The grounds for including measures of influence in this chapter's analysis of research units is explicit in the following statement: "Characterizing an organization in terms of its pattern of control is to describe an essential and universal aspect of organization, which every member must face and to which he must adjust. Organization implies control" (Tannenbaum, 1968: 33).

Organization of the chapter

This chapter presents results concerning the relationship of three classes of influence measures to the performance of research units. The first class of influence measure has to do with the total amount of influence exercised by people in selected roles over various types of decisions. The second class focuses on the differences in influence exercised by people in different roles. The third class taps differences in viewpoints (i.e., in perceptions) between people in different roles regarding the amount of influence being exercised.

In addition to this introduction, the chapter contains four other major sections. Section 2 describes the structure and nature of the data available for analyzing patterns of influence contained in Round 1 of the International Comparative Study. This section also details the construction of the various influence indices used in the analysis. Section 3 briefly sketches the major hypotheses that motivated our analysis of these data. Section 4 describes the major analytic results. Section 5 provides a summary, and some conclusions and comments.

2. Structure and nature of the data

Source of data

The data on patterns of influence that are analyzed in this chapter derive from Section L of the questionnaires that were administered to unit heads and to staff scientists.[1] In this section, the respondent is asked to rate the amount of influence that he or she believes certain groups of individuals exercise over each of nine specified types of decisions. The ratings were made using a simple five-point scale ranging from "high influence" to "low influence." The nine types of decisions include matters closely associated with the substantive content of the research, such as the "choice of specific research tasks" or "choice of methods used," and more administratively oriented decisions, such as "allocation of work within the unit" or "termination of employment of personnel." Respondents were asked to assess the amount of influence exercised by the following four groups: (1) unit heads, (2) other scientists and engineers inside the unit, (3) organizational leaders outside the research unit but within the organization to which the unit belonged, and (4) authorities or customers outside the organization.

In all, the data contain 72 distinct assessments of the exercise of influence: ratings by both unit heads and staff scientists, on the influence exercised by four groups, over nine types of decisions ($2 \times 4 \times 9 = 72$). This substantial array of basic information lends itself to combination in various ways, and the several indices constructed from it, intended to tap theoretically distinct aspects of the pattern of influence, are described below in this section.

The control graph

Before describing the indices, however, we would note the specific intellectual heritage from which this assessment of influence patterns derives. Tannenbaum and Kahn (1957) attempted to assess control in organizations by developing a method of description called the *control graph.*[2] The graph presents the control structure of an organization within a two-dimensional plot. The various hierarchical levels of an organization are arrayed along the horizontal axis of the graph. These might range, for example, from topmost organizational leaders, through various levels of supervisors, to line workers. The vertical axis represents the amount of control exercised over organizational actions, and ranges from low to high. Within the graph is plotted the average amount of control exercised by people at the indicated position in the hierarchy. By connecting the plotted averages, one obtains a *control curve.*

From the information portrayed in the control graph, Tannenbaum and his associates have derived two conceptually distinct indicators of influence patterns. The first is the *total amount of control;* this indicates how much control is exercised within the organization by all sources.[3] The second is the *distribution of control;* this is based on the relative amounts of control exercised by the different hierarchical positions. In the control graph, the total amount of control is indicated by the average height of the control curve, whereas the distribution of control is indicated by the slope of the curve.[4]

Some cautions

Although research by Tannenbaum and his associates involving the control graph clearly influenced the design of the influence questions included in the International Study, it would be inappropriate to assume that the four sources of influence identified in the International Study (unit heads, other scientists and engineers, organizational leaders, and outside clients and authorities) can be treated as analogous to the hierarchy in an industrial organization.

First, one should note that the influence source designated as "clients and authorities" is clearly outside the research organization and as such is not a part of the formal hierarchy.

Second, given that it is research units that are being examined, one should probably be cautious even about treating the three influence sources that do fall within the formal organization as constituting a functioning hierarchy. There is a real question as to whether the working processes within a research unit are regulated by the leadership of its institution in the same way as in other organizations, for instance, in businesses or voluntary associations. The institution to which a research unit belongs supports that unit and allows it to function within the resources allocated to it, but – at least in some situations – the institution to which a research unit belongs is treated by the researchers as a patron of science, not as a source that can give orders and/or grant opportunities to participate in management decisions. In some situations, research units are highly autonomous and the principal question in their functioning is how they use the resources available to them, not how they participate in decisions of interest to the institution. In such instances, the influence of the institution management on the working process in the units could be taken as an external disturbance in their autonomous functioning, not as cooperative participation in the units' lives.

The empirical data support this hesitancy to assume that institutional leaders generally constitute a level above that of unit heads in a functioning decision-making hierarchy. In all nine areas of decision referenced in the questionnaires, unit heads tended to be the most important contributors to decision formation. The scientists and engineers within the unit tended to rank second in influence to the unit heads. The only major exceptions were in the areas of personnel decisions (hiring and terminating staff), where the scientists and engineers within the unit yielded their second-place rank to leaders of the institution.

Thus, on the basis of the answers to the questionnaire, there remains considerable doubt as to whether the source of influence denoted as "leadership outside the unit but inside the organization" should be considered as a component of the decision-making hierarchy of the research unit.

Third, neither can the working relations inside a research unit necessarily be well represented by the model used for organizations with a clear-cut hierarchy of authority. In a research unit, the "unit head" may not occupy the position of a functioning supervisor, but may instead be an intellectual leader without formal status in the larger organization.

We see, then, that although the structure of the data in the International Study lends itself to analysis through the control-graph approach developed by Tannenbaum and his associates, the appropriateness of using this approach, which has not previously had major applications to R & D organizations, remains to be determined.

Interrelationships among the influence measures

As noted above, the International Study data include 72 basic influence measures. Considerable exploratory work was undertaken to find ways in which this large number of measures could be reduced to a smaller and more manageable set of variables.[5] When scores on the basic measures were related to one another, two bases for clustering emerged. The first had to do with the source of influence: The amount of influence exercised by one source (e.g., the unit head) over a particular decision area (e.g., choice of methods) tended to be correlated more with the influence exercised by this same source over other decisions than with the influence exercised by other sources. Thus it seemed reasonable to think in terms of such global notions as the influ-

Exhibit 7.1. Twelve composites from which indices were developed for assessing various aspects of the pattern of influence

Composite	Source of influence	Type of decision influenced	Respondents rating amount of influence
A	unit head	work mngt. and results	unit heads
B	unit head	work mngt. and results	staff scientists
C	unit head	personnel and equipment	unit heads
D	unit head	personnel and equipment	staff scientists
E	S & E[a] in unit	work mngt. and results	unit heads
F	S & E in unit	work mngt. and results	staff scientists
G	S & E in unit	personnel and equipment	unit heads
H	S & E in unit	personnel and equipment	staff scientists
I	org. leaders	work mngt. and results	unit heads
J	org. leaders	work mngt. and results	staff scientists
K	org. leaders	personnel and equipment	unit heads
L	org. leaders	personnel and equipment	staff scientists

[a]"S & E" means scientists and engineers (other than unit head).

ence of the unit head, the influence of other scientists and engineers in the unit, the influence of organization leaders, etc.

A second basis of clustering, subsidiary to the first, depended on the type of decisions that were being influenced. The nine decision areas referenced in the questionnaire fell into two broad groups: (1) those having to do with decisions over the management of the work in the research unit and the dissemination of R & D results,[6] and (2) those having to do with decisions over personnel and equipment.[7]

Construction of influence indices

Given the structure of the data, just described, it was reasonable to think in terms of 12 conceptual composites, which could be combined in various ways to measure different aspects of the pattern of influence. The 12 composites derive from a consideration of: (1) three sources of influence,[8] (2) two clusters of types of decisions, and (3) two types of respondents. The resulting composites are listed in Exhibit 7.1.

As an example of how to interpret Exhibit 7.1, consider the composite that is listed first and arbitrarily labeled "A." This consists of estimates of the amount of influence the head of the research unit exercises over decisions having to do with the management of the work of the unit and dissemination of its results, and is based on answers of the head of the unit himself. This composite would be based on the unit head's answers to the several questions, noted above, that clustered in this decision area. As may also be seen in Exhibit 7.1, composite B is substantively similar–head's influence over work management and results–but in this case the estimates of influence are made by the staff scientists in the unit.

The 12 composites shown in Exhibit 7.1 were combined in various ways to construct a very substantial number of influence pattern indices (more than 70).

These indices logically fall into three sets, two of which relate to the work of Tannenbaum and his associates described above. The first set consists of indices that tap the *amount of influence* exercised by various sources (this set links to Tannenbaum's notion of "total influence"); the second set consists of indices assessing the *distribution of influence* among various sources (and hence links to Tannenbaum's notion of "slope"); and the third set includes indices that tap *differences in viewpoint* between unit heads and staff scientists regarding the amount of influence exercised by various sources.

Because of the large number of indices in each set, it is not feasible to describe them all here, but some examples can be given.

Indices tapping amount of influence. Indices that tap the amount of influence exercised by various sources over various decisions involve *adding* selected composites from Exhibit 7.1. For example, the measure of total influence exercised inside the research unit (that is, by the unit head and by the other scientists and engineers, with respect to the work-management-and-results area, as rated by staff scientists) would involve adding together composites B and F. A more broadly based index tapping the same aspect of influence was also constructed–by combining the staff scientists' ratings with those of the unit head; this involved adding together composites A, B, E, and F.

Indices tapping distribution of influence. Indices that represented the distribution of influence involved either a *difference* or a *ratio* among the composites. As an example of the first, consider the difference between unit head and other scientists and engineers in the influence they exercised over decisions about personnel and equipment. This index, when based on ratings of unit heads, was constructed by subtracting composite G from composite C;

when based on ratings of staff scientists, the difference was D minus H. The rationale for these difference-based indices is straightforward: Large differences indicate uneven distributions of influence and, given that unit heads tended to exercise more influence than other scientists and engineers in the unit, a tendency toward "autocratic" decision making (and away from "democratic" decision making).

An alternative scheme, involving ratios, was also tried. The influence exercised within the unit was compared with the influence exercised by organizational leaders by considering the former *relative to* the latter. For example, a measure based on ratings from unit heads and dealing with influence over decisions in the personnel area was constructed by dividing the sum of composites C and G by composite K.[9] As the value of an index such as this rises, it indicates an increasing preponderance of influence exercised by sources within the unit relative to that exercised by organizational leaders.

Indices tapping differences in viewpoint. These indices, as the name implies, assess differences in viewpoint, or perception, between the head of a unit and the staff scientists of that unit regarding the amount of influence a given source exercises over designated types of decisions. As one example, consider the difference in viewpoint regarding the head's influence over decisions having to do with work management: This was assessed by subtracting composite B from composite A.[10] These indices provide direct assessments of any perceptual differences that may exist between the unit heads and the staff scientists.

3. Major hypotheses

The motivation for developing the three sets of measures just described was, in each case, to examine their relationship to research-unit performance.

Previous research in organizational psychology, particularly that of Tannenbaum and his associates cited above, has been concerned with the relationship between organizational effectiveness and the amount and distribution of influence in many kinds of organizations. In many of these studies, the total amount of influence was found to relate positively to effectiveness, but the "slope" of the control curve (i.e., the degree to which the influence exercised by upper levels exceeds that by lower levels) was not found to relate consistently, either positively or negatively, to effectiveness. Because major investigations of the relationship between these two aspects of influence patterns and effectiveness have not previously been made in R & D organizations, it seemed well worthwhile to make the exploration. As noted in the preceding section, however, there are doubts as to whether the notions of hierarchy that have been used for studying industrial and certain other kinds of organizations appropriately reflect the functioning of R & D organizations. Accordingly, the applicability of the concept of slope, described above, is questionable.

Measures having to do with differences in viewpoint regarding the amounts of influence exercised (the third set of measures) have not, so far as we know, been extensively investigated before. Nevertheless, the very design of the International Study and the structure of the available data on influence led us naturally to ask whether the performance of a research unit might be related to the degree of agreement (between unit heads and staff scientists) on the important topic of who exercises how much control. Other things being equal, one might expect that units in which members held congruent perceptions, that is, in which there was a mutual perception of the influence structure, would have an edge with respect to performance.

4. Results

Results on the amount of influence

Overview. A series of analyses shows that the amount of influence exercised by various sources within a research organization does indeed relate to certain aspects of research-unit performance. Furthermore, these relationships depend – in what seems a reasonable and understandable way – on the particular source that exercises the influence and on the particular aspect of performance being considered. Perhaps surprisingly, the relationships do not vary according to the types of decisions that are influenced.

Basic results. Exhibit 7.2 presents correlations between the amount of influence exercised by various sources and designated measures of performance.[11] Certain key elements of the full configuration of results are visible in this exhibit, but – as will be seen below – these particular correlations also reflect some spurious components.

Several important aspects of Exhibit 7.2 should be noted. First, the pattern of correlations for influence exercised by the unit head is virtually identical to the pattern for the other scientists

Exhibit 7.2. Performance measures in relation to amount of influence (aggregated raters, decisions)[a] (figures show Pearson *r*s)

Performance measures	Amount of influence exercised by: Unit head	Other scientists	Organization leaders
Training effectiveness	.27	.20	−.31
Recognition	.20	.22	−.21
Published written products	.11	.16	−.22
R & D effectiveness	.17	.15	.01
Patents and prototypes	−.01	−.03	.13
Applications effectiveness	.05	−.03	.18
Social effectiveness	−.02	−.04	.23
Reports and algorithms	−.09	−.08	.29

[a]Influence measures combine ratings from unit heads and staff scientists, and combine two types of decisions; see text for details.

and engineers in the unit (as shown in the first two columns). In contrast, influence exercised by organizational leaders shows a radically different pattern (as may be seen in the third column). Thus it seems that influence exercised from within the unit needs to be distinguished from that exercised from outside, but that the two within-unit sources act similarly.

Second, note that the various performance measures have been ordered so as to produce a somewhat regular progression in the sizes of the correlations, and that this ordering also results in a conceptually interesting progression in the content of the performance measures. Performance measures listed near the top of the exhibit are those that have the greatest relevance in academic settings (ratings of Training effectiveness and of Recognition, and actual outputs of Publications), whereas those near the bottom of the exhibit are, in most instances, of greatest relevance in applied settings (ratings of Applications effectiveness, and actual outputs of Patents and prototypes and of Reports). R & D effectiveness, a performance measure that has relevance in both academic and applied settings, quite reasonably falls near the middle of the sequence.[12]

Third, and perhaps most important, note the actual pattern of correlations: Influence exercised from within the unit (by the head and by other scientists and engineers) relates *positively* to academic aspects of performance (Training effectivenss, Recognition, Publications) but does *not* relate to more applied aspects of

Exhibit 7.3. Performance measures in relation to amount of influence (separate raters and types of decisions)[a] (figures show Pearson *r*s)

	Unit head's rating of influence of head & other scientists		Staff scientists' rating of influence of head & other scientists	
Performance measures	Work mngt.	Pers., equip.	Work mngt.	Pers., equip.
Training effectiveness	.23	.21	.17	.20
Recognition	.20	.16	.17	.17
Published written output	.15	.16	.03	.12
R & D effectiveness	.13	.12	.18	.16
Patents and prototypes	−.03	−.02	.02	.01
Applications effectiveness	.01	.04	.01	.03
Social effectiveness	−.01	−.04	.03	−.00
Reports and algorithms	−.06	−.03	−.07	−.00

[a]See text for details on influence measures.

performance. In contrast, influence exerted by organizational leaders relates positively to the more applied aspects of performance, but negatively to the academic aspects. (As will be seen below, the negative relationships can be explained by the intrusion of spurious effects and should probably be disregarded, but other aspects of the pattern just described remain even when later controls are introduced.)

Exhibit 7.2 presents results for some highly aggregated measures of influence. The three measures used there combine ratings from the unit heads and from the staff scientists, and combine information about both clusters of decision types (i.e., decisions in the work-management-and-publication area and in the personnel-and-equipment area).[13] Although space will not be taken to present results for all of the more detailed influence indices, it is important to report that when these were examined, highly parallel results emerged. One example appears in Exhibit 7.3. This exhibit demonstrates that ratings by unit heads show the same pattern of correlations with performance as ratings by staff scientists, and that influence exercised with respect to one cluster of decisions shows the same pattern of correlations as influence exercised with respect to the other cluster.[14] Hence, the use of aggregated influence measures, as in Exhibit 7.2, seems well justified by the empirical results.

Exhibit 7.4. Performance measures in relation to amount of influence (aggregated raters, decisions; effects associated with type of unit removed)[a] (figures show average value of Pearson *r*s in five types of research units)

	Amount of influence exercised by:		
Performance measures	Unit head	Other scientists	Organization leaders
Training effectiveness	.18	.09	−.03
Recognition	.12	.19	−.05
Published written output	.06	.14	−.04
R & D effectiveness	.17	.18	−.03
Patents and prototypes	−.03	.00	−.01
Applications effectiveness	.10	.03	.04
Social effectiveness	.08	.05	.15
Reports and algorithms	−.03	.06	.10

[a]See text for details on influence measures and analysis method.

Refinements. The correlations shown in Exhibit 7.2, as noted above, are subject to spurious effects, and a more refined analysis needs to be made. The problem arises from the fact that all types of units have been combined in the same analysis without taking account of some of the differences known to exist between them. Among these differences are the entirely reasonable phenomena that academic units tend to outrank nonacademic units with respect to Training effectiveness, Recognition, and output of Publications, whereas units with more applied orientations tend to surpass academic units on such performance measures as Applications effectiveness. These differences, combined with systematic differences between types of units in the amount of influence exercised by various sources (e.g., nonacademic units are subject to more influence by organizational leaders than are academic units), produce the spurious effects.

One way to remove these spurious effects is to perform the analysis *separately* within each type of unit. This has been done,[15] and Exhibit 7.4 summarizes the results.

The measures used for Exhibit 7.4 are identical to those in Exhibit 7.2; the only difference between the exhibits is the fact that effects attributable to type of unit have been partialed out in Exhibit 7.4. Therefore it is instructive to compare these two exhibits. Most of the relationships are weaker in Exhibit 7.4, but many aspects of the original pattern of results remain. The major exception is that the negative relationships in Exhibit 7.2 have virtually disappeared, becoming essentially zero or in some cases positive.[16]

Thus the general configuration of results suggests that the greater the amount of influence exercised by sources within the unit, the higher the unit is likely to perform on aspects of performance often associated with academic orientations – Training effectiveness, Recognition, output of Publications, and general R & D effectiveness; but that within-unit influence has little to do with aspects of performance that are relevant to more applied orientations. In contrast, the amount of influence exercised by organizational leaders is only weakly related to any aspect of performance, but shows a hint of being positively related to the more applied aspects of performance.

Comments. Two comments about the results that have just been described seem appropriate at this point.

First, as is clear from the exhibits, even the strongest of the relationships is of only modest size. Several reasons may account for this: (1) Neither these measures of influence nor the measures of research-unit performance are perfectly valid.[17] All measures probably contain certain errors, and many of these errors act to reduce the size of the correlations shown in the exhibits. (2) It would be unrealistic to expect the exercise of influence to be the sole, or even a major, determinant of research-unit performance. This is not to say, however, that influence patterns are irrelevant, or that data such as these cannot provide clues regarding preferable ways to organize R & D.

A second general comment concerns causality. The results described so far are merely relationships, and with the present data it is impossible to go beyond them to determine whether higher influence "causes" improved performance, or vice versa, or whether both are affected by some third factor. Here, again, however, the results are of interest because of the clues they may provide about the R & D process.

Implications. What is the meaning of these results? Do they support the "ivory tower" hypothesis – that is, that the best performance occurs when scientists are left to make their own decisions?

The answer is that these results clearly do *not* support the ivory tower orientation. After controlling for differences in the settings of research units, influence exerted by organizational leaders (one of the kinds of influences that would be harmful in an ivory tower) showed hardly *any* relation to performance, and the strongest of the relationships tended to be mildly positive; one certainly cannot say that influence exerted from outside had a general tendency to be harmful. Parallel comments can also be made with respect to influence exercised by the unit head, another source of influence that would surely impinge on the independent actions of other scientists and engineers within the unit: Here also the relationships tend to be close to zero or mildly positive.

To the extent that these results can be used as clues toward finding more effective ways of organizing R & D, they suggest the desirability of *mutual involvement and participation in decision making.* (Note, in Exhibit 7.4, that *all* the correlations stronger than .05 are *positive.*) Mutual influence on the part of the professionals within a research unit seems promising for most aspects of performance, and the involvement of organizational leaders seems potentially helpful with respect to some of the more applied aspects of performance.

Results on the distribution of influence

The relationships of research-unit performance to the distribution of influence depend on whether the focus is on the distribution between the unit head and other scientists, or on the distribution between influence exercised within the unit and that exercised by organizational leaders.

Distribution between unit head and other scientists. The relationships between the distribution of influence within the unit and the various aspects of performance are easy to describe: All were close to zero, and no meaningful positive or negative tendencies were found. The influence indices used in these analyses were based on the difference between the amount of influence exercised by the unit head and by other scientists within the unit, and suggest that this difference is irrelevant for any of the various aspects of performance that were examined. Units could perform well when unit heads and other scientists exercised roughly equal amounts of influence, or when the unit head's influence substantially exceeded that of his or her professional colleagues. (Recall, however, that the results described above show that higher amounts of influence on the part of both the head and other scientists were associated with enhanced performance.)

Distribution between the unit and organization leaders. A somewhat different pattern of results emerges when one compares the in-

Exhibit 7.5. Performance measures in relation to distribution of influence (separate raters and types of decisions)[a] (figures show Pearson *r*s)

	Ratings by unit heads		Ratings by staff scientists	
Performance measures[b]	Work mngt.	Pers., equip.	Work mngt.	Pers., equip.
Training effectiveness	.11	.11	.07	.04
Recognition	.08	.09	.10	.04
Published written output	.07	.11	.01	.03
R & D effectiveness	.05	.05	.10	−.01
Patents and prototypes	.08	.03	.06	.01
Applications effectiveness	−.02	.03	.01	−.04
Social effectiveness	−.09	−.06	−.04	−.11
Reports and algorithms	−.07	−.04	−.10	−.08

[a]Distribution of influence measures based on ratio of influence exercised within units (by head and other scientists) to influence exercised by organization leaders; see text for details.
[b]Performance measures have been adjusted to remove differences attributable to type of unit.

fluence of within-unit sources (head and/or other scientists) with that of organizational leaders (a source of influence external to the unit). Here the magnitude of the correlations is weak, but there is an interesting trend that is parallel to that seen above for *amount* of influence. The correlations appear in Exhibit 7.5.

Exhibit 7.5 shows that when the performance measures are ordered as in exhibits presented above (ranging from those most relevant in academically oriented units to those most relevant in units with more applied orientations), there is a consistent tendency for positive relationships to occur in the upper portion of the exhibit and negative relationships in the lower portion. In short, predominance of *within-unit* influence over external influence accompanied enhanced levels of academically oriented aspects of performance, but predominance of *external* sources of influence accompanied enhanced levels of more applied aspects of performance. As may be seen in the exhibit, the same patterns occur regardless of whether the influence ratings (from which the predominance indices were calculated) were made by unit heads or staff scientists, and regardless of whether the influence was exercised with respect to work-management decisions or with respect to personnel and equipment decisions. These results cannot be attributed to the intrusion of spurious effects because, as noted in the exhibit, the performance measures used here already incorporate adjustments to remove any differences that could be attributed to type of unit.[18]

These results concerning the *distribution* of influence complement, and seem consistent with, those presented above for the *amount* of influence. Whereas the former results indicated the potential importance of within-unit influence (particularly for academically oriented aspects of performance), the present results help to complete our understanding by allowing us to see the implications of one source predominating over the other.

As a check to see whether these internal–external distribution-of-influence measures were tapping the intended concept, their average levels were compared in various situations where the direction of the expected differences seemed reasonably clear. In each case, the comparisons proved in line with expectations: (1) When the influence exercised within the unit was compared to that exercised by organizational leaders in academic and nonacademic units, the relative influence of organizational leaders was substantially higher in nonacademic settings. (2) The relative influence of organizational leaders tended to be somewhat higher for Polish and Hungarian units than for units in Austria, Belgium, Finland, and Sweden. (3) When comparisons were made by decision areas, within-unit influence greatly exceeded that of organizational leaders in deciding on methods and allocating work; was somewhat greater with respect to choice of R & D tasks, publication of results, training, and acquisition of low-cost equipment; but tended to be about on a par with that of organizational leaders or even slightly below with respect to hiring and terminating personnel. The fact that these comparisons produced results in accord with what many informed observers would expect is evidence in support of the validity of the distribution-of-influence indices.

Results on differences in viewpoint

As noted in Section 2, a third set of indices was constructed to measure the extent to which unit heads and staff scientists *agreed* in their perceptions of the amount of influence being exercised by various sources over various types of decisions. It was expected that lack of congruency of viewpoint might represent an impediment to effective functioning, because disagreements about the exercise of influence might lead to misunderstandings and misperceptions about how decisions were actually made.

However, despite a rather extensive exploration, involving the eight aspects of performance, the two types of decisions, and the three sources of influence that appear in previous exhibits of this chapter, and using two separate ways of constructing the difference-in-viewpoint indices, no consistent relationships were noted for either the whole set of research units or for any of the five distinct research-unit types. Why the expected relationships did not appear remains unknown.

5. Summary, implications, comments

This chapter explores the statistical relationships between various aspects of research-unit performance and the exercise of influence by sources within and outside research units. The design of the original questionnaire items, and of some of the analyses reported here, were inspired by previous research on influence, control, and organizational hierarchy that has been conducted by Tannenbaum and his associates over the past 20 years. That research suggests that in industrial and certain other kinds of organizations, effectiveness is highest when the total *amount* of influence is relatively high but not necessarily when influence is *distributed* relatively evenly among the various roles in the organizational hierarchy. The chapter examines how these same concepts of amount and distribution of influence, plus one other concept – congruency in viewpoints about the exercise of influence – relate to performance of the 1,222 research units in Round 1 of the International Study. So far as is known, this is the first major exploration of these particular concepts in R & D organizations.

The statistical results show some points of convergence with those from previous research, and also some points of divergence. The amount of influence exercised by unit heads and other scientists related positively to the aspects of research-unit performance that seem most relevant to academic concerns (Training effectiveness, Recognition, output of Publications), but only weakly if at all to aspects of performance relevant to more applied concerns (Applications effectiveness, output of Patents and prototypes, etc.). On the other hand, the amount of influence exercised by leaders of the organization in which the research unit was located (a source of influence external to the unit itself), related positively to these more applied aspects of performance, but not to the more academically oriented aspects. Results for the distribution of influence trended in the same directions: higher performance on the academically oriented aspects when the relative preponderance of influence was on the part of within-unit sources, and higher performance on the applications-oriented aspects when the relative preponderance was on the part of external sources. (The intrusion of spurious effects attributable to differences in types of units was marked, and a control for type of unit was required before appropriately interpretable results were obtained.) The third area of inquiry, congruency in viewpoints, showed no consistent relations to performance.

The chapter reports statistical relationships, which ought not be interpreted as causal effects, though such effects may indeed be present. To the extent that such effects account for the observed relationships, the results provide clues to effective ways to organize decision making in R & D organizations.

The relationships reported in the chapter are consistently of rather modest size, and the reasons for this need to be considered. The chapter noted that imperfections in the measurement of the underlying influence and performance phenomena may partly account for the modest size of the relationships. Also, because performance is determined by many factors, one cannot expect any single factor to have a large effect by itself.

More fundamentally, however, one can ask about the importance of the influence factors assessed here, and about the relevance of measuring them in the present way. For example, it may be that the functioning hierarchies that matter for R & D are not primarily defined in terms of roles within a single organization, and that in this respect R & D activities differ from those conducted by many other kinds of organizations.

The very concept of influence has, in some circles, seemed antithetical to the conduct of creative science. Joseph Ben-David has pointed to the lack of organizational interests in European research institutions in the nineteenth and early twentieth centuries. He writes: "Only in the United States has there been a general and early recognition that there is no necessary contradiction between creative accomplishment in research and the organization of research. . . . The absence of prejudice against organized research and its effectiveness through standardization made it much easier to devise increasingly complex and sophisticated types of organized research. . . . By the thirties and perhaps even before, the difference reached a stage where in some fields European scientists were no longer able to compete effectively with their American counterparts" (Ben-David, 1971: 158–159).

It may be that other conceptualizations of the influence phenomena merit attention. For example, in Gaston's study on the race for priority in the large modern research organization (Gaston, 1972), we can find reason to doubt the predictive power of the kinds of variables assessed in the influence questions of the International Study. He suggests that the areas of interest for a researcher who really wants to influence the organization lie rather in the communication system and network, the organization of the experimental processes, the informal social order, and so on. It may be that interpersonal influences are more important for the effective performance of a research unit than are formal or informal control over areas of organizational decision making (Merton, 1957: Korhnauser, 1962; Pelz and Andrews, 1966; Crane, 1972; Mullins, 1973).

In conclusion, we are obliged to say that patterns of influence seem to have lower predictive power for the performance of research units than for the performance of business organizations, at least when influence patterns are conceptualized in a general form applicable to many human activities and not with a specific approach tailored toward research and development. Even using this perhaps less-than-optimal and very general approach, however, some consistent, meaningful trends have emerged. These offer leads toward ways to organize R & D decision making that may enhance research-unit effectiveness.

References

Ben-David, J., 1971, *The Scientist's Role in Society: A Comparative Study,* Englewood Cliffs, N.J., Prentice-Hall.

Burns, T., and Stalker, G. M., 1961, *The Management of Innovation,* London, Tavistock.

Crane, D., 1972, *Invisible Colleges: Diffusion of Knowledge in Scientific Communities,* Chicago, University of Chicago Press.

Gaston, J., 1972, Secret et competition chez les chercheurs, *La Recherche,* 26: 717–722.

Kornhauser, W., 1962, *Scientists in Industry,* Berkeley, University of California Press.

Likert, R., 1961, *New Patterns of Management,* New York, McGraw-Hill.

Merton, R. K., 1957, *Social Theory and Social Structure,* (Chapter 10. Patterns of Influence: Local and Cosmopolitan Influentials), London, Collier-Macmillan.

1968, The Matthew Effect in Science, *Science* 159: 56–63.

Mullins, N. C., 1973, *Theories and Theory Groups in Contemporary American Sociology,* New York, Harper & Row.

Pelz, D. C., and Andrews, F. M., 1966, *Scientists in Organizations: Productive Climates for Research and Development,* New York, Wiley.

Tannenbaum, A. S., 1968, *Control in Organizations,* New York, McGraw-Hill.

Tannenbaum, A. S., and Kahn, R. L., 1957, Organizational Control Structure: A General Descriptive Technique as applied to Four Local Unions, *Human Relations,* 10: 127–140.

Tannenbaum, A. S., et al., 1974, *Hierarchy in Organizations,* San Francisco, Jossey-Bass.

Notes

1. Major portions of these questionnaires, including Section L, are reproduced in the Appendix.

2. More recent works of Tannenbaum and his associates also make use of the control graph. See, for example, Tannenbaum (1968) and Tannenbaum et al. (1974).

3. Tannenbaum assumes that control can be exercised by many persons at all levels of the hierarchical structure in the organization, and that control tends to increase when people participate in decisions and express their opinions about situations. Empirical results support these assumptions and show that the total amount of control exercised within an organization is not limited to some arbitrary fixed amount so that increased influence gained by one group must be offset by equal losses from another. Rather, organizations differ in the amount of control being exercised, and even within one organization this total amount can change over time.

4. In some kinds of organizations the control curves approximate straight lines, and in such organizations it is reasonable to think of a steeply sloped curve as indicating a highly autocratic pattern of influence and a flatter curve as indicating a more democratic pattern.

5. Details are available in Sections 4 and 5 of an unpublished working paper (Unesco, document STP/838, 23 April 1976).

6. The relevant questionnaire items are La1, La2, Lb1, and Lb2.

7. The relevant questionnaire items are Lb3, Lb4, Lb5, and Lb6.

8. Influence exercised by the fourth source listed in the questionnaire, clients and authorities outside the organization, was not examined in the analyses reported in this chapter.

9. In actual practice, the computing formula was somewhat more complicated than (C + G)/K because of the needs to handle missing data and to bracket and reverse the result to produce an index convenient for subsequent analysis. These transformations, however, do not affect the basic logic of the index formation.

10. In some of the indices the *algebraic* difference was obtained, in others the *absolute* difference.

11. The results are based on all 1,222 research units of Round 1 of the International Study (see Chapter 2). The influence measures are described in note 13.

12. Chapter 11 describes other analyses that also indicate the differential relevance of various aspects of performance according to the organizational setting of the research unit.

13. The influence indices shown in Exhibit 7.2 involve the following composites (as these are identified in Exhibit 7.1): Influence of the head = A + B + C +D; influence of the other scientists and engineers = E + F + G + H; Influence of organizational leaders = I + J + K + L.

14. The influence indices shown in Exhibit 7.3 involve the following composites (as these are identified in Exhibit 7.1): Head's rating of within-unit influence over work-management decisions = A + E; head's rating of within-unit influence over personnel-equipment decisions = C + G; staff scientists' rating of within-unit influence over work-management decisions = B + F; staff scientists' rating of within-unit influence over personnel-equipment decisions = D +H.

15. The standard five-category classification of unit types, developed for this International Study and described in Chapter 13, was used. This typology ac-

counts for 20–31% of the variance in estimations of the influence exercised by organizational leaders, but much less (4–11%) for influence exercised by unit heads and other scientists.

16. Exhibit 7.4 reports the average value of the correlation in each of five types of research unit. A check was made to see whether these averages might hide any consistent patterns of differences in the correlations from one type of unit to another, but no consistent patterns were found.

17. Chapter 14 provides estimates of the validity of the performance measures.

18. Calculation of these adjusted performance measures is described in Chapter 2. The distribution-of-influence indices shown in Exhibit 7.5 involve the following composites (as these are identified in Exhibit 7.1): unit heads' perceptions regarding influence over work-management decisions = (A + E)/I; unit heads' perceptions regarding personnel and equipment decisions = (C + G)/K; staff scientists' perceptions regarding work-management decisions = (B + F)/J; staff scientists' perceptions regarding personnel and equipment decisions = (D + H)/L. The distribution indices were transformed to reverse the original questionnaire scales and to reduce skew.

8 The size and age of Swedish academic research groups and their scientific performance

Rikard Stankiewicz
Research Policy Program,
Lund University, Lund

1. Introduction

Until quite recently, it was almost axiomatic to consider science – especially fundamental science – as the province of individualists. Thus when in 1962 Norman Storer found that a group of fundamental researchers surveyed by him expressed preference for collaborative research, he described the result as surprising. Since then, the prevalence of the team/group organization in science has become widely recognized. The studies of multiple authorship of scientific publications (Price, 1963; Clarke, 1964) as well as sociological surveys (Hagstrom, 1967; Blume and Sinclair, 1973) demonstrated the trend. As the experience of the group organization grows, the earlier fears and objections that it inspired decrease (Weinberg, 1970; Wilson, 1970). Indeed, several recent studies of larger scientific systems such as fields and specialities indicate that these systems are best described as networks of groups rather than mere collectivities of individuals (Crane, 1972; Mullins, 1972; Price and Beaver, 1966).

The propensity to work in groups seems to reflect the intrinsic requirements of the research process. Stankiewicz (1976) found that the prevalence of group membership among Swedish academic scientists (in the natural sciences and technology) was strongly related to their research field. The frequency of group membership was the highest in the rapidly developing fields characterized by a high degree of theoretical consensus, such as physics, chemistry, and molecular biology. In these fields, more than 90% of the scientists were group members. The lowest frequencies were found in the descriptive and/or theoretically less crystallized fields such as traditional biology (67%), geography (32%), and engineering (20%).

The prevalence and advantages of team organization in industrial and other applied settings are widely known and require no special comment.

Given the general predominance of group organization, it becomes necessary to inquire about its influence on the effectiveness of research. This chapter addresses the relationship between size and age of research groups and the quantity and quality of their output. There are two major reasons why these relations must be regarded as particularly important: (1) By focusing on them we may be able to gain new insights into the nature of scientific institutions and of the research process itself. (2) Because of the tangibility and manipulability of the variables involved, our conclusions may prove important from the practical point of view. The relative size and longevity of research groups affect – among other things – the flexibility and diversification of the research program of larger R & D establishments. Such matters are of crucial importance in a wider organizational and policy perspective.

2. Some earlier investigations

Logically, one can think of four main types of hypotheses relating the size of research groups to their performance:

1 the *negative hypothesis,* which either denies that any such relationship exists or claims that effectiveness actually decreases with group size.
2 the *simple positive hypothesis,* according to which the greater the group size the higher the performance.
3 the *critical-size hypothesis,* according to which there is a dramatic improvement in performance when the group reaches a certain minimum size.
4 the *optimum-size hypothesis,* according to which the performance of groups increases with their size but only up to a certain optimum point, after which it either stabilizes or decreases.

The same set of four hypotheses could be formulated with respect to the relationship between group age and performance.

Each of the above types of hypotheses has its supporters, though the last two are the most popular. The final acceptance of any of them would have important theoretical and practical implications. It is thus surprising that there have been so few attempts to test them empirically.

The pioneering contributions to research on the effects of the size and age of research groups have been made by Wallmark and his associates (Wallmark and Sellerberg, 1966; Wallmark et al., 1973), Blume and Sinclair (1973), Shepard (1956), Wells (1962), and Wells and Pelz (1966). Related topics have been also discussed by, among others, Pelz and Andrews (1966), Hagstrom (1965, 1967), Lemaine et al. (1972), Price (1963), and Price and Beaver (1966).

Wallmark and his associates investigated the relationship between the size of research teams and the performance of their members. These data were collected from 60 teams in three specialities in applied physics. The teams were defined and identified as follows: The contributors (authors of published papers) to the selected fields were identifed; those working in a single organization/laboratory were considered as a team. Performance was measured by dividing the number of citations (excluding the self-citations) that the team's papers received by the number of the scientists in the team. After a logarithmic transformation, the performance index was related to team size in a linear regression model. The results of the analysis led Wallmark to conclude that: (1) There is a positive effect of increasing group size on performance; (2) there is no evidence of either an optimum- or minimum-size effect; (3) the improvement in performance is exponential – it was, for example, calculated that the effectiveness of a single team consisting of 50 scientists would be as great as that of 138 scientists working individually; and (4) other factors contributing to research effectiveness include material resources, selection of productive group members, and the characteristics and effectiveness of the leaders.

Blume and Sinclair (1973) investigated the relationship between group size and effectiveness using a large sample of British university chemists. Research groups were defined in approximately the same way as in this chapter. Their size was operationalized as the full-time equivalent of the number of scientists. Among the performance measures used were: the numbers of articles authored or co-authored by each scientist, the honorific awards he received, and peer ratings. The last of these measures had too high a missing-data rate to be considered seriously, and the honorific awards tend to operate with a large time lag and are therefore less interesting. This leaves us with the authorship of articles.

Blume and Sinclair set out to test the hypothesis that there exists a certain minimum size that must be reached before a group can become effective. Using linear correlations, they concluded that there was a modest positive association between individual productivity and group size (Pearson's $r = .32$). Examining the scatter diagrams, they concluded that neither critical- nor optimum-size effects occurred. The results of the investigations summarized above support what I call the simple positive hypothesis about the effect of group size on performance. There are, however, certain objections that could be posed against the conclusions:

1 The way in which Wallmark operationalizes the size of research groups will tend to underestimate the size of teams containing unproductive members.
2 Wallmark's operationalization of the concept of "research team" may also be misleading, in that some of the large teams could turn out to be clusters of smaller teams rather than truly unified entities.
3 Blume and Sinclair's measure of productivity may artificially favor the larger groups. Because such groups are likely to have large total ouputs, their members have better chances to put their names on several publications even though the per capita output of such groups may be quite modest.
4 Both investigations rely too strongly on linear models. This is dangerous because, given the skewness of group size, the measures of association and the regression slopes will be too strongly affected by what goes on in the groups of small to moderate size. A mere examination of scatter diagrams is hardly enough, especially when:
5 Both investigations fail to control other important effects that are likely to be correlated with group size and that could have "masking" effects. The potential distortions caused by the correlation between the size of groups and their age are a particular problem.

The literature on the relationship between the age of groups and their performance is even more limited than that on the effects of size. Shepard (1956) found that the creativity of research teams in industrial laboratories was highest during the first 16 months of their existence and declined thereafter. A more extensive analysis was conducted by Wells (1962) and Wells and Pelz (1966). Their study encompassed 83 research groups (49 in industry and 34 in government). The groups were reconstructed on the basis of data from a survey of individual scientists. Group age was defined as the average number of years the members belonged to the group. This means that groups with high turnover were regarded as young, even though they may have existed for a long time. As measures of performance, Wells and Pelz used the ratings of the scientists' "scientific contribution" and their "overall usefulness" to the organization. The two main conclusions of the analysis were: (1) The general scientific contribution of the groups tended to *decline* with increasing "group age"; and (2) a group's overall usefulness to the organization tended to *increase* during the first four to five years, after which it also *declined.*

Wells and Pelz found that these effects could be linked to decreasing cohesion and competitiveness and to increasing specialization in the "aging" groups.

The above results are quite striking, and one wonders whether they could be generalized to academic groups. The best guess seems to be that they are correct only in applied settings. It could be that in such settings the groups that have existed for too long a time have outlived their original purpose and therefore receive low ratings. One may also suspect that the young groups represent the high-priority projects and/or troubleshooting R & D missions, whereas the older ones consist of more bread-and-butter service and method units.

One common characteristic of the studies discussed above is that they contain conceptual ambiguities, making their interpretation difficult. In order to avoid such complications, the following are important:

1 One should use well-defined samples consisting of well-described units.
2 The organizational and institutional backgrounds of the samples should be adequately characterized.
3 The statistical models used should be multivariate and capable of handling both curvilinearities and interactions.
4 One should be aware of the danger of confusing effectiveness measures designed to operate on the individual level with those designed for groups.

In designing my analysis, I have attempted to follow these general principles.

3. The choice of data and approach

The relationships between the size and age of research groups and their performance is bound to be affected by both the nature of the groups themselves and by the institutional/organizational setting in which they operate. Thus the effects of group age reported by Shepard (1956) and Wells and Pelz (1966) reflect the realities of the industrial research environment; they are less likely to occur in academic settings. Similarly, the effects of group size can be expected to differ depending on such things as the degree of autonomy the groups have, the nature of the "social bond" holding them together, and their institutional setting. For example, when the research objectives and the resources of a group are determined externally, its performance will reflect the *balance* between the resources (including the personnel) and the objectives, rather than the *absolute level* of the resources. Autonomous groups, on the other hand, are in a better position to adapt their objectives to the available resources (which does not necessarily mean that they give up their scientific ambitions); that should strengthen the correlation between size and performance. Furthermore, a research group is more than a mere collection of individuals. The relationship between the size and age of groups and their performance will depend on the kind of social integration that exists in them, which, in turn, is likely to be related to the behavior of the leaders, and so on.

In short, it is difficult to formulate and test a hypothesis about the effect of group age and size without first defining one's empirical frame of reference. I shall therefore start by presenting the sample of research groups that will be analyzed here.

The sample

The sample that is analyzed in this chapter consists of 172 randomly selected Swedish academic research groups from the fields of natural science and technology. The relative homogeneity of the sample makes the following simplified characterization fairly adequate:

The groups composing the sample range in size from 2 to 18 scientists; when technical personnel are added, the maximum size rises to 30 persons. The typical group contains 4 to 5 scientists and is less than 8 years old. The range of group age, that is, the number of years since the group started, is 1 to 34 years.

Practically all the groups have grown around their leader, who tends to have decisive influence over the group's research program, internal allocation of resources, and recruitment of new members. The age of the groups is almost perfectly correlated with the number of years their leaders have led them.

The groups are highly autonomous in relation to their universities and departments. Nearly all of them are free to determine their own research program, but, as a rule, they have to solicit financial support from external agencies, which are predominantly the national research councils. On the average, approximately half of a group's budget comes from such external sources; the part financed by the universities/departments includes mainly salaries, stipends, heavy equipment, etc. The necessity of seeking external support introduces the element of scientific entrepreneurship into the leader's role.

Although most of the nonleaders are doctoral students, many groups, especially the larger ones, include among their members two or more persons with Ph.D. qualifications or the equivalent. The majority of the group members *and* the leaders hold temporary positions. The scarcity of permanent positions at Swedish universities increases the turnover rate and the competitive pressures. Both these circumstances influence the research groups.

The group members are connected through a variety of personal links, including direct research collaboration. If we disregard the members of the smallest groups (three or fewer scientists), a typical nonleader collaborates with two or more other group members. The number of collaborators that the nonleaders have outside their group is small. The leaders, on the other hand, have extensive collaborative links both within and outside their groups.

Hypothesis: the effects of group size

Let us now consider the possible effects of the size and age of the groups included in our sample on their research effectiveness.

One obvious effect of increasing group size is the extension of the *scale* and *pace* of the research effort. Large groups can rapidly explore several facets of a complex research problem. The pursuit of parallel strategies may help to quickly identify the fruitful lines of investigation. The collaboration of scientists representing different specialities may make feasible the solution of otherwise unapproachable technical problems. These reasons alone would be sufficient to produce a positive relationship betwen the size of research groups and their performance. However, there is still another set of factors that must be considered. The effects of those factors could be summarized with the term *intellectual synergy*. I refer here to the unplanned convergence of efforts and ideas that is likely to occur in research groups. In highly autonomous groups, the research objectives are adjustable. This flexibility permits exploration and exploitation of spontaneously arising ideas. The frequency with which such creative events occur may be a function of intellectual cross-fertilization among group members. This process is both stimulated and controlled by the propensity of small groups to strive toward consensus on the issues of central importance (see, for example, Krech, Crutchfield, and Ballachey, 1962, Chapter 13).

Given the strong need for personal autonomy that characterizes fundamental scientists, one could suspect that the true strength of academic research groups depends at least as much on such synergistic effects as on the more mechanistic division and coordination of labor. In fact, the promotion of intellectual synergy may be the main function of the leadership of such groups.

It can be argued that the intellectual synergy of research groups increases rapidly with their size. Wallmark et al. (1973) interpreted their conclusions about the effect of group size on research performance by pointing out that the number of potential interactions in a group increases exponentially with the number of members. That, however, seems to be a far too optimistic view. After all, what really matters is not so much the number of possible interactions, but the quality and number of those actually occurring. The latter are closely related to the level of cohesiveness in a group and to the properties of its leadership. The literature on small groups contains several generalizations that are relevant here. Reviewing a large body of literature, Berelson and Steiner (1964) summarize the effects of increasing group size as follows:

> The larger the informal group: . . . the greater the demands on the leader and the more he is differentiated from the membership at large; the greater the group's tolerance of the direction by the leader and the more centralized the proceedings; the more the active members dominate the interaction within the group; the more the ordinary members inhibit their participation and hence the less exploratory and adventurous the group's discussion; the less intimate the group atmosphere, the more anonymous the actions, and generally the less satisfied the members as a whole; the longer it takes to get to non-verifiable (judgmental) decisions; the more acceptable the unresolved differences; the more the subgroups formed within the membership; and the more formalized the rules and procedures of the group. [Berelson and Steiner, 1964: 358]

Berelson and Steiner go on to note that "for most of these tendencies, the watershed seems to be around size 5–7 [persons]" (1964: 358).

The gradual erosion of the cohesiveness of a group and the growing strain on its leadership are likely to neutralize some of the advantages of the increasing number of potential interactions. Indeed, the trends described above suggest that at a certain point the disadvantages of further increases in size may outweigh the advantages.

In the light of the arguments listed above, one should expect *a curvilinear relationship between the size of a group and its performance. The probable optimum point should be somewhere around five to seven scientists per group.*

As far as the possibility of the minimum-size effect is concerned, I believe that it arises only under special circumstances and should not influence the general trends in our data.

Hypothesis: the effects of group age

Turning now to the effects of group age on research performance, it seems reasonable to postulate *a positive relationship with a tendency to level off or reverse for very old groups.* The reasons for this expectaion are as follows:

1 Success in research depends at least partly on the depth of insight into the nature of the system of problems defining one's speciality; such insight can be acquired only after a period of *active* work in the speciality.
2 As time goes on, a group acquires unique skills and tacit knowledge that can only be obtained through individual experience and/or person-to-person communication.
3 At least during the earlier years of its existence, the social and intellectual cohesion of a group is likely to increase. However:
4 As a group grows old, certain negative factors are likely to appear. Thus, unless the turnover of members is sufficiently rapid, a group may suffer from too much intellectual inbreeding, causing excessive specialization and rigidity.
5 Another problem may be caused by a group being directed into areas of its leader's own special competence. In older groups, this may prevent the acceptance of necessary innovations.

An outline of the analysis

Tests of the hypotheses presented above were carried out in three stages. The first involved the examination of *overall relationships* in the data. The second consisted of a series of tests of the *strength and stability* of the relationships under a variety of conditions. The third stage focused on the *form* of the relationships (linearities and curvilinearities).

As the tool of analysis, I have used multiple classification analysis (MCA), a technique that can cope with curvilinear relationships.

Definitions of the variables

The most important variables used in this analysis are defined as follows:

1 *Group size:* the average number of scientists in a group during the three years prior to our survey. This definition has the advantage of making the variable insensitive to relatively recent fluctuations in the size of a group. The number of technicians was not taken into account because, from the point of view of the criteria of performance used in this analysis (see below), their number did not play any independent role. The choice of the "gross" *number of scientists* rather than their *full-time equivalent* as the measure of group size reflects the belief that it is the number of heads rather than mere man-hours that determines effectiveness.
2 *Group age:* the number of years since a group was formed.

Given the nature of the groups investigated here, the most appropriate performance measures seemed to be those that reflect the intrascientific criteria of value. In terms of reliability and validity, the best choices were the Total output of published papers, and the Index of scientific recognition.[1]

Although by no means identical with them, these performance measures are conceptually close to those used by Wallmark et al. and by Blume and Sinclair.

I make no attempt to evaluate performance on the level of individuals. It is doubtful whether such measurement – although theoretically desirable – is practically feasible in groups characterized by extensive collaboration. I have already mentioned the problems that arise because of the wide occurrence of multiple authorship. Wallmark's performance index, which is the ratio of the number of citations received by the team to the number of its members, is not a measure of the effectiveness of individuals. Rather, it is an index of group effectiveness with certain effects of size eliminated. In this analysis, I introduce a similar variable formed by dividing the Output of published papers by Group size and call it the index of *Output per scientist.*

The variation in Output per scientist, which is a productivity measure, accounts for two-thirds of the variation in the Total output of published papers. For this reason, the Output per scientist rather than the Total output of papers is used in most of the analyses. In a few instances, I have also examined the numbers of papers authored or co-authored by the individual group leaders/members.

The variables that were used as predictors had to be bracketed. The bracketing rules are indicated on the exhibits. As far as the dependent measures were concerned, two of them – Total output of published papers and Output per scientist – had strong skews and had to be transformed; the first was transformed logarithmically; the second according to quintiles.

4. Results

The overall relationships

Because Group age and Group size are correlated ($r = .45$), it was necessary to consider their effects jointly. The results of the analysis of variance and the MCA when the predictors are used simultaneously confirm our general hypotheses about the overall relationships between the age and size of the groups and their scientific performance (see Exhibits 8.1 to 8.6). More specifically:

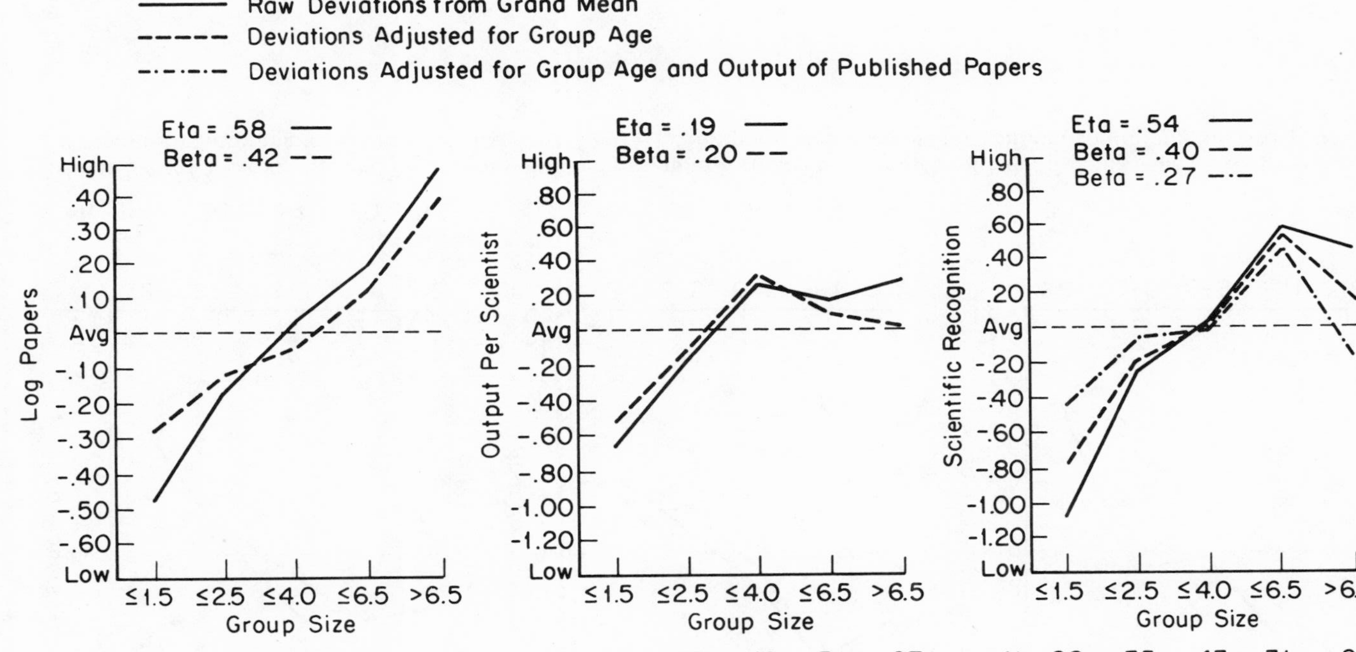

Exhibit 8.1 (*left*). Group size and Output of published papers, controlling for Group age. Exhibit 8.2 (*middle*). Group size and Output per scientist, controlling for Group age. Exhibit 8.3 (*right*). Group size and the Index of scientific recognition, controlling for Group age and Output of published papers.

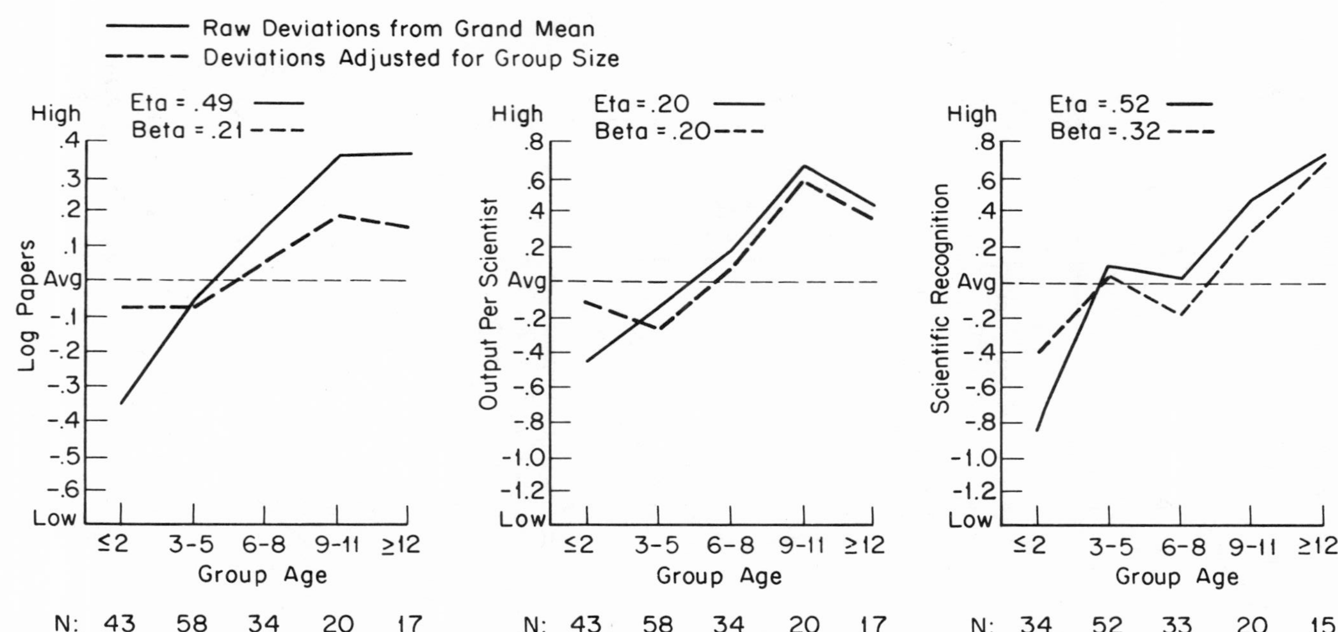

Exhibit 8.4 (*left*). Group age and Output of published papers, controlling for Group size. Exhibit 8.5 (*middle*). Group age and Output per scientist, controlling for Group size. Exhibit 8.6 (*right*). Group age and Scientific recognition, controlling for Group size.

1 Both Group size and Group age are significantly related to Output of published papers (adjusted etas are .58 for Size and .49 for Age).
2 The predictors are also strongly related to the Index of scientific recognition (adjusted etas are .54 for Size and .52 for Age).
3 There also exists a relationship between the predictors and Output per scientist; however, the levels of association are far lower here: adjusted etas are .19 for Size and .20 for Age. This result is somewhat disappointing because the effects of Size and Age on the *total* output may seem somewhat trivial. When the productivity of group members is measured in terms of the number of papers they authored/co-authored, the correlations between Group size or Group age and productivity are: (a) for the leaders, adjusted etas = .30 and .20, respectively; and (b) for the nonleaders, adjusted etas = .35 and .30. These coefficients are clearly higher than those for Output per scientist, which reflects the effect of multiple authorships. The coefficients are somewhat lower than those reported by Blume and Sinclair (1973), possibly because of the greater heterogeneity of the present sample in terms of research fields.
4 The relative importance of Size and Age seems to be about equal in the case of Output per scientist (both betas = .20), whereas for Scientific recognition the importance of Group size appears to be greater than that of Group age (betas = .40 and .32, respectively).
5 Jointly, the two predictors explain 34% of the variation in Scientific recognition, 36% of the variation in Total ouput of papers, but only 4% of the variation in Output per scientist. The figure for Scientific recognition is probably underestimated due to the limited reliability of the index. If we accept the reliability and validity coefficients developed in Chapter 14, the true percentage would rise from 34% to somewhere between 40 and 49%.
6 Group size and Age make significant marginal contributions to prediction of both Output of published papers and Scientific recognition. Their marginals are *not* significant in the case of the Output per scientist; here even the joint effects are barely significant (significance of F =.056).
7 As expected, the relation of Group size to performance is curvilinear. This is clear, especially when we look at the Index of scientific recognition. The tendency is not very striking before controlling for the effects of Group age. However, once such controls are introduced, the curvilinearities become unmistakable (see Exhibit 8.3). It seems, in other words, that the declining effectiveness of large groups is partly disguised by the fact that they are rather old. The optimum group size appears to be about five to seven scientists when we look at the Index of scientific recognition and three to four when we look at Output per scientist (Exhibit 8.2).[2]
8 The relation between Group size and Scientific recognition cannot be attributed solely to the increasing output of the larger groups. As can be seen in Exhibit 8.3, Group size relates to Recognition even if we control for *both* Group age and Output of papers. Moreover, the curvilinearity of the relationship seems to be accentuated, suggesting that when groups grow large the quality of their performance suffers more than the quantity of output. The exhibit also suggests that the low output of *small* groups is the main reason for the low degree of recognition they receive.

9 Turning now to the curvilinearities of the relationships between performance and Group age, we can conclude that although the strength of the relationship is very modest, Output per scientist seems to increase during the first 10 years of a group's existence, after which output either stabilizes or declines (Exhibit 8.5). This was confirmed when the individual output measures were examined. Both for the leaders and nonleaders, there is a noticeable decline in the number of authorships when groups were 11 or more years old.

10 When looking at the Index of scientific recognition, we can see no "optimum age" (Exhibit 8.6). The deviations from linearity are due chiefly to the unexpectedly high scores for the groups that were between three and five years old. These fluctuations could be due to overestimation of the impact of the groups' early products (which are likely to dramatically increase the "visibility" of the groups). The absence of decline in Recognition for the older groups could be the result of the fact that our sample contains very few really old groups. Another reason could be the existence of a *halo effect:* It could be argued that "fame is cumulative"; the recognition received by older research groups may continue to be high, even when their current performance no longer lives up to past standards. This constitutes another important reason for controlling group age when "impact" measures of performance are used.

To sum up: The overall relationships in the data tend to agree with our expectations. On the whole, there is a predominantly positive relationship of both group size and age with performance. The curvilinearities exist as predicted, even though the optimum size for Output per scientist is smaller than expected. However, the strength of the relationship between the productivity index and the predictors is disappointingly low, and the curvilinearity of the relationship between Group age and Output per scientist is somewhat uncertain. The absence of the curvilinearity in the case of Scientific recognition contradicts our expectations but may be due to a halo effect.

The stability and strength of the relationships

Both the size and age of research groups are related to several other factors that themselves could influence the performance of the groups. The following factors appear to be particularly relevant: (1) The *research field* of a group; (2) its *structure and composition:* the larger and the older the group, the more likely it is to evolve elaborate structures and contain large numbers of experienced scientists; (3) the structure of the *research program* may also vary with the size and age of a group; it could be that groups with broad research profiles have a wider impact and thus receive a greater degree of recognition; the heterogeneity of its research programs may enhance the creativity of a group; on the other hand, the multiplicity of projects may lead to a decrease in the cohesiveness of a group; (4) the amount of *resources* at the disposal of a group may be a factor in explaining the relations between size or age and performance; and, finally, (5) there is likely to exist a relationship between the size and age of a group and the *characteristics of its leaders;* given the importance of the leaders in groups such as ours, it is necessary to examine the effects of these characteristics.

Several different measures of the above concepts were introduced into the analysis. The additive effects of the control variables were examined first. The general conclusions that emerged were:

1 Although lowering the strength of correlations, the control variables could *not* explain away the relationship between Group size and Scientific recognition. The MCA betas for Group size fluctuated between .40 and .31, depending on which sets of control variables were introduced. The lowest beta was obtained when both Group age and Number of supervisory scientists were controlled. However, the latter variable cannot be considered as fully independent of Group size. None of the control variables changed the curvilinearity of the relationship.
2 The relationships between Group age and Scientific recognition were somewhat less stable: The betas fluctuated between .30 and .23. The latter figure was obtained when we controlled simultaneously for Group size, the status of the leader,[3] his research experience, and the amount of time he devotes to working in the group. Here again, Group age and the research experience of the leader cannot be regarded as fully independent of each other. The general form of the relationship was unaffected by the controls.
3 The relationships of Group size and Age with Output per scientist – originally weak – became even more insignificant when the controls were introduced. However, their original *form* remained unchanged.

The reduction in the strength of the relationships was to be expected, given the correlations among the predictors. What is essential here is the fact that the form of the relationships remains stable and that the marginal effects of Group size and Age are clearly significant, at least as far as the Index of scientific recognition is concerned.

Still more significant results emerge when we consider the interactions between the size and age of the groups and some of the control factors.[4] These findings throw light on the crucial role of leadership in groups such as ours.

Exhibit 8.7 shows the changes in the relationship between Group size and Output per scientist when the leader's degree of involvement with the group is controlled. The leader's involvement is defined as high if he or she devotes more than 33% of his time to the work of the group. Involvement is considered

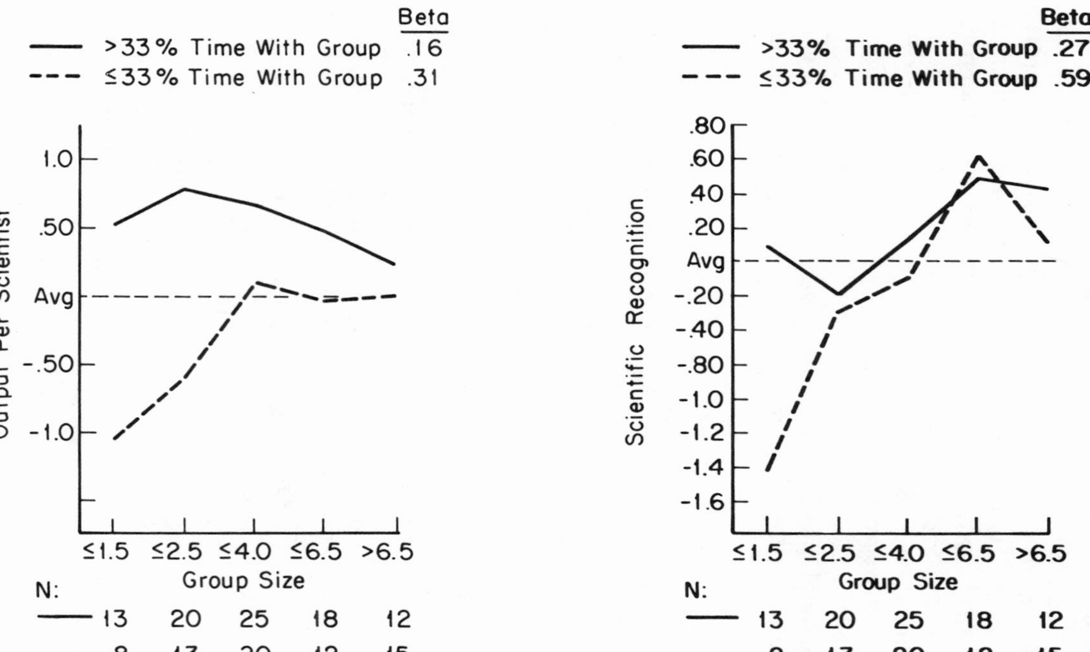

Exhibit 8.7 (*left*). Group size and Output per scientist, given the level of the leader's involvement in the work of the group and controlling for Group age. Exhibit 8.8 (*right*). Group size and Scientific recognition, given the level of the leader's involvement in the work of the group and controlling for Group age.

moderate or low if the leader devotes less than 33% of his or her time to the group. Exhibit 8.8 shows the changes in the relationship between Group size and Scientific recognition when the leader's involvement is controlled.

It is quite clear that although the performance of the groups generally improves with greater leader involvement, the relationship with Group size is most visible for groups directed by leaders with low or moderate involvement. This is understandable, for the relative importance of the nonleaders should increase when the leader's involvement decreases. Still, it is remarkable that the differences in performance between the two types of groups are so small once they reach the size of three to four scientists. I shall soon return to this point.

Another point that will be discussed in the last section of this chapter is the effect of the leader's involvement on the Scientific recognition of the large groups. Examining Exhibit 8.8, we can see that the decrease in the performance of groups larger than 6.5 scientists is very small when they are headed by highly involved leaders and quite steep when the leaders are less involved.

Another variable that interacts even more strongly with Group size and Age is the *research experience* of the leaders. Exhibit 8.9 shows the relationship between Group size and Output per scientist when we control for the level of the leader's research experience. Compared with the curves in Exhibit 8.2, the changes are quite dramatic. There appears to exist a strong *positive* correlation between Group size and productivity when the leaders have long research experience and a *negative* correlation when the leaders have short R & D experience. Note that a group size of three to four scientists seems to be a watershed in both cases: Beyond this point, the improvement in the productivity of groups with more experienced leaders becomes less pronounced, and the decline in the productivity of groups with less experienced leaders becomes quite dramatic.

When we turn to the Index of scientific recognition (Exhibit 8.10), we can again see that the performance of groups headed by experienced leaders *increases steeply* with group size up to five to seven scientists and then declines. The relationship is *far weaker* in groups headed by less-experienced scientists. Note, however, that in both cases the optimum point corresponds to five to seven scientists and that the reduction in performance when the groups grow larger is nearly identical.

The above trends can be explained if we assume that there exist two distinct types of leaders: (1) those who contribute to the total effectiveness of a group chiefly through their *own indi-*

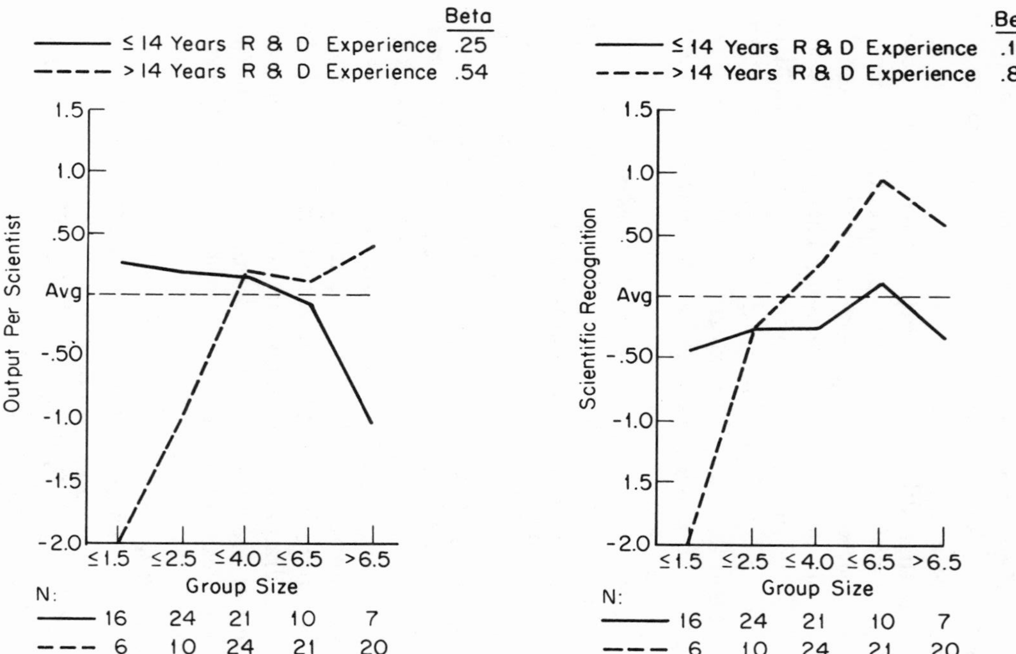

Exhibit 8.9 (*left*). Group size and Output per scientist, given the research experience of the leader and controlling for Group age. Exhibit 8.10 (*right*). Group size and Scientific recognition, given the research experience of the leader and controlling for Group age.

vidual effort but have little influence on the performance of other group members, and (2) those who contribute to a group's performance chiefly by mobilizing and directing the resources of the *group as a whole.*

In the case of groups led by scientists belonging to the first category, we could expect a decrease in Output per scientist as the group grows large simply because there would be a simultaneous decrease in the relative importance of the leader. In such groups, we would also expect a low level of correlation between their size and Scientific recognition.

In the case of groups led by scientists belonging to the second category, we would expect a positive relationship between Group size and *both* the Output per scientist and Scientific recognition.

The question is: Is there a correlation between a leader's research experience and his or her involvement with a group, on the one hand, and the type of leadership (as defined above), on the other? I think that there is such a correlation and that the reason for it is found in the organization of the Swedish academic system.

The crucial point is that nearly all the group leaders with less than 14 years' research experience hold temporary academic positions. That means two things: The leaders are under strong competitive pressure to demonstrate their own scientific merit, and at the same time – due to the nature of the job they hold – they have relatively large amounts of time for research.[5] The consequences of this situation are: (1) A leader will tend to be rather egocentric, and (2) he or she is less dependent on the assistance of the other group members. Under such circumstances, there may arise one of two diametrically different but equally unfavorable situations: (1) A leader may adopt a laissez-faire attitude, which may lead to the loss of cohesiveness in the group, or (2) he or she may attempt to completely subordinate the group to his or her own interest, which will create antagonistic tensions and the sense of being exploited among other group members.

The groups led by established and therefore more secure scientists are more likely to avoid such dangers. The fact that their leaders have only limited time for research, although in itself regrettable, may have the advantage of forcing them to learn how to work effectively *through* their groups. They have, I think, better motivation and the opportunity to create in their groups the sense of balance between challenge and security, which – as shown by Pelz (1967) – stimulates creativity and productivity in science.

What was said above does not mean that, taken as individuals, the younger scientists are less effective researchers than their older colleagues. On the contrary, many of them may be in their most creative periods (Pelz and Andrews, 1966). However, under the prevailing institutional conditions, they do not seem to be well adapted to assume the roles of group leaders.

The relationship of Group age with the measures of performance when properties of leadership are controlled is somewhat more difficult to assess, due to the considerable strength of correlations between these properties and Group age. (Some of the cells in MCA tables become too small to be analyzed.) However, the following general conclusions have emerged:

The relationship of Group age with Output per scientist was greatest in groups headed by the less-experienced leaders (beta =.45); this is quite understandable. The relationship of Group age with Scientific recognition was the greatest (beta = .44) in groups headed by highly involved leaders. Both these trends most probably reflect the fact that the effectiveness of leaders tends to improve significantly during the earlier stages of their scientific careers. Both relationships tend toward linearity. Under other conditions, the relationships of Group age with Output and Recognition were quite modest (betas between .19 and .26) and somewhat unstable in their form.

The examination of the influence of control factors has led to the identification of several additional effects. However, from the point of view of the main subject of this chapter, only a few of them are directly relevant. Especially important seems the fact that although, for the most part, the quantity and quality of scientific output have the same determinants, they also have certain unique ones. For example, Output per scientist is strongly affected by the number of projects conducted by the group (even after the effects of group size and age were removed); but the number of projects had no such effect on Scientific recognition. Similarly, the centrality of the leader (as measured by the number of scientists he directly supervises) had a positive effect on the group's productivity (over and above the effect on the group's size), but the centrality of the leader had no such effect on Scientific recognition. The latter was found to be related to the intellectual multipolarity of the groups (as measured by the number of group members with supervisory functions), but such multiploarity was unrelated to the quantitative productivity of the groups. In other words, not only the size but also the composition and structure of the groups influence their performance. However, the nature of the influence depends on whether one considers the quantity or the quality and relevance of the group's output.

This section can be concluded by saying that the tests reported in it show that the relations between Group size or Age and the measures of performance are not spurious. However, we have seen that the strength of the effects predicted by our hypotheses, and – in the case of Output per scientist – their form, are conditioned by the characteristics of the group leadership. It seems that the curvilinearities in the relationship between Group age and the measures of performance are unstable and that therefore we should adopt an agnostic attitude toward them. On the other hand, one is impressed by the persistence of the optimum-size effect. In the next section of this paper, I shall discuss possible explanations for this phenomenon.

The form of the relationships

The expectation that the relationship between Group size and research performance would be curvilinear was based on the following premises:

It was expected that the intellectual synergy of a group would go up with its size, due to the growing opportunities for intellectual interactions and collaboration among the members. However, we did not believe that the increase would be exponential and doubted whether it would even be proportional. The reason for this skepticism was the social and psychological limitations on the number of meaningful interactions in which individuals can engage. Indeed, it was suggested – on the basis of the literature dealing with small groups – that, beyond a certain point, increasing a group's size would lead to decreasing intellectual cohesion and diminishing morale in the group. Such changes would effectively neutralize the advantages of the increasing size.

Let us therefore examine the effects of Group size and Age on a set of variables designed to measure the levels of interaction, collaboration, and cohesiveness in a group. The variables were as follows: (1) *the number of collaborators*[6] that the leaders and nonleaders had in the group; (2) *the number of group members* whom the scientists considered as especially *important sources* of technical *information or ideas;* (3) the group members' (nonleaders') assessment of the *cohesiveness of the group's research program;* (4) the group members' (nonleaders') *involvement in the planning* of research in the group; and (5) the group members' (nonleaders') *sense of identification with the group.*[7]

In addition, I have examined the effects of Group size and Age on the technical roles of the group members in order to check whether the increasing differentiation between leaders and nonleaders occurs, as is predicted by small-group theory.

An examination of Exhibits 8.11 and 8.12 confirms the expectation that the number of significant partners (collaborators, communicators) increases only slowly with group size. The sole exception to this trend is the number of the leader's collaborators; here the curve is rather close to the diagonal. This reflects the influence and the sociometric centrality of the leader. It is also interesting to note the difference in the number of persons communicating significant ideas as reported by the leader and nonleaders (compare the two exhibits). Generally, the leader tends to report more such persons and seems to gain more when the size of the group increases. This again confirms the sociometric centrality of the leader's position.

The general conclusions emerging from the exhibits is that the larger the group, the relatively weaker its sociometric network. Inasmuch as the intellectual synergy would require both frequent and intensive interactions, these results would suggest that it increases only slowly with group size.

However, it could be argued that the effects of size depend more on the number of *potential* interactions than on actual ones because the larger the group, the more preselected and, therefore, better the actual interaction will be. It can also be maintained that more sporadic contacts and exchanges, which are likely to be numerous in large groups, can be as important as a relatively few intensive ones. Perhaps so. Still, one cannot help being impressed by the fact that what increases most slowly with group size is the number of persons contributing significant *ideas,* as reported by the nonleaders. This pessimistic interpretation of the effects of group size is further confirmed by the analysis described below.

In general, the technical profiles of the group leaders indicate high levels of involvement in such functions as identifying the area of interest, defining the problem, and administration. The nonleaders show moderate or low levels of involvement in such functions. The intermediate set of functions, in which both the leaders and nonleaders show similar levels of involvement, are: choosing methods, selecting hypotheses, designing the research, analyzing the data, and writing reports. The other end of the continuum consists of such functions as data collecting and literature review, where the involvement of nonleaders is much greater than that of the leaders. Now, as a result of increasing group size, the differentiation between leaders and nonleaders

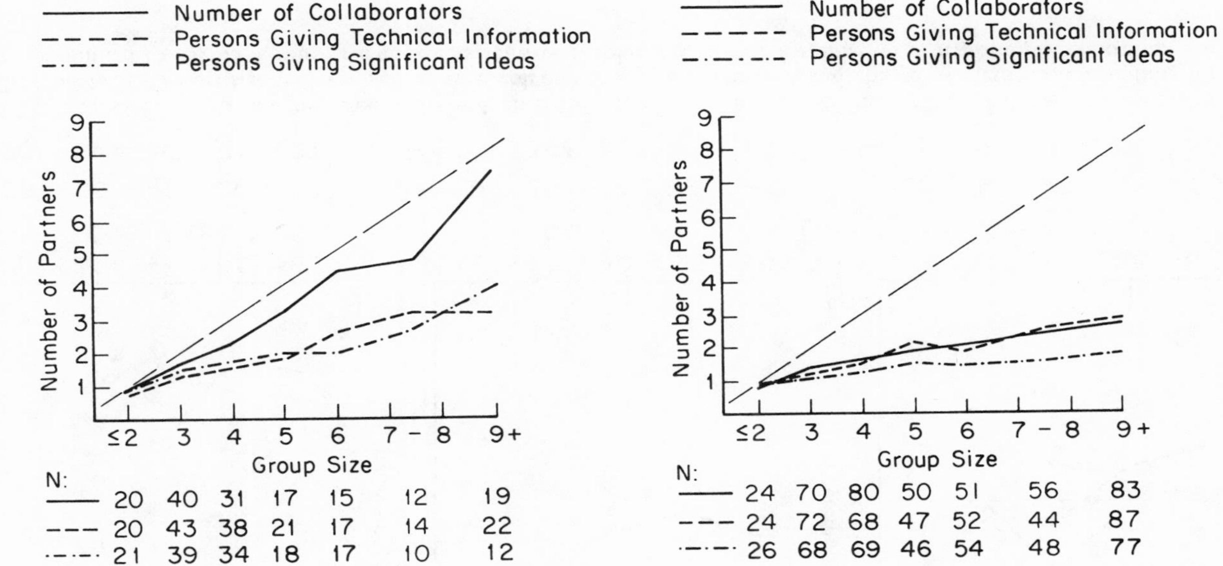

Exhibit 8.11 (*left*). The number of significant partners in the group reported by the leader, by Group size.
Exhibit 8.12 (*right*). The number of significant partners in the group reported by the nonleaders, by Group size.

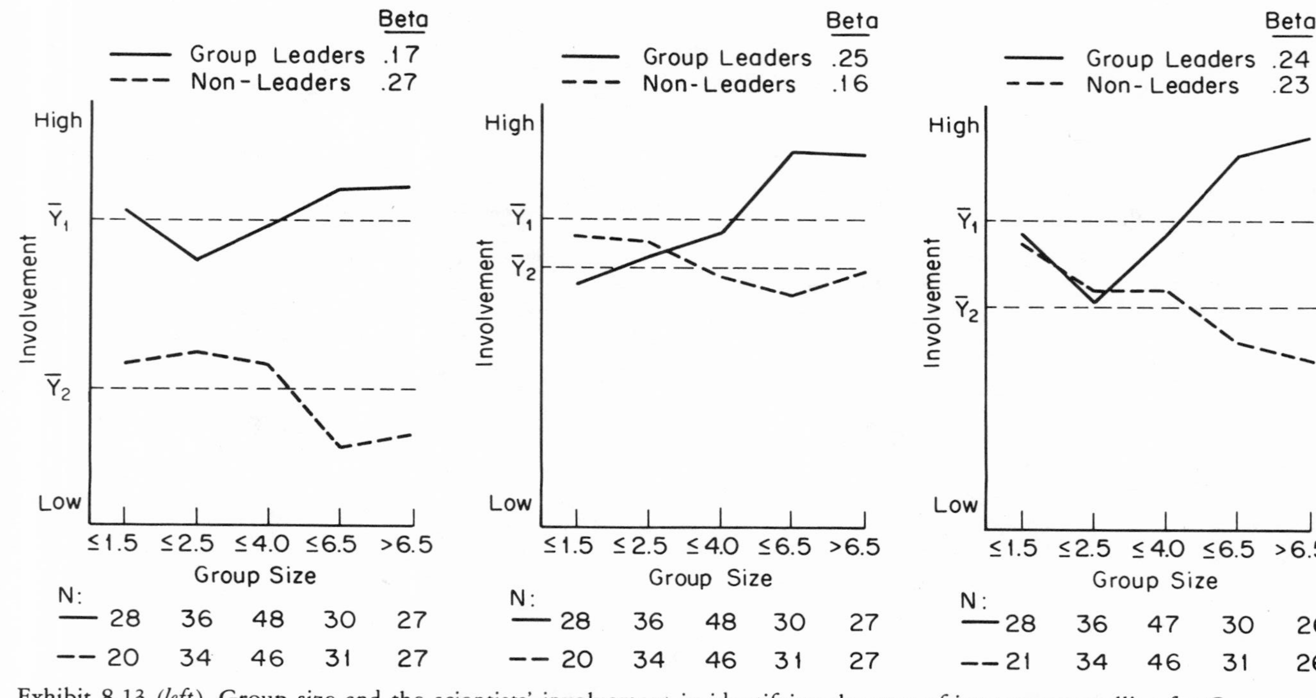

Exhibit 8.13 (*left*). Group size and the scientists' involvement in identifying the area of interest, controlling for Group age. Exhibit 8.14 (*middle*). Group size and the scientists' involvement in the perception and choice of methods, controlling for Group age. Exhibit 8.15 (*right*). Group size and the scientists' involvement in the formulation of hypotheses, controlling for Group age.

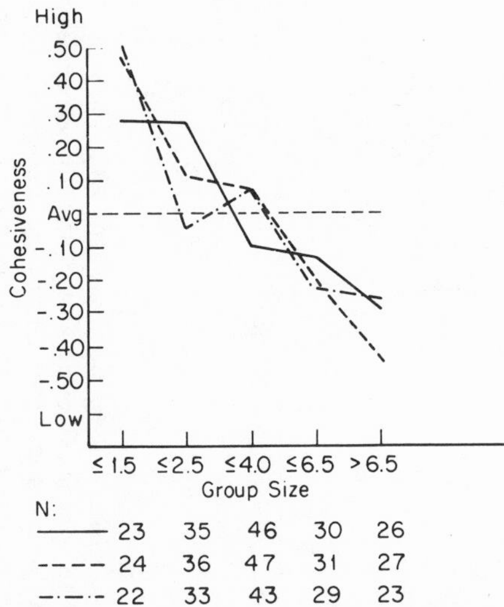

Exhibit 8.16. Group size and Cohesiveness, controlling for Group age.

tends to increase. This tendency is exemplified in Exhibits 8.13 to 8.15. It is only in two areas (data collecting and analyzing results) that the involvement of *both* the leaders and nonleaders increases with group size.

Group age appeared to have only a slight influence over the pattern of involvement in technical functions.

Although some degree of functional differentiation is both unavoidable and beneficial, the steady increase in the centrality and specialization of the leader's role and the corresponding decrease in the involvement of the nonleaders in the goal-setting functions is likely to be accompanied by declining group cohesiveness. The effects of increasing Group size on three measures of cohesiveness can be seen in Exhibit 8.16. The trends are what one would expect on the basis of small-group theory. Also expected was a tendency for cohesiveness to increase with group age. The data confirm that expectation, but the strength of the relationships is very weak; betas are .21 for Sense of belonging, .15 for Participation in the planning of research, and .18 for Coherence of the research program.

Having established that there is a relationship between the size

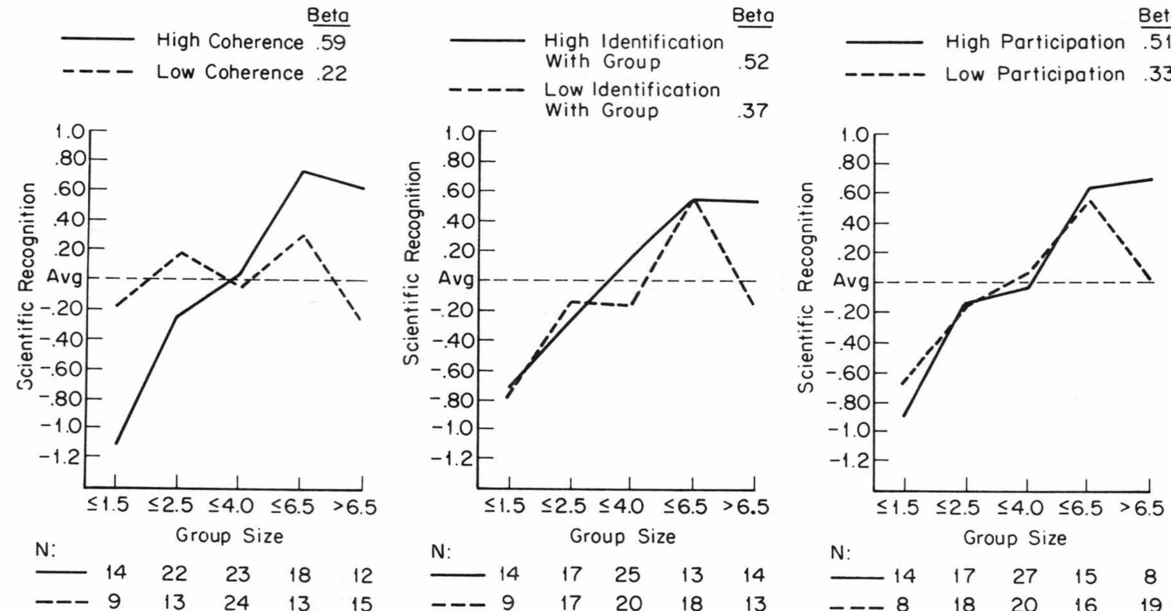

Exhibit 8.17 (*left*). Group size and Scientific recognition, given the degree of coherence of the research program and controlling for Group age. Exhibit 8.18 (*middle*). Group size and Scientific recognition, given the degree of members' identification with the group and controlling for Group age. Exhibit 8.19 (*right*). Group size and Scientific recognition, given the level of members' participation in research planning and controlling for Group age.

Exhibit 8.20. Research performance and Group size (controlling Group age) and Group age (controlling Group size), by Cohesiveness

Measures of cohesiveness	Scientific recognition and:		Output per scientist and:	
	Group size	Group age	Group size	Group age
Coherence of program				
high	.59[a]	.18	.19	.26
low	.22	.67[a]	.25	.37
Identification with group				
high	.52[a]	.24	.20	.18
low	.37[a]	.38[a]	.10	.38
Participation in planning				
high	.51[a]	.27	.30	.18
low	.33	.48[a]	.34	.43[a]

Note: Coefficients are MCA betas. Most relationships are approximately linear.
[a]Marginal contribution significant at $p < .05$ level.

of research groups and their cohesiveness, we can now consider the effects that the differing levels of cohesiveness have on the relations between the Size and Age of the groups and their performance. Some of the results of this analysis can be seen in Exhibits 8.17 to 8.19. Further information about the outcome of the tests is found in Exhibit 8.20.

Exhibits 8.17, 8.18, and 8.19 show that the degree of cohesiveness of research groups explains the curvilinearities in the relationship between Group size and Scientific recognition. The impact of cohesiveness on the performance of the large groups is rather impressive when we consider that the symmetrical dichotomization of the variables measuring cohesiveness is probably less than optimal.

The reduction of curvilinearity is most clear in the case of high Participation in research planning (Exhibit 8.19), and somewhat less certain in the case of high Coherence of research program. Note also that low Coherence of the research program nearly eliminates the relationship between Group size and Recognition.

The conclusions emerging from Exhibits 8.17, 8.18, and 8.19 are that: (1) High levels of cohesiveness are necessary for maintaining the effectiveness of large research groups; and (2) the level of cohesion plays little role in the smaller groups (with the exception of the coherence of the research program). We could interpret these findings by saying that as long as groups are relatively small, the interactions in them work satisfactorily even though the perceived cohesiveness may vary. In part, this may be due to the ease with which the leaders can direct such groups. Once, however, groups pass the critical size of five to seven scientists, centrifugal forces become too great and the maintenance of high cohesion becomes a crucial management issue.

The relationship of Group age and research performance also seems to depend on the levels of cohesiveness (see Exhibit 8.20). These effects, generally linear, are most pronounced in the groups characterized by low cohesiveness. We could therefore say that whereas highly cohesive groups can quickly achieve high performance levels by increasing their size, groups characterized by low cohesiveness have to exist for a long time to achieve nearly as good performance.

Because the shortage of data makes testing the three-way interactions impractical, I could not control leadership characteristics while examining the influence of cohesiveness on the relations between Group size and Output per scientist. Consequently, the betas in Exhibit 8.20 are quite low. Perhaps the most reliable pair of betas is that for the groups whose members showed low Participation in research planning. These relations parallel the ones observed in the case of Scientific recognition: there is a curvilinear relationship with Group size and a fairly strong positive one with Group age.

5. Conclusions and discussion

Four main types of hypotheses concerning the relationships between the size and age of research groups and their performance were given at the beginning of this chapter. Trying to predict the *overall tendencies* in the data analyzed here, I favored the *optimum-size* and *optimum-age* hypotheses. The main reason for these choices was the social-psychological changes that are likely to take place when groups grow and age and which at a certain point may outweigh the advantages of size and experience. The results of the analysis supported quite well the expectations concerning the effects of size. The relationships of group age and performance were more uncertain as far as the curvilinearity of the relations was concerned. We have also seen that changes occurred in the structure and cohesiveness of groups with increases in size that are in accord with predictions from small-group research.

Still more important results emerged when the relationships of Group size and Age were examined under varying conditions. These results indicate quite clearly that the study of overall relationships is not enough. By taking into account the levels of group cohesiveness and certain characteristics of the leaders, it is possible to define the conditions under which three of the above-mentioned four types of hypotheses are applicable. (The exception was the minimum-size hypothesis.) Thus:

1 Given a high level of cohesivenss, the effectiveness of research tends to increase with group size, and one finds no evidence – at least within our range of group sizes – of an optimum point. Under these conditions, the conclusions of this chapter's analysis and those conducted by Wallmark et al. (1973) and Blume and Sinclair (1973) coincide.
2 When cohesiveness is low, there is a strong decline in performance for groups larger than seven scientists.
3 The relationship between size and performance is strong in groups headed by leaders with long research experience. But:
4 It is weak in groups headed by younger leaders. In fact:
5 In groups headed by younger leaders, there is a negative relationship between productivity and group size.
6 In groups characterized by high levels of cohesiveness and/or directed by experienced leaders, group age has little effect on performance. On the other hand:
7 In groups characterized by low cohesiveness and/or directed by highly involved leaders, the importance of group age is considerable.

Considering the shifts in the strength and form of the relations reported above, it is hardly surprising that there circulate so many contradictory hypotheses about the virtues and vices of different sizes and ages of research groups. Indeed, I feel that the main payoffs of future research in this area will come from establishing – for specified types of research groups – the conditions under which an increase in size and/or age can be beneficial. This chapter's analysis suggests that attention should be focused on properties of leadership and on factors influencing the cohesiveness of groups.

Generally speaking, it seems risky to allow groups to grow much larger than seven scientists. If for some reason it is necessary to form larger research teams, steps must be taken to counteract the potential loss of cohesiveness. So far, our analyses have given the following hints:

1 It seems necessary to assure the participation of all group members in the overall management of the group; one must be aware of the danger of the group splitting into an active stratum and a passive stratum; for this reason one must avoid excessive differentiation of technical roles.
2 High involvement of the leaders in a group's work is crucial: It appears that there is a fairly strong negative correlation between group size and

the coherence of the research program when leaders devote 33% or less of their time to the group. This relation practically disappears when groups are headed by more involved leaders. This, incidentally, explains the fact that the curvilinearity of the relationship between Group size and Scientific recognition nearly disappears when the level of the leader's involvement is high (see Exhibit 8.8).

3 It is also preferable that groups work on few projects and have well-integrated budgets.

As we have seen, the effects of leadership are not reducible to the level of the leader's involvement with the group. It seems that, in order to be effective as leaders, scientists must be relatively free from the competitive pressures that operate on the *individual* level. Indeed, there are trends in our data that suggest that the leader's attitude toward collaboration in the group changes with his or her research experience. The older leaders appear to be more immune to external pressures and more dependent on their groups. They are also more often guided by strictly scientific criteria in the choice of their research problems. The younger leaders, on the other hand, tend to be more influenced by career considerations when choosing their research objectives and feel more independent from the rest of the group. They also tend to have fewer external contacts, which makes them less effective as "gate-keepers" for their groups. *However,* I must emphasize once again that all this does not mean that the younger leaders taken as individuals are inferior as researchers. It seems only that many of them are not well adapted to play the role of group leaders.

Finally, let me emphasize that all the above proposed conclusions and interpretations must be considered with caution. Our measurements contain errors that cannot always be detected or estimated. The causal inferences based on survey data can never be certain. The sample used here is not very large, which limits the depth of the analysis. Thus, even though further refinements and extensions of this chapter's analysis are possible and will be pursued, our understanding of the effects of the size and age of research groups can be improved significantly only by repeating the analysis on new samples. The data already collected or now being collected by the International Comparative Study on the Organization and Performance of Research Units represents a unique pool of information for this kind of research.

References

Berelson, B., and Steiner, G. A., 1964, *Human Behavior: An Inventory of Scientific Findings,* New York, Harcourt Brace Jovanovich.

Blume, S. S., and Sinclair, R., 1973, *Research Environment and Performance in British University Chemistry,* London, Her Majesty's Stationery Office.
Clarke, B. L., 1964, Multiple Authorship Trends in Scientific Papers, *Science,* 1943: 822–824.
Crane, D., 1972, *Invisible Colleges,* Chicago, University of Chicago Press.
Hagstrom, W., 1965, *The Scientific Community,* New York, Basic Books.
Hagstrom, W., 1967, *Competition and Teamwork in Science* (A report to the National Science Foundation, Washington, D.C.).
Krech, D., Crutchfield, R. S., and Ballachey, E. L., 1962, *Individual in Society: A Textbook of Social Psychology,* New York, McGraw-Hill.
Lemaine, G., et al., 1972, *Les voies du succes,* Paris, Centre National de la Recherche Scientifique (CNRS).
Mullins, N. C., 1972, The Development of a Scientific Specialty, *Minerva,* 10 (1).
Pelz, D. C., 1967, Creative Tensions in the Research and Development Climate, *Science,* 157 (3785) : 160–165.
Pelz, D. C., and Andrews, F. M., 1966, 1976, *Scientists in Organizations,* New York, Wiley. (Revised ed. 1976, Ann Arbor, Institute for Social Research, University of Michigan.)
Price, D. J. de S., 1963, *Little Science, Big Science,* New York, Columbia University Press.
Price, D. J. de S., and Beaver, D., 1966, Collaboration in an Invisible College, *American Psychologist,* 21: 1011–1018.
Shepard, H. A., 1956, Creativity in R/D Teams, *Research and Engineering,* October: 10–13.
Stankiewicz, R., 1976, Research Groups and the Academic Science Organization, *Sociologisk Forskning,* 13 (2).
Storer, N. W., 1962, Research Orientations and Attitudes Toward Teamwork, *The IRE Transactions on Engineering Management,* EM-9 (1) : 29–33.
Wallmark, J. T., and Sellerberg, B., 1966, Efficiency vs. Size of Research Teams, *IEEE Transactions on Engineering Management,* EM-13: 137–142.
Wallmark, J. T., et al., 1973, The Increase in Efficiency with the Size of Research Teams, *IEEE Transactions on Engineering Management,* EM-20(3): 80–86.
Weinberg, A. M., 1970, Scientific Teams and Scientific Laboratories, *Daedalus,* Fall.
Wells, W. P., 1962, Group Age and Scientific Performance, Ann Arbor, University of Michigan, Ph.D. thesis.
Wells, W. P., and Pelz, D. C., 1966, Groups. *In* Pelz, D. C., and Andrews, F. M., 1966, *Scientists in Organizations,* New York, Wiley.
Wilson, R. R., 1970, My Fight against Team Research, *Daedalus,* Fall.

Notes

1. This index is described in Chapter 2.
2. The absence of decline in Total output (see Exhibit 8.1) when the groups grow large is misleading: The loss of productivity is offset by the increasing number of producers.
3. An extra variable used only in the Swedish version of the questionnaires.
4. Because of the small sample size and the correlations among the predictors, the interaction tests could not be very detailed. The control factors had to be dichotomized in a symmetrical fashion to avoid too-small cell sizes. Such splits are not likely to be optimal from the theoretical point of view.

5. Although 50% of the younger leaders could devote more than one third of their time to work in their groups, the corresponding percentage among the older leaders was only 33%.

6. This is an extra variable used only in the Swedish questionnaires. As the criterion of *direct collaboration* we used the fact that two scientists either have issued, or soon will issue, a joint report or publication.

7. This is an extra attitude variable used only in the Swedish questionnaires. The scientists were asked to rate the degree to which they considered themselves as group members rather than individual workers.

9 Communication between and within research units

Nicole Visart
Division of Science and Technology Policies,
Unesco, Paris

Framework, limitations, and purposes of the chapter

Now, *here,* you see, it takes all the running *you* can do to stay in the same place. If you want to get somewhere else, you must run at least as fast as that! [Lewis Carroll]

Nihil est in intellectu quod non prius fuerit in sensu. [Thomas Aquinas]

The inner motivation of the study presented in this chapter has developed around these two ideas. It is based on the overall model of knowledge dissemination and utilization discussed by Havelock: "*Who* transfers *what* by *what channel* to *whom* to *what effect?*" (Havelock, 1969).

Communication is as old as life; it is as complex; it is the core of life and necessary to it. Human communication represents probably the most elaborate form of communication. Within human communication, communication in science and technology plays a primordial role,[1] enabling mankind to face its twofold challenge: survival and development, that is, to go against entropy. Indeed, communication in science and technology may be looked at from the point of view of *negentropy:* The challenge is whether more energy is liberated by the increase of knowledge and its use than is lost by the processes of increasing and disseminating it. In this respect, the information content and value of

The programming assistance and technical support of Cinda Gainche, without which this study could not have been realized, are gratefully acknowledged. Views expressed in this chapter are the sole responsibility of the author.

communication as a *product* (or *signal*) and the efficiency of communication as a *channel* are crucial.

It may be argued that communication in science and technology should be looked at as a holistic process in which the "what is transmitted?" and the "how is it transmitted?" are mutually complementary. The production (output) and the rated performance of research units form an integral part of that process. From such a perspective, to examine the relationships between performance and other dimensions of communication (such as the frequency of scientific and technical meetings, scientific exchanges, etc.) comes to the same thing as to find out how, and the extent to which, different elements of the communication process relate to each other. This is the approach adopted for this chapter, where channel communication and signal communication are examined as regards the way they relate to themselves, to each other, and to certain contextual dimensions. The author has indeed a preference for such a holistic approach. Type of respondent, Type of institutional/scientific setting, and Country are used as controls.[2]

Neither the data nor the resources available lent themselves to generalizations or global models of communication in R & D. The findings presented are therefore limited and fragmented. Our conviction is that a real breakthrough in the understanding of communication in R & D requires, as a prerequisite, not only that it be considered a holistic process but also that it be studied through the binoculars of various disciplines. This obviously exceeds the ability and capacity of one analysis and calls for a task-force approach.

The literature produced in the domain of communication in science and technology amounts to thousands of published documents. About 100 such papers and publications were scanned for this study, some of which were written by the "scientific stars" in the field. What was found was enough to stimulate our curiosity, not to satisfy it. Moreover, we felt that it would be unjust to quote (once more) only a few names. In the impossibility of making a fair and relevant selection, it was preferred to abstain from citing previous works, with the exception of that of Havelock. To our mind, he has made an outstanding review of the literature on the communication processes as regards the production and dissemination of knowledge. Even if this review lacks information on works published in less-developed and European countries, one of its merits is an approach both wide in scope and modest in attitude.

About the literature that we reviewed, we would like to mention that, first, it quasi-unanimously supports the importance of

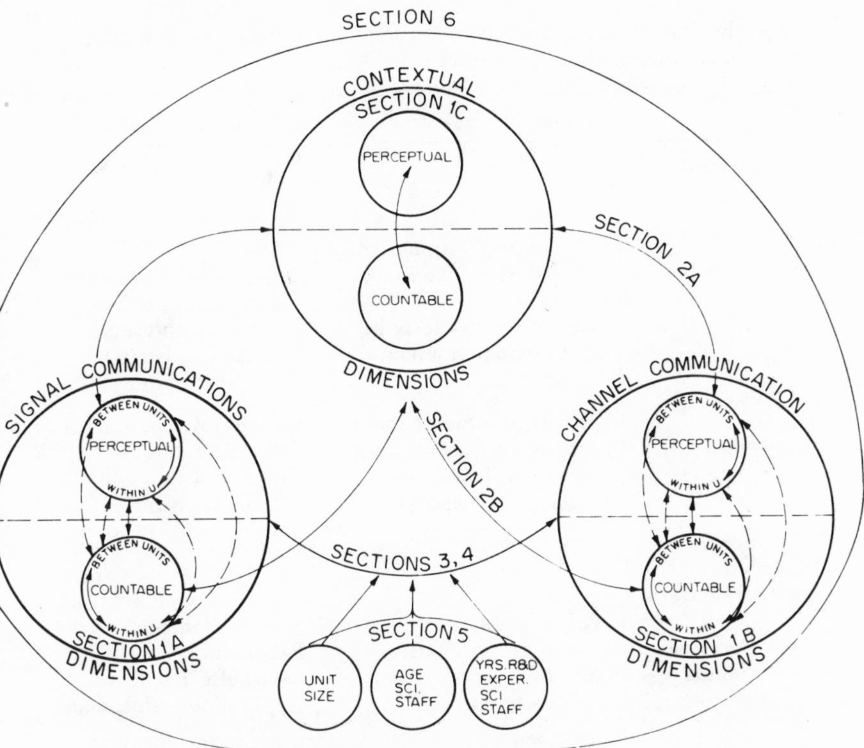

Exhibit 9.1. Relationships examined in the study
Note: Only a part of the findings have been reported in this chapter; they are indicated by the § number in which they are discussed.

communication (as a channel) (1) for the improvement of substantive information (communication as a signal), and (2) for the transmission and utilization of information; there are many variations on the subject, including the role of the scientific and institutional setting, of size, management styles, etc. Second, the literature that we have seen was quasi-unidisciplinary; there are few integrative approaches; moreover, we mostly met either facts or speculations, rarely a combination of facts and theory.

Exhibits 9.1 and 9.2 will orient the reader to the organization of this chapter's study. Exhibit 9.1 displays the complete line of reasoning that we followed in our study; however, only some of the findings are reported here: those that bear a reference to a given section or subsection of this chapter. Exhibit 9.2 gives a global picture of the communication and contextual dimensions used in the chapter. Section 1 of the chapter describes the sample and subsamples and examines the measures used, namely: (1) commu-

Exhibit 9.2. Summary table of communication and contextual measures used in the chapter

		Countable measures	Perceptual measures
Communication as channel			
	Between units	No. of S&T visits No. of publications sent No. of S&T meetings attended No. of weeks' delay in receiving communications	Contacts between units (head's rating) Contacts between units (staff scientists' rating) Contacts with users (head's and staff) scientists' ratings)
	Within units	No. of unit members providing useful information (head's and staff scientists' reports)	Contacts within units (head's rating) Contacts within units (staff scientists' rating)
Communication as signal (research-unit performance)			
	Between units	No. of published written products No. of patents/ prototypes	General contribution Recognition Social effectiveness Applications effectiveness
	Within units	No. of internal original reports	R & D effectiveness
Contextual dimensions			
		Unit size Staff composition Age of unit Years R & D experience of unit head No. of units in same/ similar fields within easy access outside organization Scientific staff turnover No. of research projects shared with other units Diversity of scientific fields borrowed by unit head in his/her research work Diversity of products resulting from unit's work	Morale as rated by unit heads Morale as rated by staff scientists Professional competence of immediate supervisor (as rated by staff scientists) Autonomy of unit

nication as a channel, (2) communication as a signal, and (3) contextual measures.[3] Each of these subsections begins with a description of the conceptual contents of the measures, first the perceptual ones, then the countable measures; then comes a review of the mutual relationships among the measures and of their level according to type of respondent and setting. Section 2 examines the relationships of contextual dimensions to communication (as channel) in two separate subsections, dealing respectively with perceptual dimensions and countable dimensions of communication.[4] Section 3 looks at the relationships of communication dimensions among themselves ("How" by "What"). Section 4 presents multivariate relationships of channel communication to signal communication (i.e., to research-unit performance). Section 5 explores the effects of some contextual dimensions (unit size, physical age, and professional age of the scientific staff) and of national setting on some of the relationships between channel and signal communication. Section 6 provides an overview of the relationships characterizing research units in terms of the compactness of their network of communication and contextual dimensions. The results are then summarized, and some conclusions for action are proposed.

In beginning the study, the following questions were posed, and the study describes the limited answers that were found in the available data:

1 How and to what extent do communication and contextual dimensions vary, according to type of respondent and type of setting?
2 How and to what extent do contextual dimensions relate to communication? Do these relationships vary according to type of respondent and type of setting?
3 How and to what extent does communication as a channel relate to communication as a signal? Do these relationships vary according to type of respondent and type of setting?
4 How and to what extent do perceptual measures of communication relate to countable measures of communication?
5 How and to what extent do *between-units* and *within-units* communications co-vary?
6 What is the pattern of multivariate relationships between channel communication and signal communication?
7 Are the multivariate relationships affected by contextual dimensions (such as size of the unit, age of the scientists) and by the national setting?

When looking at the results, it should be remembered that they derive from the research units that have been studied, and that these units exist in particular contextual environments and societies. The results do not represent a model of communication. One might perhaps question, for instance, whether written scientific communication still meets its informative purpose and, even, whether a search for other forms than verbal communication in R & D should not be encouraged.

1. Background information

The sample

The survey data used in this study come from the sample described in Chapter 2. In short, it contains 1,222 research units[5] from six European countries: Austria, Belgium, Finland, Hungary, Poland, and Sweden. The sample is rather evenly distributed across countries, but the units are unequally spread among five types of institutions[6] and nine major fields of science and technology. The data were collected mainly from four types of respondents, totaling over 10,000 individuals.[7] In order to rationalize the research effort and to preserve a certain uniformity in the presentation of the results from the primary analyses, research units have been classified according to a *performance typology*. This groups units according to their institutional and scientific setting, and is based on the similarity of units' output and rated-performance profiles.[8]

In the interpretation of the results described below, some caution should be exercised because of approximations in the allocation of fields of science and technology to research units, because of imprecisions in the performance typology, and because of noncomparabilities in the sampling design.

The analyses on communication were conducted in parallel on the whole sample and on three subsamples, categories 1, 4, and 5 of the performance typology: (1) units in academic settings and doing research in exact or natural sciences (category 1), (2) units in cooperative research institutions (category 4), and (3) units in productive enterprises and doing research in applied sciences (category 5). The subsamples were chosen to be maximally different, in order to illustrate comparisons between the results obtained for each of them separately.

The measures

Exhibit 9.2 provides an overview of the perceptual and countable measures examined in this chapter. Perceptual measures relate to ranked data only, that is, to ratings made by the respondents: unit heads, staff scientists, external evaluators; countable measures concern only discrete data as reported by the respondents. This section describes their contents, their interrelationships, and their levels according to Type of respondent, Type of institutional/scientific setting, and Country. All the measures come from the common international data file at the unit level.[9] Whenever relevant, the original ordinal scale has been reversed so that now 1 = low and 5 = high. Except where specified, all the measures have been rescaled to reduce skew in the data and to meet other requirements of the analysis techniques. For the sake of comparability, the same measures are used in all the analyses whenever possible. The use of rescaled variables sometimes slightly reduced the size of relationships. The rescaling was such as to assure a Pearson r of .95–.98 between the original continuous variables and their bracketed form.

A. *Performance measures (communication as signal)*

From the theoretical perspectives adopted for this chapter, our measures of research-unit effectiveness can be considered as indicators of communication as signal – that is, they include perceptual and countable measures of *what* is transmitted by the research unit. With one exception ("Internal original reports"), the signal communication measures have been selected from the set of performance indices developed by the International Research Team and described in Chapter 2. The selection was based on the theoretical interest of the measures for this chapter's analysis and on their estimated construct validity.[10] All measures have been adjusted to remove differences attributable to institutional/scientific setting (as is also described in Chapter 2) in order that the subgroups examined in the analysis would be on an equal footing as regards performance. Hence, any relationships found between channel communication and signal communication (i.e., research-unit performance) cannot be the spurious result of differences between types of units. (Note, however, that the adjusted and unadjusted rated-performance measures used in this analysis relate to each other in excess of r = .91.)

Five *perceptual* (i.e., rated) performance indices are used in this chapter: General contribution, Recognition, Social effectiveness, R & D effectiveness, and Applications effectiveness. Three *countable* performance measures are also used: Number of published written products of the unit, Number of patents and prototypes of the unit, and Internal original reports of the unit.[11]

B. *Communication as a channel*

Described below are the perceptual and countable measures concerning *how* the communication is transmitted. For the sake of clarity, 10 communication measures have been selected for presentation, although 56 were used during the background analyses. Data coming from support staff, despite their obvious interest in some cases, have been omitted because (1) a selection was necessary, (2) they were not indispensable to answer the questions posed in this study, and (3) they showed no strong relationships with any data except themselves. With the exception of Number of scientific and technical (S & T) meetings attended, which is a single original item, all the measures described below are composite indices. In the material that follows, we first describe 5 perceptual indicators and then turn to 5 countable measures.

Perceptual measures (rated data)

1 Contacts between units as perceived by unit heads: Five items enter this index. They represent contacts as reported by the head of the unit regarding: (1) frequency with which he or she discusses his or her work with other units within the organization, (2) frequency with which he or she visits or is visited by colleagues from other organizations (in the country or abroad) working in the same field, (3) satisfaction about opportunities for working discussions within the organization, (4) satisfaction about opportunities for visiting colleagues in other organizations, and (5) effects of contacts on his or her scientific or technical performance.

2 Contacts between units as perceived by staff scientists: The items that enter this index are parallel to those used in the previous one (Contacts between units as perceived by unit heads). These items assess contacts between units as rated by the staff scientists of the unit.

It is worth noting that the relationships between these 10 items (ratings by unit heads and by staff scientists) are stronger within the same type of respondent than between respondents. The strength of the relationships, even within types of respondents, is not very strong but (1) is fairly stable across institutional/scientific settings (although rather weaker for units from cooperative research institutions), and (2) is somewhat stronger and more compact for the staff scientists than for the head. This could be explained either by a systematic respondent bias or, and perhaps more plausibly, by a true difference in the way contacts between units are viewed and experienced. These five items are all posed in the personal form, "you." We may face here a phenomenon of perception similar to that encountered with performance ratings: Chapter 11 reports that data from heads of units and from staff scientists loaded on two separate factors for the series of items entering the indices General contribution, Recognition, and R & D effectiveness.

For the purpose of this chapter's study of communication, it was judged preferable to handle separately the data obtained from unit heads and from staff scientists when constructing indices of channel communication, except for the measure Contacts with users.

3 Contacts with users: Two items enter this index. They are the ratings by the unit head and by the staff scientists of the closeness of contacts with those ensuring the follow-up or practical application of the unit's results.

These items are related to each other in various ways, depending on the type of institutional/scientific setting (highest Pearson $r = .37$, based on all units; lowest Pearson $r = .19$, for units from cooperative research institutes).

4 Contacts within units as perceived by unit heads: Three items enter this index. They repesent contacts as rated by the head regarding: (a) frequency of staff meetings, (b) frequency of participation of support staff in staff meetings, and (c) acceptance of ideas coming from the junior staff technicians of the unit.

5 Contacts within units as perceived by staff scientists: Three items enter this index, the same as for the preceding index.

The relationships between these six last items (three for unit heads and three for staff scientists) are somewhat stronger within the same type of respondent than between respondents. These relationships, as in the case of Contacts between units, are well replicated across institutional/scientific settings and are most often stronger for the staff scientists.

Countable measures (discrete data)

1 Number of S & T visits: This is based on a combination of the number of visits, lasting at least five working days, made for scientific or technical purposes to other units inside the country, and to units abroad, by scientists of the unit during the past year (as reported by the head).

2 Number of publications sent: This is based on the number of publications sent by the unit during the past year to individuals or organizations working in the same field (as reported by the head).

3 Number of S & T meetings attended: This is based on the number of scientific and technical meetings attended by members of the unit during the past year (as reported by the head).

4 Number of weeks delay in receiving communications: This is based on a combination of the number of weeks delay in obtaining (a) a decision, and (b) satisfaction as regards (i) external information and (ii) translations (as reported by the head or the administrator of the unit).

5 Number of unit members providing useful information: This is based on the number of unit members providing technical information, original ideas, and/or administrative help (no double counting). The index represents the average between the answer of the head and the mean answer of the staff scientists. It gives a good idea of the rate of communication within the unit, especially when unit size is considered.

Relationships among channel communication measures. Exhibit 9.3 presents the interrelationships among the channel communication measures that have just been described. From Exhibit 9.3 it appears that:

1 Channel communication measures as rated by unit heads and by staff scientists have something in common. Pearson *r*s are .37, .27, and .17 between these two types of respondents for Contacts with users, Contacts within units, and Contacts between units, respectively.

2 Heads of units tend to have a more global and integrated view of the channel communication dimensions than do the staff scientists of the unit. Moreover, ratings of channel communication by the head and by

Exhibit 9.3. Relationships among the channel communication measures

	2	3	4	5	6	7	8	9	10
1. Contacts between units (head's rating)									
2. Contacts between units (staff scientists' rating)	.17								
3. Contacts with users[a] (head's & staff scientists' rating)	.11	.15							
4. Contacts within units (head's rating)	.17	−.00	.08						
5. Contacts within units (staff scientists' rating	.03	.24	.18	.27					
6. No. of S & T visits	.13	.04	−.04	.08	.01				
7. No. of publications sent	.11	.03	−.19	.03	.03	.28			
8. No. of S & T meetings attended	.14	.04	.04	.01	.01	.32	.27		
9. No. of weeks' delay in receiving communications	−.11	.07	.02	−.12	.05	.04	−.01	−.01	
10. No. of unit members providing useful information	.05	−.01	.07	.04	.07	.27	.20	.31	.08

Note: Coefficients are Pearson *r*s. Scale of original items has been reversed for perceptual measures.
[a]r = .37 between unit heads' ratings and staff scientists' ratings of contacts with users.

the staff scientists relate in a different way to contextual dimensions and to research unit performance (see Sections 2 and 3).

3 As one would expect, relationships are found between Number of S & T visits, Number of publications sent, and Number of meetings attended.

4 Two other relationships are also interesting: one between the Number of unit members providing useful information and the Number of meetings attended (r = .31); the other between Contact with users and the Number of publications sent (r = −.19). This latter negative relationship might perhaps be explained by the priority of oral contacts over written ones (whenever they exist).

5 Except for this last relationship (r = −.19), the links between perceptual and countable measures are very weak or nonexistent and, when they exist, they are systematically higher for the unit heads (in line with point 2 above).

When replicating these relationships separately for each country, one sees that the above results generally stand across countries, but one also notes that: (1) The pattern of the relationships between the perceptual and countable measures varies from country to country; and (2) there exist statistically significant differences between countries as regards the strength of the interrelationships among the countable measures;[12] but (3) there is more similarity among countries as regards the perceptual measures. The first two results probably reflect real differences due to cultural context and to the person's communication practices; the third one is perhaps due to mental adjustment processes that are common to all human beings.

In conclusion, a rather consistent pattern emerges in the national, institutional, and scientific settings under consideration in this study as regards the relationships among the channel communication measures. Although some differences exist in the strength of these relationships, a final answer regarding the sources of these differences is not available at this stage.

Mean levels of the channel communication measures. Exhibit 9.4 shows the mean strength of the channel communication measures by Type of respondent, Type of institutional/scientific setting, and Country. A few interesting trends are worth highlighting.

1 *Contacts between units:* In academic units, heads and staff scientists tend to rate communication between units in the same way, but in units from cooperative research institutions and from productive enterprises staff scientists tend to assign higher ratings. There are differences among countries in both ratings by unit heads and by staff scientists.

2 *Contacts with users:* As one would expect, contacts with users are rated much higher in units from productive enterprises (and also in units from cooperative research institutions) than in academic units. There are differences between countries, some of which obviously reflect the sampling design. For instance, it is not surprising to see the same mean for

Exhibit 9.4. Channel communication as related to Institutional/Scientific setting and to Country

Channel communication	All units	Institutional/Scientific Setting				Country						
		Acad. Nat. Sci.	Coop. Res. Inst.	Prod. Appl. Sci.	adj. etas	Austria	Belgium	Finland	Hungary	Poland	Sweden	adj. etas
Perceptual measures												
Contacts between units (head's rating)	3.4	3.5	3.5	3.5	.10	3.4	3.2	4.2	3.2	3.1	3.1	.22
Contacts between units (staff scientists' rating)	3.5	3.5	3.8	3.7	.11	3.1	3.3	4.7	3.6	3.0	3.2	.33
Contacts with users (head's & staff sci.s' rating)	3.5	2.8	4.1	4.5	.44	4.1	2.8	4.0	3.2	3.7	3.0	.30
Contacts within units (head's rating)	3.5	3.7	3.1	3.6	.12	4.2	3.2	3.2	3.3	3.9	3.7	.23
Contacts within units (staff sci.s' rating)	3.2	3.3	3.0	3.2	.08	3.5	2.7	3.1	3.2	3.1	3.4	.16
Countable measures												
No. of S & T visits	1.7	2.1	1.5	1.3	.19	1.8	1.8	1.3	2.2	1.6	1.6	.18
No. of publications sent	2.3	3.1	1.9	1.0	.19	2.0	2.3	1.8	3.0	2.4	2.1	.22
No. of S & T meetings attended	3.9	3.9	4.2	3.6	.05	3.8	4.9	3.6	4.3	4.1	2.9	.23
No. of weeks' delay in receiving communications	1.4	1.2	1.6	1.6	.15	1.1	1.1	1.6	2.0	1.7	1.0	.31
No. of unit members providing useful information	3.5	3.5	3.4	3.7	.04	3.9	3.5	2.6	5.0	3.3	2.5	.52
Number of research units	1,222	482	245	217		244	193	219	222	192	152	

Note: Figures of the form X.X are means for the designated measure of channel communication. Figures of the form .XX are adjusted etas and show the strength of relationship between the designated measure of communication and the control variable once variation due to chance alone has been eliminated.

units in Belgium, Sweden, and academic institutions when one knows that 100% of units in Sweden and 84.6% of the units in Belgium are in academic institutions.

3 *Contacts within units:* They are systematically rated higher by the head than by the staff scientists, across countries, as well as across institutional/scientific settings. The rating is about equally high in academic units and units from productive enterprises, but is lower in units from cooperative research institutes. As a general rule, the network of rated channel communication is much looser in units of cooperative research institutes than in the other two institutional/scientific settings considered here.

4 *Countable measures:* Academic units tend to report a higher number of S & T visits and publications sent than the other two settings. Units from cooperative research institutes report the highest number of meetings attended and of weeks' delay in communications received. In units from productive enterprises, one finds a somewhat larger mean number of unit members providing useful information. Countries differ as regards countable channel communication, units from Hungary being generally considerably higher than the mean, and units in Sweden tending to be lower. These mean trends bear out real-life practices; experience and literature on the subject suggest that different channels of communication are preferred in different settings.

C. Contextual measures

The contextual measures considered here tap a number of structural, environmental, climatic, and managerial features that seemed as if they might be significantly related to communication both as a channel and as a signal. The following 13 indices, developed from selections among some 160 single original items, are used in the analyses that follow.[13]

Perceptual measures (rated data)

1 Morale in the unit as rated by the unit head: This index is the mean rating by heads of units, on three single original items dealing with: innovation and pioneering spirit in the unit, dedication to working in the unit, and degree of cooperation among scientists and engineers in the unit.

2 Morale in the unit as rated by staff scientists: This index is the average of the mean ratings by staff scientists of the unit on the three same original items as in the preceding index.

3 Professional competence of immediate supervisor: This index is the average of the mean ratings by the staff scientists on two original items dealing with satisfaction with the professional ability and knowledge of one's immediate supervisor.

4 Autonomy of the unit: The "autonomy" index has been derived from patterns of influence as rated by the head of the unit. A comparison was made between: (a) the influence exercised by the head of the unit and staff scientists inside the unit and (b) leaders outside the unit but within the institution and authorities or customers outside the organization.

The latter source of influence was subtracted from the former and the scale reversed. A positive result indicates a tendency toward autonomy.

Countable measures (discrete data)

1 Unit size: This index is the number of scientists in the unit three years ago plus the number now, divided by two.
2 Staff composition: This index has two categories: (a) units in which technicians are more numerous than scientists and (b) units in which scientists are equally or more numerous than technicians.
3 Age of the unit: This is an original item: the number of years the unit has existed.
4 Number of years R & D experience of the unit head: This is an original item, reported by the head.
5 Number of units in same/similar fields within easy access outside the organization: This index is the mean of the answer reported by the unit head and the mean of the staff scientists' answers.
6 Scientific staff turnover: This index is based on the number of scientists and engineers who left the unit and the number who joined during the past three years.
7 Number of research projects shared with other units: This is an original item.
8 Diversity of scientific fields borrowed by the head in his research work: This measure is based on reports by the heads of units.
9 Diversity of products resulting from the unit's work: This measure is based on reports by the heads of units.

Mean levels of the contextual measures. Before looking at the relationships between the contextual measures and communication, we examined how the contextual measures varied in different national and institutional/scientific settings. One-way analyses of variance were then performed, first using Country and then using Institutional/scientific setting as predictors. Two-way analyses of variance were then performed using both predictors in an additive model. Country tended to be the more important of the two predictors and explained from 1% to 20% of the variance, depending on which contextual dimension was being predicted. For most contextual measures, Institutional/scientific setting explained 2% or less of the variance (data not shown).[14] In order to check whether the relationships between Institutional/scientific setting and the contextual measures would be affected by Country, one-way analyses of variance were repeated on more homogeneous subsamples of units from Austria, Finland, and Hungary. The results show that although there was a difference in the size of the relationships from country to country, the form of the relationships remained stable. From this, it was concluded that the level of the contextual measures varies among countries, but that Country has no interaction effect within the sample under consideration in the study.

2. Relationships of contextual measures to channel communication

A. Perceptual dimensions of channel communication

This section deals with *perceptual* dimensions of channel communication (rated data).[15] Exhibit 9.5 shows the relationships between the 13 contextual measures considered in this chapter and communication as a channel.

Three trends stand out amid the generally weak relationships shown in Exhibit 9.5:

1 The two Morale indices show positive relationships to both between- and within-unit contacts. Thus it seems that both communication between units and within units are strongly conditioned by the innovative spirit, the dedication to work, and the sense of cooperation among staff members of the unit.

2 Perceptual contextual dimensions as rated by unit heads tend not to be related to perceptual communication dimensions as rated by staff scientists. The reverse is also true, though to a lesser extent.[16] This again could reveal a respondent bias, a linguistic difference, or is more probably explained by the fact that contextual dimensions and communication are, in real life, perceived and experienced differently by unit heads and by staff scientists.

3 Perceptual measures of contextual dimensions are much more strongly related to perceptual measures of communication than are the countable contextual measures. This leads one to hypothesize: (a) that there may exist a psycho-mental adjustment process common to all human beings that starts to work when a minimum level of fundamental needs is attained; and (b) that perceptual measures may be more relevant and hence more "objective" in human sociology than are the countable measures, the so-called objectivity of which is often confused with the systematic methodology of the counting process.

When replicated for each country and for the three institutional/scientific settings considered in the International Study, the results were very similar.

To summarize this section on the relationships between the contextual dimensions and *perceptual* measures of channel communication, one may note that: (1) countable contextual dimensions showed practically no relations to perceptual channel communication; (2) morale in the unit as rated by the head of the unit and by the staff scientists relates relatively strongly to communication as a channel; (3) within-unit channel communication is related more or less exclusively to Morale and Diversity of products; and (4) between-units channel communication is related only to Morale.[17]

Exhibit 9.5. Relationships between perceptual measures of channel communication and contextual dimensions

	Communication between units			Communication within units	
	Contacts between units		Contacts with users	Contacts within units	
Contextual variables	Head	Staff scientists	Head and staff scientists	Head	Staff scientists
Unit size	.01	−.07	−.06	−.02	−.10
Staff composition	.04	−.04	−.13	.08	.00
Age of unit	−.03	−.10	−.04	.01	−.04
No. of years R & D experience of unit head	.03	−.12	−.10	.00	−.10
No. of units in same/similar fields within easy access	.11	.15	.02	.02	.03
Scientific staff turnover	.05	−.03	.03	.04	−.01
Morale as rated by unit heads	.24	.08	.09	.41	.18
Morale as rated by staff scientists	.09	.27	.14	.12	.57
No. research projects shared with other units	.12	.02	.09	.04	.05
Diversity of sci. fields borrowed by unit head in his/her research work	.02	−.01	.00	.05	.06
Diversity of products resulting from unit's work	.02	.03	.06	.04	.04
Profess. competence of immediate supervision (as rated by staff sci.)	−.04	.06	.06	.04	.32
Autonomy of unit	.07	−.02	−.16	.12	.07

Note: Coefficients are Pearson *rs*. Scale of original items has been reversed for perceptual measures.

B. Countable dimensions of channel communication

This subsection deals with *countable* dimensions of channel communication (discrete data). Exhibit 9.6 shows the relationship between the 13 contextual dimensions considered in this chapter and communication as a channel.

In this exhibit, it is worth noting that the channel communication measures, except for Delay in communication, are most strongly related to Unit size, to Number of shared projects, and to Diversity of products resulting from the unit's work.[18] Upon reflection, the importance of these dimensions is not surprising. In Section 5 below, we look to see what effect, if any, variables such as these may have on the relationships between communication as a channel and as a signal. One records again (in a reverse way) the absence of relationships between perceptual contextual measures and countable channel communication measures.[19]

3. Relationships of channel communication to research-unit performance (signal communication)

The relationships between measures of channel communication and measures of research-unit performance (communication as signal) were first examined by looking at the results of one-way analyses of variance performed for the whole sample, and then replicated for the three institutional/scientific settings considered in this chapter. Fifty-six single original measures of channel communication were used as predictors of 11 signal communication indices (rated performance and output). The relationships found were generally linear. Although their size varied from one setting to another, their form and direction stayed remarkably similar across settings. During a second stage of analysis, the relationships (Pearson *r*s) between 24 channel communication indices and 11 signal communication indices were examined. Only a selection is presented in this chapter. The results first obtained on the whole sample were again replicated for each of the six countries and the three institutional/scientific settings considered in the study.

Exhibit 9.7 shows the relationships (Pearson *r*s) between 10 measures of channel communication and each of the 8 signal communication indices retained for the study (5 rated-performance and 3 output measures).

A striking result emerging from the analyses is that the perceptual measures of channel communication practically never relate to countable measures of signal communication; and, con-

Exhibit 9.6. Relationships between countable measures of channel communication and contextual dimensions

	Communication between units				Comm. within units
Contextual variables	No. of S & T visits	No. of publications sent	No. of meetings attended	Length of delay in communication received	No. of unit members providing useful information
Unit size	.31	.35	.32	.00	.46
Staff composition	.00	.09	−.03	−.10	−.19
Age of unit	.13	.15	.18	.00	.21
No. of years R & D experience of unit head	.14	.28	.13	−.09	.18
No. of units in same/similar fields within easy access	.17	.16	.29	.07	.28
Scientific staff turnover	.10	.12	.14	−.08	.17
Morale as rated by unit heads	.06	.07	.06	−.17	.04
Morale as rated by staff scientists	−.02	.00	.01	−.03	.04
No. of research projects shared with other units	.29	.23	.30	.06	.25
Diversity of scientific fields borrowed by head in his/her research work	.17	.17	.16	.08	.18
Diversity of products resulting from unit's work	.28	.30	.27	.13	.35
Professional competence of immediate supervisor (as rated by staff scientists)	−.03	.08	.01	.04	.03
Autonomy of unit	.10	.14	.07	−.27	.01

Note: Coefficients are Pearson *r*s. Scale of original items has been reversed for perceptual measures.

Exhibit 9.7. Relationships between channel communication and research-unit performance (signal communication)

Channel communication	General contr.	Recog-nition	Social effect.	Applic. effect.	R & D effect.	No. of published written products	No. of patents/ prototypes	No. of internal orig. reports
Perceptual measures								
Contacts between units (head's rating)	.11	.12	.07	.12	.15	.06	−.02	.03
Contacts between units (staff scientists' rating)	.04	.12	.07	.14	.11	.06	−.10	.03
Contacts with users	.14	.08	.26	.41	.23	.02	.02	−.02
Contacts within units (head's rating)	.18	.14	.07	.21	.22	.03	.06	.04
Contacts within units (staff scientists' rating)	.17	.11	.12	.21	.31	−.01	.11	.02
Countable measures								
No. of S & T visits	.15	.25	.09	−.01	.13	.35	.13	.15
No. of publications sent	.22	.38	.10	.01	.17	.42	.15	.17
No. of S & T meetings attended	.14	.24	.09	−.04	.12	.36	.07	.20
No. of weeks' delay in receiving communications	.00	−.01	.11	−.06	−.03	.09	.01	.07
No. of unit members providing useful information	.27	.28	.17	−.05	.20	.34	.21	.23

Note: Coefficients are Pearson *r*s. Scale of original items has been reversed for perceptual measures.

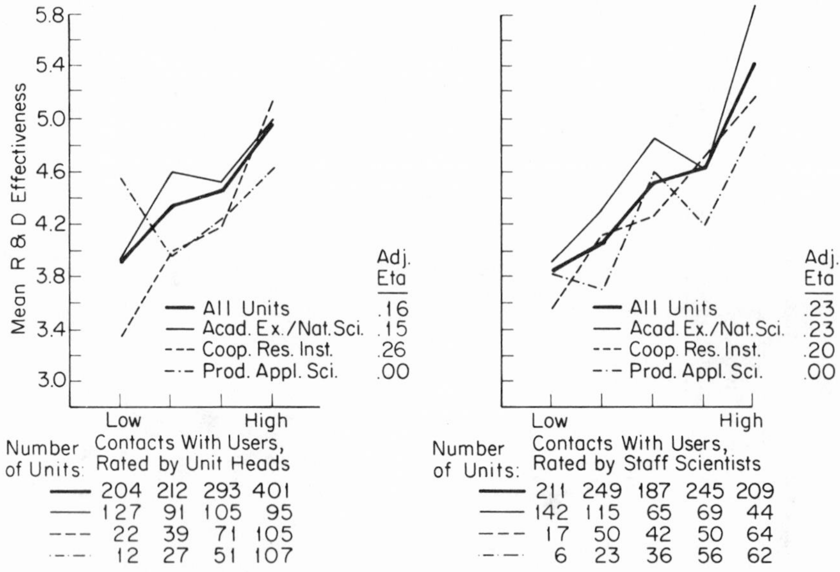

Exhibit 9.8. Mean R & D effectiveness by Contacts with users, in different settings, as rated by (1) unit heads and (2) staff scientists.

versely, the countable measures of channel communication are much more strongly related to one of the indices of signal communication (Number of published written products) than to any of the perceptual signal communication dimensions (rated performance).

As can be seen in Exhibit 9.7, each of the eight performance measures shows predominantly positive relationships to the channel communication measures. In some cases, these relationships reach the level of $r = .4$, though most are lower than this. Clearly, the trend is for more extensive communication to accompany higher levels of research-unit performance.

Replications of these results by Country and by Type of institutional/scientific setting show again an overall common pattern and, more often than not, a similar direction of relationships. However, statistically significant differences in the strength of those relationships do occur across settings. To explain these differences is beyond the scope of this chapter, but it deserves further study.

In a sort of visual conclusion of Section 3, Exhibits 9.8 and 9.9 illustrate, for a few typical cases, the general trend of the relationships and the extent to which differences exist between institutional/scientific settings.[20]

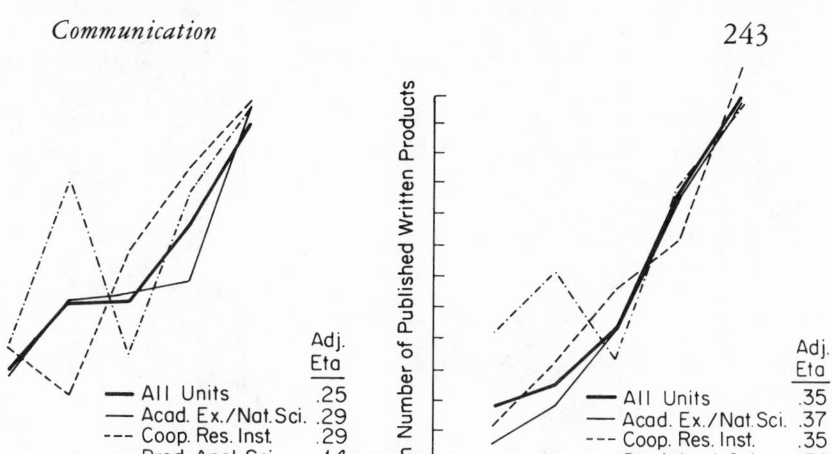

Number of Units:	0	1	2	3-4	5-8+
—— (All Units)	386	189	164	193	225
—— (Acad. Ex./Nat.Sci.)	112	79	67	93	120
--- (Coop. Res. Inst.)	86	47	30	30	40
-·-· (Prod. Appl. Sci.)	98	25	22	23	26

Number of Units:	0	1	2	3-4	5-8+
—— (All Units)	391	193	163	196	228
—— (Acad. Ex./Nat.Sci.)	111	80	66	93	120
--- (Coop. Res. Inst.)	87	48	30	30	41
-·-· (Prod. Appl. Sci.)	102	26	23	25	28

Exhibit 9.9. Mean Recognition and mean number of published written products, by Number of S & T visits, in different settings.

4. Multivariate relationships of channel communication to research-unit performance (signal communication)

On the basis of the bivariate relationships found so far between channel and signal communications (i.e., research-unit performance), we proceeded one step further to examine the multivariate relationships of the channel communication to each signal communication dimension. Multiple classification analyses and stepwise multiple regressions were performed in parallel for each performance dimension using the same seven channel communications as predictors – the seven that emerged as the most promising from the above analyses (see Exhibit 9.7). Although they differ from one performance measure to another, there is a clear preponderance of Within-unit contacts and Number of publications sent over the other channel communication measures as regards the explanation of variance in the performance measures. See Exhibit 9.10.

There are other points worthy of note:

1 For all six forms of signal communication, the first two predictors pertain in each case to between-units and to within-units channel communication dimensions.
2 The same two channel communication dimensions are the best predictors in the case of (a) General contribution and Recognition and (b)

Exhibit 9.10. Summary of multivariate relationships of channel communication to research-unit performance (signal communication)

Predictors	General contrib.	Recognition	Applic. effect.	R & D effect.	No. of published written products	No. of internal original reports
Contacts between units (head's rating)				5		
Contacts with users (ratings by heads and staff scientists)	3	3	1	2	5	4
Contacts within units (staff scientists' rating)	4	5	2	1		
No. of S & T visits		4			3	5
No. of publications sent	2	1	3	3	1	3
No. of S & T meetings attended	5		5		4	2
No. of unit members providing useful information	1	2	4	4	2	1
Percent of variance explained by model	14.8	22.4	20.9	19.2	30.9	7.0

Notes: Results are based on a series of six multiple classification analyses (Andrews et al., 1973) using, for each of the six performance measures, seven channel communication predictors. A replication with stepwise multiple regression gives nearly identical results.

Ranking of predictors is by decreasing order down to 5 (1 = most important predictor), based on ranking of MCA betas. (Betas give ability of predictor to explain variation in dependent variable after adjusting for effects of all other predictors.)

Only the first five channel communication predictors are ranked because: (1) Stepwise multiple regressions show practically no gain in explained variance after fifth predictor entered regression model (gain was less than 1% in each model), and (2) there was some disagreement between MCA and stepwise regression models for ranking of last two predictors.

Percent of variance explained by model is based on multiple R^2, adjusted for degrees of freedom.

Number of cases in each analysis is approximately 1,200.

Applications effectiveness and R & D effectiveness. For the last two, almost the same percentage of variance is explained by the whole model. One may conclude that throughout the whole chain of the R & D process, both the dialogue with the users and the contacts within units are equally important.

3 Not surprisingly, Number of published written products and Recognition are both best predicted by Number of publications sent.

4 A test was made to check the presence of first-order interactions involving the two best predictors in each case, and there were none. This result simplifies the potential application of the findings of this study to R & D management.

5. Impacts of some contextual dimensions on relationships between channel communication and research-unit performance (signal communication)

Communication is frequently considered in conjunction with the number of elements composing a network. The number of possible *connections* within a network increases much more rapidly than the number of its *elements:* The number of possible connections among n elements $= 2^n - 1 - n$. Potential relationships of the network components with the outside are even more numerous. This applies also to research units, for which it has often been argued that there is a critical size beyond which the potential channel communications are not fully exploited, or even interfere negatively with performance.

The effect of age on relationships between communication and performance has been less often considered. However, these effects also deserve attention. Section 5 attempts to evaluate how, and to what extent, the most important relationships between channel communication and performance (i.e., signal communication), identified in Section 4, are affected by three contextual dimensions: unit size, physical age of scientific staff, and professional age of scientific staff.

A summary of the results is shown in Exhibit 9.11. One can observe that the percentage of variance explained in the Recognition measure (and to some extent in General contribution and Number of internal reports) by the channel communication predictors tends to be lower in large units, units with older scientific staff, and units where the scientific staff has more years of R & D experience. Just the opposite occurs for Applications effectiveness (and to some extent for R & D effectiveness and Number of published written products). Whether these contradictory trends are each meaningful can only be answered by further research.[21]

Exhibit 9.11. Percent of variance explained in measures of research-unit performance by measures of channel communication, controlling for Unit size, Age of staff, and Experience

Performance measures	Unit size (scientists)		Age of scientific staff (years)		R & D experience of scientific staff (years)	
	1–5 (N = 708)	6 or more (N = 460)	22–33 (N = 693)	34 or more (N = 480)	1–7 (N = 702)	8 or more (N = 469)
General contribution	12	13	16	13	17	11
Recognition	25	14	24	17	24	16
Applications effectiveness	17	28	20	24	18	25
R & D effectiveness	17	17	17	21	19	19
No. of published written products	25	28	29	30	29	31
No. of internal original reports	7	1	8	9	7	7

Note: Figures are percent of variance explained (after adjusting for fluctuations due to chance alone) in indicated performance measure by four best channel communication measures (as shown in Exhibit 9.10) using multiple classification analysis.

6. Overall scheme of relationships among channel communication, contextual dimensions, and performance

Having reached the stage where the relationships of channel communication to signal communication (i.e., performance) have been somewhat clarified, as well as the relationships of contextual dimensions to both of them,[22] we have tried to throw into relief an overall scheme of relationships that might characterize research units. It was felt that such a scheme, especially if it holds across institutional/scientific and national settings, might prove useful to R & D managers, and could also serve as a departure point for further research.

Using a set of 29 measures that cover channel and signal communication and also contextual dimensions, and that seem most promising in the light of the above analyses, a series of correlation matrices were obtained (1) for all the units in the sample, (2) for each of the three institutional/scientific settings, and (3) for the six countries considered in the study. Because regression or causal analysis techniques might, in the present case, oversimplify or misrepresent reality (e.g., because of inappropriate assumptions about feedback loops, Exhibit 9.12 presents a simple summary of the general *pattern* of observed interrelationships.[23]

The following results deserve mention:

1 Two broad clusters emerge – perceptual measures and countable measures. Relationships involving Recognition constitute the only important linkages between the two clusters.
2 Within the cluster of perceptual measures, the following dimensions are more often and more strongly related to the others: (a) signal communication: Recognition, R & D effectiveness; (b) channel communication: Contacts within units as rated by staff scientists; (c) contextual dimensions: Morale as rated by the unit head and by the staff scientists, Professional competence of the immediate supervisor (usually the unit head).
3 Within the cluster of countable measures, the following dimensions are more often and more strongly related to the others: (a) signal communication: Number of published written products; (b) channel communication: Number of publications sent, Number of meetings attended, Number of scientific and technological visits, Number of unit members providing useful information; (c) contextual dimensions: Unit size, Diversity of products, Number of shared projects.

These patterns hold across institutional/scientific settings and across national settings, with a few variations.[24] Once again, this emphasizes the fact that a general common pattern exists across settings with, however, certain relationships being more relevant to one setting than another. Without going so far as to present these results as a "recipe" for R & D managers, they do throw

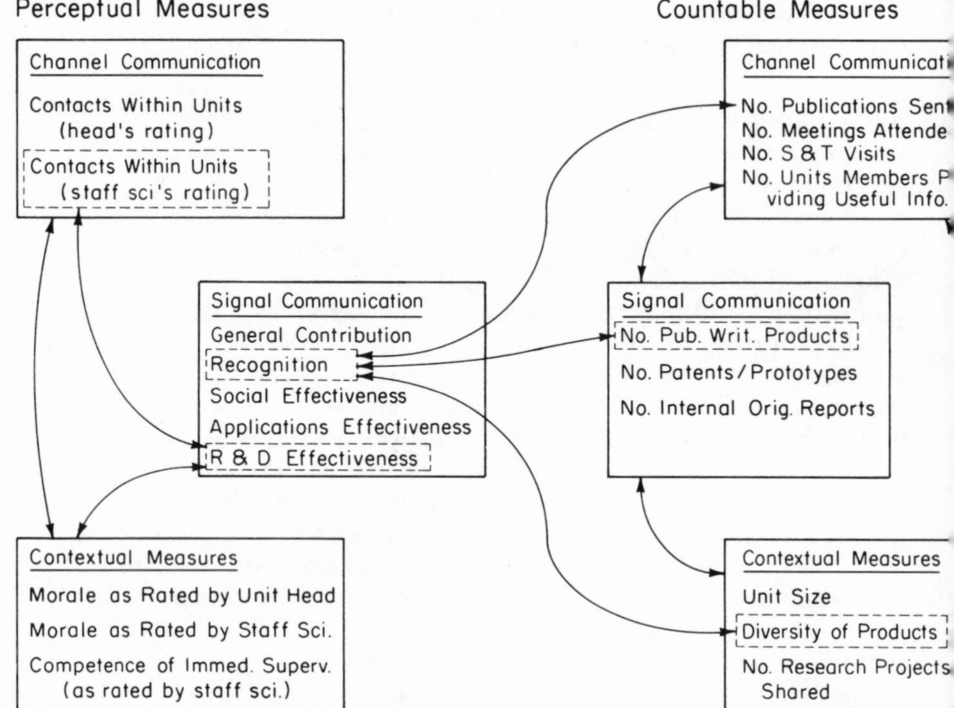

Exhibit 9.12. General pattern of relationships among measures of channel communication, research-unit performance (signal communication), and contextual dimensions.

some light on those channel and signal communication (research-unit performance) and contextual dimensions, the presence of which is crucial for the healthy functioning of the research units examined in this study.

7. Discussion

This chapter began with a series of questions. Some have been answered within the limits of the data examined; others require further thought and research.

One important result is that whatever the type of respondent, the national setting, or the institutional/scientific setting, a common *pattern* of network relationships appears between the dimensions considered in the study. On the other hand, significant differences appear as regards the *strength* of these relationships, depending upon the type of respondent and the type of setting. This indicates, we think, the presence of a macrocultural dimension over and above differences due to national, institutional, and scientific settings. The extent to which these differences are justified and must be preserved should be further investigated.

Clearly, there is a set of communication and contextual dimensions that are more strongly related to each other than to others (see Exhibit 9.12), and these give useful insight into the elements that make up the best research units.

As regards the relationships of channel communication to research-unit performance (i.e., to signal communication), it appears that both *between* and *within* communication dimensions are important, with a slight predominance of the latter. It should be recalled that (1) between-units communication is represented by *countable* measures, whereas within-unit communication is represented by *perceptual* measures; and (2) between-units and within-unit communication, appearing as the first two predictors of performance, show effects that simply add together (i.e., that show no statistical interaction).

Whatever the dimensions considered, *perceptual* measures and *countable* measures tend to relate within themselves but not to each other. This leads one to hypothesize (1) that there exists a psycho-mental adjustment process, common to all human beings, which starts to work when a minimum level of fundamental needs is attained, and (2) that perceptual measures may be more relevant in human sociology than countable measures and lend themselves better to generalization; hence they may have high potentialities for further applications. More research on the comparability and compatibility of these two types of measures, and on their respective merits, would be welcomed. The contents of the countable measures may seem, at first glance, more precise and objective than perceptual measures. However, one should not confuse precision with materiality, nor objectivity with the counting process. The perceptual measures, it is true, imply a multidimensional approach, which is less easy to delineate exactly, but which is perhaps more apt to properly reflect a sociological reality which, in any case, is operationally complex.

Heads of units tend to have a more holistic approach to channel communication than do staff scientists.

8. Conclusions for action

The results presented in this chapter on "Communication between and within research units" could be used in two different domains of action, depending on the interests at issue: R & D management and "research-on-research."

As far as R & D managers are concerned, they might wish to think of ways to provide research units with those conditions and facilities that enhance both communication between units *and* within units. Indeed, whatever the national and the institutional/ scientific settings, both between-units and within-unit communication proved to have a strong relationship with the Recognition of the units, their R & D effectiveness, their Number of published written products, and their Applications effectiveness. The importance of channel communication with regard to signal communication (research-unit performance) cannot be underestimated when one realizes that both the between- and within-units communication indices explain as much as 22% of the variance in Recognition, 21% in Applications effectiveness, 19% in R & D effectiveness, and 31% in Number of published written products.[25] This suggests that these communication dimensions are crucial to the performance of research units. R & D managers might also like to keep in mind that good communication within units seems to be even more important than communication between units.

As far as "research-on-research" is concerned, the results presented in this chapter pose a series of questions that call for further research. The following lines of inquiry could, in our mind, be usefully pursued:

1 a multi/inter-disciplinary and cross-cultural approach to the understanding of communication in R & D.
2 a study of the extent to which differences in the strength of relationships observed between national and institutional/scientific settings among the dimensions examined in this study (a) are justified, and (b) should be preserved.
3 a study on the compatibility and comparability of perceptual measures versus countable measures, and their respective merits in terms of scientific and managerial efficiency.
4 a refinement and expansion of this chapter's study as regards the role of contextual dimensions with respect to communication as a signal and as a channel.
5 an attempt to define a typology of research units based on more subtle social, cultural, and scientific affinities than the traditional approach derived from types of institutions, types of products, or broad scientific fields.

Whoever uses the results of this study should keep in mind the fact that they are only relevant to the contextual environments of the research units that have been examined. The results do not necessarily represent a model or ideal pattern of communication.

Reference

Havelock, R. G. et al., 1969, *Planning for Innovation through Dissemination and Utilization of Knowledge,* Ann Arbor, Institute for Social Research, Center for Research on the Utilization of Scientific Knowledge, University of Michigan.

Notes

1. Primordial but not unique or sufficient in itself; communication in the domains of biology, feelings, or esthetics is, for other reasons, as important.

2. As a result of an agreement between the co-authors of this book, this chapter uses the *performance typology* whose development is detailed in Chapter 13 for assigning research units to institutional/scientific settings; however, the author considers that this typology is somewhat tautological, and that it tends to reinforce existing stereotypes in the organization of science instead of opening new avenues of thought and action.

3. "Contextual measures" refer to structural, environmental, climatic, and managerial features of research units.

4. Relationships between contextual dimensions and communication as signal (i.e., research-unit performance) were also examined by the author. This portion of the analysis is not reported in this chapter in order to keep within the general organization agreed upon by the authors of this book. The reader will find similar findings in Chapters 8 and 10. Section 6 of this chapter, however, presents the author's major conclusions [editor's note].

5. For the purpose of this International Comparative Study, a research unit has been defined as follows: (1) has at least one leader who is a core member; (2) has at least three core members, each of whom has been a research-unit member for at least half a year; and (3) has a total expected life span of at least one year. A "core member" is a person who devotes at least eight hours per week to the work of the research unit and who has communication (direct or indirect) with the unit leader(s) at least once each month.

6. The five types of institutions are: (1) universities, similar institutions of higher education, and research institutes closely associated with universities; (2) institutions attached to academies of science (in the socialist countries) and to national research organizations; (3) research institutes serving wholly or partly a sector of production, a branch of industry, or a public service; (4) research laboratories of productive enterprises; and (5) contract research institutes.

7. The four main types of respondents are unit heads, staff scientists and engineers, technical support staff, and external evaluators. In most cases, the administrative questionnaire was answered by the head of the unit, but in some cases this respondent was the administrator of the unit, who constitutes a fifth type of respondent.

8. The development of the performance typology is fully described in Chapter 13.

9. In the unit-level data file, there is one record per research unit, containing, in sequence: the original data for the unit and the head; and the aggregate data for each of the three types of other respondents. The aggregate measure used in the communication analyses is exclusively the mean.

10. Chapter 14 details how estimates of construct validity were obtained.

11. The last measure is specific to the communication analyses and is based

on a questionnaire item that read "Internal reports on original R & D work within the unit's organization." We chose not to use the Reports measure developed by the International Research Team (which is described in Chapter 2) because we felt that this measure combines data that are conceptually and statistically rather distinct, i.e., it combines internal *routine* reports with internal reports on *original* R & D work.

12. Between Number of S & T visits and Number of meetings attended, Pearson *r*s are .51 in Sweden, .28 in Hungary, .26 in Austria, .18 in Poland, and .37 in both Belgium and Finland. This is because the index includes S & T visits in the country *and* abroad. Indeed, when considering only S & T visits in the country, the relationship is strong and stable across countries.

13. Age and Number of years of R & D experience of the scientific staff are used in Section 5 of the chapter but are not described here.

14. The major exception was for Autonomy of the unit; 21% of the variance of this measure could be explained by Institutional/scientific setting.

15. Subsection B of this section deals with the relationships of contextual measures to *countable* dimensions of channel communication.

16. This is true also for other dimensions not shown here, and also for the technical staff when compared with the scientific staff and with the head of the unit.

17. As noted above, findings concerning the relationships between the contextual dimensions and signal communication (research-unit performance) are not reported here. It is worth mentioning, however, that Morale is a crucial dimension also for rated signal communication within the unit and that Diversity of products is generally strongly related to measures of rated signal communication within and between units. Moreover, countable contextual dimensions show practically no relation to perceptual signal communication.

18. Replications of these relationships for each of the six countries and each of the three institutional/scientific settings led to very similar results. It is worth mentioning that the two contextual dimensions most highly related to countable signal communication are Diversity of products and Unit size.

19. This is true also with the countable signal communication measures.

20. The channel communication measures used as predictors in Exhibits 9.8 and 9.9 are *single items* (and not indices); although the results are comparable to those that would be obtained using indices, they should not be treated as identical.

21. In addition to the results reported in Exhibit 9.11, a parallel series of analyses was run to examine the gain in explanatory power when Country was added to the channel communication predictors. Although Country did show some predictive power over and beyond that of the communication measures (increasing the variance explained by up to 6 percentage points), it did not alter the basic pattern of Exhibit 9.11.

22. Details of the author's exploration of relationships between contextual dimensions and research-unit performance are not included in the chapter, for reasons described in note 4 above. Highlights of the results appear in this section [editor's note].

23. Exhibit 9.12 is a summary of a series of correlograms (single-linkage analyses). Its results are generally consistent with those from a series of principal component analyses run on the same correlation matrices, details of which are not presented here.

24. The compactness of the network of relationships is, for instance, much stronger in units from cooperative research institutes.

25. See Exhibit 9.10.

10 Motivation, diversity, and the performance of research units

Frank M. Andrews
Institute for Social Research,
University of Michigan, Ann Arbor

1. Introduction

Why do some research teams show higher levels of performance than others? It is unquestionably the case that some teams are more effective than others, and it is widely assumed that at least part of the explanation for the difference lies in the ways that teams are managed. If team leaders and members could find ways to arrange their working lives so as to increase the performance level of their units, the benefits to themselves, to science, and to the larger society could be substantial. This chapter examines two aspects of the working situation that past investigations suggest may be related to the performance of research units.

The first factor is strength of motivation. Some teams seem dedicated to the work they are doing. For them, the research or development in which they are engaged presents high challenge. They are heavily involved in what they are doing and committed to making the maximum possible progress on the task before them. In these labs, the lights are on well after the formal quitting time and there is hardly time for an extended lunch or

The assistance of Elizabeth Keogh and Marita DiLorenzi in the data processing for this chapter is gratefully acknowledged. Selected portions of this chapter have been presented at the Joint Meeting of the Society for Social Studies of Science and the Research Committee on the Sociology of Science of the International Sociological Association (Ithaca, N.Y., November 1976), and at the Annual Convention of the American Sociological Association (Chicago, Ill., September 1977).

coffee break. This chapter will show that motivation varies systematically from team to team (and hence can be considered as a characteristic of the research *unit,* as well as of the people who are members of the unit), and that where this sense of dedication is high, many kinds of research performance also tend to be high.

The second factor is diversity. In the management of research there arise numerous specific issues that revolve around the extent to which diversity is better (or worse) than focused specialization. Does modest time spent on administration, or on teaching, detract from a scientist's research output? What about time spent consulting with outside clients? Is it better to pursue several projects simultaneously within a research unit, or to concentrate all the available time and talent on just one? Is there any systematic difference in overall performance between units that bring an interdisciplinary orientation to their work and those that are more specialized? What about the number of distinct research methods in the repertoire of a unit – do units that use more different methods tend to perform at higher levels than one-method units? Does it make any difference for a unit's performance whether its scientist members are spread out along the age, seniority, or education ranges, or all rather similar? Is there any advantage in having a diversified funding base – some money coming from the host organization, some from outside grants or contracts – as compared to getting all support from a single source? Decisions about how people in units spend their time, what people are hired, what skills they bring or acquire, the methods that are used, and funding sources are all in the purview of research managers – the team leader and/or persons higher in the organization. These are factors that Managers can influence, and this chapter will show that some of these diversity factors – but not all of them – do relate to performance.

Organization of the chapter

The chapter consists of two main sections, which are followed by several smaller sections. The first main section examines motivation; the second, diversity. Each of the main sections begins by summarizing previous research on the relationship between scientific performance and the factor being considered. Next, the ways the factor was measured in this chapter's study are described. Then follow the statistical results – first, how units varied with respect to the factor; second, how different indicators of the factor relate to one another and to various aspects of research-unit performance; and third, multivariate analyses in which different indicators of the factor are combined to predict performance. Each of the two major sections winds up with a short discussion of the major conclusions. After motivation and diversity have each been explored separately, the two are considered simultaneously to see how well they can jointly explain several aspects of research-unit performance. The chapter then concludes with a general summary.

2. Motivation and performance

The idea that more dedicated scientists might do better research and development work is not a new one. It has obvious links to parallel ideas that high esprit de corps will contribute to the effectiveness of military units, that high morale will help a firm become profitable, or that high commitment is important for political party workers, monks, or bureaucrats. Although the idea is an appealing one, the expected relationship among scientists has been questioned by research results that will be cited shortly, and–so far as is now known–has never before been examined as a phenomenon characterizing research units as a whole and related to units' performance.

Some past research on motivation and scientific performance

In 1965, Lodahl and Kejner published an article titled "The definition and measurement of job involvement." They wrote: "Job involvement is the degree to which a person is identified psychologically with his work, or the importance of work in his total self-image" (p. 24). They recommended several items (to be answered on a degree-of-agreement scale) that could be used to measure workers' sense of job involvement. These included: "The major satisfaction in my life comes from my job," "The most important things that happen to me involve my job," "I live, eat, and breathe my job," and "I am very much involved personally in my work." Their concept of job involvement is essentially identical to what we shall mean by *strength of motivation* or *dedication*.

In a more recent article, Lawler and Hall (1970) distinguished between three types of attitudes that workers hold toward their jobs. The three were "job involvement," "satisfaction," and "intrinsic motivation." They accept the Lodahl and Kejner definition cited above for job involvement and include the items recommended by Lodahl and Kejner in their questionnaire. The Lawler and Hall article is interesting for two reasons. First, based on a factor analysis of questionnaire data obtained from 291 scientists in 22 American R & D laboratories, they conclude that job involvement is a concept statistically separate from both satisfaction and intrinsic motivation. Thus, Lawler and Hall plead that a sense of involvement in work should not be confused with either satisfaction with work or with a belief that specific rewards will follow from a job well done. Second, they found their measure of job involvement, which consisted of the four items cited above (selected from the earlier work of Lodahl and Kejner), to be uncorrelated ($r = .01$) with self-rated performance! Thus, here is one study in which the "obvious" relationship between strength of motivation and a measure of scientific performance did not appear.

The expected relationship also failed to appear in another study reported by Goodman, Rose, and Furcon (1970). Although they found reasonable convergent and discriminant validity for the Lodahl and Kejner measure of job involvement (Goodman, Furcon, and Rose, 1969), they found an essentially zero relationship with four measures of scientific performance (*r*s ranged from +.10 to −.07). Their finding is based on data from 66 employees of a U.S. government research laboratory.

Should we believe – on the basis of these two studies – that a scientist's motivation is unrelated to his or her research performance? This is contrary to what a naive observer would expect. It is also contrary to findings from an earlier and much larger study of American scientists by Pelz and Andrews (1966). Working at about the same time as Lodahl and Kejner, but independently from them, Pelz and Andrews incorporated in their questionnaires a set of five items that they used to measure dedication. The items asked scientists to indicate their feelings of involvement and identification with their work, and to say how challenging, important, and interesting they found it. Using data from more than 1,300 scientists, they found that these items showed significant positive relationships to both ratings of performance and actual outputs of scientific products for scientists of widely different types and in widely different types of laboratories. Relationships tended not to be very strong (most *r*s were .2 or .3), but they were consistent and positive.

When the job involvement measure proposed by Lodahl and Kejner, and subsequently administered to scientists by Lawler and Hall and by Goodman, Rose, and Furcon, seems so similar to the concept assessed by Pelz and Andrews, it seems strange that similar relationships to performance did not emerge. The explanation may reside in the relatively weak performance measure employed by Lawler and Hall, and in some idiosyncrasy of the relatively small number of cases investigated by Goodman, Rose, and Furcon, but these can be only speculations. Although the Pelz-Andrews data are undoubtedly the more extensive, and their result seems more in accord with expectation, the presence of contrary findings calls for further examination and for attempts at cross-national replication. The data of the International Comparative Study on the Organization and Performance of Research Units are well suited for such explorations.

Measurement of strength of motivation

The questionnaire used in this chapter's study included three items tapping strength of motivation. All asked respondents to indicate their answers by picking one of five categories along a scale ranging from "X" to "Y" according to the degree to which the X or Y statements applied.

In the first item, the X and Y statements were as follows: (X) "There is an atmosphere of great dedication to work in the unit"; (Y) "There is a feeling that everyone in the unit only works to make a living." We shall refer to this as the *dedication* item. For the second item, the polar categories were: (X) "I do a great deal of voluntary overtime"; (Y) "I do no voluntary overtime." This is the *voluntary overtime* item. And the third item read: (X) "The work I do is very interesting"; (Y) "The work I do is not very interesting." We call this the *interest of work* item. Note that in the first item the respondent reports a perception regarding the research unit, whereas in the latter two the reference is to a feeling or action of the individual person. Although all three items appeared within the same major section of the questionnaire, none was immediately adjacent to any other. All surveyed respondents–unit heads, staff scientists, and technical support staff–were asked the first two items; the third item, on interest of work, was not asked of the unit heads.[1] After aggregating answers from the staff scientists and from the technical support staff and computing means for each, there were eight "basic" motivation measures: two from the unit head, three from the other scientists, and three from the support staff.

Levels of motivation in different types of respondents and units

Our main interest in motivation is in how it relates to the performance of research units. However, further insight regarding the motivation measures themselves and some interesting background information will come from a brief look at how motivation levels varied for different types of respondents and in different types of units.

Types of respondents and motivation levels. In general, levels of motivation were highest for scientists who were heads of units, and lowest for people in technical support roles. Staff scientists tended to fall between these two extremes.

The biggest differences appeared with respect to voluntary overtime. On the five-point scale ranging from "I do a great deal of voluntary overtime," to "I do no voluntary overtime," the technical support members tended to put themselves about in the middle. The unit heads, however, tended to put themselves just a half-step short of the most extreme "I do a great deal. . ." answer. (Nonsupervisory scientists tended to put themselves about one full step short of the extreme answer.) This very same pattern appeared in each of the five types of research units[2] and in each of the six countries that participated in Round 1 of the International Comparative Study (data not shown).[3]

That unit heads tended to see themselves as spending more voluntary overtime than did others in their units is, of course, no surprise to anyone familiar with the organization of R & D, and, we believe, lends credence to the validity of this measure.

Unit heads were not asked how interesting they found the work, but staff scientists and technical support members were, and here again we find an absolutely consistent difference – in all types of units and in all countries. People in technical support roles tended to judge the work they performed less interesting than did the staff scientists for the work that *they* performed. Again, the difference is in accord with what informed observers would expect and hence supports the validity of the measure.

The smallest difference appeared for the item that asked about dedication in the research unit, and this also is entirely reasonable. Recall that unlike the previous two items, which inquired about personal activities and feelings, this one asked for a judgment about the unit. On this item, support personnel and nonsupervisory scientists gave – on the average – the same answer, and unit leaders gave answers that indicated only slightly higher dedication. Ideally, there would have been no differences on this item according to a person's role in the unit, because all answers referred to the same thing – the general sense of dedication in the unit. The fact that supervisors saw the unit as more highly dedicated than did the other members may be wishful misperception on their part!

Types of units and motivation levels. When we compared types of units for levels of motivation, reports of voluntary overtime stood out. There was a clear distinction between academic settings and others: Scientists (both team leaders and others) in academic settings tended to report more voluntary overtime than did scientists in either cooperative institutions or industrial organizations. Interestingly, there was *no* such difference for people in technical support roles; these people claimed about the same amount of voluntary overtime regardless of the type of unit they were in.

With respect to the interest of the work, staff scientists in academic units tended to rate their work as of slightly higher interest than did those in industrial organizations (those in cooperative institutions fell between), but the differences were rather small. As with voluntary overtime, the interest of the work to people in technical support roles did not vary much according to their type of unit.

A somewhat similar pattern emerged for dedication: a tendency for it to be rated higher in academic units than in others. The differences on this item across the five types of units were not sharp (and the staff scientists showed some exceptions), but the trend was clearly present for both the unit heads and the support staff.

Comments. These very reasonable patterns of differences, as well as being interesting in their own right, help us to have confidence that the questionnaire items intended to tap motivation levels are in fact reflecting motivation. It comes as no surprise to find that team leaders seem more motivated than the technical support staff, with the staff scientists located in between. And to find these differences bigger for the voluntary overtime and interest items than for the dedication item is just what one should expect when one realizes that the first two are descriptions of individual characteristics, whereas the latter asks for perceptions of the team as a whole. Although there might be more debate as to what differences should be expected across types of units, our finding that motivation levels, particularly voluntary overtime, were highest in academic settings will match the expectations of many observers.

Strength of motivation as a characteristic of the research unit

Relationships among the eight basic motivation measures are not strong, but are consistently positive and, in most cases, statistically significant.[4] The correlation between the two items answered by the unit heads is .19; the mean correlation among all possible pairs of the three measures based on answers by the staff scientists is .31 (range: .26–.39); and the comparable mean for measures from the technical support people is .20 (range: .14–.29). It follows, then, that items asking about dedication, voluntary overtime, and interest of the work do show modest co-variation and that this pattern is replicated for all three types of respondents. For the data from staff scientists and technical support staff, where our measures are *mean scores* from all such respondents in the unit, it is hard to attribute this co-variation to anything other than that the items all tap a common phenomenon – the level of motivation within the unit.

Two additional sets of results also suggest that motivation levels vary systematically from unit to unit.

Another way of investigating whether motivation can be regarded as a *unit* characteristic is to see whether different types of members in the same unit tend to give similar answers regarding the level of motivation in that unit. Hence, we looked to see whether there was statistically significant agreement among the answers given by the unit head, the average of the answers given by the staff scientists, and the average of the answers from the technical support people. These relationships were all positive and were all significantly different from zero.[5] Agreement was highest with respect to the dedication item (*r*s here ranged from .21 to .25) and lowest for the voluntary overtime item (range: .08–.20). Given that the dedication item asked respondents to describe a characteristic of the unit as a whole, whereas the other items asked about individual actions or feelings, it is reasonable that the dedication item showed the highest convergence. The fact that members in different roles within the same research unit tended to show at least modest agreement regarding the extent of motivation within the unit is further evidence that motivation level varies systematically from team to team.

In a different approach to this same question, we looked to see how the variation among staff scientists within the *same* unit compared with that of staff scientists in *different* units. If motivation level can be considered a characteristic of the unit, then the variation within units should be less than that between units. To test this, a *strength of motivation index* was computed for each individual staff scientist by summing his or her answers to the dedication and voluntary overtime items. Then differences between scientists within the same unit were compared with differences between scientists in different units. (The analysis was done separately in each of the five types of research units so that any motivation differences that might be attributable to type of unit could not influence the results.)

Our expectations were clearly supported. Typically, there was twice as much variation between units as within units, and the same general pattern occurred in each of the five different types of units (median value = 2.0; range: 1.7–2.5).[6]

We conclude, then, that research teams differ systematically with respect to their members' motivation levels and that it is meaningful to consider strength of motivation as a characteristic of the unit as a whole.

On the basis of the findings reported in this section, we constructed a unit-level measure, which we shall call the *Motivation index,* by summing four of the more basic motivation measures – the unit head's answers to the dedication and voluntary items, and the mean answers to these items given by the staff scientists in the unit.[7] (Other basic measures could also have been included in a general index but would have proved redundant, as will be shown in the next section.)

Relationships of motivation strength to research-unit performance

We are now ready to see how the general level of motivation within the research units related to their performance. Exhibit 10.1 provides some of the results. Shown there are correlations (*r*s) between the eight basic motivation measures, plus the Motivation index, and 10 different measures of performance. (All performance measures have been adjusted to remove variation that could be attributed to differences between types of units.)

Several types of findings emerge in Exhibit 10.1.

First, the relationships between motivation and performance tend to be positive; the few negative relationships are, without exception, all very small. As a very general statement, then, it appears that research units in which there is a higher sense of commitment are the units in which performance – at least some aspects of it – tend to be higher.

Second, nowhere in Exhibit 10.1 are the relationships very strong. Differences between units in their members' sense of dedication, voluntary overtime, and interest in the work do not by themselves explain a large part of the differences in units' performance.

Third, some aspects of performance show higher relationships to members' motivation than others. Motivation tends to be most highly related to ratings of R & D effectiveness. It seems clearly

Exhibit 10.1. Relationships of motivation strength to 10 measures of research-unit performance

	Motivation items								
	Dedication			Voluntary overtime			Interest of work		Motivation index
Performance measures	SA	SB	TS	SA	SB	TS	SB	TS	
Rated effectiveness									
General contribution	.21	.18	.06	.09	.07	.02	.20	.15	.22
Recognition	.20	.15	.08	.12	.10	−.02	.21	.08	.23
R & D effectiveness	.25	.30	.11	.15	.19	.08	.28	.12	.36
Training effectiveness	.18	.14	.06	.14	.14	.02	.12	.08	.24
Social effectiveness	.08	.15	−.02	.10	.09	.06	.19	.06	.17
Applications effectiveness	.11	.18	.09	.04	.10	.12	.09	−.01	.17
Administrative effectiveness	.17	.13	.07	−.00	−.01	.01	.06	.09	.11
Output									
Published written output	.07	−.03	.03	.12	.04	−.05	.09	.04	.08
Patents and prototypes	−.05	−.02	−.03	.05	.02	−.01	.03	.07	−.02
Reports and algorithms	−.03	−.03	−.00	.06	−.01	.05	.00	.01	−.01

Notes: SA = head of research unit; SB = staff scientist of research unit; TS = technical support personnel. N ≈ 1,222 research units in six European countries. Coefficients are Pearson *r*s. Using conventional tests, all *r*s ⩾ .06 would be statistically significant at .05 level. All performance measures have been adjusted to remove differences attributable to type of research unit; see text.

unrelated to output of Patents and prototypes and of Reports and algorithms.

Fourth, motivation reported by the *scientists* in a unit (both the unit head and staff scientists) shows somewhat stronger relationships to performance than does the motivation reported by the technical support staff. (Compare the SA and SB columns in Exhibit 10.1 with the TS columns.[8]) Although this finding might not have been predicted in advance, it does not seem unreasonable. Given that most of the initiative for the work of a research unit comes from its professional members, what may be of primary importance for the technical support staff is the conscientious application of their technical skills, and this may be possible even in the absence of a high sense of commitment to the particular projects on which the unit is engaged.

Fifth, note that the Motivation index provides a convenient summary of the general patterns just discussed and, in some cases, shows relationships to performance that are somewhat stronger than those indicated by any one of the more basic measures. This is particularly evident for R & D effectiveness and Training effectiveness, but occurs for other aspects of performance as well. We assume this results from the Motivation index being a more broadly based – and hence more valid – indicator of the sense of commitment by scientists within a research unit, and from the likelihood that it is commitment by *all* scientists that is related to unit performance.

Several checks suggest that the use of Pearson *r*s and the *adjusted* performance measures in Exhibit 10.1 is indeed appropriate. The correlation coefficient *r* indicates only the linear component of a relationship, but a careful initial exploration showed that these relationships are in fact primarily linear. (Some of the evidence for this will be seen shortly in Exhibits 10.2 and 10.3.)

With respect to the use of adjusted performance measures, we can report that the same general pattern of results also appeared for the unadjusted performance measures. However, by using the adjusted measures we are assured that differences in the focus of a unit's work (e.g., academic units give relatively more emphasis to training and publication, whereas industrial units focus more on applications and patents) did not generate spurious relationships with motivation.[9]

Having determined that across the full set of research units included in our data motivation showed modest positive relationships to some aspects of performance, it is important to check the generality of this finding. Relationships similar to those shown in Exhibit 10.1 were examined separately for each of the

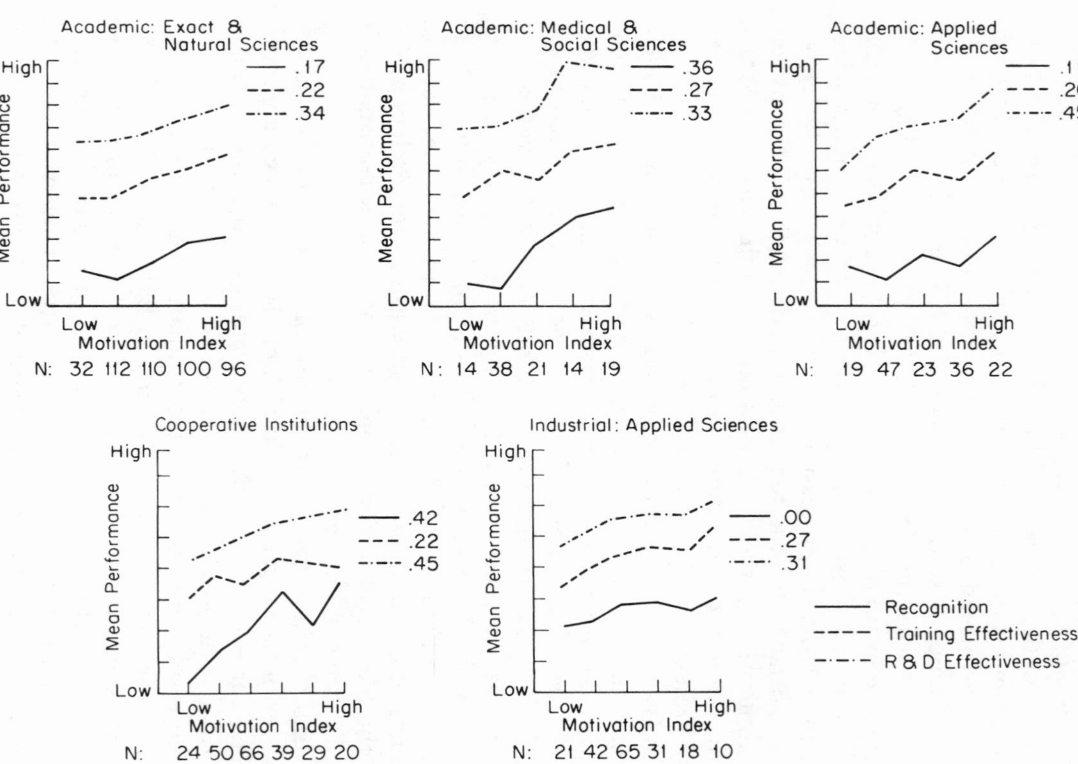

Exhibit 10.2. Mean performance by motivation in designated types of research units.
Note: All performance measures have been adjusted to remove differences attributable to type of unit. Eta statistics have been adjusted for degrees of freedom.

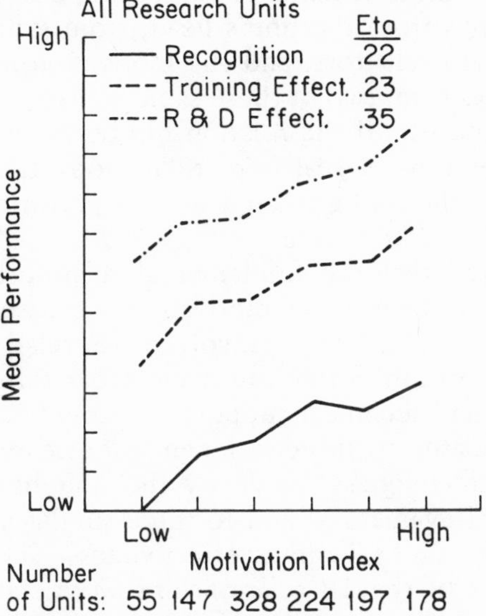

Exhibit 10.3. Mean performance by motivation.
Note: All performance measures have been adjusted to remove differences attributable to type of unit. Eta statistics have been adjusted for degrees of freedom.

five types of research units and for each of the six countries. With remarkable consistency, the same trends emerged. We conclude that the patterns shown in Exhibit 10.1 occur very generally – in units located in widely different types of organizations, investigating widely different scientific disciplines, and set in widely different national cultures.

Exhibits 10.2a–10.2e plot the relationship between the Motivation index and three selected performance measures for each of the five types of research units. Exhibit 10.3 shows the same results for all units combined.

Further checks on the motivation–performance relationship

Three further checks on the relationship between motivation and performance help to increase our confidence in the findings just presented.

The first check was to be sure the results could not be attributed to some essentially erroneous but widespread biasing of answers by respondents. Although we did not expect this to account for the relationship, this possibility existed and needed to be examined. The possibility exists because the rated-effectiveness measures used in Exhibits 10.1, 10.2, and 10.3 are indices based on ratings from the unit's head, from staff scientists, and from external evaluators, and the motivation measures also incorporate ratings from two of these same sources – the unit head and the staff scientists. If the relationship between motivation and performance were a real one, then motivation as reported by one source should be related to unit performance as reported from an *independent* source.

The analyses showed that the fundamental relationship emerges even when performance and motivation are assessed by independent observers. Our check involved 18 relationships: judgments of the motivation in the unit made separately by unit head, staff scientists, and technical support personnel (as shown in Exhibit 10.1), as related to three independent assessments of the unit's R & D effectiveness (made by the unit head, staff scientists, and external evaluators) and to three similar independent assessments of the unit's Training effectiveness. The important finding is that *all* of the 18 relationships were statistically significant and positive. On the basis of this, we conclude that the relationships shown in Exhibits 10.1–10.3 cannot be attributed simply to the fact that the performance and motivation measures came from overlapping sources.

The second and third checks were directed at the Motivation index. This index involves only four of the total of eight basic motivation items, and it combines those four in a simple and arbitrary (but not unreasonable) way. We wanted to know whether some more complex combination of the basic information might yield an index with a higher relationship to performance. The second check, then, involved computing a series of multiple regressions predicting performance from all eight basic motivation measures. Our conclusion was that the simple four-item Motivation index was doing about as well as a more complex weighted additive combination of all eight measures. For example, we found that the Motivation index correlated .35 with the (unadjusted) R & D effectiveness measure, whereas the multiple correlation of all eight motivation measures predicting the same performance measure was .40.[10] For Training effectiveness, the comparable figures were .38 and .39; for Recognition, .33 and .36; and for Published written output, .22 and .31. Although some modest gain in predictive power could be achieved by constructing, for each performance measure, a specially weighted additive combination of motivation items, it is clear that the maximum potential gain over the explanatory power offered by the Motivation index is small, and that the Motivation index is both much simpler conceptually and does not need to be reweighted for different performance measures.

These multiple regression analyses looked at *additive* combinations of the motivation items. The third check looked at certain *nonadditive* combinations. We wondered whether a multivariate relation to performance substantially stronger than that shown by the Motivation index was likely to be achieved by some complex nonadditive combination of the basic measures. We scanned the data for first-order statistical interactions, found none of note, and concluded that it was most unlikely that there was any way of combining the motivation items that would be markedly superior to that used in the Motivation index.

These three checks, then, provide added assurance that the relationship that emerges between motivation and performance is a real one, and suggest that our Motivation index provides a simple, general, and reasonably effective way of tapping it.

Discussion and conclusions on motivation and performance

Four general conclusions emerge in this section of the chapter. First, we have seen that items intended to tap strength of work motivation among members of a research unit relate to one another in expected ways and also show reasonable differences in levels between unit heads, other scientists, and technical staff. These findings support the validity of the motivation measures.

Second, we have seen that motivation levels show systematic variation across units. There is more variation between units than within, and – within a given unit – people in different roles tend to show somewhat similar motivation levels. It follows that it is reasonable to think of motivation strength as a characteristic of the *group* of people banded together to conduct a research project: Teams, as such, tend to be more or less committed to their work.

Third, we have seen that a team's commitment to its work relates to many (but not all) aspects of its research performance. The strongest relationships appear for ratings of the team's R & D effectiveness; all other ratings of effectiveness show some significant relationship to the team's motivation, and so does output of published written products. The output of patents and prototypes, and of reports and algorithms, however, seem unrelated to the team's motivation. Although the relationships are not strong, they are remarkably general, occurring for units of all five types and for units in all six countries.

Fourth, we have seen that a relatively simple Motivation index reflects most of the predictive power of the basic motivation measures and that more complicated additive or nonadditive indices offer little promise of further gains.

Before concluding this section, we would briefly consider the strength of the relationships we have observed. How should we interpret the correlations between the Motivation index and performance? Even the strongest–the .36 with R & D effectiveness–is clearly not overwhelming. It seems important to remember two things when looking at results such as these.

The first is that these data provide less than perfect indicators of the phenomena in which we are interested. Even if a pair of phenomena were highly related, an investigator would obtain only a low correlation between indicators of these phenomena if the indicators included large amounts of random measurement error. Although we have some empirical estimates of the internal validity and random error components of the performance measures (reported in Chapter 14), we have no similar estimates for the motivation measures. If, however, we were to assume that the composition of the Motivation index were identical to that estimated for the R & D effectiveness measure,[11] what would we conclude about the relationship of "true" motivation to "true" R & D effectiveness? An estimated correlation of .49 can be derived. Similarly, the underlying relationship between "true" motivation level and the "true" General contribution of the unit can be estimated at .30.[12] Thus, by applying a set of previously obtained empirical estimates and some admittedly large but not unreasonable assumptions, we generate results suggesting that the motivation level of the unit might explain 10–20% of the variance in those aspects of performance to which motivation is most relevant, after allowing for the invalidities and common biases in the measurements.[13]

The second thing to be remembered when considering the strength of the motivation–performance relationships is that one should not expect anything as complex as the performance of a research unit to be fully explained by any one factor. Experience and common sense suggest that the level of a unit's performance is determined by a multitude of factors, including such "obvious" factors as the skills and intelligence of its members and the availability of appropriate methods and materials for the task at hand. Correlations of 1.00 should not be expected in investigations such as this one, and if as much as 10% or 20% of the variance in performance can be explained by a single organizational factor we should probably be satisfied.

Finally, we would add a caution about causal assumptions.

What the statistical results show is that motivation levels are significantly related to at least some aspects of research-unit performance. The results do not prove that higher motivation causes higher performance. Given only these results, one cannot be sure that causality may not operate in the other direction – that is, that good performance leads to high motivation, or conceivably, that both motivation and performance are the result of some third factor. (However, our analyses have explicitly eliminated two of the most likely "third" factors: The relationships persist even when the performance measures are adjusted for differences between types of units; and the possibility of the results being due to simple response bias has been eliminated.) With the data presently available, it is not possible to determine the extent of causal priority (or reciprocity) between motivation and performance. For the present, we must be satisfied at having demonstrated the existence and generality of the relationship and at having obtained some approximate estimates of its strength.

3. Diversity and performance

More than a decade ago, Pelz and Andrews (1964, 1966; Andrews, 1964) showed that diversity in the professional activities and skills of American scientists related to enhanced levels of performance. Scientists who split their time among several R & D functions – basic research, applied research, development, invention, consultation – tended to be rated as making larger scientific contributions and as being more useful to their organizations, and also tended to produce more papers, patents, and/or reports. Similarly, scientists who spent less than full time on R & D, devoting some time instead to teaching and/or administration, actually outperformed those whose sole activity was research. Having current knowledge of several areas of specialization rather than just one, and being engaged in more than just a single project also were related to higher levels of performance.[14]

The positive relationships between diversity and performance were not very strong (etas ranged up to the .50s but averaged in the .20s), but were notable for their consistency. The basic data came from 1,311 scientists and engineers spread across 11 R & D organizations in the United States. Included were laboratories in university, industrial, and government settings; and labs oriented toward basic science, applied science, and engineering development. The positive relationships appeared in all of these settings. Furthermore, the positive relationships appeared for widely different indicators of technical performance: for actual counts of reports, papers, and/or patents produced over the past five years, and also for evaluations made by informed judges of the scientific contribution and usefulness of the output. And, as noted above, the relationships appeared for a variety of different indicators of diversity: diversity in R & D functions, in time allocations, in specializations, and in project commitments.

Further analysis showed that the diversity–performance relationship was not a spurious result of differences between supervisors and others, or of differences in age, seniority, or level of training.

Of course, the Pelz-Andrews analysis did not prove that increased diversity causes increased performance, but we can speculate on the dynamics by which diversity *might* enhance performance. Five reasons come to mind:

1 Through involvement in diverse activities, projects, specialities, etc., scientists may acquire substantive information that, if available, can be productively used in solving a given research problem. Thus, diversity may lead to the acquisition of *directly useful intellectual resources*.
2 Diversity may help one to acquire *knowledge and skills that can contribute indirectly* to solving a research problem. Because of the needs of one project, one may learn how to use a computer, how to hire or fire staff, who is expert in a particular subject matter, or where to find support–and then use this knowledge for later projects.
3 Diversity may enhance the effectiveness of a person's or unit's "*self-guidance*." Through contact with multiple funding sources or involvement in multiple disciplines, administrative activities, etc., there may come an expanded and better perception of the important scientific problems that might be feasibly tackled, and of the most promising ways of moving ahead on these problems.
4 Diversity may provide opportunities for *productive fallow periods*. It is widely supposed that intellectual progress occurs in spurts–periods of intense creative activity are interspersed with periods of consolidation and perhaps even neglect. When a person or unit has alternative responsibilities and projects, it may be possible to push ahead on one for a while, then turn productively to another while necessary follow-up actions occur for the first (e.g., allowing the plants to grow, the support staff to compute, or the brain to mull over an idea).
5 Diversity may offer *security*. Research is, almost by definition, an uncertain activity: Hypotheses are sometimes not confirmed, money sometimes runs out, staff sometimes leave, papers sometimes get rejected, equipment sometimes fails to arrive or breaks down. Even the best scientists and research units have "low" periods, and diversity may help to minimize the depths of the lows and ensure survival.

The positive relationships between diversity and performance raises intriguing social and psychological issues and has obvious management implications. However, diversity seems not to have been further explored until this writer undertook to see whether results similar to those that seemed broadly applicable to American scientists would also appear in other cultural and national settings.

The International Comparative Study of Research Units provides an opportunity for an extended exploration of the diversity–performance relationship in European labs. The four aspects of diversity examined for American scientists – projects, specialties, research functions, and time allocation – can each be examined here, and a substantial number of additional diversity indicators can also be considered. In contrast to the Pelz-Andrews focus on diversity in the lives of individual scientists and on scientists' individual performances, the broader European data let us focus on diversity across a whole research team and on the performance of the team as a whole.

Measurement of diversity within research units

Data from the International Comparative Study permit examination of nine conceptually distinct aspects of diversity. For most of these aspects, it was possible to construct multiple indicators and a total of 70 diversity measures have been examined. We describe each of the nine conceptual aspects and the indicators relevant to each:

1 *Diversity in projects.* On the assumption that diversity would increase with the number of projects being conducted by the unit and/or by its members, several project counts were obtained. The unit heads reported the number of research projects in which they had "been directly involved during the last three years . . . either as executor or project officer." They reported separately for projects they conducted inside the unit and projects conducted outside. The staff scientists answered an identical pair of questions. In addition, the unit heads reported the total "number of research projects carried out inside the unit at the present time." From these data, five number-of-project measures were obtained (number of projects in which the head personally was involved both inside and outside the unit, mean number of projects in which staff scientists were personally involved both inside and outside the unit, and the head's report of the total number of projects ongoing within the unit).[15]

2 *Interdisciplinary orientation.* Immediately following a series of questions on general methods used by the research unit (described below), there occurred this question: "In carrying out your research projects, do you borrow some methods, theories, or other specific elements developed in other fields, not normally used in your research?" The answer was a simple "yes" or "no" and was intended to tap the interdisciplinary orientation of the research. If respondents answered "yes," they were asked to list up to three scientific fields from which these elements were borrowed. These items were answered by both unit heads and staff scientists and yielded three diversity measures: interdisciplinary orientation as reported by the head, interdisciplinary orientation as reported by

other scientists (taken together and averaged), and a count of the number of scientific disciplines from which the unit head reported borrowings were made.[16]

3 *Diversity in specialities.* On two occasions the unit head was invited to list fields of specialization. At one point the instruction asked for "up to three . . . fields of specialization acquired in your R & D work." At another point the head was asked to list six "scientific fields in which the research unit . . . has been actively engaged during the last three years." In both cases the specialities that might be mentioned were defined by an accompanying list, the International Standard Nomenclature for Fields of Science and Technology. Many heads did not list the maximum number permitted by the instructions, and two diversity measures were constructed by counting the number of specialities actually listed.[17]

4 *Diversity in funding sources.* Several measures of diversity in support were derived from information about the percentage of the unit's income obtained from various sources. The administrative officer for the unit (or the unit head) was asked: "Please indicate the percentage distribution of last year's income of the unit according to sources of funds." Five distinct sources were given as possibilities: (a) "the organization's own funds"; (b) "grants or contracts earmarked for the unit, originating from research foundations, research councils and similar grant-giving bodies, both public and private" (within the unit's own country); (c) "grants or contracts earmarked for the unit, originating from industrial or commercial enterprises, both public and private" (within the unit's own country); (d) "grants or contracts earmarked for the unit, originating from other sources" (within the unit's own country); and (e) "foreign sources of funds."[18] Three of these five sources showed enough variation to offer possibilities as diversity measures – use of own funds; funds from foundations, research councils, etc.; and funds from industrial or commercial enterprises. For each of these three sources, diversity was scored low if the unit drew either all or none of its support (0% or 100%) from it, and high if the unit drew only part of its support from it (i.e., 1–99%). In addition, a general *funding diversity index* was derived by considering all five possible funding sources. If the unit drew 95% or more of its support from *any one,* it was assigned a low score on the funding diversity index; otherwise the unit received a high score.

5 *Diversity in R & D activities.* Questionnaires completed by both unit heads and other scientists included a series of items that asked respondents to indicate the extent of their involvement in 10 R & D activities. Involvement was indicated on a five-point scale (ranging from "very high" to "very low") for the following: (a) "perception and identification of an area of interest"; (b) "literature review"; (c) "problem precision: conceptualization, formulation, analysis"; (d) "orientation and perception of methods and techniques, apparatus, etc."; (e) "time-table, administration, organization and economic considerations"; (f) "formation and statement of hypotheses"; (g) "research design: planning, strategies and experimental outlay"; (h) "collection and production of data, including experimental work"; (i) "results, detailed analysis, interpretation and conclusions"; and (j) "report writing, e.g., for publication, dissertation, etc."[19] Two diversity measures were constructed by counting the number of different activities for which "high" or "very high" involvement was claimed. One measure was based on the unit head's response,

whereas the other was based on the means of the responses of the other professional members of the unit.

6 *Diversity in professional functions.* A series of questions directed to the professional-level members of each unit asked them to "indicate . . . in percentages how much of your total work time (= 100%) you have spent this year on" a series of nine different functions. These included: (a) "research and experimental development inside the unit," (b) "research and experimental development outside the unit," (c) "administration," (d) "teaching . . .," and (e) "consulting work . . . ."[20] Separate measures were constructed for each of the functions mentioned here, and answers by the unit head were distinguished from the mean of the answers by the other scientists. A transformation of these basic measures produced the diversity measures: When the time allocation to a given function was either very large or very small (defined as 95–100% or 0–5%), diversity with respect to that function was scored as low; when time allocations fell in the range 6–94%, diversity was scored as high. These data yielded 10 indicators of diversity in time allocation (5 for the unit head and a parallel 5 for the staff scientists).

As people spread their efforts across more different functions, we assumed that diversity would increase, and hence another pair of measures was constructed by counting the number of different functions in which the scientists reported spending at least 10% of their time. One measure was based on information from the unit head; the other, on the mean of the time allocations reported by other scientists of the unit.

7 *Diversity in methods used in the research work.* Scientists in the unit were asked to rate the significance of five general methods for their research work along a four-point scale ranging from "insignificant" to "essential." The methods were: (a) "systematic use of hypothesis"; (b) "formulation of axioms or postulates from which theorems are deduced through applications of formalized logic"; (c) "factorial analysis, multivariate analysis, probabilistic models, dimensional analysis models, etc."; (d) "operational models, morphological models, inductive models, predictive models, matrices of discovery, system analysis, etc."; and (e) "brainstorming, forecasting, synectics, etc."[21] The expectation was that use of more methods might result in more diversity, and a pair of measures was constructed (one based on answers from the unit head, the other on mean scores from the staff scientists) by counting the number of methods that were said to be either "essential" or "tending to be essential."

8 *Diversity in team leadership.* In some research units the leadership responsibilities are shared among a number of people. This was assessed by a simple questionnaire item that read: "The unit has one head/more than one head." The administrative officer of the unit (or the unit head) was asked to pick one alternative.[22] It seemed that units having more than a single head might be characterized by greater diversity, and hence answers to this item were used as a diversity indicator.

9 *Dispersion measures.* Because the data from many units include information from more than just one staff scientist, it is possible to examine the dispersion (or heterogeneity) among these people within a single research unit. The same is true for members of the technical support staff. It seemed that heterogeneity in demographic characteristics, in attitudes, in work assignments, in motivation, and the like might act as sources of diversity for the unit. A total of 39 different dispersion measures was

used at one point or another. These included: (a) 6 measures tapping heterogeneity in strength of work motivation (based on items described in the first section of this chapter – interest, voluntary overtime, and dedication of staff scientists, and a parallel set for technical support staff); (b) 9 measures tapping heterogeneity among staff scientists with respect to allocation of time across professional functions (described in group 6 above); (c) 10 indicators of heterogeneity among these same scientists with respect to R & D activities (listed in group 5); (d) 5 indicators of heterogeneity among these same people with respect to methods used in the work (listed in group 7); (e) one measure of heterogeneity in perceptions of interdisciplinary orientation of the unit (described in group 2); (f) 3 indicators of "demographic" heterogeneity among staff scientists – heterogeneity in age, in years of education, and years of R & D experience;[23] and (g) a miscellaneous collection of 5 other dispersion measures: 4 tapped heterogeneity among staff scientists with respect to frequency of discussing one's work with others in the organization, satisfaction with opportunities for these kinds of contacts, sense of time pressure, and perception of an innovative spirit within the unit; the fifth tapped heterogeneity among the technical support staff with respect to sense of time pressure.[24]

Comment. Although this list of 70 different diversity measures may initially appear formidable, it should be remembered that it is through broad exploration of the diversity concept that we stand the best chance of gaining an improved understanding of the concept itself and how it relates to the performance of research units. These are the topics to which we turn next: How do the different diversity measures relate to one another? And how do the diversity measures relate to performance? Although the scope of our exploration is broad, the answers to these questions fall into clear patterns and the basic results of the analysis are not difficult to see.

Interrelationships among diversity measures

Is *diversity* a unitary concept that varies in a simple way across research units – some units being high, others low, and still others at various intermediate levels? Or is diversity multifaceted? And if diversity is multifaceted, what are some of its aspects?

By examining interrelationships among the various diversity measures, a clear answer emerges: It is multifaceted. Units high in some aspects of diversity are not necessarily high in others.

Let us consider the diversity aspects that emerge from a statistical analysis of the 70 measures just described. (The previous classification of these 70 measures into nine *conceptual* groups anticipates some of the statistical clusters, but some conceptual groups did not produce distinct empirical clusters).

Diversity with respect to projects (conceptual group 1) is one aspect of diversity that makes both conceptual sense and that emerges as a distinct empirical cluster. Not surprisingly, units in which the head reported there being an above-average number of projects underway tended to be the same units in which scientists – both the head and others – reported themselves working on relatively large numbers of projects (average r among these 3 diversity measures = .36; range: .22–.58). Furthermore, project diversity tends to be quite distinct from other aspects of diversity.[25]

The interdisciplinary orientation of a unit (conceptual group 2) emerges as another empirically distinct aspect of diversity. Three measures are available here, and the average correlation among them is r = .50 (range: .31–.87). The fact that a very strong relationship exists between the two measures of this group that depend on data from the unit head is in part attributable to the structure of the questionnaire and is not particularly interesting. What *is* interesting, however, is that independent observers – the unit head and other scientists in the unit – were in at least modest agreement (r = .31) about whether borrowings were made from other fields. This cluster of measures is either statistically independent or only weakly related to all other diversity measures, thus suggesting that the interdisciplinary orientation of a unit should be treated as another distinct aspect of diversity.

The third conceptual group has to do with the number of scientific specialities in which the unit's head is skilled and the number of specialities that the unit itself uses. The correlation between the two measures in this group proved to be .33, and neither measure showed any strong relationships to any other diversity measure. We expected that this aspect of diversity might be related to the interdisciplinary orientation of the unit, but the statistical results show this not to be the case (average r among measures assessing these two aspects of diversity = .01), hence we treat diversity in specialization as distinct from interdisciplinary orientation.

A fourth cluster of measures emerging in the data has to do with support sources. The basic structure of the questionnaire – which asked for a percentage allocation of the unit's funding across several support sources – suggested that a cluster of diversity measures should appear here, and in fact it did (average r among diversity measures based on the three major sources = .40). The adequacy of the Funding diversity index, described above, is indicated by substantial correlations between the index and its major components (range: .44–.82). Funding diversity is virtually unrelated to any other diversity measure (with the minor exception of a weak relationship – r about .15 – between Funding diversity and the number of specialities claimed by the unit leader).

These first four conceptual groups of measures – diversity with respect to projects, interdisciplinary orientation, specialities, and funding sources – were the only ones to produce substantial empirical clusters. The agreement between unit heads and staff scientists regarding the number of methods used in their work (conceptual group 7), although statistically significant, was rather modest at $r = .14$. The same is true for the agreement between heads and staff scientists regarding the number of professional functions performed (group 6), for which $r = .10$. The two measures of diversity in R & D activities (conceptual group 5) showed virtually no relationship to one another ($r = .03$), and only weak relationships to any other diversity measures. Interestingly, none of the large group of dispersion measures (conceptual group 9) was related to any other measure of diversity either within or outside its group.

Thus, it seems that diversity is not a unitary concept. Rather, one must speak of diversity with respect to a particular matter, and consider the relationship of each aspect of diversity to the performance of research units.

Relationships between diversity and performance

Basic results. Exhibit 10.4 presents some of the relationships that have motivated our exploration of diversity. Shown there are correlations between selected diversity measures and three measures of research-unit performance.

Two things stand out in this exhibit. All relationships are positive; none is very strong, but nearly all are statistically significant. It follows, then, that some aspects of diversity do tend to accompany higher levels of certain types of performance in these European data. Although the trends are modest, they do appear and they operate in the expected direction. Furthermore, analogues to each of the four aspects of diversity investigated previously by Pelz and Andrews – time allocation to professional functions, number of activities performed, number of specialities, and number of projects – are included in Exhibit 10.4 and show results that replicate the American findings.[26]

Supporting analyses. The analysis reported in Exhibit 10.4 was undertaken only after several preliminary explorations of the underlying relationships, a few of which appear in Exhibits 10.5 and

Exhibit 10.4. Relationships of selected diversity indicators to three aspects of research-unit performance

	Rated effectiveness		Output
	Recognition	R & D effectiveness	Publications
Diversity in Projects			
No. of projects in RU	.19	.11	.25
No. of SA's projects within RU	.17	.15	.20
No. of SB's projects within RU (mean)	.12	.12	.16
Interdisciplinary orientation			
SA report	.20	.11	.15
SB report (mean)	.15	.11	.11
No. of other discip. borrowed from	.18	.11	.16
Diversity in specialities			
No. of SA's specialities	.15	.11	.23
No. of active specialities in RU	.08	.06	.05
Diversity in funding sources			
Index of funding diversity	.13	.14	.13
Diversity in R & D activities			
No. of R & D activities of SA	.13	.15	.00
No. of R & D activities of SB (mean)	.14	.08	.06
Diversity in professional functions			
SA spends part time on R & D in RU	.10	.17	.09
SBs spend part time on R & D in RU	.09	.10	.07

Notes: SA = head of research unit; SB = staff scientist of research unit. N ≈ 1,222 research units in six European countries. Coefficients are Pearson *r*s. Using conventional tests, all *r*s ⩾ .06 would be statistically significant at .05 level. All performance measures have been adjusted to remove differences attributable to type of research unit.

10.6. It was important to know, for example, whether performance tended to increase regularly with each added discipline, speciality, project, or R & D activity – or whether, after showing initial increases, performance peaked and then stayed constant, or peaked and then declined, as diversity increased. With minor exceptions, the general trend for the diversity measures that are based on counting potential inputs tended to be reasonably linear. At least within the range of alternatives offered in the questionnaire and chosen by the respondents, the more disciplines, specialities, projects, and R & D activities, the better. Exhibit 10.5 shows plots for one of these "counting" type measures.

The major complement to the diversity measures based on

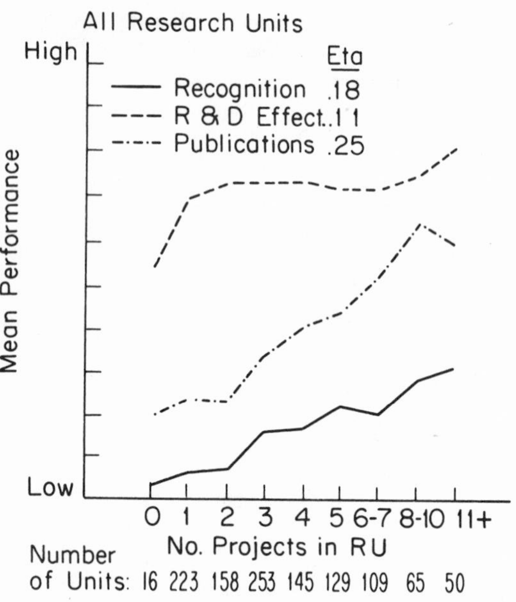

Exhibit 10.5. Mean performance by number of projects in the research unit.
Note: All performance measures have been adjusted to remove differences attributable to type of unit. Eta statistics have been adjusted for degrees of freedom.

counts are those derived from percentage allocations. When respondents indicated the percentage of their time spent on various functions, or the percentage of the unit's income coming from various sources, the basic diversity hypothesis suggests a *curvilinear* relationship. For example, scientists who spent some of their time on R & D within the unit, and also some time on other functions, would experience more diversity and hence be expected to show higher performance than those who spent either all or none of their time on the R & D function. Curvilinear relationships with performance did indeed tend to appear for these percentage-based measures, a few of which can be seen in Exhibit 10.6. [As noted in the section on measurement of diversity, it was necessary to transform the data of these percentage items to produce a measure of diversity per se. Once the high and low values had been grouped together as indicating less diversity, and the intermediate values treated as indicating more diversity, linear relationships with performance were expected (and found), and it became reasonable to use the product-moment correlations shown in Exhibit 10.4 to measure their strength.]

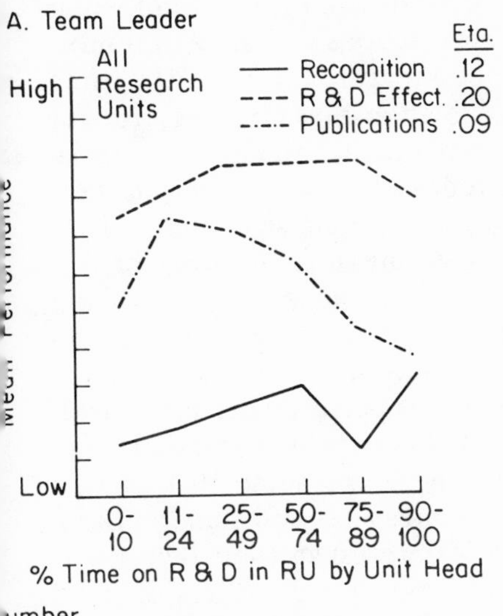

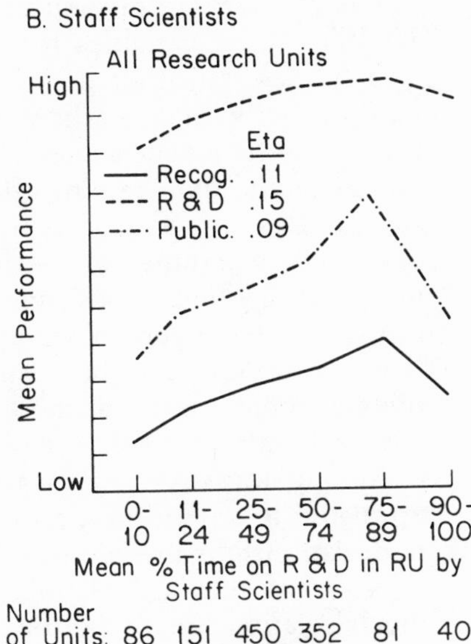

Exhibit 10.6. Mean performance by percent time spent by (A) team leader and (B) staff scientists on R & D within the unit.
Note: All performance measures have been adjusted to remove differences attributable to type of unit. Eta statistics have been adjusted for degrees of freedom.

A second preliminary exploration checked to see how stable the diversity–performance relationship might be across the different European countries and across the five types of research units (described in note 2 above) represented in the data. Although there was some variation in the relationships from country to country, and from one type of research unit to another (as one would expect, given the modest size of the correlations in Exhibit 10.4 and the much smaller number of cases available for these subgroup analyses), the general trend seemed replicable. More than 400 diversity–performance relationships were examined, and there was no country and no type of unit that consistently gave results contrary to those in Exhibit 10.4.

The results in Exhibit 10.4 suggested that perhaps differences in unit size might account for the diversity–performance relationship. Could it be that larger units would be more likely to have multiple projects, skills, funding sources, etc., than smaller units and also be performing at higher levels? Several checks showed that the positive relationship between diversity and performance could not be explained by size differences alone; it persisted even when size was controlled.

The measures of diversity and performance included in Exhibit 10.4 are those variables for which relationships appeared most clearly. Several other performance measures showed the same patterns but with generally weaker relationships. This was true for the rated-effectiveness measures of General contribution, Social effectiveness, and Training effectiveness, and for the output measures of Patents and prototypes and Reports and algorithms. However, the remaining two performance measures – ratings of Administrative effectiveness and of Applications effectiveness – did not replicate the general trends. For these two measures all correlations were low, and there were about as many negatives as positives. It seems clear that these aspects of performance have virtually nothing to do with any of the diversity factors assessed here.

Among the diversity measures, there are some that proved unrelated to any of the performance measures and some of these nonrelationships are of considerable interest in their own right.

None of the large number of dispersion measures showed much relationship to performance. This suggests that whether the staff scientists and technical support personnel of a research unit are heterogeneous or homogeneous (in age, education, seniority, or any of various attitudes or behaviors relevant to the unit) has little to do with the unit's performance. Although there may be valid reasons for trying to build some degree of demographic heterogeneity into the membership of research units (as is common practice in some organizations), these data suggest that short-term performance reasons should not be among them.

A second interesting nonrelationship pertains to the number of broad methodological approaches used by members of the unit. There was no evidence that use of a variety of methodological approaches was in any way superior to exploitation of just a single methodological approach.[27]

Other potential aspects of diversity that were unrelated to performance include whether leadership of the research team was vested in just one person or divided among several persons, and the number of projects the unit head or staff scientists happened to be involved in outside the unit.

We would comment on the effect of adjusting the performance measures to remove differences associated with type of research unit. With only a few exceptions, all the relationships in Exhibit 10.4 held for the raw measures as well as for the adjusted ones. The exceptions seem attributable to essentially spurious linkages between the type of unit, diversity, and performance. One obvious example occurred for diversity in time devoted to teaching (none versus some) and Training effectiveness. Using the raw performance measures, this relationship stood at .4 for both unit heads and other scientists (higher than any of the relationships shown in Exhibit 10.4). With the adjusted measures, however, this relationship dropped to .1. Given that most aspects of diversity tended to be somewhat higher in research units located in academic institutions than in units located elsewhere,[28] it seems clear that the previously strong relationship was the result of combining academic and nonacademic units in the same analysis. The weaker relationship seems a truer representation of the possible effects of diversity.

By considering the relationships among the full set of diversity and performance measures, we can see the results of Exhibit 10.4 in better perspective. Some forms of performance (Applications effectiveness and Administrative effectiveness) seem unrelated to any form of diversity, and some aspects of diversity (intragroup heterogeneity, use of multiple methods, and multiple leadership) seem unrelated to any form of performance. Nevertheless, we have identified a rather wide range of distinct diversity measures that do show consistently positive relationships to various forms of research performance.

Combinations of diversity measures. No one of the diversity measures, by itself, showed very strong relationships to performance. However, given that diversity is a multifaceted phenomenon, one wonders whether stronger relationships would emerge if several different aspects of diversity were to be considered simultaneously. Do research units in which two or three (or more) aspects of diversity are present tend to outperform those in which only one aspect is present? Do effects of diversities cumulate?

A series of stepwise multiple regressions was run to obtain the answer, and the answer is clearly "yes." Diversity effects "add."

Three multiple regressions were run, one for each of the performance measures shown in Exhibit 10.4 – Recognition, R & D effectiveness, and Published written output. Each regression used the same nine diversity measures to predict performance. These nine were selected from those shown in Exhibit 10.4, so as to tap each of the six aspects of diversity shown there. (Measures that prior analysis had shown to be largely redundant were omitted.)[29] The multiple correlations between the nine diversity measures and the (adjusted) performance measures were as follows: for Recognition, $R = .32$, for R & D effectiveness, $R = .30$, for Published written output, $R = .36$.[30] Thus, we find that the nine diversity measures together could explain about 10% of the variance of these performance measures.[31]

As in the analysis of the simple motivation–performance relationship discussed above in this chapter, we can here ask how one should interpret this 10% explanatory power of the multiple diversity measures. Again, one must recall that the observed relationship is affected by various types of measurement errors and that the true relationship is almost certainly higher. How much higher? Making the same assumptions as was done above, that is, that the diversity measures have compositions roughly similar to those that are estimated for the performance measures in Chapter 14, one would conclude that the joint predictive power of the diversity measures fell in the 20–30% range.[32] Without more detailed information about the diversity measures (information that is not available), the precise value cannot be determined, but even this approximate calculation is sufficient to suggest that diversity factors, as a group, are potentially important for explaining why some research units outperform others.

Discussion and conclusions on diversity and performance

Earlier in this chapter, it was noted that research performance was almost certainly affected by a large number of influences and that we should not expect any single phenomenon to account for a substantial portion of the variation. What we have seen here is that single diversity measures relate weakly but positively to performance, and that diversity as a general phenomenon can explain roughly 10% of the variance in some forms of performance. When we consider that this 10% is almost certainly a low estimate because of imperfections in the measures of diversity and performance, it seems obvious that the possible effects of diversity, as a general phenomenon, are well worth our attention.

Of course, the demonstration of a relationship says little about the causal dynamics of the underlying phenomena, and this is an area that is ripe for exploration. Why does this diversity–performance relationship occur so generally? Five reasons why diversity might enhance performance have been listed above in the chapter, and these provide starting points for further investigation. One should also consider the possibility that performance enhances diversity. A third possibility – that the diversity–performance relationship is a spurious one – has been checked by introducing controls and adjustments for the more obvious sources of spuriousness and, so far, has not been found applicable, but this alternative cannot be totally eliminated with the presently available data. At this point, we do not know for sure whether diver-

Exhibit 10.7. Multiple relationships of diversity and motivation to aspects of research-unit performance (in percent)

	Performance measures		
Percent of variance explained by:	Recog-nition	R & D effectiveness	Publi-cations
A. Motivation and diversity together	15	19	13
B. Motivation alone	5	13	1
C. Diversity alone	10	9	12
Relative marginal predictive power of motivation [(A – C)/B]	100	77	100
Relative marginal predictive power of dedication [(A – B)/C]	100	67	100

Notes: Coefficients in lines A–C are based on adjusted R^2s and show percentage of variance in performance measure explained by 9 diversity measures and/or Motivation index, after allowance for capitalization on chance when fitting model. See text for list of 9 diversity measures. All performance measures have been adjusted to remove differences attributable to type of unit.

sity enhances performance. We do know, now, that they co-vary. And it is not hard to imagine ways in which diversity *might* influence performance and thereby explain the relationships we have observed.

4. Motivation, diversity, and performance

So far in this chapter, it has been shown that both motivation and diversity relate to the performance of research units. It has been shown that the Motivation index, which summarizes the several more basic motivation measures, can explain 5–10% of the variation in at least some of the performance measures. We have also seen that a simultaneous consideration of several different aspects of diversity can also explain roughly this same amount of variance in some of the performance measures. The question that logically follows concerns the predictive power of motivation and diversity *together*. Is the variance that one factor explains different from that explained by the other – in which case the total explanatory power rises if we put the two together? Or do they somehow offer alternative explanations for the same portion of variance?

Exhibit 10.7 demonstrates that motivation and diversity operate relatively independently, and that one can do a better job of accounting for differences in research-unit performance if one considers both factors than if one considers either factor alone. The exhibit shows results for the three aspects of performance that show the strongest relationships to diversity, two of which also show relatively strong relationships to motivation.

One can see in the exhibit that motivation and diversity together can explain 15% of the variance in Recognition, 19% of the variance in R & D effectiveness, and 13% of the variance in Published written output.[33] (All performance measures have been adjusted to remove effects attributable to differences between types of units.) For Recognition, the exhibit shows that the relative marginal predictive power of motivation and diversity is, in each case, at 100% – that is, neither factor explains any part of the variance that can be explained by the other, and hence each contributes at its individual maximum to the joint explanation. The identical pattern holds true for Published written output, though the individual predictive power of motivation for this aspect of performance is small. For R & D effectiveness, the relative marginal predictive powers are 77% and 67% for motivation and diversity, respectively, suggesting that here also the major part of the individual explanatory powers are reflected in the joint explanation.

What this analysis shows is that the relationships of motivation and diversity to performance are independent, or nearly independent, phenomena. Each factor merits attention in its own right, and each can contribute to predicting and understanding research-unit performance.

5. Summary

The chapter explores relationships of the performance of research units to two factors, motivation and diversity. Motivation is examined first, then diversity, and finally the two together.

Previous investigations of motivation and scientific performance have produced mixed results. One relatively large study showed consistently positive but modest relationships; two smaller studies found no relationships. The present investigation differs from these previous ones in its assumption that motivation and performance can be considered as characteristics of the research unit as a whole.

Three basic questionnaire items were used to assess strength of motivation. These asked about the sense of dedication in the unit, about each respondent's own interest in the work, and about the amount of the respondent's voluntary overtime. These items showed modest co-variation, which supported the combination of some of them into a Motivation index. Reasonable variations across different types of respondents (unit heads, staff scientists, and technical support staff) enhanced the credibility of the measures, and the finding of systematic variation from unit to unit supported the assumption that motivation might be treated as a unit characteristic.

When motivation measures were related to performance, a pattern of modest, positive correlations emerged. The relationships were stronger for the unit heads and staff scientists than for the technical support staff, and were stronger for performance assessed by ratings than by output. The strongest relationship was between the Motivation index and ratings of R & D effectiveness (adjusted to remove differences attributable to type of unit); $r = .36$. Further checks showed that the positive relationships could not be solely attributed to respondent biases, and that the rather simply constructed Motivation index would not be markedly improved by inclusion of more variables and/or a more complicated weighting of the variables. With respect to the strength of the relationships, it is noted that scientific performance is determined by multiple influences and that the measures of performance and motivation are less than perfectly valid; both considerations lead us to expect relationships of only modest size. It is concluded that although these results cannot prove that motivation enhances performance, they suggest that this possibility may well exist.

Previous research on the topic of diversity has suggested that diversity in the working roles and intellectual resources of scientists accompanies higher levels of performance. The International Comparative Study offers a chance to check these results at the level of the research unit and to explore further the diversity concept.

Using the present data, a total of 70 potential diversity measures have been examined; these can be conceptually grouped into nine different aspects of diversity. Interrelationships among the diversity measures show that diversity is a multifaceted concept; units high on one aspect of diversity show no necessary tendency to be high on other aspects.

Six aspects of diversity proved to be positively related, at modest levels, to measures of research-unit performance: having an interdisciplinary orientation, engaging in multiple scientific specialities, incorporating multiple projects, drawing funding from multiple sources, and arranging the work so scientists engage in multiple R & D activities and/or multiple professional functions. Positive relationships occurred between diversity and most measures of performance (even after the performance measures were adjusted for differences between types of units and after controlling for unit size), with the stronger relationships occurring for R & D effectiveness, Recognition, and Published written output. However, diversity did not relate to either the Applications effectiveness or Administrative effectiveness of the units. Although single diversity measures rarely explained more than 2% or 3% of the variance in any performance measure, combining measures tapping a half-dozen aspects of diversity raised the explanatory power to approximately 10%. Again, the reader is reminded that performance is multiply determined, that imperfections in the measures can be expected to reduce the apparent strength of the relationships, and that demonstration of a relationship does not prove a causal connection. One can imagine, however, a number of reasons why diversity might enhance performance and, hence, why the observed relationships may have occurred. These include the possibilities that diverse activities, responsibilities, contacts, etc., may help scientists acquire new knowledge that is either directly or indirectly useful in solving research problems, that diversity may lead to more effective and enlightened self-guidance, that diversity may enhance the productivity of what would otherwise be fallow periods, and that diversity may introduce a degree of security into an otherwise risky situation.

In a final analysis, it is shown that motivation and diversity tend not to overlap much in their predictive powers, and that therefore it is helpful to consider both factors when attempting to account for the performance of research units.

References

Andrews, F. M., 1964, Scientific Performance as Related to Time Spent on Technical Work, Teaching, or Administration, *Administrative Science Quarterly,* 9: 182–193.

Cochran, W. G., 1970, Some Effects of Errors of Measurement on Multiple Correlations, *Journal of the American Statistical Association,* 65: 22–34.

Goodman, P. S., Furcon, J. E., and Rose, J. H., 1969, Examination of Some Measures of Creative Ability by the Multitrait-Multimethod Matrix, *Journal of Applied Psychology,* 53: 240–243.

Goodman, P. S., Rose, J. H., and Furcon, J. E., 1970, Comparison of the Motivational Antecedents of the Work Performance of Scientists and Engineers, *Journal of Applied Psychology,* 54: 491–495.

Lawler, E. E., III, and Hall, D. T., 1970, Relationships of Job Characteristics to Job Involvement, Satisfaction, and Intrinsic Motivation, *Journal of Applied Psychology,* 54: 305–312.

Lodhal, T. M., and Kejner, M., 1965, The Definition and Measurement of Job Involvement, *Journal of Applied Psychology,* 49: 24–33.

Pelz, D. C., and Andrews, F. M., 1964, Diversity in Research, *International Science and Technology,* July: 21–36.

Pelz, D. C., and Andrews, F. M., 1966, *Scientists in Organizations: Productive Climates for Research and Development,* New York, Wiley. (Revised ed. 1976, Ann Arbor, Institute for Social Rearch, University of Michigan.)

Notes

1. In the questionnaire answered by heads of units, these were items J2d and J3b; in the questionnaires answered by other scientists and by technical support staff, these were items J2c, J2f, and J3b.

2. The five types of research units are: (1) units engaged in exact and natural sciences and located in academic organizations; (2) units engaged in medical and social sciences and located in academic organizations; (3) units engaged in applied sciences and located in academic organizations; (4) units located in cooperative R & D institutions; (5) units engaged in applied sciences and located in industrial organizations. For a description of the statistical explorations that led to this typology, see Chapter 13.

3. The six countries are Austria, Belgium, Finland, Hungary, Poland, and Sweden.

4. When correlations are computed using data from all 1,222 research units, conventional tests of statistical significance would show any correlation larger than .07 to be statistically significant beyond the .01 level. Although the sampling design of the present study does not match assumptions built into conventional tests, making proper allowance for these differences would not markedly change the level required for significance.

5. $p < .01$ in all cases.

6. Statistically experienced readers will recognize this as a one-way analysis of variance in which unit identification was used as the independent variable. The values cited are those of the F statistic. Given the numbers of units having two or more staff scientists (this ranged from 86 to 371 across the five types of units) and the number of staff scientists in units where there were at least two such people (range: 238–1,057), all Fs were statistically significant, most beyond the .001 level.

7. Given that the variances of the four basic measures were all approximately equal (about 0.9) and that the typical unit included more than one staff scientist, the effect of these operations is to give somewhat greater weight in the final motivation index to answers from the unit head, a procedure that did not seem unreasonable. The multiple regressions reported below in the chapter support this implicit weighting.

8. In the exhibits of this chapter, measures based on information obtained from the unit head will carry the designation "SA," those from staff scientists, "SB," and those from technical support staff, "TS."

9. There is no doubt that differences between types of units in both goals and motivation levels did influence the correlations between motivation and some of the unadjusted performance measures: Compared to the figures shown in Exhibit 10.1, those for the unadjusted measures were somewhat higher for Training effectiveness, Recognition, and Published written output; and were somewhat lower (less positive or more negative) for Applications effectiveness, Output of patents and prototypes, and Output of reports and algorithms.

10. All multiple correlations cited in this paragraph are adjusted for degrees of freedom (i.e., for "shrinkage").

11. The R & D effectiveness measure used in this chapter has been estimated to consist of 58% valid variance, 4% variance attributable to SA bias/halo, 4% variance attributable to SB bias/halo, 11% variance attributable to EV bias/halo, and 23% random error (see Chapter 14).

12. These values were obtained by applying the formula presented in the Annex to Chapter 14.

13. Recall that the square of a correlation shows the percentage of variance in one variable that can be explained by another. Similarly, the square of a multiple correlation shows the percentage of variance in the dependent variable that can be explained by an optimally weighted additive combination of the independent variables.

14. The results contained various hints that there was such a thing as too much diversity – e.g., for some types of scientists performance rose as the number of R & D functions increased from one to four, but then declined if time was split among five functions. Nevertheless, the basic trend was positive, and it is on this trend that we shall focus here.

15. The relevant items appear in sections C2 and E2 of the SA and SB questionnaires.

16. The relevant items appear in section D2 of the SA and SB questionnaires.

17. The relevant items appear in sections A2e and E1 of the SA questionnaire.

18. The relevant items appear in section 4.2 of the RU questionnaire.

19. The relevant items appear in section C3 of the SA and SB questionnaires.

20. The relevant items appear in section C1 of the SA and SB questionnaires.

21. The relevant items appear in section D1 of the SA and SB questionnaires.

22. The relevant item appears in section 1.2 of the RU questionnaire.

23. The relevant items appear in section A2 of the SB questionnaire.

24. These are items Q2a, Q3a, J2g in the SB questionnaire and item J2g in the TS questionnaire.

25. There is just one possible exception. Units engaged in many projects also tended to be actively using more scientific specialities (group 3 of the diversity measures). Although such a relationship is reasonable, the relationships between these two conceptual groups are rather weak (average r = .09; range: .23 to −.06), and it seems best to treat diversity in projects and in specialities as two separate aspects of diversity.

26. With respect to number of projects, Pelz and Andrews found "a very slight tendency for scientists to perform better if they worked on two or three projects, rather than on one or none" (Pelz and Andrews, 1966: 75), but because of the weakness of the relationships Pelz and Andrews concluded that number of projects made little difference. The fact that diversity in projects shows positive correlations to certain performance measures in the present data suggests that the interpretation of the American results may have been overly cautious.

27. Unfortunately, in an attempt to capture the essence of a whole methodological tradition within the few words of a questionnaire item, the descriptions of methods became very abstract, and it may be that this series of items was simply not well understood by many respondents. This could explain why relationships to performance failed to appear.

29. Differences in diversity levels across types of units were not great (etas varied from .07 to .22), but were consistently larger than could be attributed to chance alone.

29. These were: Number of other disciplines from which the unit borrowed methods, theories, etc.; Number of specialities in which the unit head was

expert; Number of projects within the research unit in which the unit head was involved; and the Mean number of projects in which staff scientists were involved within the unit.

30. Adjusting these *R* values for capitalization on chance when fitting the model (i.e., for "shrinkage") decreased each *R* by .01. A check of what were considered to be the most likely sources of interactions showed none of noteworthy size, thereby suggesting that the multiple regression results reflect most of the predictive power potentially obtainable from these diversity measures.

31. Given that the regressions were run stepwise, it is possible to tell whether one particular subset of the diversity measures was consistently the most useful combination for predicting performance. No consistent pattern emerged. Generally the explanatory power rose little if at all after the number of diversity indicators used for the predictions was up to about six, but the optimal set was a different six for each dependent variable. (If use of nine diversity measures proved too cumbersome in some future undertaking, it would seem reasonable to use just six – being sure that each of the six aspects of diversity shown in Exhibit 10.4 was represented.)

32. Formula 3.6 in Cochran (1970) is helpful in deriving these estimates. The exact estimate would depend on the correlations between measurement biases in the performance and diversity measures.

33. Results in Exhibit 10.7 were obtained by multiple regression. A check of the most likely sources of statistical interaction involving motivation, diversity, and performance showed none of marked size, thereby suggesting that other multivariate analysis techniques would not have produced explanatory powers much greater than those shown here.

Part 3. Methodological reports

11 Ratings of research-unit performance

Joseph Bonmariage, Edmond Legros, and Michel Vessière

Belgian Archives for the Social Sciences, Catholic University of Louvain, Louvain-La-Neuve

1. Introduction

The International Comparative Study on the Organization and Performance of Research Units has as its primary objective the development of a *methodology* for assessing and improving the effectiveness and efficiency of research units for the benefit of all member states of Unesco.

This primary concern with methodological aspects led us to focus our research interest on the various measures of effectiveness, because they constitute the basic dependent variables of the whole project. As we delved further into this study, we became more and more aware of the fact that, whatever the strategy used for constructing performance indices, their validity is conditioned by the tools of observation used in the collection of data: The operationalization of the theoretical dimensions fixes from the beginning all subsequent possibilities for further analysis.

In order to assess the effectiveness of research units, this project has chosen to use two sets of performance indices. The first takes into account the output of a research unit, such as books, articles, patents, algorithms, etc. The second relies on a battery

In addition to the authors of this paper, the Belgian research team included Claire Demain, data collection manager, and Anne Magits, analyst programmer. The authors would also like to acknowledge the collaboration of those interested, especially the members of the research units, without whose support this research could not have been achieved.

of items that involved asking members of each research unit to rate different aspects of the effectiveness of their unit.

The focus of this chapter is to try to evaluate how these "subjective" ratings perform as measures of effectiveness.

Motivations for the chapter

This chapter is intended to obviate three kinds of criticism that have been addressed to other investigations.

First, we would like to avoid a criticism made of Lazarsfeld and Thielens' study, *The Academic Mind* (1958). These authors have been suspected of defining the eminence of universities from the vantage point of a person in a position of power and authority, and perhaps even of capitalizing upon the particular vantage point of Columbia University, where Lazarsfeld was employed (Sjoberg and Nett, 1968: 305–306). It seems thus appropriate to check if we have not also projected a particular point of view as a general framework for outlining effectiveness at the theoretical as well as at the operational level.

A second criticism that we would like to examine is the assumption that the respondent's own frame of reference constitutes the basic reality. The well-known hierarchy of professional prestige produced by the ranking of respondents used by Warner (1960) as an identification tool for social class is a typical example of what can occur when utilizing such an approach. It must be admitted that the International Study doesn't totally escape this criticism. In fact, we have also considered from the beginning that effectiveness is what people in the research units say it is. Having constructed the effectiveness measures on this basis, our objective in this chapter is then to try to further explore their meaning.

Third, the International Study will presumably result in various recommendations for political decisions in the field of science management. It seems appropriate to check that such recommendations are based on valid empirical statements and not on merely artificial results produced by the particular measurement tool that has been used.

Organization of the chapter

One approach for assessing the subjective performance measures would be to examine the links between the conceptual dimensions of effectiveness and their operationalization in terms of questionnaire items. This would constitute an investigation of validity and would require a review of the conceptual frame of reference from which the concept of effectiveness used in this study was derived. However, the lack of theory in this field, and the concern for empirical results that has characterized the project from its start, limit us to the available data. A more practical alternative strategy for bringing to light some of the implicit or hidden assumptions that might be unconsciously present in the effectiveness measures is to consider the consistency of these measurements. We shall explore this at two levels:

1 Are the meanings of the performance measures consistent across subsets of research units, and are these measures reasonably independent of the environment in which the unit operates?
2 Is the configuration of the relationship between the performance measures and other variables assessed in this study reasonably stable or does it depend on the contextual setting of the research units? If the last were to be the case, it would no doubt be illusory to expect to identify a unique set of factors that affect the effectiveness of research units based on the data collected in this project.

It should be clear from the above that the analysis in this chapter of the relationships between effectiveness scores and other variables has no explanatory or causal purpose; rather, it is essentially directed toward an *exploration* of the latent structure and is intended to allow a more informed reading of the rated-performance measures used in this project.

The ultimate goal is to answer the question: Does there exist a unique stable pattern of relationships between the characteristics of a research unit (e.g., its size, experience, activities, climate, leadership, resources, communication, equipment, etc.) and the sets of scores that are supposed to measure the different dimensions of its effectiveness?

After Section 1, which consists of a brief presentation of the rated-performance indices used in this chapter and some comments about how these indices relate to the performance measures used elsewhere in the book, the chapter will consist of three main sections.

Section 2 reports analyses on the global sample level – that is, results that emerged after all the surveyed units from the six countries that participated in Round 1 of the International Comparative Study had been analyzed together. This section begins by examining the relationship of rated-performance indices to *objective* outputs of the research units. Next, it identifies other items in the questionnaire that have strong relationships to the effectiveness indices in order to enlighten the empirical meaning of each *subjective* performance measure. Then follows a general appraisal of the whole structure of relationships between effectiveness scores and all the other dimensions included in the project. This first section winds up with some partial conclusions suggesting hypotheses for further analyses that involve the division of research units into homogeneous types in terms of country, institution, and scientific field.

In Section 3, we examine how the main contextual variables affect the various measurements of effectiveness. The results encouraged us to go further to a more specific analysis of homogeneous subsets of research units, their homogeneity being defined in terms of context. The results of these analyses constitute our Section 4, which examines the stability of the relationships between effectiveness and other factors. Repeating the correlation analyses of Section 2 for each dimension of effectiveness, it becomes evident that some starting hypotheses are at least not rejected by the data.

The chapter ends with some conclusions on the generalization of results arising from this study, on the validity of the applications of these results in science management, and on some possible future developments if further research should be planned concerning the effectiveness of research units.

Presentation of the rated-performance measures

With respect to the construction of rated-performance measures, the merits of developing orthogonal measures versus related scores was discussed at some length by members of the team that conducted Round 1 of the International Comparative Study. The discussion centered around two basic arguments: preference toward univocal dimensions or preference toward indices that best fit the observed data. It is clear that the first argument calls for an orthogonal solution and that the second favors instead oblique measurements.

We have maintained that the more realistic point of view when faced with this dilemma was to explore the feasibility of orthogonal approaches, keeping in mind that the test of fitting reasonably the original observations remains the final criterion for acceptance. In other words, it seems reasonable to sacrifice a minimum of fit in order to preserve univocal dimensions for further analysis.

We have thus developed a series of factor and principal components analyses of the 17 performance ratings made by heads of research units, plus 17 comparable ratings made by staff scientists.[1] These analyses were performed on the full set of 1,222 research units included in Round 1 of the International Comparative Study. Among the solutions obtained, the first seven factors produced by a principal components analysis, when orthogonally rotated, provided an attractive solution. While preserving orthogonality between dimensions, this solution keeps, in seven dimensions, 59% of the total variance of the 34 original items. From this model, corresponding scores for these seven factors have been computed for all the units in the sample and are considered as *the seven basic dimensions of rated effectiveness* in this chapter.

The correlations between the original items and the rated-effectiveness factors are presented in Exhibit 11.1. It immediately appears that, for factors 1 and 2, corresponding variables in questionnaires answered by unit heads and staff scientists converge rather well on the same dimensions. Factors 1 and 2 focus on Productiveness, Innovativeness, R & D effectiveness, Quality of research-unit work, and General contribution. The first factor is uniquely related to the staff scientists' answers; the second, to the same items as answered by the heads of the units. We propose therefore to name these two dimensions "R & D effectiveness" and "General contribution" (or "General effectiveness"), as assessed by staff scientists and heads of units, respectively.

The label of "Recognition" seems well suited for the third dimension. Its two highly related items are applicable to both the head of the unit and the staff scientists and refer to the response of the scientific community to the activities of the research unit: Publications in high demand and International reputation.

The fourth dimension shows a heavy loading only with the item Training effectiveness, and will be named from that.

The fifth factor is clearly related to those items dealing with the applications of the results obtained by the research units, and is therefore presumably well designated by the label "Applications effectiveness."

The high loadings on the sixth factor of the items concerned with Social value and Usefulness of the work of the units indicates that this dimension is presumably an indicator of what may be called the "Social effectiveness" of research units.

If we assign a title to the last dimension, its unique high correlation with the item assessing the extent to which the unit remains within its operating budget, and its lower correlation with an assessment of the way the unit meets its schedules, suggests that this factor be designated "Administrative effectiveness."

These seven effectiveness factor scores seem to be remarkably well related to the performance measurements produced by other approaches that have been used elsewhere in this book.

Exhibit 11.1. Principal components analysis of performance ratings, all units combined (figures are factor loadings after varimax rotation)

Questionnaire items	Factors: 1. Gen. eff.: staff sci.	2. Gen. eff.: unit heads	3. Recognition
Head's responses			
SA: Result follow-up?	−.08	−.25	.05
SB: Experimental development used?	−.04	−.25	−.04
SC: Outside pressure for research use	−.06	−.12	−.04
SD: Contact with users	−.07	−.14	.04
TA: Productiveness	.17	*−.73*	.11
TB: Innovativeness	.20	*−.73*	.05
TC1: R & D effectiveness	.15	*−.64*	.08
TC2: Training effectiveness	−.10	−.40	.13
TD: S & T objectives not R & D	−.10	−.18	.13
TE1: International reputation	.02	−.34	*.77*
TE2: Publications in high demand	−.00	−.35	*.73*
TF: Social value	−.07	−.39	.01
TG: Usefulness	−.06	−.25	.02
TH: Quality of RU work	.02	*−.63*	.14
TJ1: RU meets schedules	.05	−.42	.03
TJ2: RU stays in budget	−.12	−.14	.05
TK: General contribution to S & T	.10	*−.62*	.38
Staff scientists' responses			
SA: Result follow-up?	.43	.07	−.08
SB: Experimental development used?	.41	.04	−.12
SC: Outside pressure for research use	.23	.05	−.18
SD: Contact with users	.39	.09	−.10
TA: Productiveness	*.76*	−.21	.15
TB: Innovativeness	*.74*	−.21	.09
TC1: R & D effectiveness	*.71*	−.11	.11
TC2: Training effectiveness	.32	.04	.12
TD: S & T objectives not R & D	.42	.14	.09
TE1: International reputation	.43	−.01	*.75*
TE2: Publications in high demand	.39	.00	*.71*
TF: Social value	.39	.01	−.04
TG: Usefulness	.32	.11	−.00
TH: Quality of RU work	*.59*	−.11	.12
TJ1: RU meets schedules	.50	−.03	−.02
TJ2: RU stays in budget	.16	.07	.01
TK: General contribution to S & T	*.65*	−.13	.32
Factor contributions	4.28	.44	2.66

4. Training effect.	5. Applications effect.	6. Social effect.	7. Admin. effect.	h^2 Communalities
.08	*−.74*	.01	.01	.63
−.00	*−.76*	.06	.04	.65
−.25	*−.62*	.21	−.02	.51
−.05	*−.68*	.20	.01	.53
−.05	−.12	.05	.00	.59
.01	−.11	.08	−.05	.60
.19	−.19	.09	.08	.53
.68	.14	.12	.06	.69
.12	−.24	.44	.19	.36
.08	.07	−.03	.02	.72
.15	.11	.04	.04	.68
.08	−.26	*.52*	.02	.50
.04	−.06	*.79*	.01	.70
.10	−.08	−.05	.21	.49
.06	−.11	.12	*.56*	.52
.07	−.05	.03	*.73*	.58
−.03	.03	.19	.09	.59
.08	*−.68*	−.00	−.02	.67
.06	*−.69*	.00	.02	.66
−.22	*−.56*	.23	−.06	.50
−.08	*−.60*	.18	.00	.57
.03	−.11	.00	−.07	.66
.01	−.14	.08	−.08	.64
.22	−.14	.06	.01	.59
.76	.09	.05	.03	.70
.04	−.24	.44	.17	.48
−.02	.02	−.03	−.01	.74
.10	.08	.11	.04	.69
.02	−.20	*.58*	−.01	.53
−.05	−.08	*.75*	.05	.69
.01	.00	−.01	.24	.44
−.05	.01	.11	*.50*	.51
−.01	.10	.02	*.69*	.52
−.01	.03	.26	.07	.62
1.35	3.99	2.54	1.79	20.07

(59% of total variance explained)

They also pass quite satisfactorily the test for orthogonality: The correlation among them never exceeds .03, and most of the correlations are lower. Exhibit 11.2 shows that the rated-effectiveness factor scores correlate fairly well with most of the comparable performance indices built up by the a priori summing of individual items. All Pearson *r*s between effectiveness scores and indices used in other chapters of this book are above .80 between corresponding dimensions except for R & D effectiveness, where answers from the heads of units and from staff scientists were combined in the a priori approach.[2] Nevertheless, this last dimension remains correlated at .60 with our effectiveness factor scores.

The conclusion of this factor analysis of rated-performance measures is that the factor analysis and the more a priori approaches lead to generally convergent indices. The most striking difference is the absence of a single factor tapping both the staff scientists' and the unit heads' ratings of general effectiveness.

2. Exploring the meaning of the rated-effectiveness factor scores

Objective and subjective measures

Having described how the seven dimensions of rated effectiveness were analytically derived, it now seems appropriate to test their meaning with regard to the classical measures of the output of research units. It is reasonable to hypothesize that if the rated-effectiveness dimensions are in some way indicators of the actual effectiveness of a research unit, we should observe some relationship between our factor scores and the output measures.[3]

Exhibit 11.3 gives the Pearson *r*s between the rated effectiveness factor scores and the bracketed measures of research-unit output, both before and after the output measures were adjusted to remove effects attributable to the type of unit. Several interesting observations emerge in this table.

First, the two dimensions of General effectiveness are very poorly related to any raw output measure: The two highest correlations are only .13 and .16. Thus, it appears that ratings of General effectiveness by the head of the unit and by staff scientists are by no means significantly related to the output of the unit. Adjustment for type of unit does not modify this statement.

Second, Applications effectiveness is moderately correlated with technical outputs (.25 with algorithms, .21 with prototype devices) and with internal research reports (.21). This correlation

Exhibit 11.2. Relationships between rated-effectiveness factor scores and a priori rated-effectiveness measures (figures are product moment *rs*)

Performance measures of International Research Team	Factor scores						
	Gen. eff.: staff sci.	Gen. eff.: unit heads	Recognition	Training effect.	Applications effect.	Social effect.	Admin. effect.
Original indices[a]							
General contribution	.44	.42	.44	−.02	−.04	.20	.02
Recognition	.25	.20	*.90*	.04	−.09	.02	.03
Social effectiveness	.18	.09	.01	−.03	.17	*.84*	.05
Training effectiveness	.12	.20	.18	*.81*	−.17	.06	.03
Admin. effectiveness	.20	.18	.02	.01	−.00	.09	*.90*
R & D effectiveness	*.62*	*.58*	.18	.08	.15	.04	−.05
Applications effectiveness	.22	.12	−.05	.08	*.87*	.00	.01
General R & D effectiveness	*.61*	.57	.27	.06	.10	.09	−.01
Residualized indices[b]							
General contribution	.45	.41	.40	−.05	−.00	.20	.07
Recognition	.30	.19	*.84*	−.03	.06	.05	.02
Social effectiveness	.20	.14	.06	.04	.11	.77	.02
Training effectiveness	.19	.19	.06	.72	.02	.10	.01
Administrative effectiveness	.22	.19	.00	.01	.00	.05	.86
R & D effectiveness	*.61*	.57	.19	.09	.13	.06	−.04
Applications effectiveness	.20	.15	.06	.20	.74	−.03	.01
General R & D effectiveness	.61	.57	.27	.06	.10	.10	−.00

[a]These indices combine data from unit heads, staff scientists, and external evaluators (see Chapter 2).
[b]These indices are as above, but with effects attributable to type of research unit removed.

Exhibit 11.3. Relationships between rated-effectiveness factor scores and research-unit products (figures are product moment *rs*)

Output measures	Factor scores						
	Gen. eff.: staff sci.	Gen. eff.: unit heads	Recognition	Training effect.	Applications effect.	Social effect.	Admin. effect.
Separate outputs of the research unit[a]							
Books	.00	−.01	.24	−.00	−.08	.17	.02
Articles pub. within country	.05	.03	.31	.03	−.11	.29	.10
Articles pub. outside country	.11	.16	.43	.14	−.26	−.15	−.06
Patents within country	.12	.13	−.11	−.12	.14	.04	−.06
Patents outside country	.12	.10	−.04	−.10	.12	−.04	−.06
Algorithms	−.02	.05	−.11	−.06	.25	−.02	−.08
Reviews, bibliographies	.01	.05	.19	.06	−.06	.07	−.02
Internal reports	.06	.02	−.02	−.11	.21	.14	−.05
Routine reports	.07	−.03	−.06	−.20	.20	.15	−.02
Prototype devices	.05	.11	−.06	−.06	.21	−.08	−.15
Prototype materials	.11	.05	−.03	−.02	.05	.06	−.03
Output indices (raw form)[b]							
Published written output	.07	.09	.45	.09	−.21	.12	.01
Patents & prototypes	.14	.15	−.08	−.12	.18	−.02	−.10
Reports & algorithms	.05	.02	−.08	−.15	.30	.12	−.08
Output indices (residualized)[c]							
Published written output	.12	.09	.37	−.02	−.04	.11	−.01
Patents & Prototypes	.10	.16	.04	−.03	.04	.03	−.08
Reports & Algorithms	.01	.05	.08	−.02	.10	.12	−.07

[a] Variables have been rescaled to reduce skew. [b] Construction of these indices is described in Chapter 2.
[c] These indices are as above, but with effects attributable to type of research unit removed.

reaches .30 when a weighted index for reports and algorthms is used (but this drops to .10 when the index of reports and algorithms is adjusted to remove variations that could be attributed to differences between types of units). On the other hand, this dimension is negatively correlated (−.26) with the production of articles.

Third, positive relationships exist between Recognition and output of written products by the unit: .43 with articles published outside the country, .31 with articles published inside, and .24 for books. The highest coefficient of the whole table is between this dimension and a weighted composite index for publications: .45. This coefficient is not greatly modified after adjustment for type of unit (.37).

Fourth, Social effectiveness and Training effectiveness show fewer and weaker relationships. For Training effectiveness, these disappear completely with adjustment for type of unit. As a matter of fact, the type of the unit–presumably the distinction between academic and nonacademic units–heavily affects this last dimension.

Fifth, Administrative effectiveness is, as in the factor analysis, a very poor dimension: We observe only one *r* higher than .10, a −.15 with output of prototype devices.

In summary, a careful examination of this exhibit suggests that rated-effectiveness measurements are not direct indicators of the outcome of the work of research units: They show no correlations with the outputs, or the correlations that appear seem attributable–at least in part–to the type of unit analyzed. The higher correlation between Recognition and Written output does not contradict that reading of the results. Indeed, Recognition is based primarily on the items "Publications in high demand" and "International reputation," and there are academic pressures that may lead researchers to believe that their reputation is produced by the quantity of papers they publish.

If we believe that effectiveness ratings measure "something else" than objective output, as suggested by the results just examined, the question is, what do they measure?

Happily enough, the project has included a wide range of dimensions that could be related to effectiveness. We propose to utilize these dimensions to shed some light on the meaning of the rated-effectiveness scores.

Significance of the rated-effectiveness dimensions

For the maximum utilization of the information at hand, we will now direct our analysis toward a systematic exploration of the

Exhibit 11.4. Items with strongest relationship to General effectiveness as rated by staff scientists

	Item[a]	*r*
P1b:	Interest in research activities	.48
J3a:	Sense of innovation and pioneering	.47
P1a:	Adequacy of research planning	.44
J3c:	Consideration of new ideas	.44
J3b:	Dedication to work	.42
P1c:	Coherence of research program	.40
M1b:	Effect of contact with supervisor	.40
M2f:	Support of staff scientists by supervisor	.39
M2d:	Supervisor's knowledge of research field	.37
M2a:	Supervisor's professional ability	.37
M2e:	Amount of work supervisor performs	.36
J3f:	Cooperation among scientists in unit	.36
J2c:	Interest of work	.35
M2c:	Supervisor's leadership qualities	.34
J3g:	Frequency of scientific and technical staff meetings	.33

[a]For all these items, respondents were staff scientists.

whole data set in order to explore what the factor scores of rated effectiveness seem to measure. We have identified all items that are empirically related to any of the seven rated-effectiveness scores with a Pearson *r* of at least .20. From these correlations, it is possible to identify those items that are the most related to each rated-effectiveness dimension and, by so doing, hopefully to gain a better understanding of the empirical meaning of what the rated-effectiveness factor scores actually measure.

The procedure followed here is to list, in decreasing order, up to 15 items that are most correlated with each dimension and to try to point out the conceptual links between these items and the effectiveness scores.

General R & D effectiveness as assessed by staff scientists. Exhibit 11.4 lists the 15 items that showed the highest correlations with the staff scientists' assessments of General R & D effectiveness. This measure of effectiveness seems clearly related to three dimensions: Planning of the research work (P1a, P1b, P1c), General atmosphere of the unit (J3a, b, c, f, g), and Satisfaction with supervisor (M1b, M2a, c, d, e, f). The last item, Interest of work, used as a measurement of individual attitudes, does not disturb the logic of the pattern.

There seems to be a clear positive relationship between this first dimension of effectiveness and the way in which the organization of research work is perceived: interesting and conceptually exciting activities, well-conceived planning, and a highly coherent research program. Then comes the general atmosphere of the unit, in which we can distinguish two types of items. The first, which is the more related to General effectiveness, taps the morale of the research unit: a very innovative spirit and sense of pioneering, an adequate consideration of new ideas, and a great dedication to work. The second type of item is a more organizational one; these items refer to the cooperation among scientists and engineers of the unit and to the frequency of scientific and technical staff meetings. Finally, satisfaction with one's supervisor correlates well with General effectiveness: In a research unit where the scientists think that the contacts they have with their head are highly beneficial for their scientific performance, they also rate highly the effectiveness of the research unit. The same occurs when there is great satisfaction with the supervisor as regards his support of the work of scientists, his knowledge of the field in which the unit is active, his professional ability, the amount of work he does, and his leadership qualities. Interesting enough, satisfaction with the personality and character of the supervisor correlates lower at .27.

General R & D effectiveness as assessed by the unit head. With respect to the general effectiveness of the research unit as rated by the unit head, we find, as for staff scientists' ratings, a significant relationship with the general "climate" in the research unit. The same indicators of the morale of the research unit – innovation and pioneering spirit, acceptance of new ideas, and dedication to work – are the three items most related to this dimension of effectiveness (see Exhibit 11.5). These are followed by items tapping more organizational characteristics, such as the cooperation of scientists and engineers in the research unit, invitations of technical workers to scientific meetings, and the frequency of scientific and technical meetings. These assessments may be viewed as substitutes for the indicators of satisfaction with the immediate head. Then we find a set of items dealing with the personal involvement of the head of the research unit in three areas of R & D activity: development of analysis results, interpretations, and conclusions; conceptualization and formulation of problems; and identification of areas of interest. The structure of all these items seems to find its source of coherence in the same dimensions as those identified for staff scientists' ratings.

Recognition. With the Recognition rating we come to a seemingly well-structured set of items dealing with scientific exchanges, production of articles, duration and number of research projects, and individual characteristics of heads of units. (See Exhibit 11.6.)

Exhibit 11.5. Items with strongest relationships to General effectiveness as rated by unit head

	Item[a]	*r*
J3a:	Innovation and pioneering	.40
J3c:	Consideration of new ideas	.34
J3b:	Dedication to work	.30
J3f:	Cooperation among scientists in unit	.28
J3h:	Technicians invited to meetings	.24
J3d:	Consideration of nontechnical ideas	.24
J3g:	Frequency of meetings	.23
J2f:	Knowledge of assessment	.22
C3j;	Involvement in developing results	.22
C3c:	Formulation of problems	.21
J3e:	Acceptance of ideas from junior staff	.21
C3a:	Involvement in identifying research themes	.21

[a]For all these items, respondents were unit heads.

Exhibit 11.6. Items with strongest relationships to Recognition

	Item	Respondents	*r*
F3a2:	No. of publications received by unit	unit head	.36
R1b:	No. of research unit articles published abroad	unit head	.33
F3a2:	No. of publications sent	unit head	.32
A1a:	Years member this research unit	unit head	.29
A2d:	Years R & D experience	unit head	.30
H1v:	Importance of scientific significance in choosing research themes	unit head	.26
R1b:	No. of research unit articles published within country	unit head	.26
E3:	Years going on: project 5	unit head	.23
A1c:	Years as head	unit head	.22
E3:	Years going on: project 2	unit head	.22
E3:	Years going on: project 4	unit head	.22
A2a:	Age	unit head	.22
F1b1:	Technical advancement of visitors from own country	unit head	−.22
La1:	Influence of organization leaders in choosing research tasks	staff scientists	−.21
A1:	Years member this research unit	staff scientists	.20

Exhibit 11.7. Items with strongest relationships to Training effectiveness

Item	Respondents	*r*
C1b2: % time teaching	staff scientists	.32
C1b2: % time teaching	unit head	.30
J2f: Amount voluntary overtime	staff scientists	.24
H1v: Importance of scientific significance in choosing research themes	unit head	.22
1.4b: No. of staff engaged in R & D in organization	admin.	.22
La1: Influence of organization leaders in choosing research tasks	staff scientists	−.22
La1: Influence of organization leaders in choosing research tasks	unit head	−.21
Lb3: Influence of staff scientists on use of training facilities	unit head	.21
Lb3: Influence of organization leaders on cooperation	unit head	−.20
Lb5: Influence of organization leaders on terminating staff	unit head	−.20

Again, the scientific significance of results is directly related to Recognition, as well as to the influence that leaders inside the organization have on the choice of research tasks. All these items seem to indicate that research work and management are centered around a stable research staff, whose activity is oriented toward such scientific exchanges as publications arising from long-term research projects chosen for their scientific significance.

Training effectiveness. The next dimension of effectiveness, Training effectiveness, is remarkably related to the part of working time devoted to teaching by unit heads and staff scientists, as can be seen in Exhibit 11.7. (This seems to be the inverse of the correlations that will be described next for Applications effectiveness.)

In the units rated as highly effective in training, voluntary overtime is common. Also, leaders outside the units (but inside the organization) are perceived by the unit head and/or staff scientists as having rather low influence on the choice of research tasks, on the unit's cooperation with other units, and on termination of employment of personnel. Heads think also that scientists and engineers inside their units tend to have high influence on the use of training and career facilities. Finally, high Training effectiveness tends to be positively related to the total number of scientists paid by the organization who are engaged in R & D

Exhibit 11.8. Items with strongest relationships to Applications effectiveness

	Item	Respondents	r
H1v:	Importance of scientific significance in choosing research themes	unit head	−.38
La1:	Influence of organization leaders in choosing research tasks	unit head	.29
C1b2:	% time teaching	unit head	−.27
C1b2:	% time teaching	staff scientists	−.26
C1b6:	% time on design studies	staff scientists	.25
R1d:	No. of research-unit algorithms, etc.	unit head	.24
La1:	Influence of organization leaders in choosing research tasks	staff scientists	.24
C3b:	Involvement in literature review	staff scientists	−.24
C3f:	Involvement in formulating hypotheses	staff scientists	−.24
La1:	Influence of outsiders in choosing research tasks	unit head	.24
J2e:	Other employment opportunities	staff scientists	.23
La1:	Influence of outsiders in choosing research tasks	staff scientists	.22
N2b:	Use of formal research scheduling methods	unit head	.22
La3:	Influence of organization leaders on publishing of research results	staff scientists	.22
Lb2:	Influence of organization leaders on cooperation	staff scientists	.22

activities and to the use of scientific importance as a criterion for choosing research themes. Clearly, these characteristics may be viewed as related to a research unit's environment and structure.

Applications effectiveness. As can be seen in Exhibit 11.8, the items related to ratings of Applications effectiveness are quite different.

The first item, with a correlation of −.38, has to do with the factors that influence the choice of research themes in the unit. If the scientific significance of the research is a very important factor, the rated Applications effectiveness tends to be low. Conversely, the rated Applications effectiveness tends to be high if leadership outside the unit (but inside the organization) has a high influence on decisions concerning the choice of specific research tasks (.29). Applications effectiveness is negatively related to the percentage of total work time devoted to teaching by the head of the unit (−.27) and by the staff scientists (−.26).

The set of items whose relationships with Applications effectiveness range from .25 to .22 suggests that this measure of effectiveness is highly related to the nature of task allocation in the research unit and to patterns of influence on decisions concerning the research work and management of the research unit.

As indicators of the nature of work, we find, beyond the teaching activities just mentioned, the percentage of time allocated to design studies, the personal involvement of scientists in literature review and in formulation of hypotheses, and the number of algorithms produced by the research unit.

All the other items, with the exception of J2e, Other employment opportunities, may be considered as indicators of the way decisions are made in the life of the research unit: choice of tasks, cooperation with other units, and formal planning methods.

In summary, Applications effectiveness seems to be more related to the structural characteristics of the research unit than to any other dimensions. None of the 15 items that related to R & D effectiveness relates as much as .20 to Applications effectiveness.

Social effectiveness. The underlying structure of items related to the ratings of Social effectiveness seems more difficult to clarify. At first glance, they appear to be spread across conceptual areas without clear links. Nevertheless, it finally appears that rated Social effectiveness may be viewed, like Applications effectiveness, as related to a certain way of organizing the research.

As shown in Exhibit 11.9, when Social effectiveness is highly rated, the themes of research are heavily dependent on science policymaking bodies, and the choice of research tasks is perceived as largely influenced by authorities outside the organization. The scientific significance and promise of the research seems secondary for making such choices. The delays in buying or hiring expensive equipment are rather short, but unit heads seem to be rather dissatisfied with their scientific equipment and technical assistance. Some kind of formal planning of the research is undertaken, and all scientists in the units feel a rather strong restriction imposed by administrative regulations. Systematic evaluation of the work of the research unit by persons higher up in the hierarchy of the organization is rather frequent, and leaders inside the organization seem to have – for scientists – a high influence on decisions concerning the use of training and career-development facilities. Finally, the presence of an interdisciplinary orientation and the number of articles published inside the country seem to be directly related to Social effectiveness. In summary, the structural characteristics of the research work again seem predominant in coherently organizing the items related to this dimension of effectiveness.

Exhibit 11.9. Items with strongest relationships to Social effectiveness

	Item	Respondents	*r*
La1:	Influence of outsiders in choosing research tasks	unit head	.28
D2a:	Interdisciplinary orientation	staff scientists	.28
La1:	Influence of outsiders in choosing research tasks	staff scientists	.27
5b2:	Delay satisfaction: expensive equipment	administrators	−.25
Kb:	Rating of scientific equipment	unit head	−.24
N2a:	Use of formal research-planning methods	unit head	.24
H1v:	Importance of scientific significance in choosing research themes	unit head	−.23
R1a:	No. of research-unit articles published in country	unit head	.23
Lb3:	Influence of organization leaders on use of training facilities	staff scientists	.22
H1i:	Importance of science policymaking bodies in choosing research themes	unit head	.22
Kf:	Rating of technical assistance	unit head	−.22
J3j:	Amount of administrative restrictions	staff scientists	−.21
J3j:	Amount of administrative restrictions	unit head	−.21
G2c:	Work of unit is evaluated by organization hierarchy	unit head	.21

Exhibit 11.10. Items with strongest relationships to Administrative effectiveness

	Item[a]	*r*
Kj:	Adequacy of budget	.23
P1a:	Adequacy of research planning	.17
A2a:	Age	.16
P1c:	Coherence of research program	.14
A2d:	No. of years R & D experience	.14

[a]For all these items, respondents were staff scientists.

Administrative effectiveness. This dimension of effectiveness is poorly correlated with all the items included in the survey, as can be seen in Exhibit 11.10. One item does show a correlation greater than .20: Adequacy of budget as perceived by the scientists (.23). Good planning of research work (P1a and P1c) is slightly related to this dimension, and when scientists advance in age and in R & D experience, they seem to rate the administrative effectiveness of their unit higher.

Comments. What did we learn by identifying the items that are most related to the ratings of effectiveness?

Except for Administrative effectiveness,[4] which seems very poorly related to any dimension in the data, the six other factor scores of effectiveness may be viewed as empirically related to underlying structures for which some sources of coherency can be identified at least at the hypothetical level.

For example, items related to Training effectiveness could be viewed as a description of the characteristics of the special kind of scientist corresponding to the academic researcher. He devotes a lot of his time to teaching, accepts voluntary overtime, and has relatively high influence in managing, training, and career facilities. Scientific significance is important in choosing his research themes, and leaders outside research units have little influence over the choice of tasks. Such characteristics could easily be used as indicators for academic freedom, which is a distinctive attribute of university academic members. Finally, the number of paid staff engaged in R & D in the organization is high. Given that this number is counted at the total-university level, this also contributes to the support of our hypothesis. Indeed, universities are among the largest organizations performing research activities.

The same hypothesis could be made mutatis mutandis for Recognition and for Applications effectiveness.

Social effectiveness could also be attributed to a specific way of organizing research activities. Here the scientific significance and promise of the research give way to themes decided by science policymaking bodies. Similarly, authorities outside the organization have a relatively high influence on the choice of research tasks. This seems to go with formal planning of the research and a feeling of administrative restrictiveness by the scientists.

The general hypotheses arising from those four dimensions may be summarized in a more theoretical way: The effectiveness measures are at least partly produced by the institutional setting to which research units belong and not only by "true" variations in effectiveness.

As to the meaning of ratings of General effectiveness, there are also some pieces of evidence that allow speculation as to the existence of a basic framework that induces the scientific community to adopt somewhat of a consensus on how to be effective in today's world. This consensus is reflected in the way the topic of effectiveness is approached by some leading researchers in the field (cf. Georgopoulos and Tannenbaum, 1957; Orth, 1959; Pelz and Andrews, 1966; Price, 1968, 1972). Should we attribute the remarkably parallel correlations observed across data from heads of units and from staff scientists to a causal relationship or to adhesion to a common ideology of "modern" effectiveness? Our hypothesis here is that the ideological interpretation may in part be relevant.

The rest of this chapter is devoted to the exploration of these rather disturbing hypotheses. In our mind, their rejection is required before the rated-performance measures we have constructed can be utilized any further.

Overall appraisal of the rated-performance measures

We have summarized in Exhibit 11.11 the relationships of each effectiveness measure to all the dimensions assessed in the questionnaire directed to administrative officers, heads of units, and staff scientists. The idea was that a global appraisal of those relationships would perhaps lead to a more thorough understanding of the meaning of the factor scores of rated effectiveness.

The first observation worth noting is the difference between the columns: Some dimensions of effectiveness are related to topics scattered across all three questionnaires, some are related to topics concentrated in only one questionnaire, whereas others are poorly related to any topic.

Among these last, Administrative effectiveness is so isolated in the whole set of variables that – as it is now measured – this dimension has very little interest and may perhaps be recommended for exclusion from further analyses.

With respect to General effectiveness as rated by staff scientists, apart from the items of research planning, general atmosphere, and immediate supervisor (which we have presented above), we find that individual attitudes, such as satisfaction with job security and the system of manpower recruitment, are also related. Likewise, satisfaction with remuneration and advancement and with contacts with other units are positively related to this dimension. This may reinforce the hypothesis that what we have called "General effectiveness" reflects a general attitude regarding the activity of the research unit.

More precisely, General effectiveness seems to be a good indicator of the degree of *integration* of scientists in their research units in terms of relations with their supervisor,[5] of the organization of research work and of communication networks, and of the degree to which scientists share the common ideology of the productive climate for research and development (e.g., regarding the importance of innovativeness, new ideas, pioneering spirit, dedication, etc.).

As regards General effectiveness as rated by heads of units, the same ideological components as for staff scientists is clearly present, but this dimension seems also to reflect a certain representation of the role of the unit head in terms of the activities to be performed: identification of areas of interest, formulation of problems, and analysis of results. This new dimension does not conflict with the assumed underlying ideology: A leader should be involved in the most critical tasks to be achieved in research.

When we consider the last four dimensions, the most important result is clearly the links observed between them and the nature of research units. Even the quantitative relationships between technical products and Applications effectiveness, or between written products and Recognition, are better understood at the qualitative level: They support the hypothesis that research units oriented toward specific goals should demonstrate differential scores in terms of Applications, Recognition, Social effectiveness, and Training effectiveness.

This proposition nevertheless needs further testing before being accepted. These tests are the main concern of the next two sections.

3. Rated-effectiveness scores: sensitivity to context

One way of testing our hypothesis regarding the effects of specific goals on certain of the performance scores is to return to Exhibit 11.2 and examine how the adjustment for type of research unit affects the correlations between the orthogonal rated-effectiveness scores and the a priori effectiveness measures. For General effectiveness as rated by staff scientists and by heads of units, and for Administrative effectiveness, the correlations remain stable: The highest difference is .01. In contrast, the adjustment drops the correlation from .87 to .74 for Applications effectiveness, a difference of .13. The differences for other dimensions are, respectively, .09 for Training effectiveness, .07 for Social effectiveness, and .06 for Recognition.

These observations led us to run a multiple classification analysis (MCA) on each rated-effectiveness score, using Country, Type of unit, and Scientific field as predictors. The results of

Exhibit 11.11. Synopsis of the highest correlations between rated-effectiveness factor scores and major groups of items[a]

	Factor scores							
Item groups	Articles pub. within country	Gen. eff.: staff sci.	Gen. eff.: unit heads	Recognition	Training effect.	Applications effect.	Social effect.	Admin. effect.
Administrator questionnaire								
1. Type, field, size, etc., of research unit	—	—	—	X	XXX	XXX	X	—
2. Facilities/equipment of unit	—	—	—	—	—	X	—	—
3. Training and career development facilities	—	—	—	—	—	—	—	—
4. Human and financial resources	X	—	—	—	—	—	—	—
5. Delays in satisfaction of needs	—	—	—	—	—	—	X	—
Unit head questionnaire								
A. Individual profile	XX	—	—	XX	—	—	—	—
A3. Contribution to unit products	X	—	—	XX	—	X	—	—
B. Remuneration and advancement	—	—	—	—	—	—	—	—
C. Activities and tasks performed	—	—	X	X	XX	X	—	—
D. Methods used in research work	—	—	—	—	—	X	—	—
E. Scientific fields and research projects	—	—	—	X	—	—	—	—
F. Scientific exchanges	X	—	—	XX	—	—	—	—
G. Evaluating work	—	—	—	—	—	—	X	—
H. Choice of research themes	—	—	—	X	X	XX	X	—

J. Working climate	—	—	—	—	—	—	—	—
J2. Individual attitudes and perceptions	—	—	X	—	—	—	—	—
J3. Gen. atmosphere of unit	—	—	XXX	—	—	—	X	—
K. Budget, facilities, and services available	—	—	—	—	—	—	X	—
L. Patterns of influence	—	—	—	—	X	X	X	—
N. Organization and planning of research work	—	—	—	—	—	X	X	—
Q Contacts with other units	—	—	—	—	—	—	—	—
R. Products of research unit	X	—	—	XX	—	X	X	—
Staff scientist questionnaire								
A. Individual profile	X	—	—	X	—	—	X	—
A3. Contribution to unit products	X	—	—	X	—	—	—	—
B. Remuneration and advancement	—	X	—	—	—	—	—	—
C. Activities and tasks performed	—	—	—	X	XX	X	—	—
D. Methods used in research work	—	—	—	—	—	—	X	—
J. Working climate								
J2. Individual attitudes and perceptions	—	XX	—	—	—	X	—	—
J3. General atmosphere of unit	—	XXX	—	—	—	—	X	—
K. Budget, facilities, and services available	—	—	—	—	—	—	—	X
L. Patterns of influence	—	X	—	X	X	X	X	—
M. Immediate supervisor	—	XXX	—	—	—	—	—	—
P. Research planning in unit	—	XXX	—	—	—	—	—	—
Q. Contacts with other units	—	X	—	—	—	—	—	—

[a]*Key:* X: at least one $r \geq .20$; XX: at least one $r \geq .30$; XXX: at least one $r \geq .40$.

Exhibit 11.12. Relationship between rated-effectiveness factor scores and Country, Type and Field (figures show R^2 or eta^2)[a]

	Factor scores						
Predictors	Gen. eff.: staff sci.	Gen. eff.: unit heads	Recognition	Training effect.	Applications effect.	Social effect.	Admin. effect.
Country (alone)	.02	.02	.05	.02	.22	.23	.03
Type (alone)	.02	.00	.09	.17	.16	.10	.02
Field (alone)	.00	.02	.07	.03	.21	.13	.00
Country + Type	.03	.02	.14	.19	.30	.25	.03
Country + Field	.02	.03	.11	.04	.33	.29	.02
Type + Field	.02	.02	.12	.18	.26	.20	.02
Country + Type + Field	.03	.03	.16	.20	.36	.30	.03

[a] Adjusted for degrees of freedom.

Exhibit 11.13. Analyses of variance: rated-effectiveness factor scores by types of research units (figures show eta-squares)

Factor scores	Classification of research units		
	(Type/Field)[a]	(Typology)[b]	(Country/Type/ Field)[c]
General effectiveness as rated by staff scientists	.01	.02	.05
General effectiveness as rated by unit heads	.00	.02	.04
Recognition	.06	.11	.12
Training effectiveness	.15	.15	.23
Applications effectiveness	.22	.23	.38
Social effectiveness	.04	.13	.28
Administrative effectiveness	.01	.01	.06

[a] A priori typology of research units: academic vs. nonacademic and technological vs. nontechnological fields.

[b] This typology of research units was prepared by International Research Team by using configurations of objective and rated-performance variables (see Chapter 13).

[c] Same as in note *a,* but combined with the 6 countries.

these analyses are presented in Exhibit 11.12. There is no doubt that these three contextual variables explain – in the "statistical sense" – a significant part of the variance of Applications effectiveness (36%), Social effectiveness (30%), Training effectiveness (20%), and Recognition (16%). On the other hand, General effectiveness and Administrative effectiveness were clearly independent of those variables.[6]

To examine the variation of rated performance in different settings, we have run three analyses of variance. Their results appear in Exhibit 11.13. In the first, the rated-performance scores were predicted by a four-category typology of research units derived by distinguishing among research units in academic versus nonacademic settings[7] on one hand, and in technological versus nontechnological fields[8] on the other.

The generally weak relationships from this analysis (shown in the first column of Exhibit 11.13) suggested we try predicting performance with another typology used by the International Research Team for removing the Type of institution and Scientific field effects from effectiveness measures.[9] As can be seen in column 2 of Exhibit 11.13, this typology did not perform better than the first–except perhaps for Social effectiveness.

We then moved to an a priori typology that combined Type of institution and Scientific field (as defined in our first analyses) and each of the six countries. Thus, we ended up with 24 possible types, of which 22 are present in the data. The analysis of variance using these 22 types produced the results in column 3 of Exhibit 11.13, which replicate fairly well the magnitude of effects identified by MCA (shown in Exhibit 11.12). We think that this convergence may be viewed as a good estimate of the true effects of contexts, and thus we use these subsets of research units for examining the stability of the means for each effectiveness dimension when Country, Type of institution, and Scientific field are controlled.

Some of the most striking results observed when comparing the mean scores across the 22 subsets of units are in support of the proposed hypothesis: The range of mean scores in the academic nontechnological unit subsets varies from −.213 to .238 for R & D effectiveness rated by scientists, and from −.261 to .288 for the same dimension rated by heads of units. All the mean scores on Training effectiveness for nonacademic units are below the general mean, whereas academic units rate higher on this dimension. If we consider all seven dimensions, the highest scores seem to be concentrated in certain countries and the lowest in certain others.

These findings can be interpreted in two ways: Either the levels of performance are really different according to their contextual environments, or the differences in rated effectiveness merely reflect an appraisal that is attributable to contextual effects such as cultural, political, or institutional patterns.

There is no empirical criterion for choosing between these two interpretations. But whichever we decide to favor, it seems necessary to perform a detailed analysis of the stability of the relationships between rated effectiveness and other characteristics of research units in different countries, types of institutions, and scientific fields. Thus, we shall repeat the correlation analysis that was conducted on the total sample (described in the first main section of the chapter), now exploring systematically within subsets of units that are homogeneous in terms of Country, Type, and Scientific field. This analysis will be centered on the set of variables that were identified in the global analysis as showing the strongest relationships.

The hypothesis of the proposed analysis is that if our measurements of effectiveness are not too sensitive to context effects, their relationships to other unit characteristics should remain more or less constant.

4. Stability of relationships between rated effectiveness and other dimensions

In order to have a sufficient number of cases in each subset, the correlation analysis has been run only on 6 types of units. From the 22 types identified in the preceding section, 4 consist of units in academic settings in nontechnological fields; these units are in four countries. The 2 other types consist of units in nonacademic settings in technologically oriented fields; these come from two countries. The sizes of these subsets range from 90 to 140 units, with a mean size of 106. This seems reasonably large for our analytical purpose.

Exhibits 11.14 to 11.20 summarize the most salient results. We shall comment on these exhibits according to the lines of interpretation established in the previous section.

With regard to the dimension of General effectiveness, the idea that the relationships discussed in our first section could be produced by a general ideology regarding modern research seems to find some support.

First, it is clearly shown in Exhibits 11.14 and 11.15 that items proposed as indicators of people sharing that ideology demonstrate relatively strong relationships in each of the four subsets of units coming from academic nontechnological settings. (One can even imagine that the proliferation of publications devoted to demonstrating the relationship between effectiveness and such indicators will increase still more the strength of such correlations by reinforcing that ideology!) Compared to the values observed for academic settings, there is a marked decline in the strength and stability of the relationships in the two nonacademic settings.

Second, when we move out from this set of items, the variability of the relationship increases remarkably. For example, the correlation coefficient between General effectiveness as rated by staff scientists and Number of publications received moves from −.02 to .31, and for Adequacy of budget the range is from −.22 to .33. The same result occurs with the age of the head of unit (−.33 to .08), for his experience (−.22 to .35), and for articles from the unit published outside the country (−.19 to .36). The stability of ideological items in academic settings when compared with the variation observed for other items suggests that we should question the validity of General effectiveness as rated by

Exhibit 11.14. General effectiveness as rated by staff scientists: pattern of relationship in six types of research units (figures show Pearson *r*s)

	Item	Respondents[a]	Academic units in nontechnological fields				Nonacademic units in technological fields	
			Hungary	Belgium	Sweden	Austria	Austria	Finland
J3c:	Consideration of new ideas	SB	.54	.54	.33	.59	.45	.28
J3a:	Sense of innovation and pioneering	SB	.48	.52	.52	.44	.44	.29
J3b:	Dedication to work	SB	.45	.43	.35	.38	.38	.46
M1b:	Effect of contact with supervisor	SB	.46	.36	.44	.44	.38	.26
M2a:	Supervisor's professional ability	SB	.45	.38	.30	.44	.38	.13
M2d:	Supervisor's knowledge of research field	SB	.35	.32	.39	.39	.45	.28
M2f:	Supervisor's support of staff scientists' work	SB	.54	.34	.42	.51	.26	.28
P1a:	Adequacy of research planning	SB	.50	.48	.42	.59	.39	.45
P1b:	Interest in research activities	SB	.45	.59	.43	.58	.44	.40
P1c:	Coherence of research program	SB	.41	.50	.32	.34	.16	.43
Kj:	Adequacy of budget	SB	.33	−.22	.05	.10	.35	.07
F3a2:	Number of publications received by unit	SA	.07	.31	.05	.23	−.02	.12
R1b:	Number of research unit articles published abroad	SA	.22	.19	.17	.17	.13	.06

[a]SA = unit heads; SB = staff scientists.

Exhibit 11.15. General effectiveness as rated by unit head: pattern of relationship in six types of research units (figures show Pearson *r*s)

Item		Respondents[a]	Academic units in nontechnological fields				Nonacademic units in technological fields	
			Hungary	Belgium	Sweden	Austria	Austria	Finland
J3a:	Sense of innovation and pioneering	SA	.57	.42	.41	.35	.28	.24
J3b:	Dedication to work	SA	.33	.22	.46	.33	.24	.35
J3c:	Consideration of new ideas	SA	.47	.44	.33	.37	.24	.18
J3d:	Consideration of nontechnical ideas	SA	.33	.41	.18	.27	−.01	.26
J3f:	Cooperation among scientists in unit	SA	.26	.30	.31	.41	.25	.15
J3g:	Frequency of meetings	SA	.20	.19	.21	.33	.14	.11
J3h:	Technicians invited to meetings	SA	.23	.24	.33	.42	.09	.16
A1c:	Years as head	SA	−.29	−.25	−.10	−.12	−.21	.06
A2d:	Years R & D experience	SA	.10	.33	.08	−.09	.11	.10
Kb:	Rating of scientific equipment	SA	.24	.32	.18	.10	.17	.08
A2a:	Age	SA	−.33	−.14	−.02	−.22	.08	−.07
A2d:	Years R & D experience	SB	.35	−.02	−.07	−.22	.20	−.02
M2a:	Supervisor's professional abilities	SB	−.18	−.01	−.06	−.06	−.39	−.09
R1b:	No. of research-unit articles published abroad[b]	SA	−.19	.36	.25	.08	−.08	.20

[a] SA = unit heads, SB = staff scientists.
[b] Rescaled version of item.

Exhibit 11.16. Recognition: pattern of relationship in six types of research units (figures show Pearson *r*s)

Item		Respondents[a]	Academic units in nontechnological fields				Nonacademic units in technological fields	
			Hungary	Belgium	Sweden	Austria	Austria	Finland
Indx:	Research unit's published written output[c]	SA	.33	.48	.40	.38	.34	.33
A1a:	Years member this research unit	SA	.35	.17	.34	.23	.32	.25
A2d:	Years R & D experience	SA	.25	.16	.37	.20	.37	.19
E3:	Years going on: project 2	SA	.29	.21	.33	.24	.21	.24
R1b:	No. of research unit articles published within country[b]	SA	.21	.14	.25	.19	.37	.47
R1b:	No. of research unit articles published abroad[b]	SA	.35	.49	.34	.14	.37	.49
R1b:	No. of research unit articles published abroad	SA	.32	.48	.26	.15	.21	.42
F3a2:	No. of publications received by unit	SA	.24	.34	.17	.40	.12	.34
F3a2:	No. of publications sent by unit	SA	.16	.33	.05	.33	.33	.31
A1c:	No. years as head	SA	−.07	−.12	−.32	−.10	−.26	−.21
H1v:	Importance of scientific significance in choosing research themes	SA	.09	−.01	.22	−.08	.25	.20
R1b:	No. of research articles published in country	SA	.24	.10	.22	.20	.26	.37
Kb:	Rating of scientific equipment	SA	.01	.14	−.04	.31	.18	−.15
R1d:	No. of algorithms, etc.	SA	−.11	.16	−.04	.15	−.36	−.18
Kj:	Adequacy of budget	SB	.08	.05	.01	.14	.00	−.31
M2a:	Supervisor's professional ability	SB	.34	.34	−.04	−.14	−.05	.31
R1d:	No. of research unit algorithms[b]	SA	−.06	.14	−.02	.16	−.36	−.15

[a]SA = unit heads, SB = staff scientists. [b]Rescaled version of item. [c]Index residualized for type of unit (see Chapter 2).

Exhibit 11.17. Training effectiveness: pattern of relationship in six types of research units (figures show Pearson *r*s)

Item		Respondents[a]	Academic units in nontechnological fields				Nonacademic units in technological fields	
			Hungary	Belgium	Sweden	Austria	Austria	Finland
1.4b:	No. of staff engaged in R & D in organization	RU	−.04	−.00	.09	−.02	.01	.18
C1b2:	Percent time teaching	SA	.30	−.01	−.03	.36	.07	−.00
H1v:	Importance of scientific significance in choosing research themes	SA	.06	.23	.01	.14	.10	.25
J3f:	Cooperation among scientists in unit	SA	.03	.32	.11	.19	−.10	.08
J3g:	Frequency of meetings	SA	.09	.36	−.03	.07	−.04	−.02
La1:	Influence of organization leaders in choosing research tasks	SA	−.04	−.07	−.03	−.14	−.01	.03
C1b2:	Percent time teaching	SB	.40	.02	.07	.10	.06	−.26
J3b:	Dedication to work	SB	−.07	.37	.09	−.01	.05	.19
J3c:	Consideration of new ideas	SB	.04	.34	.05	.13	.10	−.10
La1:	Influence of organization leaders in choosing research tasks	SB	−.19	.14	.04	−.08	−.23	.17
P1b:	Interest in research activities	SB	.12	.36	.18	−.07	−.13	.24
R1a:	No. of research-unit books[b]	SA	−.13	−.16	.09	−.33	−.03	−.14

[a]SA = unit heads, SB = staff scientists, RU = administrators.
[b]Rescaled version of item.

staff scientists and by heads of units. How, indeed, could we explain that sometimes the R & D experience of the head of a unit has a positive effect and at other times a negative effect?

As expected from the results of previous analyses, the instability across type of unit is fairly high for rated Applications effectiveness (Exhibit 11.18). Except perhaps for the number of algorithms produced by the unit (in either raw or adjusted form) there is no stable correlation with any variable across the six types of units analyzed. For example, Invitations to technical staff to attend scientific meetings shows correlations ranging from −.09 to .27, and Influence of authorities outside the organization varies from −.06 to .39. It would be hard to ignore this lack of stability when proposing some general theory or policy recommendations in the field of applications effectiveness.

As for Social effectiveness, there seems to be some stability of the relationships involving outputs of research units and items related to the organization of research activities (the influence of science policymaking bodies, of authorities outside the organization, external formal planning, etc.). The other items are significantly unstable across types of units. It seems that the hypothesis that Social effectiveness is a rating heavily influenced by the type of unit is somewhat supported by these results (Exhibit 11.19).

The same conclusion, concerning Recognition and Training effectiveness, arises from an examination of Exhibits 11.16 and 11.17. Except for items that identify a specific type of research unit (e.g., the number of written products, percentage of time spent on teaching, etc.) there is no salient stable relationship.

This analysis does not permit us to reject completely the question of validity of the rated-performance measures. We have the feeling, considering all the available evidence, that we should not make a premature interpretation of these relationships.

5. Summary and conclusions

This chapter tries to assess the validity of the rated-performance measures used in the International Comparative Study.

The logic of our analysis has been to explore the meaning of rated-performance measures by utilizing the relationships they show with other dimensions in the study. It appears that the context in which research units are working introduces significant variation into those indices. For that reason, we subset the individual research units into more homogeneous groups, within which we repeated the analysis performed at the global level. This approach allowed us to evaluate the stability of the previous patterns.

Exhibit 11.18. Applications effectiveness: pattern of relationship in six types of research units (figures show Pearson *r*s)

Item		Respondents[a]	Academic units in nontechnological fields				Nonacademic units in technological fields	
			Hungary	Belgium	Sweden	Austria	Austria	Finland
R1d:	No. of research-unit algorithms, etc.	SA	.22	.21	.01	.03	.17	.25
Indx:	Research-unit's reports & algorithms[b]	SA	.38	.18	.02	.22	.10	.12
5b2:	Delay satisfaction: expensive equip.	RU	.06	.09	.16	.00	.24	.05
C1b2:	% time teaching	SA	.07	−.07	−.03	−.17	.03	.08
H1i:	Importance of science policymaking bodies in choosing research themes	SA	.00	.24	.01	.12	−.16	−.04
H1v:	Importance of scientific significance in choosing research themes	SA	−.23	.08	−.04	−.19	−.08	.07
J3a:	Sense of innovation and pioneering	SA	.19	−.01	−.06	−.12	.25	.15
J3d:	Consideration of nontechnical items	SA	.16	.09	.02	.15	.16	.33
J3f:	Cooperation among scientists in unit	SA	.09	−.00	.10	.07	.31	.07
J3g:	Frequency of meetings	SA	.17	.12	.02	−.07	.21	.11
J3h:	Technicians invited to meetings	SA	.09	.10	−.09	.25	.14	.27
Kb:	Rating of scientific equipment	SA	.22	.32	.06	.04	.04	.00
La1:	Influence of organization leaders in choosing research tasks	SA	.16	.25	.20	.12	−.05	.03
La1:	Influence of outsiders in choosing research tasks	SA	.17	.31	.39	.23	.02	−.06
N2a:	Use of formal research-planning methods	SA	−.12	.14	.02	.26	−.07	−.09
C1b2:	% time teaching	SB	.12	−.17	−.18	−.16	−.06	.17
La1:	Influence of organization leaders in choosing research tasks	SB	−.10	.23	−.04	.09	−.06	−.14
La1:	Influence of outsiders in choosing research tasks	SB	−.06	.40	.40	.18	.13	−.07
R1f:	No. of research-unit internal reports[c]	SA	.32	.17	.00	.01	.04	.03
R1g:	No. of research-unit routine reports[c]	SA	.21	.09	.06	.33	.16	.01

[a] SA = unit heads, SB = staff scientists, RU = administrators. [b] Index residualized for type of unit (see Chapter 2). [c] Rescaled version of item.

Exhibit 11.19. Social effectiveness: pattern of relationship in six types of research units (figures show Pearson *r*s)

Item		Respondents[a]	Academic units in nontechnological fields				Nonacademic units in technological fields	
			Hungary	Belgium	Sweden	Austria	Austria	Finland
R1b:	No. of research-unit articles published within country	SA	.34	.16	.04	.11	.22	.23
R1b:	No. of research-unit articles published abroad	SA	−.09	−.24	−.00	−.06	−.03	.09
R1d:	No. of research-unit algorithms, etc.	SA	−.10	−.09	.07	.21	.01	−.20
R1a:	No. of research-unit books[b]	SA	.24	.17	.20	.01	−.24	.20
R1b:	No. of research-unit articles published within country[b]	SA	.42	.17	.07	.15	.22	.28
R1b:	No. of research-unit articles published abroad[b]	SA	−.12	−.25	−.13	−.08	−.06	.17
R1d:	No. of research-unit algorithms, etc.[b]	SA	.05	.01	.06	.26	.04	−.13
R1e:	No. of research-unit reviews, bibliographies[b]	SA	.25	.13	.09	.04	.02	.27
R1g:	No. of reserch-unit routine reports[b]	SA	.23	.17	.09	.16	−.10	.13
R2b:	No. of research-unit prototype materials[b]	SA	.16	−.17	−.06	−.03	.20	.10
Indx:	Research unit's published written output[c]	SA	.26	.02	.04	.03	.09	.28
Indx:	Research unit's reports and algorithms[c]	SA	.20	.13	.19	.23	.04	.04
H1i:	Importance of science policymaking bodies in choosing research themes	SA	.08	.30	.20	.14	.03	.12
N2a:	Use of formal research-planning methods	SA	.12	.24	.11	.07	.03	.24
1.4b:	No. of staff engaged in R & D in organization	RU	−.23	.26	−.03	−.07	−.19	−.10
A1a:	Years member of this research unit	SA	−.02	−.10	−.00	.06	.35	.14
A1c:	Years as head	SA	−.01	−.06	−.00	−.09	.23	.12
A2d:	Years R & D experience	SA	.18	−.09	−.09	.06	.29	.23
C1b2:	% time teaching	SA	−.17	−.05	−.13	−.13	−.13	.23

E3:	Years going on: project 2	SA	.06	−.02	.12	.05	.06	.27
F3a2:	No. of publications received by unit	SA	.04	−.22	.14	−.05	.03	.27
G2c:	Work of unit is evaluated by organizational hierarchy	SA	.14	−.05	.00	.36	.14	−.03
H1v:	Importance of scientific significance in choosing research themes	SA	−.30	−.13	−.16	−.40	.10	.28
Kb:	Rating of scientific equipment	SA	−.21	−.12	−.16	−.19	−.06	−.17
La1:	Influence of organization leaders in choosing research tasks	SA	.04	.01	.11	.07	.05	−.23
La1:	Influence of outsiders in choosing research tasks	SA	.23	.24	.39	.45	.08	.21
A2a:	Age	SB	.09	.08	.04	.12	.23	.10
C1b2:	% time teaching	SB	−.00	−.06	−.27	−.16	−.06	−.02
C1b6:	% time on design studies	SB	.21	.07	−.09	.08	−.14	−.21
D2a:	Interdisciplinary orientation	SB	.12	−.04	.18	.10	.08	.36
J3a:	Interest in innovation and pioneering	SB	.14	−.10	.13	−.25	.25	−.04
J3c:	Consideration of new ideas	SB	−.06	.01	−.23	.18	−.09	−.10
Kj:	Adequacy of budget	SB	.04	.06	−.29	−.21	−.14	−.28
La1:	Influence of outsiders in choosing research tasks	SB	.09	.20	.45	.22	−.06	.01
M1b:	Effect of contact with supervisor	SB	.05	−.04	−.03	.08	−.16	.24

[a]SA = unit heads, SB = staff scientists, RU = administrators.
[b]Rescaled version of item.
[c]Index residualized for type of unit (see Chapter 2).

Exhibit 11.20. Administrative effectiveness: pattern of relationship in six types of research units (figures show Pearson *r*s)

			Academic units in nontechnological fields				Nonacademic units in technological fields	
Item		Respondents[a]	Hungary	Belgium	Sweden	Austria	Austria	Finland
1.4b:	No. of staff engaged in R & D in organization	RU	−.26	.05	.02	.05	−.11	−.11
C1b2:	% time teaching	SA	.16	.11	−.30	.05	.09	−.01
J3d:	Consideration of nontechnical ideas	SA	−.03	.16	.28	.11	.05	−.04
Kb:	Rating of scientific equipment	SA	−.09	.16	.20	.16	.18	.30
R1d:	No. of research-unit algorithms	SA	−.00	.16	−.09	−.09	−.28	−.12
A2a:	Age	SB	.04	.07	.11	.21	.16	.27
A2d:	Years R & D experience	SB	.08	.04	.12	.20	.06	.17
Kj:	Adequacy of budget	SB	.04	.36	.22	.30	.14	.16
P1a:	Adequacy of research planning	SB	.29	.03	.20	.04	.24	.30
P1c:	Coherence of research program	SB	.22	.01	.08	.15	.27	.20
R1b:	No. of research-unit articles published abroad[b]	SA	.09	−.16	.05	−.30	−.09	−.10
R1d:	No. of research-unit algorithms[b]	SA	−.05	.09	−.01	−.01	−.31	−.11

[a]SA = unit heads, SB = staff scientists, RU = administrators.
[b]Rescaled version of item.

The major results suggest that there are very few constant relationships across different types of units.

There are, however, two sets of exceptions. The first appears to be for General effectiveness, but we believe that stability here, across academic settings, may be viewed at least partially as an indicator of adhesion to a common notion about "modern" effectiveness, which in turn is part of the global ideology of our modern social system in highly developed countries. The second exception seems to result mainly from the tools used for measuring effectiveness as well as some other dimensions (Recognition and written products, Training and teaching, Applications and algorithms).

Referring to the first motivation of this chapter, these last findings seem to demonstrate that the effectiveness measures are not completely free of influences from particular institutional settings. It seems that these measurements capitalize primarily upon the dimensions recognized in the academic or technological arenas in developed Western countries.

The opportunity given to scientists to assess the effectiveness of their research units seems also questionable. The absence of marked relationships observed between the subjective appraisals and the objective outputs of the units should not be taken for granted without further thought. This lack of relationship, however, does not necessarily mean that the subjective measures are invalid for their purpose. Indeed, we have no formal evidence that countable outputs really measure the effectiveness of research units, though they have been classically used – in the literature and in the management of science – to assess scientists' productivity. Nevertheless, it would be extremely difficult to believe that the outputs of a unit are completely independent of its effectiveness, and that the absence of relationships does not by itself question the validity of the rated-performance measures. The sensitivity that they demonstrate to the typology of units reinforces our doubts. It seems that a unit's members, like any other social actors, behave according to the context in which they carry out their activities. Their attitudes in assessing the effectiveness of their units may consequently be related to the specific features of that context, or, more precisely, to their position in it.

These findings do not detract from the interest of the study. Many aspects of the life of research units may be analyzed with benefit so long as the rated-performance measures are not asked to indicate more than they can.

Summarizing our previous conclusions, it seems appropriate to be rather cautious in making any generalization about the effectiveness of research units using rated-performance scores. Their sensitivity to the context of the unit, and the relative instability of their relationships, seem to call for care concerning any evaluation of research units by means of those measurements. It would be unwise to derive from those measurements any premature recommendations regarding the improvement of the effectiveness of research units. Nevertheless, this does not mean that no feedback can be undertaken on many aspects of the life of the units. In that process, we could learn something from the criticism and suggestions coming from the researchers themselves, provided that the feedback procedures allow for a two-way flow of information.

A final conclusion can be formulated at the level of suggestions for further studies on research effectiveness. It seems that the repetition of what already has been used in this study does not offer any further promise for the improvement of our understanding of the phenomenon. On the contrary, we would suggest that some effort be devoted to more theoretically oriented studies with the purpose of defining the concepts of research units and of their efficiency and effectiveness, taking into account the institutional setting and the general social framework in which they operate. This would primarily include a theory of the objectives of research units, covering the aims of governments, institutions, and individual researchers, and coping, for example, with the problems of possible conflicts arising between these different social actors.

A second type of research that may be worthwhile would consist of empirical, in-depth investigations of the functioning of research units in homogeneous contexts. The instability of measurements and of relationships observed in our research seems to indicate that appropriate performance measures can only be built for subsets of units belonging to a similar environment. Science policies, the sources of financial support, the status of the researcher, the links between scientific and economic activities, etc., should – at least hypothetically – be considered from that perspective.

Those two approaches seem, according to our results, to offer the most promise for moving toward a better understanding of the effectiveness of scientific activities.

References

Georgopoulos, B., and Tannenbaum, A. S., 1957, A Study of Organizational Effectiveness, *American Sociological Review,* 22: 534–540.

Lazarsfeld, P., and Thielens, W., 1958, *The Academic Mind,* New York, Free Press.

Mott, E., 1972, *The Characteristics of Effective Organizations,* Harper & Row, New York.

Orth, C. D., 1959, The Optimum Climate for Industrial Research, *Harvard Business Review,* 37: 135–147.

Pelz, D. C., and Andrews, F. M., 1966, *Scientists in Organizations, Productive Climates for Research and Development,* New York, Wiley.

Price, J. L., 1968, *Organizational Effectiveness: An Inventory of Propositions,* Homewood, Ill., Irwin.

Price, J. L., 1972, The Study of Organizational Effectiveness, *The Sociological Quarterly,* 13: 3–15.

Sjoberg, G., and Nett, R., 1968, *A Methodology for Social Research,* Harper & Row, New York.

Warner, L. W., 1960, *Social Class in America,* New York, Harper & Row.

Notes

1. For details, see the items in sections S and T of the questionnaire (reproduced in the Appendix to this volume). These sections refer to the Application of the results obtained by the research unit, and to the Value of the work of the research unit, respectively.

2. All correlation coefficients exhibit signs that allow them to be interpreted in the classical way: Positive correlations mean that two variables vary in the same direction in terms of meaning (regardless of original scaling).

3. The problem of validity of effectiveness measures is discussed by Mott (1972: 189–199). He accepts the self-evaluation approach if respondents use viable professional standards. The definition of these remains in our mind the key issue.

4. Some people might question the appropriateness of considering Administrative effectiveness as a dimension of scientific performance, on the basis that this view reflects an approach to the management of research that is too bureaucratic.

5. It seems that the attitude regarding one's immediate supervisor is a core variable, highly correlated with perceptions of patterns of influence and of the planning of research.

6. Similar findings occurred using the AID technique.

7. Academic units include units located in the following types of institutions: (1) universities and similar institutions of higher education; (2) research institutes closely associated with and often managed by universities; and (3) institutions attached to academies of science (in the socialist countries) and to national research organizations [such as Toegepast Natuurwetenschappelijk Onderzoek (TNO) in the Netherlands, Centre National de la Recherche Scientifique (CNRS) in France, Institute Max Planck in the German Federal Republic, atomic energy commissariat and commissions, national space agencies, etc.]. The category of Nonacademic units includes units located in institutions characterized as: (1) research institutes serving, wholly or partly, a sector of production, a branch of industry, or a public service; (2) research laboratories of productive enterprises; and (3) contract-research institutes.

8. Scientific fields and disciplines considered as technological are: agricultural sciences, medical sciences, and technological sciences (i.e., categories 31 to 33 in Unesco's International Standard Nomenclature for Fields of Science and Technology).

9. This typology is described in Chapter 13. Its use for adjusting performance measures is described in Chapter 2.

12 The analysis strategy of the Hungarian Research Team and some results on R & D facilities

Peter Hunya
Laboratory of Cybernetics, Jozsef Attila University, Szeged
Arpad Halász and Csaba Fajszi
Biological Research Center, Hungarian Academy of Sciences, Szeged

1. Introduction

The authors have sought to gain an overall picture of the variables used in the International Comparative Study on the Organization and Performance of Research Units and to acquire an insight into some relationships among the objective and rated input measures and output measures.

A careful planning of the analysis seemed to be desirable. Thus, we have defined the following main subgoals: (1) to elucidate the structure and properties of groups of variables and of the whole data step by step; (2) to elaborate and apply an appropriate methodology both for structural analysis and for the investigation of relationships; and (3) to identify the topics that seem essential for further analysis.

This chapter describes the logical succession of the phases of analysis, the methods and results of the structural analysis, and some results related to the effectiveness of research units.

The Unesco data from Round 1 of the International Study (archived in the Belgian Archives for the Social Sciences) served as the basis for the analyses. Prior to beginning the work, we had to decide if some selected portions of the data or all the material would be analyzed. We chose to investigate the whole data set. Although this significantly increased the amount of work that was necessary, it enhanced the probability of our finding a reliable approach to the goals mentioned above.

The heterogeneity of these international data needs always to be borne in mind. This heterogeneity was one of the facts that turned our attention to the analysis of the effect of Country as a control variable.

2. Analysis

Examination of the variables

Conceptual survey of the variables

Before the statistical analyses, we performed a thorough review of both the variables in the questionnaires and of the answers given to them. We asked whether the variables – in the form given or in any other form – could yield information on the questions that we thought to be important. As a result of this review some variables were omitted from further consideration, while others were selected for use in constructing composite measures.

Univariate and bivariate statistical analyses

Before undertaking any structural analyses, a variety of univariate and bivariate analyses was performed. Scientific discipline, Type of institution, and Country served as control variables. The univariate analyses showed that these three control variables were associated with substantial differences in the distributions of the majority of variables.

The bivariate analyses (involving computation of the chi-square, F, t, and/or d tests) provided a more exact statistical investigation of the "country effects" revealed by the univariate analyses. About 90% of the variables had relationships to Country that were strong enough to reach statistical significance.

Study of the control variables

The results described above led to the following questions: Which of the three control variables mentioned above determined the main tendencies in the data? Are there any other important control variables?

In order to answer these questions, we undertook a structural search, using the AID computer program (Sonquist, Baker, and Morgan, 1973). Those output variables that we thought to be most important and subjective ratings of research-unit effectiveness were used as dependent variables. The results of these analyses once more turned our attention to the effects of the three main control variables, particularly Scientific discipline and Type of institution.

Country, however, seemed to be of only secondary importance. Considering the strong Country effects found in the univariate and bivariate analyses, and the differences in the samples of research units in different countries, it seemed reasonable to assume that the Country effects were mainly attributable to the effects of the former two control variables.

There seemed no reason to use any other variables as controls in the succeeding analyses. Although the R & D experience of the researchers showed a considerable relationship to some dependent variables, we decided not to treat it as a control variable.

Creation of a refined discipline code

The analyses described above demonstrated the roughness of the stratification by disciplines and suggested the desirability of creating a more refined set of categories for scientific field.

Two sets of data provided by heads of units permitted classification of the units on the basis of their scientific fields. The first derived from a supplementary question (not part of the main Round 1 questionnaires) that used the two-digit discipline categories from Unesco's Proposed International Standard Nomenclature for Fields of Science and Technology (Unesco, 1973). (In our univariate analysis, this is the variable that was used.) The second set of data was based on questions E1a–f, where the six scientific fields most important for the unit were to be identified according to the same nomenclature, using a six-digit classification.[1]

The two-digit classification of the research unit's scientific field seems more prone to error because: (1) It was based on the last question asked of unit heads, after two or three hours of previous questions; (2) the answer was coded by the interviewer; and (3) some disciplines occur in the nomenclature at more than one place. Therefore, the answers to question E1 were thought to be the more suitable ones for further use. However, these six-digit discipline codes did not give a unique assignment to Scientific field and were too detailed for analysis. Hence, a more appropriate code system had to be created.

Only the first four digits of the listed six-digit disciplines were taken into account (this was possible because of the hierarchical structure of the nomenclature), and the most frequently occurring four-digit discipline was accepted as characteristic of the unit's work. (In the case of ties, the code appearing first was selected.) Even this classification was too detailed. Therefore, we consulted with researchers and created 25 science-field groups, on the basis of the similarity of the disciplines with respect to facility requirements and type of output. The original and the new discipline codes proved to be substantially related (Cramer's V = .95), yet the distribution of the new code categories is much more homogeneous among countries than that of the two-digit codes.

Structural analysis and construction of representative measures

After a thorough preliminary study of the whole set of data, we sought to identify areas worth further, deeper analysis and to explore the overall structure of the questionnaire.

One of the main difficulties in the realization of this task was the great number of variables involved: It greatly exceeded the number of variables that could be simultaneously handled by the currently available computing facilities.[2] Therefore, the first step was to split the variables into meaningful conceptual clusters, with at most 60 variables in each cluster. The variables of a cluster of such size could be handled simultaneously by any of several different analysis techniques.

Thus, there were two fundamental stages of the structural analysis: (1) a conceptual analysis to clear up the logical structure of the data, based upon examination of the meaning of the questions; and (2) an empirical analysis of the conceptual clusters formed in the previous stage. In this second stage, the meaning of the questions was ignored and only the values of the answers to them were used.

The data base used in the structural analyses is described in detail in a working paper (Fajszi, Halasz, and Hunya, 1975).

Conceptual grouping of the variables

After studying several possible groupings, we determined a final clustering, which appears in Exhibit 12.1.

Empirical analysis

In the first step of the empirical study, the conceptual clusters were analyzed one by one. Composite measures (called *representative measures*) were constructed and stood for the empirically identified factors. The analyses were performed on both the re-

Exhibit 12.1. Conceptual grouping of the variables

Content	Reference letter	Questionnaire items[a]
Output variables		
Respondent-level output	A	SA,SB:A3,C1a2,C1b2,C1b3,C2
Unit-level output (resources[b])	B	SA:R1–3; RU:4
Performance measures of International Research Team	C	
Rated performance variables		
Internal evaluations	D	SA,SB:S,T
External evaluations	E	EV:Ta–d,f–h
Variables influencing performance		
Objective inputs (facilities available, delays in meeting needs)	F	RU:2,5
Internal & external connections	X	SA:F1–3; SA,SB:Q1–4
Activity distribution, general	T	SA,SB:C1b1–7,G1a2,G1c1
Activity distribution in R & D	U	SA,SB:C3a–k
Supervision, control	K, L, M	SA,SB:L; SA:G
Research themes, planning	V	SA:D,E2,H,N; SB:D,F2,P1; RU:2.4b
Subjective influence, judgments	N, O, P, R, S	SA,SB,TS:B,J,M
Satisfaction with level of inputs	G	SA,SB:K
Other general and personal data	Z	SA,SB:A1b–c,A3g–h,R1g–h SA,SB,TS:A2; RU:1a

[a]Codes appearing before colon indicate particular questionnaire(s) in which items appeared; codes after colon indicate relevant questionnaire section(s). Unless indicated otherwise, all items within indicated section were considered as belonging to group.
[b]This group also includes indices expressing changes in resources of unit. In our opinion, resources at a given period can only slightly influence output in same period but instead reflect recognition of past results and expectations of future production.

spondent and unit levels. In the second stage, an overall investigation of all representative measures was performed.

Empirical analysis of conceptual clusters. In order to explore the internal structure of the conceptual clusters, several well-known methods of structural analysis were applied.

Taking the matrix of similarity measures (Pearson *r*s) among the variables as a starting point, the following analyses were performed: (1) factor analysis (Harman, 1967); (2) correlogram (Sibson, 1973); (3) hierarchical cluster analysis (Johnson, 1967); and (4) multidimensional scaling (Shepard, 1962).

The purpose of this many-sided examination was to go somewhat beyond the restrictions inherent in the basic assumptions of the methods and to obtain information concerning the structure of the groups from different points of view.

The fundamental features of the structures obtained using the different methods proved to be similar, and the results concerning each cluster could be represented in one combined picture. Exhibit 12.2 provides an example and shows the structure of group D, the internal evaluations. This presentation highly facilitated the identification of structural patterns within the conceptual clusters. The internal structures of all conceptual clusters as obtained were laid down in 22 combined pictures and were presented in a working paper (Fajszi, Halasz, and Hunya, 1976).

Construction of representative measures. On the basis of the above results, *primary representative measures* were constructed for each conceptual cluster. The variables that proved to be independent of the other variables in the cluster were taken as representatives. From the strongly related variables, an index was constructed (in most cases the mean of the original or of the standardized variables), and this index was later used as the representative measure for those variables. (Exhibit 12.2 indicates which variables were treated as, or combined into, primary representative measures.)

The structural analysis and index construction were then repeated on several *combined* conceptual clusters, using the primary representative measures as starting variables. Thus, *secondary representative measures* were obtained. This was done for two reasons. First, to avoid the danger that the initial cluster boundaries might cause a substantial restriction in the analysis. Second, to generate a set of representative measures that would be as orthogonal as possible for use in further investigations.

By this multilevel structural analysis, we proceeded from the original data through the primary, secondary, etc., representative measures, to develop a pyramid-like system of representative measures.

The representative measures contain, in a concentrated manner, the original measures. We checked to see the extent to which the representative measures preserved (and hence could be used to predict) the variance of the original variables. These analyses showed that the representative measures reproduced quite well the original variance of the variables. Multivariate re-

Notations used in the figures

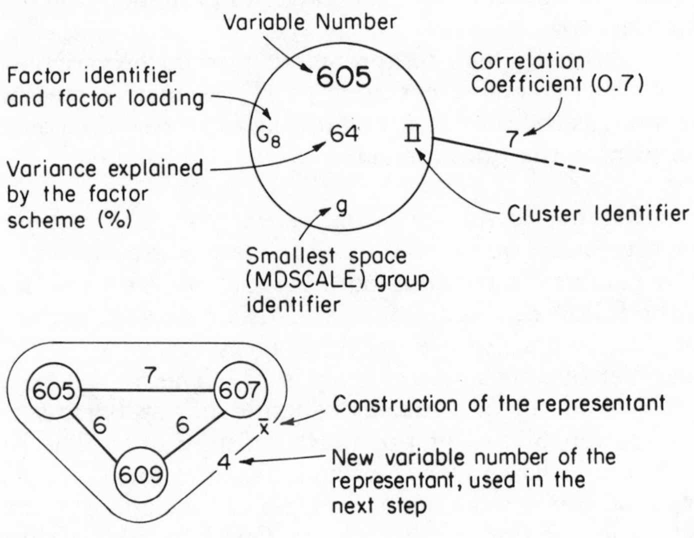

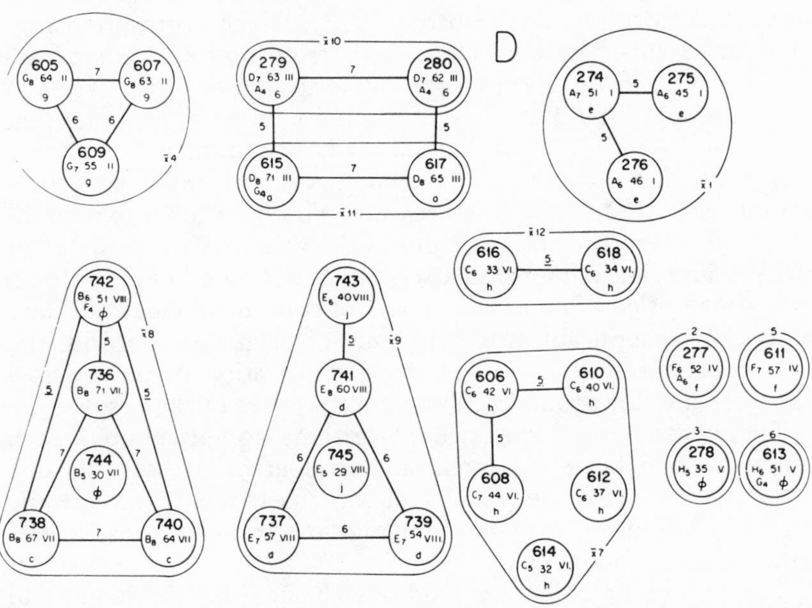

Exhibit 12.2. Structural relationships among variables in conceptual group D.

gression was used as the analysis technique, and an average multiple *R* of .75 was obtained for the variables examined (the minimal value was .44).

Based on this fairly high representative power, the variables at the top of the pyramid-like system of representative measures were accepted as the ones that empirically expressed the content of the answers to the questionnaire.

Overall investigation of the representative measures. The system of representative measures derived using the procedures outlined in the above paragraphs contains both respondent- and unit-level data. In the following discussion, we restrict ourselves mostly to presenting the analysis of the unit-level measures.

The number of unit-level variables is 273. The overall examination of such a set of variables required new programs that exceeded the capabilities of previously existing ones. The programs reported in Fajszi (1976) provide facilities for hierarchical clustering and for producing correlograms, including a semi-graphical representation of the results. Our hierarchical cluster analysis program is based on Johnson's algorithm (1967). Our hierarchical correlogram comprises a series of the well-known single-link correlograms (Sibson, 1973), which correspond to a predefined cut-point list. The results from both techniques can be presented in the form of contour maps, an example of which is shown in Exhibit 12.3. The maximum number of variables that can be accessed in one run is 400 for both programs.[3]

We decided to apply these two less-sophisticated structure-exploring procedures for two reasons. First, the other two methods used to explore the structure of the original variables – factor analysis and multidimensional scaling, as described in the subsection above titled "Empirical analysis of conceptual clusters" – are practically inapplicable for problems of such size. Second, the four procedures used for structural exploration of the original variables did not produce essential differences in the results.

The outcomes of the two algorithms complemented each other. Although the hierarchical correlogram stresses the disjunctions between the groups of variables, the results of the hierarchical cluster analysis emphasize the compact, close aggregations of the measures.

The two complementary methods characterize the lower and upper bounds of the relational strength between variables. In the correlogram, any connection between two groups separated by a contour line was smaller than the level of this contour line. In the cluster structure, the level corresponded to the minimal

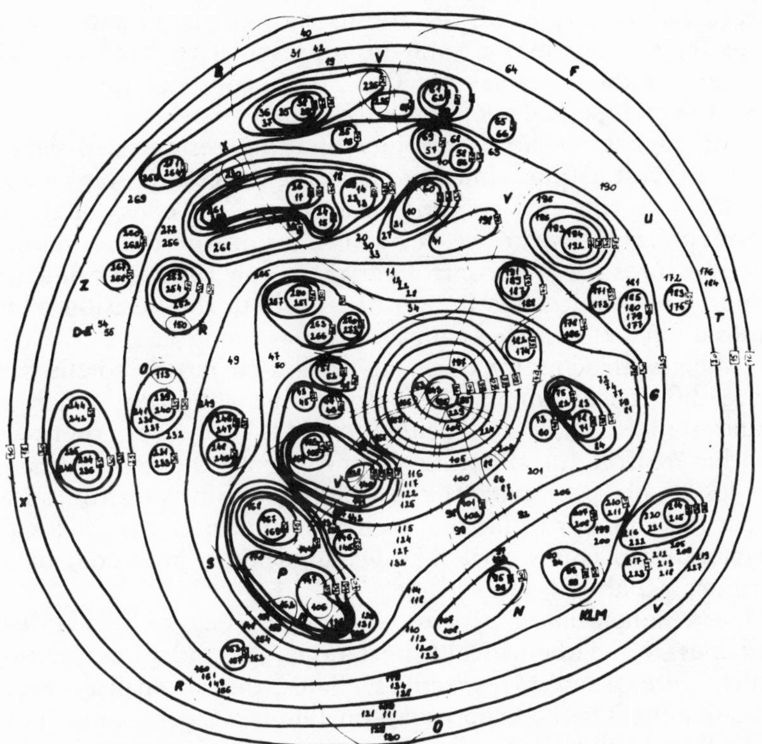

Exhibit 12.3. Contour map showing hierarchical correlogram of representative measures.

value of the relationship between any two variables within the contour line. This difference was reflected in the survey maps in their degree of disaggregation.

It seems that the correlogram patterns corresponded to more identifiable concepts than those of the cluster structures.

Control variables and representative measures

In the subsection above titled "Study of the control variables," the effects of the basic control variables were reported. It is a question for further investigation whether the previously observed relationships could be found for the representative measures as well.

Effects of Country, Scientific field, and Type of organization

In order to answer the question, Cramer's Vs were computed between the three basic control variables and the representative measures.[4] As expected, the results showed significant relationships for the vast majority of the representative measures. (The medians of the V values are 0.32, 0.25, and 0.25 for Country, Scientific field, and Type, respectively.)

This suggested the desirability of using residualized data in further investigations aimed at exploring the relationships among the facilities, internal conditions, and productiveness of the research units. However, we decided to residualize the representative measures for two control variables only (Scientific field and Type). This choice was in accord with both the decision of the International Research Team and the assumption that the relationships with Country could be attributed mostly to the sampling differences among the participating countries, which are manifested in Type and Scientific field. Moreover, there was another reason for omitting Country from the residualization process: This preserved the possibility of investigating differences in a number of factors, such as science-policy practices and organizational issues, that may be implicitly represented in the Country variable.

The residualization process generated a set of standardized variables, the mathematical expectation and standard deviation of which were 5 and 2, respectively. Thus, the residualized representative measures: (1) appeared on a uniform, comparable scale, and (2) had values in a range appropriate for the programs of the Osiris computer software package. (It is to be stressed tht correlational relations are invariant under linear transformation.)

Control variables and residualized representative measures

The assumptions concerning the sampling and Country effects were checked using the residualized measures. Two indicators were considered: (1) One-way analysis of variance (Bock, 1963) was performed for certain variable groups; and (2) Cramer's Vs between Country and all the residualized representative measures were computed. Both tests showed that the Country dependence, although at a decreased level, remained for many of the variables. (The analysis of variance gave significant F ratios for more than 80% of the variables examined. The median of the Cramer's V values was .17.)

In order to find the source of the dependency on Country, further examinations were made using country averages (i.e., means) for the residualized variables. These searches considered: (1) the unit-level countable output, (2) the size and dynamics of staffing, (3) the rated-performance and recognition measures, (4) the external evaluations, (5) the equipment available to a research unit and members' satisfaction with it (available/needed), (6) the ratings of available facilities, (7) the communications of the unit, and (8) the age and experience of the personnel and of the unit.

The results of the analysis and the procedures applied are detailed below in the subsection titled "Country-level analysis."

Structure of the residualized representative measures

An overall structural analysis of the full set of data was performed using the residualized variables in the same way as described in the subsection above titled "Overall investigation of the representative measures" for the unresidualized representative measures. We found that eliminating the effects of Type and Scientific field produced some changes in the empirically determined structure of the data.

The hierarchical correlogram map based on residualized data showed many interesting patterns. For example, the subjective answers coming from different types of respondents generally were separated: There was a segregation between data from staff scientists and from the technical support staff, and a further one between data from these groups and heads of units. This pattern of aggregation by content and separation by respondent appeared for the following types of variables, among others: ratings of available facilities, estimations of the importance of scientific significance in choice of research themes, reports on the patterns of influence within the research unit, and information regarding the linkage of the research unit to external groups. However, for objective (countable) output variables, the type of respondent seemed not to be a strong separator. Rather, these variables are separated according to the type of output: books, articles, patents, algorithms, prototype devices, and internal and routine reports.

Besides the variable separation, some connections that are interesting for further investigation should be noted. For example, it is remarkable, from a management point of view, that the number of people nonadministratively attached to a research unit was related to indices of the growth of the unit (personnel, expenditure, and financial level). Also interesting was the aggregation of variables expressing the patterns of influence within the unit and the extent to which practical needs and scientific significance affected the choice of research themes. Another example is that, for data from unit heads, the measures of Rated general effectiveness and Recognition were close to the composite measure of Within-unit collectivity; however, the same connection did not appear for staff scientists. Finally, we noted that the age of the research unit and the experience of its personnel were related to per capita output of articles for both heads of units and staff scientists. It is intersting, however, that the number of books was only very slightly related to age or experience.

Multivariate predictive analysis

The multivariate predictive analysis aimed at examining multivariate relationships between the facility variables (conceptual group F, as described in the subsection above titled "Conceptual grouping of the variables" and Exhibit 12.1), the countable outputs, and the rated-performance and resource measures. The analysis was conducted at three levels: for respondents, for research units, and for countries.

Respondent-level analysis

In the first step, the respondent-level nonresidualized representative measures were used. The main countable outputs were taken for dependent variables one by one and the input variables (facilities available and delays in meeting needs) for predictors.

The regression computations, when performed on all the respondents, yielded multiple *R*-square values of .02, .03, and .02 for books, articles, and patents, respectively. This extremely low predictive power motivated a repeated calculation using a subset of respondents, because a great number of them did not produce any output of this or that type, and this may have hidden the actual relationships. The subset consisted of those respondents who had produced at least one of the outputs (books, articles, or patents) being examined. The corresponding multiple *R*-squares were .02, .02, and .03. We conclude that there were no essential relationships (in either of the populations examined) between R & D facilities that were available or delays in meeting needs for facilities and outputs of books, articles, or patents – at least when the analysis was conducted at the respondent level.

Unit-level analysis

For the unit-level analysis, we focused our attention on the residualized representative variables (which were described in the subsection above titled "Effects of Country, Scientific field, and

Type of organization"). In searching for relationships, the AID program (Sonquist, Baker, and Morgan, 1973) was applied, and regression analysis was also used. Two topics were investigated: (1) prediction of the rated-performance measures on the basis of the countable outputs, and (2) prediction of the countable outputs on the basis of the R & D facilities available to the unit.

Countable output and rated performance. From the correlations among the variables and the hierarchical correlogram derived from these correlations, we found that there was no marked direct relationship between the countable outputs and the rated-performance measures (the maximum r was .23), that is, no one of the performance measures could be unambiguously related to any of the countable outputs. For this reason, multivariate analysis was attempted.

We expected that the main countable outputs (books, articles, and patents) would jointly show at least a modestly strong correlation with the rated-performance measures. It was known from an earlier stage of the study that the experience of scientists/engineers has a relatively strong relationship with both the countable output and the rated performance (as described in the subsection above titled "Study of the control variables"). Therefore, preliminary computations were made in which the outputs of books, articles, and patents, and also the experience variables, were used as predictors of the performance ratings. The explained variance proved to be relatively low (R-squares averaged .05 and ranged from .01 to .14, the highest being for prediction of Recognition as rated by the heads of units).

We then tried a more complete and detailed predictor set and added variables that could be taken as official reflections on the unit's results in a former period (specifically, the growth of expenditures and personnel). These measures indicate the development of the unit; consequently, they may have a positive effect on the internal evaluations. A series of multiple regression analyses was performed and the results show that modification of the predictor set enhanced the explanatory power (mean R-square = .10, maximum R-square = 0.17 – for Recognition – and minimum R-square =.04 – for Administrative effectiveness as rated by unit heads).

Facilities and countable output. Parallel to the analyses performed at the respondent level (reported in the subsection above titled "Respondent-level analysis"), the possibility of predicting countable output from the facility variables was examined at the unit level as well. First, the relaionships were studied by AID, and in a second step a refinement was attempted using regression techniques. Again, we concluded that the countable outputs (the number of books, articles, patents, etc., produced by a research unit) were almost independent of the supply of facilities and services, and of the speed with which facility needs were satisfied.[5]

Country-level analysis

As we reported in the subsection above titled "Control variables and residualized representative measures," the residualization of the representative measures did not eliminate their relationships to Country. In this subsection, we try to find the basis of this dependence. First, we consider a general procedure for ranking countries on the basis of a combination of several variables; then, we examine the degree of match between various rankings.

A ranking procedure. When combining several variables into a composite measure, summing of the (weighted, standardized) values is a generally used procedure. For variables tapping the same concept, this is a proper solution. However, if the underlying dimensions of the variables to be combined are different, such a composite measure will not necessarily reflect the original vector-variable at all.

In the case of one ordinal-scale variable, each of two objects can be compared, but if the comparison should be made on the basis of two variables, we have the following alternatives: (1) Both components of one of the objects are greater than or equal to the components of the other object; or (2) the deviation of the two components is not in the same direction. The first condition permits a fair ranking of the objects. However, if the second condition holds (e.g., the first component of the first object is less but the second one is greater than the corresponding components of the second object), there is no well-founded ranking possibility on the basis of the variables considered. So the objects yield a partially ordered set rather than an ordered one when more than one criterion is used in ranking.

A scaling procedure based on the partially ordered set has been developed (Hunya, 1976), and it yields a unique (composite) ordinal scale, provided the original variables are measured on the same type of scale. Using this scaling procedure, any two objects of the set can be compared, that is, we can transform the partially ordered set into an ordered one even if there are originally uncomparable objects.

The scaling procedure is as follows. The partially ordered set can be very well displayed by a directed graph. The new ordinal-scale value of an object depends on only one property of this structure: the number of the preceeding and succeeding objects in the set. The ratio of these two figures determines the composite score based on the hierarchical position the object has in the structure. (The Annex to this chapter illustrates an application of this ranking procedure.)

This ranking algorithm gives a result that may be different from that of the summing procedures. Furthermore, the intermediate graph representation step may itself provide a very good insight into the internal structure of a modest-sized population.

Relations among country rankings based on various composite scores. Using the procedure for deriving rankings based on combinations of variables that has just been described, various rankings of the six countries that participated in Round 1 of the International Study were determined. Eleven such rankings are graphically portrayed in Exhibit 12.4. (In these graphs, the six countries are arrayed along the horizontal axis in an arbitrary but always constant sequence, and their relative position on the particular composite being considered is indicated along the vertical axis.) The degree of similarity of the rank orderings on different composites can be determined by inspecting the plots in Exhibit 12.4 (plots with similar shapes indicate similar rank orders).

As one can see in Exhibit 12.4, at the country level there is a perfect relationship between the composite output index (which is based on a joint consideration of the number of books, articles, and patents) and the combined rated effectiveness–recognition measures, that is, the rank orders of the six countries on these two composite measures is identical. With one exception, the rank order of the countries is also the same for the external evaluations (labeled "EV" in Exhibit 12.4).

Among the set of objective input variables shown in the exhibit – age-experience, frequency of contacts, personnel turnover, size of staff, and growth in personnel – only the age-experience index and the personnel growth index show rank orders approximately the same as the composite countable output measure.[6] (Rankings on the two other personnel indexes are similar to one another, but different from the rankings on the performance measures.)

We must call attention to the objective and the rated facilities indices (labeled "Equipment number and price," "% satisfaction," and "Rating of input" in Exhibit 12.4), which consist of a number of measures. Their shapes are identical between them-

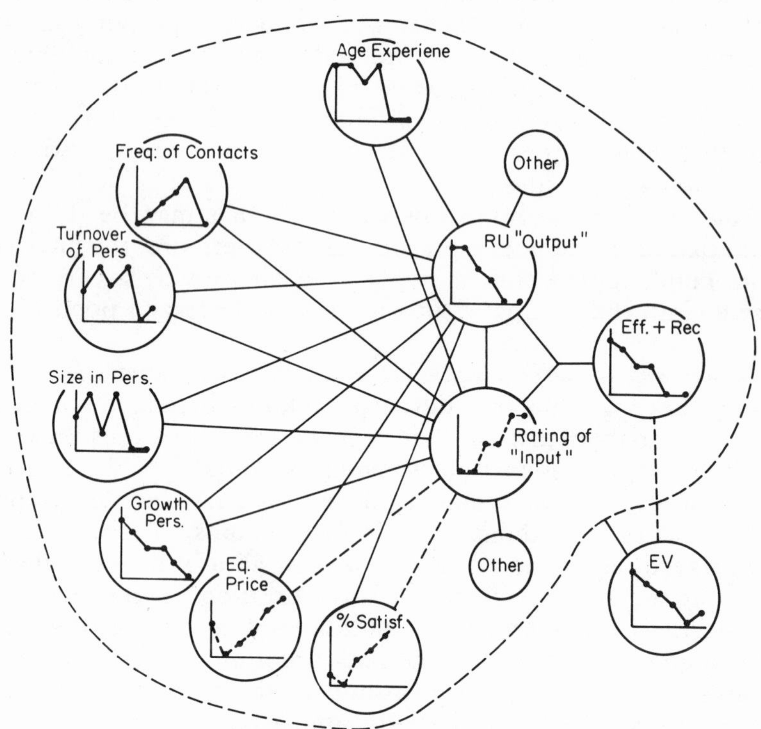

Exhibit 12.4. Six countries ranked on various composite measures of input and performance.

selves, but are opposite to the rankings on output and rated performance. However, it does not seem reasonable to assume a negative effect; therefore, this connection should be the subject of further investigations. (We see an example here of the necessity for a careful interpretation of the connection of two variables, even if it is very strong.)

The relation of the rated input and the countable output fairly fit the shape of the effectiveness-recognition measure. It is obvious that a higher input/output ratio results in a higher rated-effectiveness measure as well.

3. Conclusion

On the basis of a substantial uni- and bi-variate statistical analysis, which highly facilitated the final correction process and gave a good insight into the data, a well-founded conceptual clustering of the original variables could be made. As a result of this clustering, the number of variables to be analyzed simultaneously decreased to such an extent that sophisticated methods for empirical structural analysis could be applied. The preliminary clusters proved to be stable and conceptually acceptable, and the need for further aggregation did not arise even in the later stages of the study.

What kind of empirical groups were identified? There seemed to be two main tendencies in the separation of the variables: separation by content and by type of respondent. These tendencies appeared to be of different extent in the cases of both the nonresidualized and residualized representative measures. In the correlogram of the residualized measures, the separation by respondents became more pronounced.

For example, the *residualized* performance measures from unit heads were disjoint from the corresponding staff scientist performance variables, whereas in the *nonresidualized* case they were aggregated. A similar disaggregation of certain data from the technical support staff was also observed.

However, we also found some definite separations and aggregations according to item contents. The main output clusters became more independent after residualization, but they did not separate by respondents at all. Other favorable changes included the gathering of articles and age variables, and the separation of Land used by the research unit from the Number of books produced. (This latter connection was a hard-to-explain pattern of the nonresidualized measures.)

The contour maps drawn on the basis of the hierarchical correlogram and cluster analyses helped to identify a variety of interesting problems for further analysis. Because the cluster mapping and hierarchical correlogram programs can give a clear overview of the structure of a large number of variables, the use of these programs may be suggested for other studies as well, especially in the early stages.

On the basis of the unit-level multivariate predictive analyses, we concluded that output of articles could be relatively well predicted by the age of the unit and the experience of the researchers. The objective input measures (facilities available) did not show substantial connections with the countable output.

Among the rated-performance measures, General effectiveness and Recognition seemed to be fairly related to the countable output and to the age-experience variables when data were analyzed at the country level.

A thorough investigation of the control variables Country, Scientific field, and Type of organization showed their importance. However, at the same time, the necessity of a careful interpretation of the relationships to the control variables became clear. The control variable Country should be mentioned as an example. Significant differences in the distribution of a number of variables could be found by countries, but these differences seemed to be caused not simply by "country itself," nor by association of Scientific field and Type of organization with Country. It may be supposed that there are more specific relationships behind these associations and that Country is only an indicator of other relevant differences.

In the International Study data, the country means are different and mostly in a well-identifiable system. This kind of heterogeneity, however, enhances the probability of having a sample with a great variety of research units and therefore it is an advantage instead of a handicap.

Our results concerning the input/output-rated performance connections and the fact that, according to expectations, they are not directly related, turn attention to the importance of taking into account the personality (motivations, etc.) of the researchers in investigations of research-unit effectiveness.

4. Annex

This Annex illustrates the ranking procedure by which several distinct ordinal-scale variables may be combined into one composite measure. This procedure is described in the subsection of this chapter titled "Countable and rated performance."

In this example, shown in Exhibit 12.5, we rank the six countries with respect to a composite measure of research-unit inputs. The composite measure is derived from a joint consideration of the following four facilities and services: (1) scientific equipment, (2) library and information services, (3) the availability of administrative and technical assistance, and (4) human resources.

The upper portion of Exhibit 12.5 displays country means on each of the four research-unit inputs. (Countries have arbitrarily been designated by letters A through F.) Based on the relative positions of the countries on these four factors, one can derive a partial ordering of the countries and, from this, a composite measure – as described in the subsection of this chapter titled "Countable output and rated performance." This partial ordering, displayed as a directed graph, and the composite numerical scores on the composite measure, appear in the middle portion of Exhibit 12.5. Finally, scores on the composite measure can be plotted, as is shown in the lower portion of Exhibit 12.5.

References

Bock, R. D., 1963, Programming Univariate and Multivariate Analysis of Variance, *Technometrics,* 5: 95–117.

Exhibit 12.5. Illustration of derivation of composite rankings

A. Mean scores of 6 countries on 4 variables

Country	Scientific equipment	Library & information services	Adm. & tech. assistance	Human resources
A	5.10	5.16	4.89	5.30
B	5.46	5.19	5.48	5.02
C	5.34	5.08	5.33	4.94
D	4.88	5.22	4.95	4.93
E	4.44	4.84	4.83	4.50
F	4.59	4.43	4.58	5.13

B. Composite scores for 6 countries

Country	Score
A	0.00
B	0.00
C	0.50
D	0.50
E.	1.00
F	1.00

C. Directed graph of composite scores for 6 countries

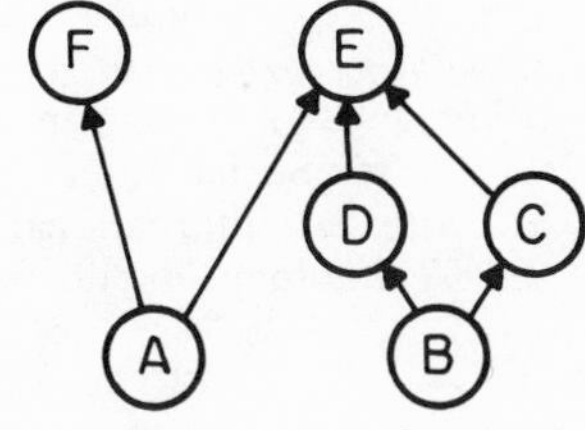

D. Plot of composite scores for 6 countries

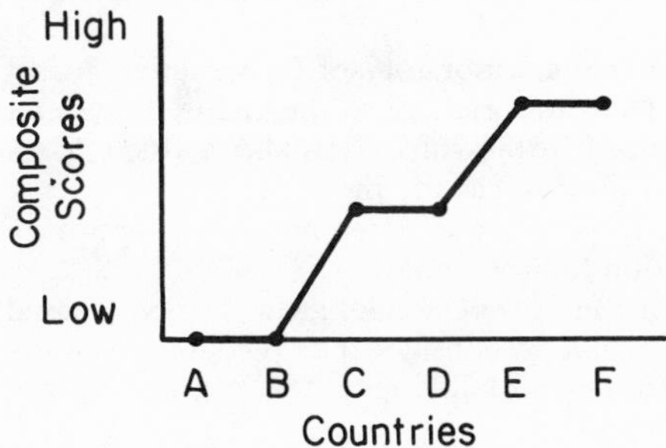

Fajszi, C., 1976, HICOR Procedure (internal report), Szeged, University JATE, Laboratory of Cybernetics.

Fajszi, C., Halasz, A., and Hunya, P., 1975, Structure of the Hungarian Work File (unpublished report presented at the 12th working session of the International Comparative Study), Szeged, Biological Research Center, Hungarian Academy of Sciences.

Fajszi, C., Halasz, A., and Hunya, P., 1976, Empirical Structure of Conceptual Clusters (unpublished report presented at the 14th working session of the International Comparative Study), Szeged, Biological Research Center, Hungarian Academy of Sciences.

Harman, H. H., 1967, *Modern Factor Analysis,* Chicago, University of Chicago Press.

Hunya, P., 1976, A Ranking Procedure Based on Partially Ordered Sets (internal report), Szeged, University JATE, Laboratory of Cybernetics.

Johnson, S. C., 1967, Hierarcical Clustering Schemes, *Psychometrika,* 32: 241–254.

Shepard, R. M., 1962, The Analysis of Proximities: Multidimensional Scaling with an Unknown Distance Function, I, II, *Psychometrika,* 27: 125–140, 219–246.

Sibson, R., 1973, SLINK: Optimally Efficient Algorithm for Single-link Cluster Method, *Computer Journal,* 16: 30.

Sonquist, J., Baker, E. L., and Morgan, J. N., 1973, *Searching for Structure,* Ann Arbor, Institute for Social Research, University of Michigan.

Unesco, 1973, Proposed International Standard Nomenclature for Fields of Science and Technology (document NS/ROU/257/rev. 1), Paris, Unesco.

Notes

1. The exact wording of these questions appears in the Appendix.

2. Computations were performed using the Osiris III software system, which was developed at the Institute for Social Research, University of Michigan, Ann Arbor, Mich., USA. This system is intended for use with large, complex data sets and is one of the most powerful and sophisticated systems available.

3. The programs were developed at the Laboratory of Cybernetics, Jozsef Attila University, Szeged, Hungary. They are oriented to the Osiris III system.

4. The Scientific field code described in the subsection above titled "Creation of a refined discipline code" was used to classify the units.

5. Chapter 5 examines the same topic using a different analysis approach and reaches the same general conclusion [editor's note].

6. As mentioned above, we do not consider personnel growth to be a causal factor for output. It seems more reasonable to consider it as recognition of the productiveness or effectiveness in a former period.

13 Classifying research units by patterns of performance and influence: a typology of the Round 1 data

Gerald A. Cole
Division of Science and Technology Policies, Unesco, Paris

1. Introduction

Policymakers, particularly those operating at the national level, are generally constrained to formulate their plans and execute their programs in terms of broadly defined, macrolevel concepts. The difficulties inherent in information analysis, program implementation, and the instruments of policy enactment (budgets, guidelines, tax incentives, etc.) frequently preclude the formulation of an intricate, detailed program for social, economic, or science policies. From the vantage point of the policymaker, therefore, a premium is placed on those methodologies that promise both breadth and parsimony in their resolution of a recalcitrant social question. This perspective explains, in part, the continued popularity of *systems approaches* in the analysis of social issues (Rivlin, 1971).

The hallmark of such a systems approach is to develop a statistical model that will both highlight the essential (and hopefully

The research reported in this chapter was conducted while the author was a member of Unesco's Division of Science and Technology Policies. The completion of these analyses would not have been possible without the support of the Division's director, M. Yvon de Hemptinne, and the technical assistance of Cinda Yates-Gainche. The author also wishes to thank F. M. Andrews, Karin Knorr, Roland Mittermeyer, and Peter Hunya for their comments on earlier versions of the chapter. The opinions expressed in this chapter are the sole responsibility of the author, who is presently associated with the University of Michigan's Institute of Public Policy Studies, Ann Arbor, Mich., USA.

malleable) parameters of the question, and predict the likely outcomes of selected policy interventions. Whether the attempt is a general exploration of an evolving policy concern, such as the Unesco International Comparative Study of Research Units, or the evaluation of an existing social program (Weiss, 1972), the analyst is led to employ statistical techniques that assume both consistency and homogeneity in the data. With respect to science policymaking, proposals have been put forth for the development of deterministic models (Roberts, 1964) and the increased use of operations-research techniques (Lakhtin, 1968).

This trend toward the reflexive use of statistical models and their associated research methodologies has elicited both caution and critique. Statistical handbooks generally caution the analyst to check for linearity and interaction effects before proceeding with correlation and regression techniques (Blalock, 1960; Draper and Smith, 1966; Johnston, 1972; Hays, 1973). Other methodologists have underscored the normative implications associated with common statistical techniques and have questioned their value in sociological research (Cicourel, 1963; Phillips, 1973). Despite these well-known and generally acknowledged problems with abstract, statistical models, the search for a set of broadly defined structural relationships represents a major confluence of interest between the policymaker and the practicing social scientist. Research in this tradition has been directed toward the activities of scientists by Kornhauser (1962), Marcson (1960, 1966), and Pelz and Andrews (1966), to name but a few examples of well-known studies. The Unesco Secretariat has sought to capitalize on this perspective by launching the International Comparative Study of Research Units.

The search for a general model of research-unit behavior is an ambitious undertaking. To command the attention of the policymaker, as well as the sociologist of science, such a model would have to demonstrate its efficacy across a variety of *organizational settings* and within different *scientific fields*. Previous research suggests that research activities differ considerably with respect to these two categorical distinctions, and these distinctions constitute two obvious points of reference for the assessment of a model's descriptive and predictive capabilities. The design of the International Study reflected these considerations by deliberately seeking to sample research units in several organizational settings (academic, governmental, and industrial) and across a selection of scientific disciplines (chemistry, physics, medical sciences, technological sciences, and the like).

In fairness, it should be noted that the identification of differences in performance levels associated with organizational or disciplinary distinctions do not, in themselves, invalidate the utility of a structural model. Indeed, the members of the International Research Team expected to isolate some differences between research units with respect to activities such as the publication of research articles (generally associated with academic research) and the registration of patents (an industrial or applied research output). Well-known techniques exist to cope with such perturbations in the data, including scale transformations and statistical residualizations. Of more pressing concern was the possibility of encountering entirely different patterns of behavior within selected research settings. These would be evidenced by inconsistent patterns of correlations or significant nonadditive properties in the data. To treat these types of problems, it would be necessary to split the Round 1 data into homogeneous subsets of research units that would exhibit internally consistent behavioral characteristics.

In response to the issues outlined above, the Round 1 data were analyzed to identify dissimilar subsamples in the data. If distinctive subgroups of research units were present in the data, and if they could be identified, steps might be taken to reduce the potential for making inappropriate comparisons when assessing performance characteristics. This chapter reports the means by which the 1,222 research units were eventually split into five subgroups characterized by relatively distinct performance patterns. The resulting performance Typology was employed extensively in the analysis of the Round 1 data.[1]

Section 2 of this chapter reviews the theoretical arguments for grouping research units on the basis of both the scientific disciplines that characterize their work and the organizational settings within which they operate. After outlining the methodology employed in the chapter's study (Section 3), the results of several clustering analyses will be presented, thereby demonstrating that the research units in the Round 1 data can be broken into five subgroups distinguished by their performance and influence patterns (Section 4). The chapter closes with an analysis of the performance and influence profiles that characterize each of these subgroups (Section 5), and relates these results to the literature on the development of scientific specialties and the impacts of organizational characteristics (Section 6).

2. Grouping research units according to scientific field or organizational setting: theoretical considerations and previous investigations

It has been noted that the research units in the international study might conceivably group themselves along disciplinary lines and/or according to organizational setting. In the subsections that follow, a series of arguments will be presented to support these propositions. Reference will also be made to the intellectual tradition that stresses the unity of science, for this literature, in the abstract, could be taken as a justification for the *null hypothesis* of there being no specific groupings whatsoever.[2]

Unity in science: the null hypothesis

Three broadly defined, unifying trends can be identified in previous research and writing concerned with scientific development. Within the philosophy of science, considerable effort has been expended to demonstrate that, though the immediate subject matter of individual scientific disciplines may differ, the logical and semantic operations associated with observation, theory construction, and hypothesis testing could be (and should be) standardized across all science. According to this widely held viewpoint, the maturity of a science may be judged by its ability to state theoretical propositions, and rules for observation and verification, in the form of logical and mathematical axioms. Furthermore, through the careful formulation of all scientific theory in this fashion, metaphysical concepts could be purged from scientific thought, thereby achieving a broader unification of science as a whole. This received view of scientific theories, based upon the work of the logical positivists, held sway in the philosophy of science from the 1920s to the early 1960s (Ayer, 1959: Suppe, 1974).

Logical positivism, with its assumptions of timeless criteria for the assessment of scientific validity, has had its echo in the history of science. In seeking to provide thorough and detailed expositions of major scientific theories, historians of science have often referenced earlier developments as precursors or significant antecedents, thus giving scientific progress the image of a gradual but continuous accumulation of factual observation and verified hypotheses (Cohen, 1974).

Within the sociology of science, there has been a tradition of viewing science as a single subculture with its own well-defined norms and value structures. These norms have been discussed by Merton (1957) and Barber and Hirsch (1962), among others, and have been used as the working assumptions for studies and commentary in the sociology of science (Shepard, 1956; Reif, 1961). A parallel theme in the sociology of science has been the *exchange theory,* whereby scientists are seen as exchanging their creativity and research findings for professional recognition

(Hagstrom, 1965; Storer, 1966). Here, too, resides an implicit assumption of stable and pervasive criteria for the evaluation of scientific excellence.

Taken together, these three unifying trends describe science as an essentially rational, stable, and monolithic social enterprise. Both the *cognitive* and *social* aspects of scientific research are taken as describable by a set of relatively simple, well-defined rules and norms.

Lines of cleavage: the scientific speciality

The unified image of science has been challenged for both its cognitive and social presuppositions (Toulmin, 1961; Kuhn, 1962, 1970c; Feyerabend, 1975). Within the sociology of science, the work of Thomas Kuhn has had a particular impact (Kuhn, 1963, 1970a, 1970b, 1974). The principal feature of this work, as well as the greatest source of confusion in Kuhn's writing, is the specification of the scientific "paradigm" as the central mechanism at work in the development of a scientific speciality. A paradigm, which is taken to govern the practice of research within a given scientific speciality, involves not only a theoretical (or "cognitive") framework, but entails an explicitly sociological dimension as well. In reviewing Kuhn's discussion of the paradigm, Masterman (1970) points to three aspects of the functioning paradigm that serve to foster common perceptions and approaches among its adherents while distinguishing them from scientists who hold contrasting "world views."

Thus, one may argue that the members of a scientific speciality form a loosely bound social unit (Crane, 1972), whose research activities are concentrated in relatively narrow topic areas and whose training has equipped them with a set of commonly recognized symbols, analogies, and language elements for use in professional communication. Precedent-setting research accomplishments establish standards in research design and scientific argumentation for members of the speciality. Furthermore, advanced education in a scientific field provides a sense of common history and identity to the members of that field. It can be argued that the modes of correct research procedure and the accepted forms of professional interaction become subjectively defined for the members of a scientific specialty. In Van Rossum's view, membership in a scientific speciality involves no less than the acceptance of a social construction of reality (Van Rossum, 1973; Lammers, 1974). Consequently, the hypothesis of a general model capable of describing all research activities, as well as claims regarding universal scientific "truth," are rendered problematic (Whitley, 1972). Speculations of this sort have contributed to a marked shift of focal concerns within the sociology of science: The social structure associated with a scientific speciality has taken on renewed importance as a factor that might directly affect the development of scientific knowledge (Martins, 1972; Weingart, 1974; Knorr et al., 1975; Mullins, 1972, 1973). Detailed studies of scientific specialities comprise one aspect of this new trend (Lemain et al., 1976).

Interpreting data across scientific fields

A recurring problem in the literature on research specialities has been to define the boundaries of a speciality in terms of its fields of inquiry and its membership. One approach has stressed the use of sociometric networks to identify groups of scientists who regularly interact in the course of their professional activities (Crane, 1972). A related approach has emphasized the use of co-citations to identify clusters of scientists who reference each other's work (Griffith et al., 1974; Small and Griffith, 1974). Though such studies have opened new directions for research, they have also met with critical review in that the substantive content of the scientists' interactions has not received as detailed an analysis as the structure of their communication network. The charge of "black-boxism" (Whitley, 1972) has been leveled by sociologists who have attempted to explicate the links between the cognitive and social aspects of a research speciality (Whitley, 1974). Thus, one proposition posits the juxtaposition of subject matter and social interaction such that the basic model for scientific activity is taken to be two scientists engaged in dialogue concerning a specified object or phenomenon (Bohme, 1975). Reporting on a survey of Austrian scientists, Knorr uses styles of scientific argumentation among members of specified disciplines as a means of clustering and categorizing research workers (Knorr, 1975). A case study of X-ray crystallographers leads Law to conclude that the members of a scientific speciality can be organized around theoretical issues, substantive questions, and techniques and methodologies (Law, 1973).

Such theoretical debates raise questions concerning the interpretation of data describing scientists and research units operating within different scientific specialities. Several studies have reported differences in publication rates across scientific fields and specialities (Crane, 1972; Blume and Sinclair, 1973b; Hagstrom, 1974). Hagstrom attributes this, in part, to differing levels of competition within disciplines which, in turn, may be due to the extent of consensus concerning the relative importance of problem areas and approaches to their solution: High consensus may foster high levels of competition (Hagstrom, 1965, 1974). Blume and Sinclair note differing levels of competition among British chemists, but stress, as well, the differential levels of prestige associated with selected specialities, and the appearance of topically focused professional journals (Blume and Sinclair, 1973b). Either high prestige associated with a particular subject, or the existence of a specialized journal, would facilitate publication for scientists in the favored areas. Studying the publication patterns in a physics speciality over a 25-year period, White and his colleagues suggest that publication rates will surge as "hot" research topics come into focus and concerted attempts are made to resolve the associated theoretical and experimental problems (White et al., 1976). On the basis of his case studies, Mullins indicates that publication patterns may become engrained in the "folkways" of a speciality: Within the Phage group, the emphasis was placed upon the publication of a relatively small number of high-quality papers (Mullins, 1972), whereas ethnomethodologists have tended to circulate their findings informally rather than publish them at all (Mullins, 1973). These findings argue for caution when comparing individual and group publication patterns across research disciplines and speciality areas. Preliminary statistical investigations might yield scale transformations or other statistical adjustments that would permit direct comparisons of publication rates.

As a supplementary approach to the assessment of research performance, one might employ indicators of research quality that were independent of publication counts. Most studies, including this one, have sought to incorporate one or more such qualitative assessments of research performance (Pelz and Andrews, 1966; Cole and Cole, 1968; Cotgrove and Box, 1970). Note, however, that the arguments concerning the uniqueness of scientific disciplines would apply to qualitative, as well as quantitative, indicators of research performance. Maverick researchers, choosing to work at the fringes of the prevalent topic areas in their discipline, might receive low marks from their colleagues regardless of the originality or rigor of their research efforts (Mullins, 1973). Conversely, scientists working in prestigious areas might benefit from a "halo effect," such that relatively sloppy research performance would, nonetheless, earn high recognition from members of the field (Cole and Cole, 1968). Within research specialities where competition is high, unusually strict precautions may be necessary in research design and data presentation in order to attain even moderate professional regard

(Hagstrom, 1974). Finally, scientific disciplines may give differential emphasis to fundamental research as opposed to teaching or the development of applications-oriented findings (Lodahl and Gordon, 1972). Thus, statistical adjustments of qualitative indicators, similar to those suggested for publication counts, may be required before performing cross-discipline comparisons.

Taking neo-Kuhnian theory to its limits, though, one might argue that the research processes within separate disciplines are fundamentally different, such that a socio-psychological model for the description of research in chemistry, for example, would not hold at all when applied to research in biology or economics. Within this context, where relationships and interactions as well as levels of output differ, any simple statistical adjustment for selected indicators would be insufficient, if not inappropriate. For example, Blume and Sinclair have explored the effects of research-team size on research effectiveness and have reported differential correlation patterns for several specialities within British academic chemistry (Blume and Sinclair, 1973a; Chapter 8 above). Complex or intricate instrumentation may require management procedures and working patterns tailored to the specific technical requirements of a laboratory setting. Even within the studies of communication networks, both the size of the networks and the intensity of interactions may vary not only across disciplines but also within a discipline as major topics are defined and then resolved (see Visart, Chapter 9 above). Summarizing their data, Lodhal and Gordon state that "the structure of scientific fields has important differential correlates in the attitudes and activities carried on within them . . . which go to the heart of teaching, research and student–faculty relationships" (Lodahl and Gordon, 1972: 70–71). Hagstrom is equally emphatic in stating that specialities "vary enormously in characteristics of interest to the sociologist of science" (Hagstrom, 1974: 10). These suggestions of statistical interactions argue for analytic procedures that extend to the replication of key analyses within subgroups of demonstrated homogeneity vis-à-vis the relevant sets of indicators. A typology, perhaps based upon distinctions by scientific disciplines, would provide a statistical control variable for the execution of such analyses.

Research activities and organizational settings

Though differences between scientific disciplines are rarely disputed by scientists themselves, or by science policymakers and management personnel in scientific organizations, their importance in terms of the planning and financing of research is often discounted. Consider the following statements of Harvey Brooks:

> People who write about planning of or for science usually seem to be talking primarily about fundamental science, and the planning process is thought of in terms of relative governmental funding of different scientific disciplines. In fact, this is a grossly over-simplified view of planning [in that] the scientific discipline is only one of many dimensions of planning, and probably the one least susceptive to non-expert judgement. . . . the categorization of research for planning purposes is most easily done in an institutional context. [Brooks, 1968: 97–98]

Salomon echoes these feelings in stating that "the essential feature of research can be considered to be the institutional environment in which it is conducted rather than whether [it is fundamental or] applied. The institutional framework is what determines the character of research, and accordingly how it can be conceived, managed, administered and oriented. . . ." (Salomon, 1968: 9).

One of the most noticeable aspects of modern science has been its growing institutionalization. Particularly since the end of the Second World War, major scientific activities have become grouped within institutional frameworks and increasingly dependent upon state planning agencies or major industrial programs for their financial support (OECD, 1968; Krohn, 1972). For some, this has been viewed as a positive trend, particularly among those concerned with national development. They argue that, with appropriate planning, science would contribute more directly and fruitfully toward the goals of national and industrial development (Unesco, 1976c, 1976d, 1977; UN General Assembly, 1977). For others, the presumed advantages of institutionalization have been outweighed by the difficulties of integrating science within an organizational framework (Drucker, 1952, 1963), or by the signs of bureaucratic encroachment upon the freedom for scientific investigation (Kowalewska, 1974). Organizational theorists and industrial psychologists have debated the potential for conflict between the professionally oriented scientist and the bureaucratically structured institution (Moore and Renck, 1955; Orth, 1959; Burns and Stalker, 1961; Blau and Scott, 1962; Kornhauser, 1962). Sociologists concerned with the postulated "norms of science" have speculated upon the types of incentives that must be offered by industry and government to offset the supposed "deprivations" suffered by scientists who leave the university environment (Storer, 1972: 250). Still other researchers, who have been less quick to place academic research at the epicenter of the scientific world, have examined the impact of differing organizational reward systems upon the types and quality of research conducted within those organizations (Pelz and Andrews, 1966; Cotgrove and Box, 1970; Krohn, 1971). Finally, a concern for the role played by the institution in shaping the directions of research, and thereby the types of knowledge produced, led members of a consortium of European sociologists (the PAREX organization) to conduct a special survey of European social science research organizations (Crawford and Perry, 1976). Thus, in addition to entertaining hypotheses about the differences in research-unit performance across scientific disciplines, one should consider arguments for grouping research units on the basis of their organizational affiliation as well. This subsection will summarize several of the relevant studies.

Marcson has examined scientists operating in a number of differing organizational contexts and concludes that a typology of research settings should distinguish among four types of organizations, three of which warrant particular attention because of their importance within a national research effort (Marcson, 1960, 1966). He highlights, therefore, the differences between academic, governmental, and industrial research operations. In doing so, he gives particular attention to such issues as organizational objectives, methods for selecting research topics, procedures for organizing research work, and the availability of career-advancement opportunities for dedicated, practicing research scientists (Marcson, 1972). With respect to university-based research, he recalls that the institution is definitionally committed to training and the advancement of knowledge along disciplinary lines; Teaching, publication, and professional recognition are the primary concerns of the faculty. Despite evident changes in the past 30 years, control and influence are still vested in the faculty, which operates through a system of "colleague authority." The "executive authority" of the administration carries considerably less weight than is the case in industry. Consequently, research priorities are generally established within a disciplinary perspective (though entrepreneurship in obtaining government contracts is valued), and senior faculty members enjoy considerable discretion in the organization and execution of their personal programs.

Government research institutes present a different picture, however. Here, research activities are often cast in a supportive role and are expected to help further one or more socially or politically determined programs. The main goals of such social programs often evolve within a nonscientific context and are difficult to restate in terms of explicit research objectives. Under such circumstances, the goals and objectives of the government research organization may be both complex and subject to rapid change. The organizational structure is often hierarchical and formal in conception, which generates tensions for scientists who wish to set their own research priorities, adopt unorthodox working patterns, or pursue a problem beyond the requirements of the larger program within which it has been conceived.

Within industry, research priorities are typically set by market conditions and a tactical concern for updating and renewing the firm's basic product line. Cost-effectiveness and potential payoffs are major criteria for evaluating research projects; this may result in the abrupt launching and/or canceling of a project as market conditions or cost factors shift (Disman, 1962; Baker and Pound, 1964; Cetron et al., 1967; Souder, 1969, 1973a, 1973b; Baker and Freeland, 1975). Shifting research priorities, as well as hierarchical management structures, can cause severe strains between scientists committed to exacting professional standards (the "norms of science"), and an administration that looks primarily toward production and sales operations (Marcson, 1972; Cotgrove and Box, 1970). Publications and professional recognition are not heavily weighted in the determination of promotions or salary increases, and patent rights are generally signed over to the company. Usefulness to the organization and administrative potential are key concerns. Marcson summarized the import of his typology by stating that research settings "constitute subcultures with their own organizational work environment characteristics, their own standards of performance, their own norms of autonomy, their own criteria of creativity, their own incentive systems, their own patterns of conflict, and their own definitions of innovation" (Marcson, 1972: 163).

Pelz and Andrews used survey techniques to study the performance of 1,311 scientists and engineers working within industrial, governmental, and university research laboratories. They developed a series of performance indicators that resemble those used in the Unesco International Study, and found that the mean levels of those indicators varied according to such factors as degree level and years of training and experience (Pelz and Andrews 1966: 275–283). What should be noted here, however, is that mean levels of performance varied by type of organization as well. (Adjustment factors were introduced to statistically remove these effects before predictive analyses were performed.) Furthermore, exploratory investigations indicated differences in correlational patterns among subgroups of the data, which suggested the need to substantiate major findings through repeated analyses within such subgroups. The typology used for such analysis purposes incorporated three qualitatively distinct dimensions: (1) possession of the Ph.D. degree, (2) domination of the scientist's department by Ph.D.s, and (3) distinction of a *research* or *development* orientation within the scientist's department. The first two dimensions reflected differences in status hierarchies and management patterns for the relevant labs. The third dimension was tied closely to type of organization, with all the university scientists being categorized as members of research labs and all the industrial scientists tagged as members of development labs. When this typology was used in the analysis of questions concerning a scientist's relative freedom, degree of coordination in research tasks, and level of work satisfaction, important differences by category were evident. A careful sifting of these data revealed that these differences were persistent and that they precluded the formulation of a single statistical model capable of describing research activities within all organizational settings.

Cotgrove and Box studied the research activities and job satisfaction of British industrial chemists, but included within their survey a special subsample of graduating chemistry students to shed light on the factors that shaped career choices (Cotgrove and Box, 1970). They introduce their study by asking whether all scientists should be viewed as having internalized Merton and Barber's "norms of science" and, therefore, whether the recurrent speculations about an "inherent" conflict between scientists and industrial management could be justified. Arguing against the assumption of a universal acceptance of the norms of science, they suggest not one but three roles and identities for scientists, only the first of which (the *academic* scientist committed to publication) corresponds to the image portrayed in the writings of Merton, Barber, and Storer. The other two roles, the *instrumental* scientist concerned with applications and development work for a parent organization, and the *organizational* scientist who has moved into management ranks, predominate among industrial scientists. Furthermore, they find little evidence to support the contention of an inherent conflict between scientists and industrial bureaucracies. Drawing upon their subsample of chemistry students, they seek to explain the relative absence of academic scientists within industry, as well as the relatively moderate levels of job dissatisfaction, by arguing that scientists search for employment situations that are compatible with the scientific role they have assumed during their student years. In particular, the academic student is generally recruited on the spot by the members of his faculty, and may never give serious considerations to a position in industry. On the basis of these findings, Cotgrove and

Box propose a typology of scientists that incorporates both scientific identity and type of organization. They further specify an "interactionist" hypothesis for the levels of performance and job satisfaction that accompany the degree of congruence between a scientist's internalized role and the nature of the organization within which the scientist works. The typology is used as a major control variable in all their analyses.

Summarizing some of the principal results of their study, one should note that the occurrence of job dissatisfaction was most evident for publication-oriented scientists located within industry. Points of particular concern for these scientists were methods employed for the selection and termination of research projects, the sensed lack of participation in long-range planning, procedures for managing daily research activities, and the inability to follow up on scientifically appealing ideas or publication possibilities (Cotgrove and Box, 1970: 91–115). The analysis of scientific productivity by Cotgrove and Box also demonstrates different results for different categories of their typology, supporting the thesis that high publication rates are achieved most readily by publication-oriented scientists working within settings that grant some influence in the selection of research topics and the organization of laboratory work. (No clear patterns emerged for the production of patents, however.) Expanding upon the theme of an interaction between a scientist's relative commitment to pure research and publication, and the patterns of influence that govern an organization's working conditions, Cotgrove and Box conclude by stating that "the prescriptions for the most effective use of instrumental scientists in development work are not necessarily the same as those for the public scientists in basic/applied research; nor are the factors which maximize publications necessarily the same as those for optimum performance in the kind of research most likely to lead to patents" (Cotgrove and Box, 1970: 157).

Krohn reports rather similar findings from his earlier study of scientists working in the Minneapolois–Saint Paul area of the United States (1971). His sample was broader than that of Cotgrove and Box and included scientists from three fields of research (physical and biological, basic medical, and clinical medical) located within three types of organizations (university, governmental, and industrial). In reviewing his data, Krohn takes issue with much of the literature treating the "norms of science" and argues that it has focused too heavily upon academic scientists and their particular organizational base, the university (1971: 20–21). Consequently, he proposes a three-fold typology of scientists similar to that of Cotgrove and Box, and distinguishes organizational settings with respect to their differential emphasis upon such scientific activities as research toward publication, research toward applications, training, and patent licensing. He argues that a reciprocal selection process, similar to that described above, is at work between scientists and their prospective employers. His analysis of scientific productivity underscores systematic differences between types of organizations and, in particular, the contrasting patterns of influence that operate to determine research priorities and to manage the work within the laboratory. In summary, Krohn's study would support the thesis that the major differences in research activities are based in organizational distinctions rather than disciplinary perspectives.

Summary regarding organizational settings. The studies just cited have offered arguments and evidence for a distinction among research activities on the basis of the organizational context in which they are performed. With respect to scientific productivity, these authors have reported substantial differences in publication patterns and in emphasis upon applications research as a function of type of organization. University-based scientists tend to emphasize research toward publication and training, whereas industrial scientists concentrate upon research toward applications and patents. Work by Marcson implies that scientists in government laboratories are directed toward areas of socially determined, practical payoffs.

In addition to the differences in types of research orientation and research output, it would appear that research organizations can be distinguished in terms of both their internal operating procedures and also the characteristics and interests of the researchers they attract. Of particular interest is the repeated suggestion that institutional differences can be characterized by the patterns of influence that operate to determine research priorities and to organize work in the laboratory. The studies by Cotgrove and Box and Krohn indicate that these patterns of influence affect a researcher's motivation, job satisfaction, and long-range career opportunities. Such considerations imply that organizations act to maintain research settings that differ fundamentally in terms of the standards of performance and creativity by which researchers are evaluated, as well as in terms of the norms of autonomy and discretion in the conduct of research. These arguments are sufficiently persuasive to submit the Round 1 data from the International Study to a series of statistical tests to assess whether a grouping of research units on the basis of organizational affiliation would be warranted.

3. Measurement

This section of the chapter describes the basic measures used in the typological analyses to be presented in Section 4. Detailed here are the classification of research units according to scientific discipline and type of organization and the indicators of research-unit performance and influence patterns.

Classification of research units by Scientific field

Attempts to develop classifications of scientific activities on the basis of disciplinary distinctions encounter both theoretical and practical problems. This is especially true when studying research specialities that are undergoing rapid development (Menard, 1971). Scientists themselves frequently take issue with attempts to construct rigid classifications of their activities, thereby complicating the lot of the census taker and interviewer (Hagstrom, 1974). The classification of scientific fields and disciplines used in this study was developed by the Unesco Secretariat for the purposes of science administration and the presentation of detailed national science statistics. It covers 24 main fields of science and technology, including approximately 240 subfields of scientific disciplines. Each subfield can, in turn, be broken down into an averge of 10 specialities. In field tests of the classification, interviewers reported relatively little difficulty classifying scientists in the traditional "exact" and "natural" sciences, but met with considerably more resistance among scientists in the social sciences and new multidisciplinary fields, thus reinforcing the impressions noted above.

Of the 24 scientific fields represented in the classification, 9 were included in the national sample designs of the Round 1 data collection. Data within these 9 field classifications could be further subdivided into as many as 50 scientific disciplines and research specialities. The actual assignment of a research unit to a disciplinary classification was accomplished in two ways. In the design of the national sampling plans, the data-collection teams contacted the research institutions to be surveyed and obtained an indication from the institution's administration of the scientific fields represented within that institution.

As a check against this rather general classification, the heads of the research units were asked to list up to six scientific specialities that would best describe the work of the research unit over the past three years. The detailed responses of the research unit heads were then aggregated to the level of scientific disciplines and analyzed for frequency of mentions. A research unit was assigned to the discipline most frequently named as characterizing current research activities. This process generated a regrouping of the data into 26 subgroups, each of which could be considered as relatively homogeneous with respect to the self-reported focus of recent research.[3]

The scientific fields included in the Round 1 data and the number of research units from each are as follows: technological sciences and engineering (N = 345); chemistry (N = 240); life sciences (N = 215); agricultural sciences (N = 125); physics (N =77); social sciences (N = 75); earth and space sciences (N = 69); medical sciences (N = 57); and a selection from mathematics, astronomy, and astrophysics (N =19).

Classification of research units by Type of organization

Research units in the Round 1 data were also classified according to their institutional affiliation. The classification used in this process was a slightly modified version of a classification of research organizations developed originally by the UN's Economic Commission for Europe (see Exhibit 13.1) and was selected because it could accommodate the institutional frameworks of both the Western and Eastern European countries participating in Round 1. National sampling frames were developed using this classification with the specific goal of obtaining data from research units located within several different institutional settings. The assignment of research units to a category of the classification was determined through direct contact with the administration of the institution within which the research unit operated.

During the actual sampling and data-collection process, categories 1 and 2 of the classification were treated as functionally equivalent, thus providing a single, broadly defined classification for university-based research. As can be seen by the frequencies reported in Exhibit 13.1, university-based research units constitute the largest single group in the data. By comparison, research units attached to the academies of science (category 3) are only weakly represented, an artifact of the sampling designs in the two socialist countries. Government-operated research units serving industry or public service (category 4) and research units located within private enterprise (category 5) have been heavily sampled, however. Consequently, four distinct types of institutionally defined research settings are represented in the Round 1 data, three of which (university, government, and industry) have been frequently discussed in the literature.

Exhibit 13.1. Classification of Type of organization in the Round 1 data

Code name	Number of units	Code number	Category description
Academic research	694	1	Universities and similar institutions of higher education
		2	Research institutes closely associated with (and often managed by) universities
Academies of science	45	3	Institutions attached to academies of science (in the Socialist countries) and to national research organizations (such as TNO in the Netherlands, CNRS in France, Max Planck Institute in German Federal Republic; atomic energy commissions, national space agencies, and the like)
Government/ cooperative laboratories	257	4	Research institutes serving, wholly or partly, a sector of production, a branch of industry, or a public service (usually managed by the government in cooperation with, and for benefit of, industry or public service)
Private enterprise	217	5	Research laboratories of productive enterprises
Other	9	7	Contract-research institutes and other nonspecified institutes
Total	1,222		

A cross-classification of Scientific field and Type of organization

In the preceding sections, arguments have been presented for analyzing research activities according to their classification by Scientific field and Type of organization. Such hypotheses suggest the creation of a typology of research units that would fall largely along one or the other of these two dimensions. However, alternative outcomes could be proposed. First, as was mentioned above, it could happen that neither classification served to group the data in analytically meaningful patterns. Second, it could be that the best grouping, from the standpoint of controlling for statistical interactions, involved some combination of the two classifications. The analytical procedures to be used in exploring these hypotheses have been designed to bring out the effects attributable to either or both of these classifications; the possibility of joint effects is specifically explored. To facilitate this approach, it is necessary to classify each research unit in the data with respect to both its Scientific field and the Type of organization within which its research activities take place.

A two-way cross-classification of research units by Scientific field and Type of organization yields a 9-by-5 table with a total of 45 cells, each representing a unique combination of scientific field and type of organization. Of these 45 cells, only 35 include research units assessed during Round 1 of the International Study; the rest are empty. Exhibit 13.2 presents the details of this cross-classification, including the percentage of research units that falls within each cell. These percentages vary considerably, ranging from as much as 12.8% (or approximately 155 research units) in some cells down to 0.1% or 0.2% in others. These substantial differences in cell size can present problems for statistical analyses, and two sets of precautions have been taken. First, the principal results, to be reported below, are based on the patterns in the 21 cells containing 10 or more research units, as the descriptive statistics and correlations for these subgroups tended to be more stable. Second, a series of replications has been carried out to check for statistical artifacts stemming from the differing cell sizes. The details of these replications are reported in the Annex to this chapter. In the sections that follow, this cross-classification will be referred to as the *Pattern variable.*

Indicators of research-unit performance and patterns of influence

The literature cited in the preceding sections suggests three related areas in which the hypothesized differences between scientific fields and types of organizations should be most clearly evident. First, there is the question of research orientation: whether the research unit stresses research leading toward publication, research leading toward applications or patents, the training of new researchers, or research with a social significance. Second, the literature has reported systematic differences in research output as a function of organizational affiliation, and has suggested that such differences, because of levels of competition or the availability of specialized journals, are characteristic of scientific disciplines as well. Of particular note would be publication patterns for articles and books, and development work on applications such as prototype devices and patents. Third, the literature relating to differences in research settings underscores the contrasting patterns of influence that operate to determine research priorities and the organization of work in the laboratory. Measures for each of these three facets of a research unit's operations will be presented next.

Exhibit 13.2. The cross-classification of Scientific discipline and Type of organization (N = 1,222)

Scientific discipline	Type of organizations	Percent of all units	Plot label
Subgroups containing more than 10 research units			
Math/Astronomy/Astrophysics	Academic research	1.5	1
Physics	Academic research	5.9	2
Chemistry	Academic research	12.4	3
Life sciences	Academic research	12.8	4
Earth & space sciences	Academic research	3.0	5
Agricultural sciences	Academic research	2.3	6
Medical sciences	Academic research	3.2	7
Technological sciences	Academic research	11.0	8
Social sciences	Academic research	4.8	9
Chemistry	Academy of science	1.0	10
Life sciences	Academy of science	1.7	11
Chemistry	Government/cooperative	2.5	12
Life sciences	Government/cooperative	2.8	13
Earth & space sciences	Government/cooperative	2.1	14
Agricultural sciences	Government/cooperative	5.5	15
Medical sciences	Government/cooperative	0.9	16
Technology	Government/cooperative	5.9	17
Economics	Government/cooperative	1.1	18
Chemistry	Private enterprise	3.8	19
Agriculture	Private enterprise	1.9	20
Technology	Private enterprise	11.3	21
Subgroups with 10 or fewer research units			
Earth & space sciences	Academy of science	0.2	—
Agricultural sciences	Academy of science	0.3	—
Medical sciences	Academy of science	0.3	—
Physics	Governement/cooperative	0.2	—
Math	Private enterprise	0.1	—
Physics	Private enterprise	0.2	—
Earth & space sciences	Private enterprise	0.2	—
Medical sciences	Private enterprise	0.2	—
Economics	Private enterprise	0.1	—
Life sciences	Other	0.3	—
Agricultural sciences	Other	0.2	—
History	Other	0.1	—
Technology	Academy of science	0.1	—
Earth & space sciences	Other	0.1	—

Research orientations: the rated-effectiveness measures. The International Study has utilized two distinct types of performance-evaluation measures. The first approach, to be discussed here, is based on a battery of Likert-type rating scales that permit the members of a research unit, and selected external evaluators, to indicate their qualitative assessment of the unit's performance according to several different criteria.[4] Following an extensive series of analyses (some of which are reported in Chapters 2, 11, and 14), these scales were combined to form seven composite indicators of research-unit performance, which have been called the *rated-effectiveness measures.*

These seven measures were designed to be used as qualitative indicators of research-unit performance along dimensions suggested by structural analyses of the item pool. There has been debate about the general applicability of these measures as indicators of research-unit performance (e.g., see Chapter 11), and in a separate analysis Cole explored this question in detail (Unesco, 1976a). Cole concludes that certain rated-performance indicators are more relevant within some research settings than within others, and that the set of relevant rated-effectiveness measures can be taken as a general indication of the research orientations of the units within that group. Four of the measures that might be viewed in this light are the Recognition, Applications, Social-effectiveness, and Training-effectiveness scales. A fifth scale, R & D effectiveness, has shown moderately high construct validity across all the research units in the data, and can be taken as a general qualitative indicator of research effectiveness (see Chapter 2). These five measures provide a general profile of research orientation (as well as an indication of assessed quality) and will be used as one of the bases for grouping research units within the Round 1 data.[5]

Research products: the output items. The second approach to the assessment of research-unit performance is based upon a battery of questions that requested an accounting of all the research products generated by the unit over a three-year period. Fourteen categories of research products were suggested for this exercise, including books, articles, patents, reviews, reports, and prototypes.[6] In the process of developing composite indicators of research-unit output, these items were submitted to a series of structure-seeking analyses (including factor analysis and monotone distance analysis) to explore the basic, underlying dimensions (Unesco, 1975c). On the basis of those analyses, seven items were selected as representing the three or four basic dimensions in the most statistically efficient manner.[7] These items include the number of books written by the unit as a whole, the number of articles published both inside and outside the research unit's country, the number of patents the unit has registered within its country, the number of algorithms and prototype devices the unit has developed, and the number of internally distributed research reports the unit has authored.

Patterns of influence: choice of research themes and organization of the work. The literature that raised arguments for the classification of research activities on the basis of organizational differences focused repeatedly on the contrasting patterns of influence that operate in different organizational settings. Two issues were of concern to those authors, as well as to the scientists they studied: methods for the selection (and termination) of research projects; and procedures for the organization of work in the laboratory. The Round 1 questionnaire contained questions that touched upon both these issues; they will be introduced below.

The questionnaire addressed to heads of units contained a series of six items under the heading "Choice of Research Themes of the Research Unit."[8] These items were presented in the format of a dominance-ranking task: The head of the research unit was asked to indicate, in percentage terms, the amount of influence exercised in the choice of the unit's research themes by the guidelines of three types of management groups, as well as by recognized scientific and practical considerations. Preliminary analyses determined that four of the six items warranted retention in further analyses. These four items indicate the reported influence of guidelines issued by national science policymaking bodies, guidelines from the governing organ(s) of the research unit's parent institution, practical needs identified by the unit, and the scientific significance and promise of the research. For the sake of convenience, these items will be referred to as "S. p-making bodies," "Management," "Practical needs," and "Sci. significance."

The unit head's questionnaire contains an additional series of questions about influences that operate within the research unit and guide the conduct of research. This substantial set of questions, titled "Patterns of Influence," was modeled upon Tannenbaum's studies of organizational behavior (Tannenbaum, 1968, 1974) and has been analyzed extensively by Kowalewska and other members of the International Research Team (see Chapter 7).[9] Following Tannenbaum's suggestions, the items were structured so that several participants in a decision process could be reported as exercising high levels of influence; the possibility of expanding "total control" within an organization has been one of Tannenbaum's principal interests (Tannenbaum, 1968: 3–30). This theme has found its echo in the study of research operations, as well in the fact that neither complete autonomy for the scientist nor total control by the managers has been found to be associated with high productivity (Pelz and Andrews, 1966: 3–34; Cotgrove and Box, 1970: 140–162).

Previous analyses by Cole have demonstrated that the 36 items in this pool will group primarily with respect to the potential participants mentioned in the items; hence, a series of composite indicators of influence were developed for each of these actors (Unesco, 1976b).[10] Of particular interest for this analysis is the amount of influence exercised by "leadership outside the unit but inside the organization" (Organization leader), by the unit's head, and by "Scientists and engineers inside the unit" (Staff scientists) in determining the organization and management of research work within the unit. Parallel composite indicators were developed for each of these three actors indicating their influence over: the choice of specific research tasks, the choice of research methods, the allocation of work within the unit, coordination with other research units, and the publication and circulation of research results. It will be recalled from the literature that these topics are among the key considerations of young scientists when evaluating their prospective employers, and are among the principal sources of concern for dissatisfied scientists working within industry (Cotgrove and Box, 1970; Krohn, 1971). It has also been reported that differences in the levels of management intervention in the organizational and control of laboratory work provide one of the most striking contrasts between academic research, on the one hand, and government and industrial research, on the other (Marcson, 1972). Consequently, a research unit's pattern of scores on these three indicators, as well as on the four choice-of-research-themes items discussed above, should provide an indication of the influences that determine the types of research questions that are addressed, and the procedures by which the laboratory work is organized.[11]

4. Clustering the research units: methods and results

A preliminary check; variations by Pattern-variable categories

In the preceding sections, it was noted that the development of a typology of research units in the Round 1 data would be based on a systematic examination of the performance and influence *profiles*. The term profiles is used here in the sense of distinct patterns of mean values across the measures introduced in Section 3. This type of statistical profile can be developed for each subgroup within the cross-classification of Scientific discipline and Type of organization, and can then be analyzed across all subgroups for similarities and differences. From a technical perspective, the examination of such characteristic profiles becomes an analysis of co-variance patterns among subgroups of research units, as calculated across the sets of measures introduced above.

For such an analysis to be feasible, and to have subtantive meaning, the statistical profiles must demonstrate appreciable statistical variation: Neither weak and random fluctuations among categories of the Pattern variable, nor the presence of a single dominant pattern, would allow for the designation of distinct subgroups of research units.[12] A simple test for the presence of the requisite variation can be performed through an analysis of variance; the cross-classification of Scientific discipline and Type of organization, combined in the form of the Pattern variable, is used as the control for variance in the performance and influence measures. The results of this test are displayed in Exhibit 13.3 and indicate that there is considerable variation across the categories of the Pattern variable. Indeed, the Pattern variable demonstrates a strong capability to control the variance in most of these measures.[13]

Column 1 of Exhibit 13.3 indicates the percentage of variance in the performance and influence measures that can be explained by the full Pattern variable (35 categories); column 2 gives the same information for the reduced Pattern variable, representing only the largest subgroups in the data (21 categories). Looking first at the figures reported for the measures of rated effectiveness, one can see that the Pattern variable accounts for as much as 25% of the variance in Training effectiveness and only slightly less for the measures of Applications effectiveness, Social effectiveness, and Recognition. Among these measures of research orientation, only R & D effectiveness shows no relationship to the Pattern variable.

Strong variations by category of the Pattern variable are evident for the measures of research outputs as well. Here the percentage of variance explained ranges from a low of 13% for Number of books published in the past three years, to a high of 23% for Number of articles published outside the country during the same period.

Finally, turning to the seven measures-of-influence patterns,

Exhibit 13.3. Correlation ratios between designated control factors and indicators of research-unit performance and decision making (Figures show adjusted eta-squares; N = 1,222)

	35-category pattern variable[a]	21-category pattern variable[b]	Typology[c]	Country	Country and typology[d]
Research orientations					
Recognition	.17	.15	.13	.06	.18
Social effectiveness	.18	.17	.11	.17	.23
Training effectiveness	.25	.25	.22	.03	.24
Applications effectiveness	.20	.20	.16	.20	.27
R & D effectiveness	.00	.00	.01	.05	.05
Research outputs					
No. of books	.14	.13	.08	.07	.12
No. articles in country	.16	.15	.09	.14	.20
No. articles out of country	.23	.23	.22	.07	.24
Internal research reports	.17	.17	.16	.03	.17
Patents in country	.16	.15	.11	.07	.17
Prototype devices	.19	.18	.09	.09	.15
Algorithms	.13	.14	.09	.11	.15
Influence measures					
Choice of research themes					
S. p-making bodies	.16	.14	.07	.20	.24
Management	.18	.18	.18	.06	.23
Practical needs	.10	.10	.09	.04	.12
Scientific significance	.40	.40	.37	.12	.40
Organizing lab work					
Organization leaders	.33	.33	.28	.17	.36
Unit leader	.07	.07	.05	.02	.06
Staff scientists	.09	.09	.07	.05	.10
Composite output indicators					
Published written materials	.23	.22	.20	.11	.27
Patents and prototypes	.18	.17	.15	.08	.20
Internal reports, algorithms	.22	.23	.21	.06	.23

[a]35-category cross-classification of Scientific discipline and Type of organization.

[b]21-category cross-classification of Scientific discipline and Type of organization containing only subgroups of 11 research units or more.

[c]Typology variable developed after clustering 35 categories of pattern variable.

[d]R^2 adjusted statistics taken from MCA analysis–equivalent to joint explanation of variance, and comparable to adjusted eta-squares.

the analyses of variance confirm once again the presence of significant variations among subgroups of the research units. As much as 40% of the variance in the measure of Scientific significance can be explained by the cross-classification of Scientific discipline and Type of organization. The figure is only somewhat smaller for the indicator of the influence exercised by the organization's leaders in managing the research work in the laboratory.

These figures indicate that the analysis of co-variance patterns in the Round 1 data is at least feasible, that is, differences *are* evident among subgroups of research units and, therefore, the null hypothesis may be rejected. Furthermore, the statistics in columns 1 and 2 of Exhibit 13.3 indicate that the reduced Pattern variable, representing only the major subgroups within the data, is as powerful a control variable as the original Pattern variable, which represents all 35 cells within the cross-classification.[14]

The task before us now is to systematically analyze those intergroup differences and represent them in such a way as to determine whether they are a function of disciplinary distinctions, organizational characteristics, or both. Following a discussion of analysis methods, the results of the search for consistent clustering patterns will be presented.

Analysis methods

The objective of the clustering analysis is to identify groups of research units that exhibit broad similarities in their orientations toward research and in their conduct of research. As suggested above, this objective will be approached by analyzing sets of performance indicators so as to reveal distinctive scoring patterns characteristic of large segments of the data. This procedure should be contrasted with standard multivariate analyses, which test for similarities among variables. This latter approach assesses the strength of association among variables by analyzing patterns of scores across objects in the data. What is proposed here is to numerically assess for the similarities among objects by analyzing patterns of scores across selected sets of variables in the data. Indeed, this is a deliberate inversion of the usual correlational analysis traditionally employed in survey research; this inverted form is sometimes referred to as a "pattern similarity" or "Q-type" analysis (Rummell, 1970).

To prepare for the Q-type analyses, the measures introduced above were first standardized and then aggregated within categories of the Pattern variable to obtain a mean value on each of the indicators for each of the distinct subgroups within the data. The data matrices containing the standardized, aggregated indicators were then transposed and submitted to a computer program that calculated pattern similarity coefficients between each of the subgroups of units represented by the Pattern variable. Thus, all possible pairs of subgroups were compared with respect to the similarities of their profiles across the performance and influence indicators. In order to represent these sets of pair-wise comparisons in a fashion that lends itself to visual inspection, the matrices of pattern similarity coefficients were then submitted to a technique known as "monotone distance analysis" (Lingoes, 1972).

Monotone distance analysis, as used here, portrays the objects of an analysis as points in geometric space such that the interpoint distances are indicative of the relative dissimilarities between the objects. Thus, two objects that are highly similar, as described by their similarity coefficient, will be positioned a short distance apart within the spatial configuration; conversely, objects that are highly dissimilar will be positioned far apart. The program actually used for these analyses, Minissa-I, was developed by Lingoes and Roskam (1973) and modified by Rattenbury (1975).

Once developed, these spatial configurations can be manipulated, through rotation techniques, to highlight relational patterns and regional densities (Green and Rao, 1972; Shepard, 1972). Additionally, two or more different configurations may be compared to assess the similarity with which matched points are arrayed within the configuration spaces (Schonemann and Carroll, 1970; Lingoes and Schonemann, 1974; Borg and Lingoes, 1976a, 1976b). Both techniques have been used in this analysis to examine evidence in favor of clustering on the basis of either Scientific discipline or Type of organization. If the comparison across configurations reveals a consistent clustering pattern, one can then classify the objects (the research units) into qualitatively distinct groups, each of which will correspond to one consistently defined cluster within the configuration spaces.

Finally, as a means of demonstrating the modal performance and influence patterns that characterize each of the categories of the Typology, an additional analysis technique, multivariate nominal scale analysis (MNA), has been employed (Andrews and Messenger, 1973). Through MNA, the performance and influence indicators, across which the pattern similarity coefficients were calculated, are used to predict each unit's group classification. The results indicate the probability of a unit's being assigned to a given category for each scoring level on the performance and influence indicators.

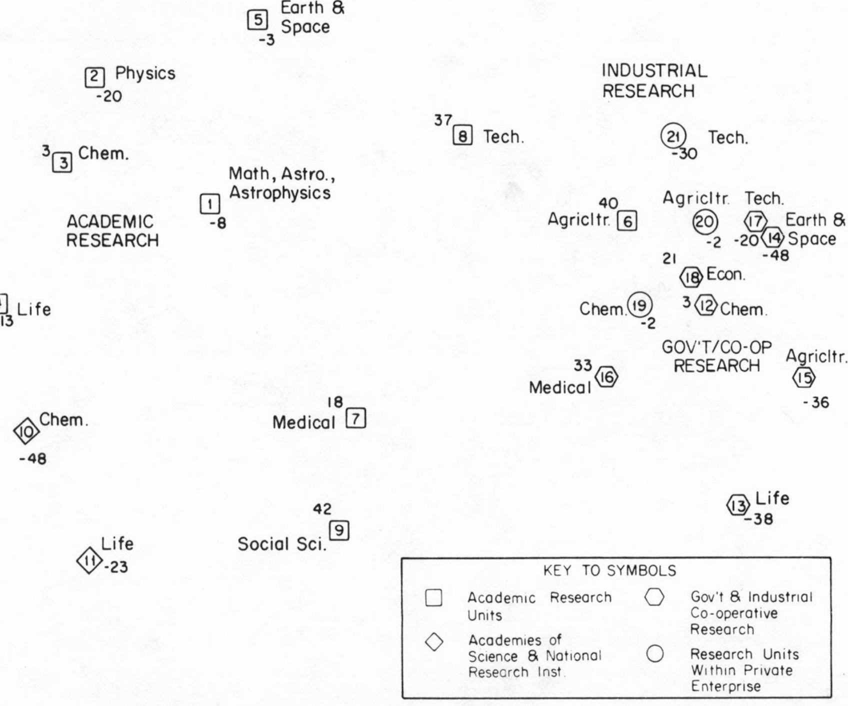

Exhibit 13.4 Clustering subgroups of research units on the basis of patterns of research orientations.
Note: MINISSA–I; G-L Stress = 0.020.

Results of the clustering analysis

Using the methodology outlined above, spatial configurations were obtained to represent profile similarities across the performance and influence indicators for all designated subgroups of research units in the Round 1 data. Exhibits 13.4 and 13.5 indicate these similarities for profiles calculated across the Rated-effectiveness and Research output indicators, respectively.[15] The 21 points depicted in these two configurations represent the 21 subgroups within the cross-classification of Scientific discipline and Type of organization that contained 11 or more research units. The enclosed numbers in the configuration plots correspond to the numbering system given in Exhibit 13.2, and the sets of symbols and abbreviations indicate the subgroup's specific organizational affiliation and scientific field, respectively. The numbers inserted at the upper left or lower right of each point in the configuration indicate the point's elevation above, or below, the two-dimensional surface represented in the exhibit.

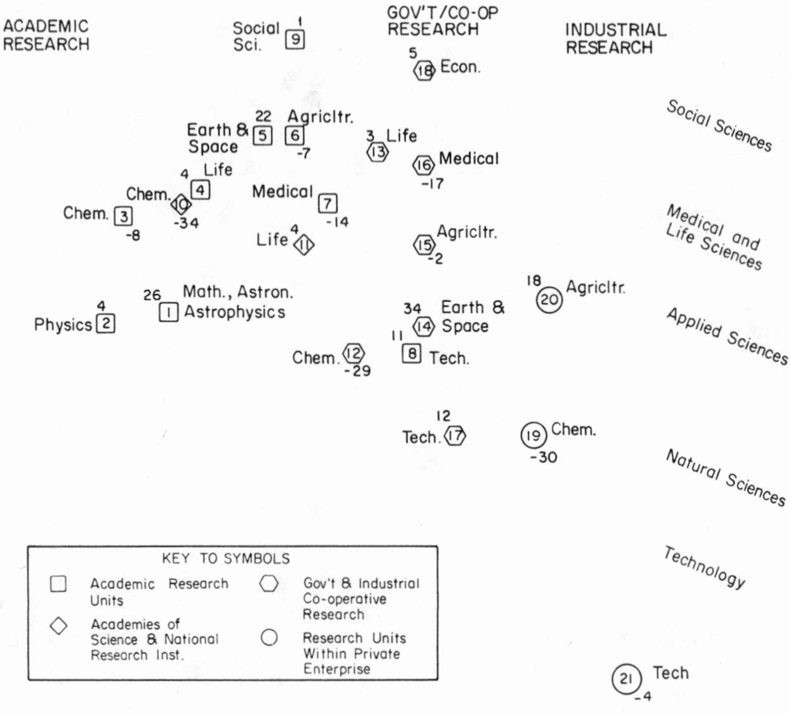

Exhibit 13.5. Clustering subgroups of research units on the basis of patterns of research outputs.
Note: MINISSA–I; G-L Stress = 0.042.

Clustering by research orientation. Recalling the hypotheses for clustering on the basis of scientific disciplines and types of organizations, one notes that in Exhibit 13.4, which represents similarities in research orientations, the major trend in clustering is on the basis of organizational affiliation. The two-dimensional surface that summarizes this three-dimensional configuration indicates a rather tight clustering of industrial and government/co-operative research units at the positive extreme of vector 1, with the academic research units spread across this vector's negative range.[16] The dominant trend of clustering on the basis of organizational setting is underscored by comparing the positioning of subgroups of research units of the same scientific discipline, but operating within different types of organizations. Consider, for example, the four points representing research units in chemistry (going from negative to positive on vector 1, these subgroups are numbered 10, 3, 19, and 12). The groups of units associated with universities and academies of science are at one extreme in the configuration space; those operating within government and industry are at the other extreme. Recalling that large distances within the configuration space indicate large dissimilarities in profiles, it becomes clear that chemistry research units in academic settings have very different research orientations from those in government and industry. The same type of tracing procedure can be repeated for the research units in the life sciences (numbers 1, 11, and 13) and reveals, once again, that research units of a different scientific discipline, but operating within the same type of institution, are more closely associated than research units of the same scientific discipline but differing organizational affiliation.

Reversing this procedure, one can review the positioning of units within a single type of organization, the government/cooperative research units (numbers 12–18), conducting research within a variety of scientific disciplines. Exhibit 13.4 indicates that these subgroups of research units are tightly clustered together, demonstrating that the potential differences in research orientations due to differences across scientific disciplines are effectively overridden by the dominant perspective of the organizational setting.

Considering the compelling arguments in favor of clustering on the basis of scientific discipline, the results presented in Exhibit 13.4 might seem curiously at odds with the literature cited in Section 2 of this chapter. It should be recalled, however, that most of that literature deals with research groups either directly or indirectly associated with the academic research tradition. A reexamination of Exhibit 13.4 for similarities and differences among academic research units reveals a substantial spread among these points, particularly within the two-dimensional projection of vector 1 by vector 2.[17] Here, for example, it is apparent that the academic research units in the medical and social sciences (numbers 7 and 9, respectively) are at some distance from those in chemistry, physics, the earth and space sciences, and technology (numbers 3, 2, 5, and 8, respectively). Thus, there appears to be some differentiation in research orientations among the academic research units. Extensive analysis of this configuration, and several others like it, has demonstrated that three subgroups of academic research units may be identified.

The most distinct subgroup would be the academic medical

and social sciences (points 7 and 9), which occupy a position in the lower-left quadrant of Exhibit 13.4. An analysis of the interpoint distances demonstrates that points 7 and 9 are at a considerable distance from the rest of the academic research units. A second subgroup could be identified as the academic "applied" sciences, comprised of points 5, 6, and 8. These points define an arc-shaped subspace that extends from the predominantly academic region on vector 1 across to the predominantly industrial region.[18] The remaining points, including math, astronomy, and astrophysics (point 1); physics (point 2); chemistry (point 3); and the life sciences (point 4) could be seen as the third major collection of academic research units, focused on the more traditional topics in the exact and natural sciences. The two points representing research units operating in the academies of science (point 10, chemistry; and point 11, life sciences), though difficult to categorize unambiguously in this configuration, appear similar in their research orientations to the subgroup of academic units in the exact and natural sciences.

Summarizing the discussion of Exhibit 13.4, it would appear that the clustering patterns based on research orientations lend primary support to the hypothesis of clustering by organizational affiliation rather than by scientific discipline. Only within the academic setting is there any evidence for distinguishing between research units on the basis of their disciplinary concerns. These findings are consistent with the clustering trends discussed next and depicted by Exhibit 13.5, where the underlying profiles, across which the pattern similarity coefficients were calculated, refer to research outputs.

Clustering by research outputs. Looking first at the distribution of points along vector 1 in Exhibit 13.5, it is again apparent that the subgroups of research units in the Round 1 data form consistent groupings on the basis of their organizational affiliation.[19] At the left end of this vector are located the academic research units, followed by the government/cooperative units in the center regions, with the industrial research units at the far right. One should recall that the government/cooperative and industrial units were grouped closely together in the configuration based upon research orientations. In this configuration, the industrial research units tend to distinguish themselves quite clearly (note the differences in elevation for neighboring points), a trend that was even more apparent in an earlier analysis of these data (Unesco, 1975b). Consequently, it could be argued that the industrial research units should be considered separately from the government/cooperative settings, particularly with respect to the quantities and types of research outputs.

In addition to grouping research units on the basis of organizational setting, Exhibit 13.5 demonstrates consistent patterns with respect to scientific discipline as well. Vector 2 is of particular interest here, as it tends to order the research units along a continuum from the social sciences, through the medical, applied, and natural sciences, to the technological sciences. This pattern can be detected within each of the three major organizational settings and is sufficiently consistent in its ordering of the research units to suggest a well-defined, functional relationship in the data.

An examination of the data across which the pattern similarity coefficients were calculated indicates that the spread of research units along vector 2 is a direct function of the production of books and articles and of patents and prototype devices (data now shown here). The greatest proportion of books and articles, relative to total research output, is reported among the academic social sciences (point 9) and the government/cooperative economic sciences (point 18). This proportion declines steadily along vector 2 such that the industrial research units in technology (point 21) produce virtually no books or articles. An exactly opposite trend is apparent for the proportion of patents and prototype devices, relative to total output: The industrial units in technology produce the largest proportion, and the economic and social sciences produce the smallest. Section 5 provides a more general overview of such trends.

Though the configuration in Exhibit 13.5 reveals patterns attributable to disciplinary differences, the primary clustering is on the basis of organizational affiliations: The distances separating subgroups of the same discipline but differing organizations (e.g., chemistry) are considerably greater than the distances separating subgroups of differing disciplines but the same organization (e.g., academic or government/cooperative). Vector 1, which represents the major source of variance in this configuration, groups research units with respect to their type of organization, and the composition of these groupings is much like that of Exhibit 13.4.[20] Despite the disciplinary differences that surface in this configuration, the spatial array of points serves more to reinforce organizational distinctions, in particular by splitting the industrial research units apart from those in government/cooperative settings.

Clustering by patterns of influence. The configurations displayed in Exhibits 13.4 and 13.5 indicate that the research units in the

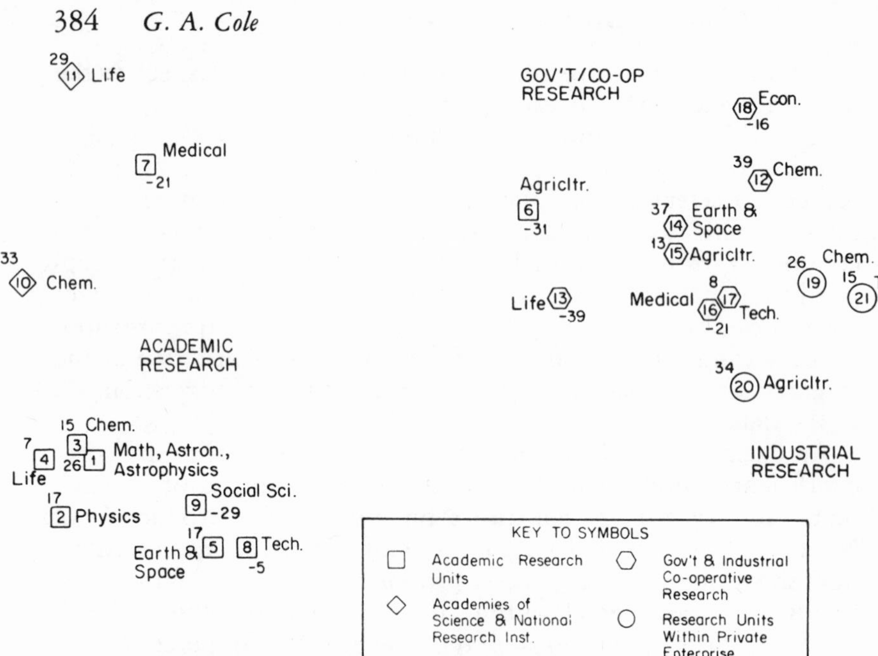

Exhibit 13.6. Clustering subgroups of research units on the basis of patterns of influence.
Note: MINISSA–I; G-L Stress = 0.064.

Round 1 data cluster primarily with respect to their organizational settings, regardless of whether the basis of comparison is research orientation or types of research output. These distinctions along organizational lines recall the comments in the literature indicating that a major difference among research organizations was the patterns of influence operating within the organization's decision-making structure. If we adopt, for the moment, the hypothesis that a major characteristic distinguishing one type of organization from another is its internal pattern of influences, then the groupings of research units described above should be replicated when the research units in the Round 1 data are analyzed with respect to their influence profiles. Seven indicators of influence, governing the choice of research themes and the organization of work in the laboratory, were described in Section 3, and Exhibit 13.6 presents the configuration that is generated when the same 21 subgroups of research units are compared for similarities in profiles across these measures.[21]

An examination of Exhibit 13.6 strongly confirms the hypothesis presented above. Once again, the primary grouping of research units in these data is defined by organizational differences. Furthermore, and this may be the most striking aspect of the analysis, those organizational differences can be effectively summarized by sets of profiles calculated across a relatively limited number of influence measures. As one traces across vector 1, a sharp distinction becomes evident between the academic research units, on the far left, and the government/cooperative and industrial research units on the far right. In addition, the distinction between the industrial research units and their government/cooperative counterparts, which was revealed in Exhibit 13.5, is apparent here as well. Finally, by reviewing the elevations of these points, differences among the academic research units reported for Exhibit 13.4 become evident once again, thereby reinforcing the previous conclusion that these research units may be divided into three groups. In a concise manner, the three-dimensional configuration presented in Exhibit 13.6 not only summarizes the conclusions derived from the two previous spatial arrays of these points, but goes on to suggest an intimate linkage between the patterns of influences operating within an organization and both the research orientations and the profiles of research outputs for units within the organization.

This latter hypothesis can be given a partial statistical test by using the spatial array of points in Exhibit 13.6 to predict the placement of points in Exhibits 13.4 and 13.5. This test has been performed by using the Schonemann-Carroll technique for achieving a Procrustean fit of two configuration matrices (Schonemann and Carroll, 1970).[22] When the configuration derived from the influence profiles (Exhibit 13.6) is used to predict the configuration based on similarities in research orientations (Exhibit 13.4), the resulting fit is remarkably close: The normalized symmetric error, comparable to the error variance in a regression analysis, is only .074, indicating that nearly 93% of the variance among the array of points in Exhibit 13.4 can be accounted for by the patterns of influence that characterize organizational differences. When the configuration based on patterns of influence is then used to predict the spatial configuration summarizing profiles of research outputs (Exhibit 13.5), the normalized symmetric error is .090. Thus, more than 90%of the variance within the research output configuration can be explained by similarities in influence patterns for research units in the Round 1 data. Despite the existence of a sizable literature that discusses the impacts of decision-making processes on the conduct and orientation of laboratory research, and the availability of relatively powerful multivariate statistical techniques for structural analyses and hypothesis testing, we had *not* anticipated encountering a set of results that were as clear and consistent as those reported here.

Exhibit 13.7. Composition of the Typology of research units in the Round 1 data

Category	Title	Points included	Number of units	Percent of units
1	Academic exact and natural sciences	(1–4, 10–11)	437	38.8
2	Academic medical and social sciences	(7, 9)	103	8.4
3	Academic applied sciences and technology	(5, 6, 8)	208	17.0
4	Government/cooperative research units	(12–18)	254	20.8
5	Research units in private enterprise	(19–21)	220	18.0
	Totals		1,222	100.0

Defining a Typology of research units

The confirmatory nature of the clustering analyses suggests that the research units in the Round 1 data can be partitioned into five major groups, as shown in Exhibit 13.7. The category definitions in Exhibit 13.7 are based on the clustering patterns of the 21 major subgroups contained within the cross-classification of Scientific discipline and Type of organization. The 14 remaining, smaller subgroups have been assigned a position within the Typology following a secondary analysis of the data. The procedures employed were similar to those described for the replication analyses (see Annex), and the assignment of the smaller subgroups to a category in the Typology depended upon their proximity to one of the five previously identified clusters.[23]

To check the actual degree of similarity among the profiles for the subgroups of research units clustered together by this Typology, the average Q-type correlation in each category of the Typology, as well as the standard deviations for those correlations, were calculated. The average correlations ranged from a low of .69 among the points in category 3 (academic applied sciences and technology), as calculated across the rated-effectiveness measures, to a high of .91 for the points in category 5 (private enterprise), as calculated across the same measures. The standard deviations for these Q correlations were all less than .21. These statistics show that the subgroups within each category of the Typology are very similar to one another with respect to their patterns of performance and influence.

Using the Typology as a statistical control variable

The Typology, Pattern, and Country variables. As was mentioned in the introduction to this chapter, the Typology was foreseen to play a significant role in the analysis of the Round 1 data, and moving from 35 categories in the cross-classification of Scientific discipline and Type of organization to 5 in the Typology provides a noteworthy gain in parsimony. A question that remains, however, is whether this gain in parsimony was not purchased at the expense of explanatory power. The 35-category cross-classification, by virtue of its construction, was capable of capturing the statistical explanatory power attributable to the disciplinary classification, the organization code, and any interaction effect involving them. One might reasonably ask whether a 5-category control variable could perform as well. The results are presented in Exhibit 13.3.

Exhibit 13.3 contains the previously reported analyses of variance, which demonstrated the impact of the Pattern variable on several performance and influence indicators. The additional columns expand on that analysis to demonstrate the explantory power of the new Typology and, for purposes of comparison, Country as well. When comparing the columns containing correlation ratios (eta-squares adjusted for degrees or freedom) for the Pattern variable and the Typology, one notes that the Pattern variable, as expected, explains more variance in the performance and influence indicators than does the Typology. A continued examination of these statistics reveals, however, that the five-category Typology retains an impressive capacity to control for explained variance. In most cases the decrease, when compared to the Pattern variable, is but 2 to 5 percentage points. These findings suggest that the Typology, with its relatively small number of distinctions, captures nearly all the variance uniquely attributable to the effects of Scientific discipline and Type of organization. Indeed, in those instances where the loss of explanatory power by the Typology relative to the Pattern variable exceeds 5%, one suspects the Pattern variable of having captured country effects as well as those for which it was created. This conclusion is reinforced if one compares the explanatory powers of the Pattern variable, Typology, and Country (Exhibit 13.3).

It should be recalled that the relatively unique sampling plans adopted by the six countries participating in Round 1 serve to link, indirectly, the Country code and the cross-classification of Scientific discipline and Type of organization. In particular, the

Pattern variable, with its large number of categories, tends to capture a good deal of the variance that actually stems from country effects.[24] The data in Exhibit 13.3 indicte that whenever the Typology shows a marked decline in explanatory power compared to the Pattern variable, the Country code appears to be a relatively strong predictor (e.g., Social effectiveness, Number of books, Number of articles in the country, Number of prototype devices, and S. p-making bodies). When the Typology and Country variables are then used as joint predictors in an additive model (multiple classification analysis), the total explanation of variance returns to levels that equal or exceed those reported for the Pattern variable alone. Though the Typology and Country variables are not completely independent (note the statistics for the joint and separate predictions toward Applications effectiveness), they are much less intertwined than the Country and Pattern variables. As the findings in this volume indicate, both the Typology and Country variables have proved to be consistently important control variables in the analysis of the Round 1 data.

Alternate versions of the Typology. As another check on the construction of the Typology, a series of statistical analyses was performed to see whether all five categories of the Typology were necessary. Two tests were run. First, all the academic research units (categories 1, 2, and 3) were collapsed into a single category and the resulting three-category typology was used in a series of one-way analyses of variance to test for a possible loss of explantory power. The second test was similiar to the first, but specified two categories of academic research units: the original category 1 (academic exact and natural sciences), and a composite of categories 2 and 3.

The results of the first test were quite clear: The analysis of variance using only a three-category Typology showed a marked decline in its power to control for explained variance as compared to the original five-category Typology. The drop-off was most noticeable for the rated-effectiveness measures, where the clustering analyses had indicated the greatest differences among the academic research units. The comparable test with a four-category Typology showed a less dramatic, but consistent, decrease in predictive power when compared to the five-category Typology. This drop-off was most noticeable for measures relating to applications orientations within the research unit. Furthermore, when predicting toward a series of measures concerned with sources of research funds, the four-category Typology was appreciably less effective in controlling for explained variance.

Consequently, it was concluded tht the five-category Typology was preferable as a general control variable for use in the Round 1 analyses.

Though the statistical properties of the Typology have been thoroughly demonstrated, some might legitimately question whether this categorization of research units will prove fruitful for future research. Visart, in Chapter 9, comments that the Typology has proven useful in the analysis of the Round 1 data, but fails to break new conceptual ground. She calls for a fresh approach to the study of research activities that goes beyond the time-worn distinctions of scientific discipline and type of organization. Visart's suggestion is an interesting one and deserves serious consideration. Preliminary investigations along these lines have been conducted. After speculating that the Typology described here might be only one of many categorical dimensions underpinning the Round 1 data, the data set was scanned for additional control variables that would be *both* conceptually interesting *and* statistically efficient. Unfortunately, the search generated little information that is not reported in other chapters of this volume. Thus, this author knows of no other sets of variables or categorizations that could have generated a radically different Typology. The conceptual interpretability of the present Typology, as well as its proven statistical capacities, recommend it for further use in the analysis of these data.

5. A summary of profiles of research orientations, output, and influences for the five Typology categories

The results of the clustering analyses have demonstated that the research units in the Round 1 data group themselves in a consistent fashion, regardless of whether they are analyzed for patterns of research orientations, patterns of research outputs, or patterns of influences. In order to highlight the substantive basis of the resulting Typology, the structural characteristics of the clustering configurations and the composition of certain clusters have been emphasized more than the scoring profiles upon which they were based. In this section, the scoring profiles associated with the categories of the Typology are summarized.

As a means of identifying and assessing the category-specific profiles, an extensive series of secondary analyses has been performed on the Typology using the technique of multivariate nominal scale analysis (MNA) (Andrews and Messinger, 1973). The MNA technique not only indicates the profiles characteristic of each category of the Typology, but determines, as well, their relative distinctiveness and coherence. The multivariate relationship between a selected set of variables, such as those of research orientations or research outputs, and the Typology are calculated, and the relative statistical importance of each variable in a given set is assessed. Limitations of space preclude a full exposition of these results, but the major findings are summarized below. In order to obtain stable estimates of these statistical parameters, the analyses have employed data from all 1,222 research units in the Round 1 data.[25]

Three separate MNA analyses have been performed, one each for the measure of research orientations, research outputs, and organizational influences. In summarizing the results of these analyses, the emphasis is placed on the superior predictive power of the influence measures. As was shown for the clustering analyses, these measures play a central role in the formation of the clustering configurations and this impact carries over to the MNA analyses of the resulting Typology.[26] By drawing upon theoretical arguments in the relevant literature, plausible scenarios can be constructed in which organizational influences act as determinants of both research orientations and patterns of research outputs.

The hypothesis for clustering on the basis of scientific disciplines emphasized the interplay between a discipline's cognitive and social structures. In particular, a research question, defined within some generally accepted theoretical perspective, assumes a degree of importance only when the members of the discipline jointly recognize the question as essential to their shared research program. Consequently, the potential *scientific significance* of a research topic cannot be determined without reference both to the body of theory and research practice tht underlies the discipline and to the general sense of priorities that develops among the discipline's active members. The dependence upon the larger research community for the ratification of an individually defined research program recalls, as well, the need for *recognition* among one's colleagues. The quest for professional recognition has been put forth as a primary motivating factor in the work of the professional scientist, and this recognition is most frequently obtained through the *dissemination* of one's research results within the professional literature.

The results of the clustering analysis, however, suggest that the proposed scenario is characteristic of academic research units only. This conclusion is supported by the analysis of performance and influence profiles, especially for academic research units in the traditional exact and natural sciences. The MNA pattern analyses indicate that for research units in category 1 of the Typology, a preponderant weight is given to potential *scientific significance* in the choice of research themes. The scientists in the laboratories, as opposed to the organization's management, play the leading role in the planning, organization, and execution of the unit's research work. Furthermore, the research orientations of these units stress *professional recognition* (and training) at the expense of applications, and the dominant form of research output is shown to be *published written materials.* If one accepts the theoretical propositions that have been put forth concerning the distinguishing characteristics of disciplinary research, then the results of these analyses can be seen as both consistent and cohesive for research units in the exact and natural sciences.

With respect to category 2, academic medical and social sciences, and category 3, academic applied sciences and technology, the analysis results are less sharply defined. Though the clustering analysis based upon research orientations demonstrates that these two groups are qualitatively different from those in the exact and natural sciences, the MNA pattern analyses indicate that those differences are more of degree than of fundamental direction. If, however, the patterns of influence and decision-making structures are more or less equivalent for all three subgroups of academic research units, as is indicated by the MNA analysis, then the reasoning applied to category 1 should apply to categories 2 and 3 as well. Thus, one could argue that the scientists in the academic medical, social, and applied sciences look to the theory and practices of their disciplines, and to their professional colleagues, for cues concerning appropriate research topics, and seek to disseminate their research results through the accepted literature. The main differences among the three groups of academic research units are those of *research orientations,* and these differences comply with expected divergences in disciplinary concerns. For units in the medical and social sciences, the emphasis is more on social effectiveness than upon recognition per se. As for the academic units in the applied sciences and technology, the research orientations stress applications in addition to recognition.

When writing about research practices in industrial settings, Cotgrove and Box, Kornhauser, Krohn, and Marcson have emphasized the contrasts with academic research and, in particular, the differing patterns of influences that govern the choice of research themes and the management of work in the laboratory. The MNA analyses of these data not only exhibit the contrasts outlined by previous researchers in this field, but demonstrate as well that they are aligned with complementary patterns of research orientations and research outputs. The conclusion is that the members of industrial research units do not look to the priorities of their discipline for the outline of their research program, but rather to the organization's goals as articulated by the management. *Management* plays a large role in the daily operations of the unit, including the choice of research themes, and the stress is placed on practical *value* and *applications* in research work. Publications are eschewed in favor of *internal research reports, prototypes,* and *patents.* In brief, the scoring profiles for the research units in industrial settings (category 5) contrast sharply with those for research units in the exact and natural sciences (category 1).

The remaining group of research units, those in government/cooperative laboratories (category 4), exhibited an influence profile that resembled, in certain respects, that of the research units in private enterprise. The weight given to scientific significance in the choice of research themes was quite low, and the role played by the *organization's leaders* in the management of the research work was quite high. Here again, one could argue that the members of these research units find their research priorities defined by the objectives of their organization (and the environment in which it operates) rather than the priorities established by the members of their discipline. The evidence provided by the MNA pattern analyses indicates that these organizational objectives stress research on issues of *social concern* that lead toward *practical applications.* The primary forms of research output are articles published within the country, internal reports, and patents registered within the country.

Cautionary note

Though the impacts of organizational influences on research orientations and types of research outputs have been stressed in these discussions, one should *not* conclude that deliberate manipulations of those influence patterns will, in themselves, bring about planned reorientations in the laboratory. The influence measures used in this analysis have served to explicate some of the major differences between research institutions represented in this sample. Recall, however, that previous work by Cotgrove and Box, and by Krohn, has shown that institutions differ, as well, with respect to the scientists who have chosen to work there; and furthermore that occupational choice is based, in large part, on the scientist's perceptions of the decision-making structure and working environment that characterize the organization. An abrupt change in organizational influence patterns might lead to declines in research effectiveness unless compensatory policies, such as increased opportunities for job mobility, were instituted at the same time. The potential social costs, in terms of disruptions of continuing research work, and the relocation of valuable manpower, should be considered carefully in advance of policy initiatives of this type. In the short run, the policymaker might do well to more carefully direct research proposals toward institutions with a demonstrated capacity to perform research work of a given type. The strengthening of institutional capabilities, involving a comprehensive manpower policy, suggests itself as the medium-term approach.

6. Summary and conclusions

The International Comparative Study of Research Units was conceived with the general objective of identifying basic, structural relationships that describe the behaviors and performance characteristics of research units. Literature in the sociology of science and in organizational theory suggests, however, that research-unit performance should vary substantially according to distinctions by scientific discipline and organizational setting. The possibility of identifying a single structural model, capable of assisting science policymakers, is therefore open to question.

The analyses reported in this chapter approach these issues from an empirical perspective, using multidimensional scaling techniques to cluster research units in the Round 1 data on the basis of their patterns of performance and reported organizational influences. The results demonstrate that the data may be divided into five groups of research units that exhibit internally consistent performance and influence patterns. The primary distinction in the resulting Typology is that of organizational setting, with striking differences in performance and influence patterns evident for research units in academic, government/cooperative, and industrial settings. The academic and industrial settings, in particular, exhibit antipodal patterns of performance and influences. Distinctions on the basis of scientific discipline are evident only within academic environments, where clusters comprised of the exact and natural sciences, the medical and social sciences, and the applied sciences and technology may be identified. Differences in patterns of influences can effectively account for the reported differences in both research orientations and types of research outputs for the units represented in this study.

The performance Typology that derives from this analysis has been used extensively in the analysis of the Round 1 data. In some instances, it has been used to determine statistical adjustments for the study's measures of performance, thereby sharpening the definition of structural relationships that were masked in the original data (see Chapter 10). In cases where a general model was shown *not* to hold for all research units in the data, the Typology was employed as a means of subsetting the data for a detailed analysis of selected subsamples (see Chapters 3 and 4). The results of this chapter's analysis indicate that structural models of research-unit performance, based on data from Round 1, are more appropriate when developed within categories of the Typology, where similarities in performance and influence profiles have been demonstrated. Replication analyses within other categories of the Typology would argue for wider application of such a model.

Neo-Kuhnian theory, which has stimulated much of the research on scientific specialities, stresses the interactions between the cognitive and social aspects of research work, arguing that research specialities form distinctive sociological entities possessing norms of behavior, lines of communication, hierarchies of interest, and criteria for the evaluation of originality and innovation. Those who have studied differences among research organizations have voiced similar convictions, stating that institutional settings determine the "character" of research, the way in which it is conceived, and the criteria by which it is evaluated. In either case, the basic expectation is that the social setting in which research takes place will shape the nature of the research work and, in turn, the type of knowledge that is produced. At this level of abstraction, these two perspectives hold much in common. Consequently, those concerned with the social factors affecting the content and direction of research might reconsider and reemphasize the role played by the institution in shaping research practices.

Annex: verification of the cluster analysis results

It is of interest to reconsider the original cross-classification of research units by Scientific discipline and Type of organization. In particular, it might be argued that the seeming dominance of organizational differences over scientific discipline in the clustering process was merely a statistical artifact stemming from the rather broad classification used to define scientific disciplines. One might speculate that the hypothesized distinctions among research specialities were effectively glossed over by an aggregation process that, for instance, lumped together all academic units performing research in chemistry (point 3 in Exhibits 13.4–13.6) or all industrial research units in technology (point 21). This possibility was explored in some detail by reanalyzing the data using a classification of scientific speciality groups that made much finer distinctions in terms of the types of research work actually being performed by the members of the unit.

As was mention in Section 3, two methods were used to classify units according to the scientific content of their work. The first method, a broad classification along major disciplinary lines, has been used for the analyses reported in the main body of this chapter. The second method involved a series of questions answered by the unit leader concerning the scientific specialities that characterized the work of the research unit. Whereas the first method generated 9 scientific discipline groups, the second approach generated 26. When this expanded disciplinary classification (which was developed by the Hungarian National Research Team), was used in conjunction with the code for types of organizations, a very finely defined grid was developed, which split the research units of the first round into 130 relatively small subgroups. Indeed, the grid was too fine in that many of the 130 cells contained 0, 1, or 2 research units. Consequently, this second cross-clssification of Scientific discipline and Type of organization was not used directly to recluster the Round 1 data; but employed, instead, as a means of subdividing the largest aggregations of research units entering the initial clustering analysis. Using the more detailed classification of scientific groups to define cutting points, the 8 largest parent groups were each split to form 2 or more children. The analysis procedure described in the body of the chapter was then repeated incorporating the new children subgroups into the original configuration spaces.

During the reclustering procedure, a special feature of the Guttman-Lingoes monotone distance analysis technique was utilized, allowing for the specification of a "fixed" initial configuration. In this instance, the fixed input configurations were those generated during the initial cluster analyses, *minus* the parent points, whose exact position in the configuration space had been predetermined. The analytic test, therefore, was a rather specific one: Would the children points position themselves in approximately the same region of the configuration as was occupied by their parents? Here again, the results were confirmatory. There was no appreciable drift in the positioning of these points that would have given additional support to the hypothesis for clustering on the basis of scientific discipline. Despite the substantial increase in the number of points being fit within this space, the calculated stress values were remarkably low: The Guttman-Lingoes Coefficient of Alienation, when calculated across the additional 29 children points, was only .004; no stress value associated with a single point exceeded .017.

Hence, the reanalysis of the data using the more detailed classification of scientific disciplines confirms the initial findings that disciplinary distinctions are evident only within academic settings. One should note that *none* of the children points originating within an academic cluster shifted across the configuration space to position themselves within the region occupied by the government/cooperative or industrial clusters of research units. Conversely, none of the government/cooperative or industrial children points drifted into the academic regions to form new linkages by disciplinary similarities. Consequently, one is again led to conclude that the fundamental cleavages within the data are defined along organizational lines, and that only within academic settings does a broadly defined disciplinary perspective become apparent.

References

Andrews, F. M., and Messenger, R. C., 1973, *Multivariate Nominal Scale Analysis: A Report on a New Analysis Technique and a Computer Program,* Ann Arbor, Institute for Social Research, University of Michigan.

Ayer, A. J. (ed.), 1959, *Logical Positivism,* New York, Free Press.

Baker, N. R., and Freeland, J., 1975, Recent Advances in R & D Benefit Measurement and Project Selection Methods, *Management Science,* 21 (June).

Baker, N. R., and Pound, W. H., 1964, R & D Project Selection: Where We Stand, *IEEE Transactions in Engineering Management,* EM-II (December) : 124–134.

Barber, B., and Hirsch, W. (eds.), 1962, *The Sociology of Science,* New York, Free Press.

Blalock, H. M., 1960, *Social Statistics,* New York, McGraw-Hill.

Blau, P. M., and Scott, W. R., 1962, *Formal Organization: A Comparative Approach,* San Francisco, Chandler.

Blume, S. S., and Sinclair, R., 1973a, Chemists in British Universities: A Study of the Reward System in Science, *American Sociological Review,* 38: 126–138.

Blume, S. S., and Sinclair, R., 1973b, Research Environment and Performance in British University Chemistry, *Science Policy Study Number 6,* London, Her Majesty's Stationery Office.

Bohme, G., 1975, The Social Function of Cognitive Structures: A Concept of the Scientific Community within a Theory of Action. *In* Knorr, K. D., Strasser, H., and Zilian, H. G. (eds.), 1975, *Determinants and Controls of Scientific Development,* Dordrecht, Holland, D. Reidel, 205–225.

Borg, I., and Lingoes, J. C., 1976a, A Direct Transformational Approach to Multidimensional Analysis of Three-way Data Matrices: Theory and Applications, Ann Arbor, Mich., Michigan Mathematical Psychology Program, technical report MMPP-76-1.

Borg, I., and Lingoes, J. C., 1976b, What Weight should Weights have in the Analysis of Individual Differences?, Ann Arbor, Mich., Michigan Mathematical Psychology Program, technical report MMPP-76-5.

Brooks, H., 1968, Can Science be Planned?. *In* Salomon, J. J. (ed.), 1968, *Problems of Science Policy,* Paris, OECD, 97–112.

Burns, T., and Stalker, G. M., 1961, *The Management of Innovation,* London, Tavistock.

Cetron, M. J., Martin, J., and Roepcke, L., 1967, The Selection of R & D Content–Survey of Quantitative Methods, *IEEE Transactions in Engineering Management,* 14 (March): 4–13.

Cicourel, A. V., 1963, *Method and Measurement in Sociology,* New York, Free Press.

Cohen, I. B., 1974, History and the Philosopher of Science. *In* Suppe, F. (ed.), *The Structure of Scientific Theories,* Urbana, University of Illinois Press, 308–349.

Cole, S., and Cole, J. R., 1968, Visibility and the Structural Bases of Awareness of Scientific Research, *American Sociological Review,* 33: 397–413.

Coleman, J. S., Campbell, E. Q., Hobson, C. F., McPartland, J., Mood, A. M., et al., 1966, *Equality of Education Opportunity,* Washington, D.C., U.S. Government Printing Office.

Cotgrove, S., and Box, S., 1970, *Science, Industry and Society: Studies in the Sociology of Science,* London, Allen and Unwin.

Crane, D., 1972, *Invisible Colleges: Diffusion of Knowledge in Scientific Communities,* Chicago, University of Chicago Press.

Crawford, E., and Perry, N., 1976, *Demands for Social Knowledge: The Role of Research Organizations,* London, Sage.

Disman, S., 1962, Selecting R & D Projects for Profit, *Chemical Engineering,* 69 (December): 87–90.

Draper, N., and Smith, H., 1966, *Applied Regression Analysis,* New York, Wiley.

Drucker, P. F., 1952, Management and the Professional Employee, *Harvard Business Review,* 30: 84–90.

Drucker, P. F., 1963, Twelve Fables of Research Management, *Harvard Business Review,* 41: 103–114.

Feyerabend, P., 1975, *Against Method,* London, New Left Books.

Green, P. E., and Rao, V. R., 1972, *Applied Multidimensional Scaling: A Comparison of Approaches and Algorithms,* Hinsdale, Ill., Dryden Press.

Griffith, B. C., Small, H. G., Stonehill, J. A., and Dey, S., 1974, The Structure of Scientific Literatures II: Toward a Macro- and Microstructure for Science, *Science Studies,* 4: 339–365.

Hagstrom, W. O., 1965, *The Scientific Community,* New York, Basic Books.

Hagstrom, W. O., 1974, Competition in Science, *American Sociological Review,* 39: 1–18.

Hays, W. L., 1973, *Statistics for the Social Sciences,* London, Holt, Rinehart and Winston.

Johnston, J., 1972, *Econometric Methods,* New York, McGraw-Hill.

Knorr, K. D., 1975, The Nature of Scientific Consensus and the Case of the Social Sciences. *In* Knorr, K. D., Strasser, H., and Zilian, H. G. (eds.), 1975, *Determinants and Controls of Scientific Development,* Dordrecht, Holland, D. Reidel, 227–256.

Knorr, K. D., Strasser, H., and Zillian, H. G. (eds.), 1975, *Determinants and Controls of Scientific Developement,* Dordrecht, Holland, D. Reidel.

Kornhauser, W., 1962, *Scientists in Industry: Conflict and Accommodation,* Berkeley, University of California Press.

Kowaleska, W., 1974, Bureaucratic Trends in the Organization and Institutionalization of Science Activity. *In* Whitley, R. (ed.), 1974, *Social Processes of Scientific Development,* London, Routledge and Kegan Paul, 269–280.

Krohn, R. G., 1971, *The Social Shaping of Science: Institutions, Ideology and Careers in Science,* Westport, Conn., Greenwood.

Krohn, R. G., 1972, Patterns of Institutionalization of Research. *In* Nagi, S. Z., and Corwin, R. G. (eds.), 1972, *The Social Contexts of Research,* New York, Wiley-Interscience, 29–66.

Kruskal, J. B., 1964a, Multidimensional Scaling by Optimizing Goodness of Fit to a Nonmetric Hypothesis, *Psychometrica,* 29: 1–27.

Kruskal, J. B., 1964b, Nonmetric Multidimensional Scaling: A Numerical Method, *Psychometrika,* 29: 115–129.

Kuhn, T. S., 1962, *The Structure of Scientific Revolutions,* Chicago, University of Chicago Press.

Kuhn, T. S., 1963, The Function of Dogma in Scientific Research. *In* Crombie, A. C. (ed.), *Scientific Change,* London, Heinemann, 347–369.

Kuhn, T. S., 1970a, Logic of Discovery or Psychology of Research. *In* Lakatos, I., and Musgrave, A. (eds.), 1970, *Criticism and the Growth of Knowledge,* Cambridge, Cambridge University Press, 1–23.

Kuhn, T. S., 1970b, Reflections on my Critics. *In* Lakatos, I., and Musgrave, A. (eds.), 1970, *Criticism and the Growth of Knowledge,* Cambridge, Cambridge University Press, 231–278.

Kuhn, T. S., 1970c, *The Structure of Scientific Revolutions* (enlarged ed.), Chicago, University of Chicago Press.

Kuhn, T. S., 1974, Second Thoughts on Paradigms. *In* Suppe, F. (ed.), 1974, *The Structure of Scientific Theories,* Urbana, University of Illinois Press, 459–482.

Lakhtin, G. A., 1968, Operational Research Methods in the Management of Scientific Research, *Minerva,* 6: 524–540.

Lammers, C. J., 1974, Mono- and Poly-paradigmatic Developments in Natural and Social Sciences. *In* Whitley, R. (ed.), 1974, *Social Processes of Scientific Development,* London, Routledge and Kegan Paul, 123–147.

Law, J., 1973, The Development of Specialties in Science: The Case of X-ray Protein Crystallography, *Science Studies,* 3: 275–303.

Lemain, G., MacLeod, R., Mulkay, M., and Weingart, P. (ed.), 1976, *Perspectives on the Emergence of Scientific Disciplines,* Chicago, Aldine.

Lingoes, J. C., 1966, New Computer Developments in Pattern Analysis and Non-metric Techniques. *In Uses of Computers in Psychological Research,* Gauthier-Villars, Paris, 1–22.

Lingoes, J. C., 1968, The Multivariate Analysis of Qualitative Data, *Multivariate Behavioral Research,* 3: 61–94.

Lingoes, J. C., 1971, Some Boundary Conditions for Monotone Analysis of Symmetric Matrices, *Psychometrika,* 36: 195–203.

Lingoes, J. C., 1972, A General Survey of the Guttman-Lingoes Nonmetric Program Series. *In* Shepard, R. N., Romney, A. K., and Newlove, S. B. (eds.), *Multidimensional Scaling: Theory and Applications in the Behavior Sciences,* New York, Seminar Press, 52–68.

Lingoes, J. C., and Roskam, E. E., 1973, A Mathematical and Empirical Analysis of Two Multidimensional Scaling Algorithms (*Psychometrika* monograph supplement, mongraph no. 19), *Psychometrika,* 38 (4, part 2).

Lingoes, J. C., and Schonemann, P. H., 1974, Alternative Measures of Fit for the Schonemann-Carroll Matrix Fitting Algorithm, *Psychometrika* 39: 423–427.

Lodahl, J. B., and Gordon, G., 1972, The Structure of Scientific Fields and the Functioning of University Graduate Departments, *American Sociological Review,* 37: 57–72.

Marcson, S., 1960, *The Scientist in American Industry,* New York, Harper & Row.

Marcson, S., 1966, *Scientists in Government,* New Brunswick, N.J., Rutgers University Press.

Marcson, S., 1972, Research Settings. *In* Nagi, S. Z., and Corwin, R. G. (eds.), 1972, *The Social Contexts of Research,* New York, Wiley-Interscience.

Martins, H., 1972, The Kuhnian "Revolution" and its Implications for Sociology. *In* Nossiter, T. J., Hanson, A. H., and Rokkan, S. (eds.), *Imagination and Precision in the Social Sciences: Essays in Honor of Peter Nettl,* London, Faber and Faber, 13–58.

Masterman, M., 1970, The Nature of a Paradigm. *In* Lakatos, I., and Musgrave, A. (eds.), 1970, *Criticism and the Growth of Knowledge,* Cambridge, Cambridge University Press.

Menard, H. W., 1971, *Science: Growth and Change,* Cambridge, Mass., Harvard University Press.

Merton, R. K., 1957, *Social Theory and Social Structure (revised ed.)*, New York, Free Press.

Moore, D. G., and Renck, R., 1955, The Professional Employee in Industry, *Journal of Business* (January): 58–66.

Mullins, N. C., 1972, The Development of a Scientific Specialty: The Phage Group and the Origins of Molecular Biology, *Minerva,* 10 (1): 51–82.

Mullins, N. C., 1973, The Development of Specialities in Social Science: The Case of Ethnomethodology, *Science Studies,* 3: 245–273.

OECD, 1968, *Problems of Science Policy,* Paris, OECD.

Orth, C. D., 1959, The Optimum Climate for Industrial Research, *Harvard Business Review,* 35: 55–64.

Pelz, D. C., and Andrews, F. M., 1966, *Scientists in Organizations: Productive Climates for Research and Development,* New York, Wiley.

Phillips, D. L., 1973, *Abandoning Method,* San Francisco, Jossey-Bass.

Rattenbury, J., 1975, Smallest Space Analysis (MINISSA): OSIRIS-III Version (unpublished report), Ann Arbor, Institute for Social Research, University of Michigan.

Reif, F., 1961, The Competitive World of the Pure Scientist, *Science,* 134: 1957–1962.

Rivlin, A. M., 1971, *Systematic Thinking for Social Action,* Washington, D.C., Brookings Institution.

Roberts, E. B., 1964, *The Dynamics of Research and Development,* New York, Harper & Row.

Rummell, R. J., 1970, *Applied Factor Analysis,* Evanston, Ill., Northwestern University Press.

Salomon, J. J., 1968, A Review of the Seminar. *In* OECD, 1968, *Problems of Science Policy,* Paris, OECD.

Schonemann, P. H., and Carroll, R. M., 1970, Fitting One Matrix to Another Under Choice of a Central Dilation and a Rigid Motion, *Psychometrika,* 35: 245–255.

Shepard, A. H., 1956, Basic Research and the Value System of Pure Science, *Philosophy of Science,* 23: 48–57.

Shepard, R. N., 1972, Introduction to Volume 1. *In* Shepard, R. N., Romney, A. K., and Nerlove, S. B., 1972, *Multidimensional Scaling,* New York, Seminar Press, 1–22.

Small, H., and Griffith, B. C., 1974, The Structure of Scientific Literatures. *In* Identifying and Graphing Specialties, *Science Studies,* 4: 17–40.

Souder, W. E., 1969, The Validity of Subjective Probability of Success Forecasts by R & D Project Managers, *IEEE Transactions on Engineering Management,* 6: 35–49.

Souder, W. E., 1973a, Analytical Effectiveness of Mathematics Models for R & D Project Selection, *Management Science,* 19: 907–923.

Souder, W. E., 1973b, Utility and Perceived Acceptability of R & D Project Selection Models, *Management Science,* 19: 1384–1394.

Storer, N. W., 1966, *The Social System of Science,* New York, Holt, Rinehart and Winston.

Storer, N. W., 1972, Relations among Scientific Disciplines. *In* Nagi, S. Z., and Corwin, R. G. (eds.), 1972, *The Social Contexts of Research,* New York, Wiley-Interscience.

Suppe, F. (ed.), 1974, *The Structure of Scientific Theories,* Urbana, University of Illinois Press.

Tannenbaum, A. S., 1968, *Control in Organizations,* New York, McGraw-Hill.

Tannenbaum, A. S., 1974, *Hierarchy in Organizations,* San Francisco, Jossey-Bass.

Toulmin, S., 1961, *Foresight and Understanding,* London, Hutchinson (New York, Harper & Row Torchbook, 1963).

UN General Assembly, 1977, Report of the Preparatory Committee for the United Nations Conference on Science and Technology for Development: Official Records: Thirty-Second Session; supplement no. 43 (A/32/43).

Unesco, 1975a, Identification of the RU Output Clusters – A Preliminary Analysis Report (document STP/524), Paris.

Unesco, 1975b, Development of a Performance Typology for Research Units in the First Round Data – A Preliminary Analysis Report (document STP/525), Paris.

Unesco, 1975c, Constructing and Testing of RU Output Composite Measures – A Preliminary Analysis Report (document STP/1713), Paris.

Unesco, 1976a, Assessing the First Round Performance Measures for their Potential Use within Categories of the Unesco Typology Variable: An Application of the MNA Program (document STP/836), Paris.

Unesco, 1976b, Preliminary Analyses of the Delays and Patterns of Influence Items – The Development of Composite Indicators, (document STP/838), Paris.

Unesco, 1976c, *Science and Technology in the Development of the Arab States* (Castarab working document), Paris.

Unesco, 1976d, *Program Plan and Budget 1977–1978* (document 19 C/5), Paris.

Unesco, 1977, *Medium Term Plan 1977–1982* (document 19 C/4), Paris.

Van Rossum, W., 1973, Informal Communication and the Development of Scientific Fields, *Social Science Information* 12 (6): 63–75.

Weingart, P., 1974, On a Sociological Theory of Scientific Change. *In* Whitley, R. (ed.), 1974, *Social Processes in Scientific Development,* London, Routledge and Kegan Paul, 45–68.

Weiss, C. H., 1972, *Evaluation Research: Methods of Assessing Program Effectiveness,* Englewood Cliffs, N.J., Prentice-Hall.

White, D. H., Sullivan, D., and Barboni, E. J., 1976, Growth, Changes and Dynamics of Scientific Specialties: The Interdependence of Theory and Experiment in the Life-Cycle of a Specialty in Elementary Particle Physics (paper presented at the International Symposium on Quantitative Methods in the History of Science, Berkeley, Calif., 26 August 1976).

Whitley, R., 1972, Black Boxism and the Sociology of Science. *In* Halmos, P. (ed.), *The Sociology of Science,* Keele University (sociological review monograph no. 18, September 1972).

Whitley, R. (ed.), 1974, *Social Processes of Scientific Development,* London, Routledge and Kegan Paul.

Notes

1. The analyses presented in this chapter represented a replication and slight refinement of analyses that were performed at an early stage in the International Study. The Typology described here, and the analysis methods used to develop it, are similar to the results reported by Cole (Unesco, 1975a) and subsequently employed by members of the International Research Team. The only substantive differences between the original Typology (used by authors of other chapters in this book) and that described here derived from the more stringent methodological criteria employed in the replication analysis. As a

result of this reanalysis, 60 research units, less than 5% of the data, were reassigned to new categories. The category most affected by this change was category 3, academic applied sciences, which was augmented by 45 units originally classified in category 1, academic exact and natural sciences. Numerous analytic tests indicate that the differences between the original and refined classifications are statistically inconsequential.

2. In fact, either of two hypotheses could be derived. The first would argue for no specific groupings; i.e., a random distribution of empirically observed "disciplinary" effects due to inconsequential differences among the research units represented in the data. The second, more stringent, hypothesis would argue for a single, undifferentiated clustering of all units in the study.

3. The development of this detailed classification by scientific discipline was carried out by members of the Hungarian national research team, and the author wishes to express his appreciation for their cooperation in conducting the analysis.

4. This battery is summarized in Exhibit 2.3, and the exact item wordings appear in questions S and T, reproduced in the Appendix.

5. As will be discussed in Section 4, the analysis techniques to be used in clustering the research units will rely upon the co-variance patterns, and not on absolute values of the measures in question. Thus, the argument for viewing these five measures for providing a "profile" of research orientation is justified and does not prejudice their later use as direct indicators of research-unit effectiveness.

6. These items are summarized in Exhibit 2.3 and appear in question R, reproduced in the Appendix.

7. Items were selected with respect to the magnitude of their factor loadings in a varimax factor rotations, and in consideration of their spatial positioning within a three-dimensional monotone distance analysis. In reviewing the monotone distance solution (Minissa-I), items that tended toward the periphery of the three-dimensional configuration were selected because these items exhibited maximum dissimilarity, thereby lending the greatest degree of conceptual coverage to the analysis.

8. See question H, which is reproduced in the Appendix.

9. The items appear in question I and are reproduced in the Appendix.

10. The questionnaire addressed to staff scientists contained a parallel set of items that also clustered in the manner described here. For the purposes of the analyses reported in this chapter, however, the data from staff scientists were not necessary and are not reported. See Chapter 7 and Unesco (1976) for further details.

11. Some readers may question whether the influence measures discussed here demonstrate more variance with respect to Country than as a function of Type of organization or Scientific discipline. Exhibit 13.3 presents the relevant figures, and it can be seen that some Country effects are evident, particularly for the S. p-making bodies and Organization leader measures. Only with the S. p-making-bodies measure, however, does the statistical effect attributable to Country exceed that reported for the Pattern or Typology variables. With the exception of this one influence variable, the reported organizational and disciplinary effects outweigh those of national and cultural differences.

12. Such results would provide statistical evidence in support of the null hypothesis. The first would lead to no evident clustering of the research units. The second would lead to a single, massive cluster.

13. The statistics reported in this exhibit are taken from a series of standard

one-way analyses of variance and represent the variance in the dependent measure that can be accounted for by the control variable. The statistic, eta-square, has been adjusted for degrees of freedom in all cases and is comparable across columns despite the differences in the numbers of categories for the control variables. An explanation for the columns titled "Typology," "Country," and "Country and Typology" will be presented below in the chapter.

14. A careful review of the two-way tables generated during the analyses of variance (data not shown here) indicates that the correlation ratios reported in Exhibit 13.3 are *not* statistical artifacts due to the presence of two or three deviant subgroups, but indeed reflect differing patterns of values across the bulk of the categories in the control variable. F ratios have not been reported, as they were felt to be redundant: With 1,222 cases in the analysis, a relationship accounting for as little as 1% of the variance in the dependent variable is statistically significant beyond the .01 level.

15. The technique that generated these configurations, Minissa-I, operates iteratively to develop a spatial representation in which the interpoint distances retain a high monotonic fit with the original pattern similarity coefficients (Lingoes, 1966, 1968, 1971, 1972). For Exhibits 13.5 and 13.6, the goodness of fit, as assessed by the Guttman-Lingoes Coefficient of Alienation, was .020 and .042, respectively (an alternate measure, Kruskal's Formula I for Stress, yields values of .015 and .034). These values indicate that a very good fit has been obtained in only 3 dimensions. For further details, see Lingoes and Roskam (1973) and Kruskal (1964a, 1964b). Because all multidimensional-scaling techniques are subject to local minima traps that can terminate the computations before a best-fitting configuration has been found, the configurations presented throughout this chapter have been subjected to a procedure of additional iterations using both arbitary and preselected starting configurations. In all cases, the Minissa-I program returned to a spatial array of points that was stable and consistently defined. Thus, the author is confident that the configurations presented here are truly representative of the underlying structure of the data.

16. The reference to vectors in this and the following discussions is for the purpose of focusing the reader's attention on specific segments of the configuration space; the vectors, themselves, have no particular substantive meaning. In fact, all these configurations have been rotated to highlight certain clustering features. Consequently, the distribution of research units in Exhibit 13.4 along vector 1, from academic to government/cooperative, has not been determined by the Minissa-I program, and the reader is cautioned against imputing a precise numerical interpretation to the positioning of research units along this or any other vector.

17. When examining these configuration plots, recall that the diagrams represented here are two-dimensional projections of what is, in truth, a three-dimensional space. The precise interpoint distances will appear somewhat distorted in a projection of lower dimensionality, as some points must be, figuratively, "squeezed" into place. To obtain a more accurate conception of the true interpoint distances, it is necessary also to consider the points' positions on the third dimension. Although space limitations preclude presentation of plots for vectors 1 by 3 and 2 by 3, the nonenclosed numbers associated with each point in Exhibit 13.4 provide this information.

18. The proposal for grouping points 5, 6, and 8 may seem curious given the seemingly great distance that separates points 5 and 6 and the comparatively short distance that separates points 1 and 5. Clarifications can be made here. First, the projection given in Exhibit 13.4 tends to distort the distance separat-

ing points 1 and 5, making it seem shorter than it in fact is. The corresponding projection on vectors 2 and 3 (not presented here) indicates that points 1 and 5 are separated by a substantial distance and that points 5, 6, and 8 occupy a relatively compact and distinct subspace. Furthermore, when other measures are used as the basis for the clustering (e.g., as in Exhibit 13.5), it becomes evident that points 5 and 6 have more in common than is immediately apparent here.

19. The reader is again cautioned about seeking a precise numerical interpretation for the location of points along vector 1. The projection that comprises Exhibit 13.5 has been both rotated and translated to represent organizational distinctions along vector 1, and disciplinary differences along vector 2. Vector 3, which is not plotted here, has relatively little variance, but serves to tap muted disciplinary distinctions: i.e., chemistry units tend to be located low on vector 3; astronomy and earth/space sciences high; and life sciences, technological sciences, agriculture, and medical sciences seem to form "layers" in the middle of this vector. Had the Round 1 sampling plan been more complete in its coverge of scientific disciplines, it is possible that this configuration would have exhibited a "lattice" structure.

20. A statistical comparison of the two configurations in Exhibits 13.4 and 13.5 reveals that they are closely related with respect to the array of points in space. The configuration-fitting operation, calculated according to the Schonemann-Carroll technique (1970), reports a normalized symmetric error of only .098; this can be interpreted as indicating that more than 90% of the spatial variance in these two configurations is commonly shared.

21. As with the two configurations presented above, the spatial array of points displayed in Exhibit 13.6 was developed by the Minissa-I technique and then rotated to highlight certain clustering characteristics. In 3 dimensions, the fit is very good; Kruskal's Stress I = .053; Guttman-Lingoes' Coefficient of Alienation = .064.

22. Readers familiar with the technical literature in this field may have noted that improvements have been suggested in the original Schonemann-Carroll technique (Lingoes and Schonemann, 1974) so as to facilitate comparisons of the type made here. These suggestions have been incorporated into the computations.

23. The fitting of these additional points proved rather straightforward for the Minissa-I program. The average stress values (G-L K coefficient) calculated across all 14 additional points never exceeded .076 for any of the 3 previously defined configuration spaces. With but 3 exceptions, the assignment of the 14 additional points followed directly from their positioning in the configuration space. For the 3 most troublesome points, which represented only 5 research units in total, the assignment was made first with respect to Type of organization, and second with respect to Scientific discipline.

24. Note that in all but two cases the Pattern variable explains considerably more variance than Country alone, and that whenever the Country code does explain as much as 14–20% of the variance in a performance or influence measure, the Pattern variable does as well or better. The only major exception is for the S. p-making bodies indicator, which is heavily dependent upon whether a given country possesses a vigorous science policymaking agency at the national level.

25. The pattern similarity coefficients, upon which the clustering analyses were based, were calculated across data that had been aggregated within the cross-classification of Scientific discipline and Type of organization. These aggregated data constitute but 35 cases, corresponding to the 35 cells in the cross-classification table, and this number is too small for the reliable estimation of the statistical parameters of the MNA model. The return to the disaggregated, unit-level data provides more cases for the statistical computations (N = 1,222) but incorporates more random variance as well.

26. Without entering into a lengthy explanation of the statistics generated by the MNA program and their interpretation in this analysis, it can be stated that the measures of organizational influences showed a stronger capacity to predict toward the Typology, and evidenced more distinctive category-specific profiles, than either the measures of research orientations or research outputs.

14 Estimating the construct validity and correlated error components of the rated-effectiveness measures

Frank M. Andrews
Institute for Social Research,
University of Michigan, Ann Arbor

1. Introduction

The International Comparative Study on the Organization and Effectiveness of Research Units includes various measures of research-unit performance. An important qustions is: How good are these measures?

There are various ways in which goodness might be assessed. The one to be addressed here is the matter of *internal validity.* Internal validity coefficients provide estimates of construct validity – that is, they estimate how closely an observed measure reflects the theoretical construct it was intended to represent. This is to be distinguished from various forms of *criterion validity* (predictive criterion validity, concurrent criterion validity), which refers to a different issue – that is, how closely an observed measure relates to other observable measures (criteria) that are believed relevant to it. Although an investigation of criterion validity would also be interesting, this is not the present topic.

The International Study assesses various different facets of research-unit performance. Included among them are the following seven aspects: General contribution, Recognition, Social value, Training effectiveness, Administrative effectiveness, R & D effectiveness, and Applications effectiveness. Measures of the performance of each research unit with respect to these seven as-

Nicole Visart, Gerald Cole, and Cinda Gainche have contributed in numerous ways to the analyses and discussions presented in this chapter.

pects have been derived from ratings provided by three types of respondents: unit heads (Type A scientists–SA), other professional-level members of the unit (Type B scientists–SB), and external evaluators (EV).[1] This chapter estimates the validity with which these three types of raters evaluated the seven aspects of performance. The analysis is based on the full set of research units (N = 1,222).

We shall use a structural measurement model that is derived from a set of interrelated causal theories as to what influences each of the performance measures. The model is based on the premise, widely accepted in psychometric theory, that an observed measure reflects three types of influences: (1) the true state of whatever is being measured, (2) other conditions that affect more than just one measure (e.g., common biases or *halo*), and (3) other conditions that affect only the given measure. These influences produce, respectively, three types of variance: (1) true variance, (2) correlated error variance, and (3) residual or random error variance. The problem is to decompose the total variance of each measure into its three components. By knowing the proportion of total variance that is valid variance, one can determine the internal validity of the measure, and from the proportion of variance that is correlated error variance one can determine the extent to which the measure has been influenced by the undesired effects of biases, halo, and the like.

2. Methodological development

The analyses reported in this chapter depend on several previously separate streams of methodological development. One is the notion of *construct validity* itself. This term was introduced in the psychological literature by Cronbach and Meehl (1955). They noted that construct validity depends on both (1) a network of relationships among a set of observed measures and (2) a series of theoretical assumptions about the relationships of a set of hypothetical constructs (i.e., unobserved variables) to one another and to the observed measures. A more recent and very useful treatment of the subject is provided by the sociologists Heise and Bohrnstedt (1970), who distinguish construct validity (which they suggest depends on the valid variance in a measure) from reliability (which depends on the *sum* of the valid variance and the correlated error variance).

Direct estimates of construct validity have been very few. The use of a multimethod-multitrait matrix, suggested by Campbell and Fiske (1959) seemed to offer a promising approach, but it turned out to be insufficient until the data collected by this approach could be analyzed using sophisticated causal models (Alwin, 1974; Boruch and Wolins, 1970). The models include unmeasured variables (Costner, 1969; Land, 1970), and it was only with the development of powerful computerized algorithms by Joreskog (1969, 1970, 1973; Joreskog and Van Thillo, 1972) that it became feasible actually to estimate sufficiently complex structural models. The validity coefficients derived from these models are not, in a strict sense, construct validity coefficients but rather what we shall call *internal* validity coefficients. However, given appropriate models and data – both of which we believe are present in the current analysis – *estimates* of construct validity can be obtained.

3. The model

This paper reports results from three separate structural modeling analyses. All three derive from one basic model, the "full form" of which is shown in Exhibit 14.1. The analytic task is to estimate a set of parameters for this model that will come as close as possible to accounting for the correlations among the observed measures, given what is assumed to be their linkages to the unmeasured causal variables (the theoretical constructs) and the presumed linkages among these unmeasured variables.

In Exhibit 14.1, the 18 rectangles represent the observed effectiveness measures. The circles on the left are intended to stand for *true* levels of performance. There are 7 such circles, one for each aspect of performance being considered. The circles on the right are intended to represent sources of correlated error arising from bias and halo effects that influence more than a single measure. There are 3 such circles, one for each separate source of data – the SA, SB, and EV raters. In speaking of "true performance" and "sources of correlated error," we are referring to theoretical constructs that are not (and could not be) actually measured. Thus, our measurement model involves a mixture of measured and unmeasured variables, a mixture of data and theory.

The fact that we want a particular circle to stand for a particular construct (e.g., true General contribution, SA bias/halo, etc.) does not, of course, make it so. Unmeasured variables – our circles – take on particular meanings according to the way they are linked to other variables in the model, both measured and unmeasured, and according to the constraints imposed on the strengths of their linkages. Given the way the model has been specified, we believe it reasonable to think that the circles mean

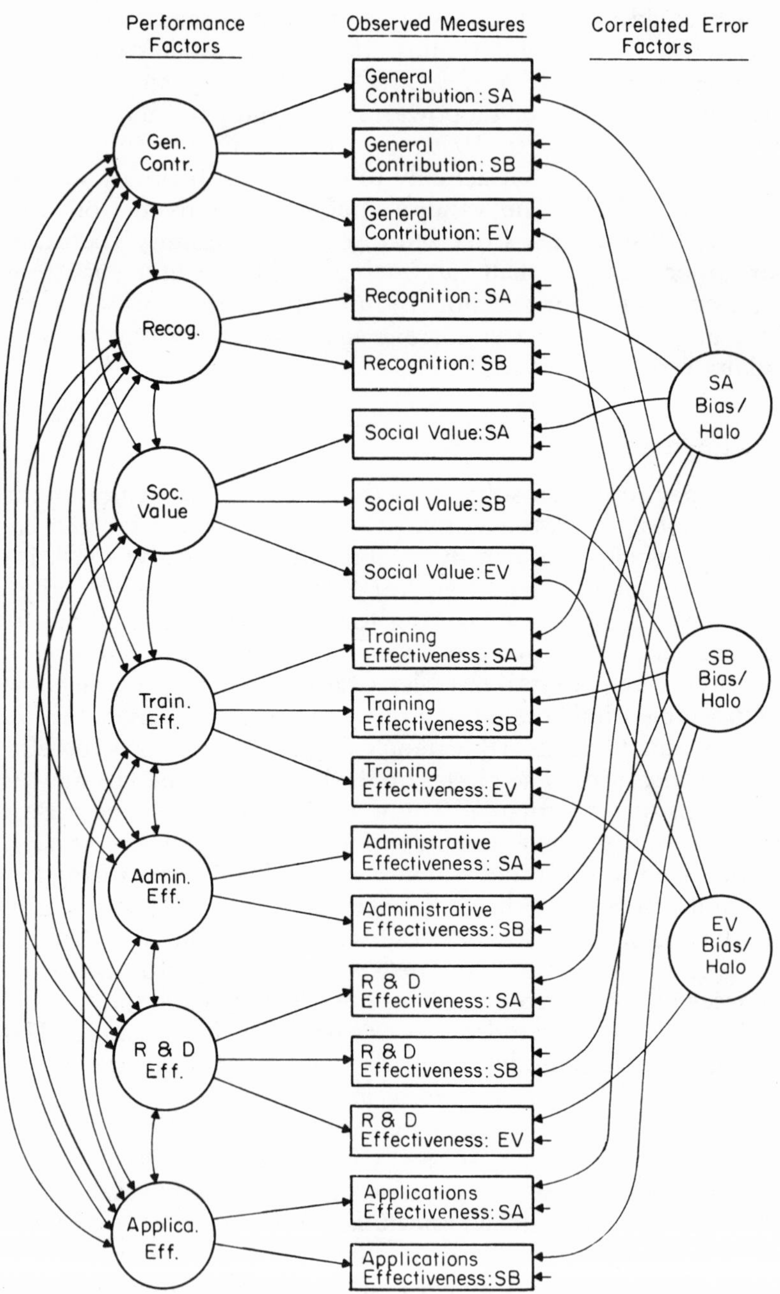

Exhibit 14.1. Full form of measurement model.

what we have said they do; hence, it is reasonable to think that this model can provide estimates of construct validity and correlated error effects. It should be explicitly recognized, however, that the appropriateness of interpreting the results in this way is dependent on a set of theoretical assumptions. This is the essence of the notion of construct validity.

The linkages shown in Exhibit 14.1 represent both our theories about what influences each of the observed measures and the parameters of the model that are to be estimated. Note that three arrows enter each rectangle: one (from the circles on the left) representing an input of true variance, one (from the circles on the right) representing the input of correlated error variance, and the last representing the input of residual variance. There is also a set of linkages among the circles on the left, the true performance factors. These linkages correspond to our theoretical expectation that one aspect of true performance will likely show some co-variation with other aspects of performance. Although this measurement model allows for expected co-variation among these true performance variables, it makes no assumptions about the causal priority among these variables (note that these linkages are shown by two-headed arrows).

The absence of possible linkages is also a significant aspect of the model. The true performance factors have direct causal impacts *only* on the measures directly relevant to them, and the bias/halo factors are linked *only* to measures based on the same data source. Note, also, that the three bias/halo factors are constrained to be independent of one another (i.e., there are no links between them). This reflects our theoretical expectation that the correlated errors attributed to one data source will be independent from those associated with another source. Finally, the bias/halo factors are constrained to be independent from all the true performance factors.[2]

When estimating the model, all the linkages coming from any one bias/halo factor were constrained to have equal values (though the magnitude of this value was left to be determined by the model-fitting algorithm). There are two reasons for introducing such a constraint. First, this corresponds to our theoretical expectation about the nature of a bias/halo effect, and by constraining the parameters in this way we help to ensure that the circles on the right take on the meanings intended for them. Second, introduction of this constraint ensures that the model will be identified – that is, that there will be only one set of parameter estimates that provides the best fit to the data.

Three forms of this measurement model have been estimated.

One is the model actually shown in Exhibit 14.1; we shall call this form 1. Another is similar to that shown in the exhibit, but deletes the four measures derived from the EV raters (and, of course, the EV bias/halo factor); we shall call this form 2. The third (form 3) deletes all EV-based measures and *all three* bias/halo factors.

The parameter estimates to be presented were derived by the Lisrel computer program (Joreskog and Van Thillo, 1972). Lisrel provides a set of parameters that comes closest to reproducing the observed intercorrelations among the measures, given the way the model is specified and the constraints imposed, under the maximum-likelihood criterion.

The parameters that are of perhaps greatest interest are those associated with linkages between the circles on the left and the measures. These represent the input of valid variance, and can be interpreted as estimates of *construct validity coefficients* when all variables are in standard-score form (i.e., with variance = 1.0). The other sets of parameters, however, are also interesting. Those associated with linkages from the bias/halo factors can be interpreted as *correlated error effects.* And those associated with linkages among the true performance factors (i.e., *between* the circles on the left) show the estimated correlations between the theoretical constructs after removing the effects of correlated and random errors.

4. Analysis results

Goodness of fit to the data

Before considering any of the individual parameters, it is important to examine the degree to which the whole set of parameters fit the data. Models that fit the data well may or may not be "correct" (this cannot be determined by examining the modeling results, but depends on external considerations, including the applicability of one's theory), but models that do not fit the data are certainly unsatisfactory.

One indication of fit is provided by the discrepancy between the variances and co-variances actually observed for the measures and the variances and co-variances that would be predicted by using the specified model and the obtained parameter estimates. By this criterion of fit, form 1 of the measurement model fits rather well, but involves a few substantial discrepancies. The average (absolute) deviation between the observed values and the fitted values for the variances and co-variances was .039.[3] There are 171 such deviations, and the largest was .294.

We observed that all the larger discrepancies involved data from the EV raters, and consequently developed form 2 of the model, in which the EV data were omitted. Here the fit turned out to be excellent: average discrepancy = .027, largest discrepancy = .086.

To check whether the bias/halo factors were important, we tried form 3 of the model, which is the same as the nicely fitting form 2, but from which the bias/halo factors have been completely omitted. The result was clear: The model fit much worse when these factors were not present. For form 3, the average discrepancy was .138 and the largest was .246.

Our conclusions are that form 2 of the model is the most elegant, that form 1 is not bad, that it is the EV data that cannot be well represented within the additive linear constraints of this general measurement model, and that inclusion of the bias/halo factors are needed if the model is to fit the data well.

Estimated validity and correlated error effects

Exhibit 14.2 presents validity coefficients and correlated error effects as estimated in each of the three forms of the model. Although our discussion will focus primarily on results from forms 1 and 2, which fit the data better than form 3, it is important to note that the estimates of the validity coefficients were essentially identical regardless of which form of the model was used.

The exhibit shows that the median estimated construct validity of measures derived from the SA raters is .58, from SB raters .67, and from EV raters .40. None of the individual validity coefficients deviate from these median values by as much as .15. The exhibit also shows bias/halo effects estimated at just over .40 for the SA and SB ratings,[4] and at .72 for the EV ratings. Based on these figures, we can say that a typical SA-based rating is composed of 34% valid variance, 18% correlated error variance, and 48% random error variance.[5] Because *reliable* variance includes both the valid and common-error components, we can also say that the typical SA-based measure includes 52% reliable variance, and hence has an estimated reliability coefficient of .72.[6] Comparable figures for a typical SB-based measure are: 45% valid variance, 18% correlated error variance, 27% residual error variance, and reliability = .79. For EV-based data, the figures are: 16% valid variance, 52% correlated error variance, 32% residual error variance, and reliability = .82.

Exhibit 14.2. Coefficients of construct validity and correlated error as estimated by three forms of the measurement model, for three types of raters[a]

	Form 1 (full model)			Form 2 (EV omitted)		Form 3 (no bias or EV)	
	SA	SB	EV	SA	SB	SA	SB
Validity coefficients							
General contribution	.57	.63	.38	.59	.65	.55	.67
Recognition	.71	.76	—[b]	.70	.75	.71	.76
Social value	.60	.72	.54	.60	.73	.58	.75
Training effectiveness	.58	.58	.41	.59	.55	.61	.58
Administrative effectiveness	.51	.56	—[b]	.47	.59	.55	.57
R & D effectiveness	.57	.67	.37	.59	.67	.54	.66
Applications effectiveness	.63	.69	—[b]	.62	.71	.59	.78
Median validity	.58	.67	.40	.59	.67	.58	.67
Correlated error effects	.43	.41	.72	.43	.42	—[c]	—[c]

[a]The three raters are: SA = research unit heads; SB = other professional-level unit members; and EV = external evaluators

[b]This aspect of effectiveness not rated by external evaluators.

[c]Bias/halo factors were not included in form 3 of the model.

The fact that the SB-based measures have the highest estimated construct validities and the EV-based measures the lowest is not surprising when it is recalled how the measures were derived, nor is it surprising that the EV-based measures include a much greater proportion of bias/halo variance than the others. We suspect that the SB-based measures show higher validity than the SA-based ones because the SB measures are *mean* scores, which combine independent judgments from several individual SB raters. One of the major reasons for computing the mean was to increase the validity of the measure, and it seems that this was in fact achieved.[7] The relatively low construct validity of the EV-based measures and their high bias/halo component is probably the result of asking people to evaluate a research unit who were not intimately familiar with the many different facets of the work of that unit.

Exhibit 14.2 is also interesting for what it shows about the validity differences between the various aspects of performance. Here also, results are highly consistent for all three forms of the measurement model. Recognition is the aspect that seems to be rated with the highest validity. Social value and Applications effectiveness also tend to show relatively high validities. The least valid ratings were of Administrative effectiveness. General contribution and R & D effectiveness show validities that are at or below the median. The validities of the Training effectiveness ratings vary on both sides of the median.

Estimated validity and error composition of composite scores

Use of the measurement model has provided estimates of the construct validity of ratings produced by individual sets of raters, but the performance measures actually used in the International Study are *composites* that combine data from the several types of raters. Given the results in Exhibit 14.2, however, we can apply a formula provided by Bohrnstedt (1969) and derive estimates of the validity and error components of various performance indices.

Exhibit 14.3 shows estimated construct-validity coefficients for the SA + SB combination and also for the SA + SB + EV combination.[8] (For comparison purposes, it also repeats the estimates for the individual components, as shown in Exhibit 14.2, for form 1 of the model.) One can see that combining the SA- and SB-based ratings produced a rather substantial increase in estimated construct validity. The median validity of the composite is estimated at .75, whereas that of the individual components was .58 and .67. Adding in the EV-based data, however, had very

Exhibit 14.3. Estimated construct validity and correlated error for individual and composite performance measures, for three types of raters[a]

	SA	SB	EV	SA + SB	SA + SB + EV
Validity coefficients:					
General contribution	.57	.63	.38	.73	.76
Recognition	.71	.76	—[b]	.84	.84[c]
Social value	.60	.72	.54	.77	.81
Training effectiveness	.58	.58	.41	.71	.72
Administrative effectiveness	.51	.56	—[b]	.66	.66[c]
R & D effectiveness	.57	.67	.37	.75	.76
Applications effectiveness	.63	.69	—[b]	.77	.77[c]
Median validity	.58	.67	.40	.75	.76
Correlated error effects					
SA correlated error	.43	—	—	.26	.20
SB correlated error	—	.41	—	.25	.19
EV correlated error	—	—	.72	—	.33

[a]The three raters are: SA = research-unit heads; SB = other professional-level unit members; EV = external evaluators.
[b]This aspect of performance not rated by external evaluators.
[c]This value repeated from SA + SB combination; no separate EV data exist.

little effect on the validity: It produced a small gain in validity for each of the measures, but the maximum gain was only .04 (for Social value). It would seem that including the EV data neither improves nor detracts from the measures, and that decisions about whether these data should be collected and used must be based on considerations other than their contribution to estimated construct validity. On the basis of the estimates shown in Exhibit 14.3, one can infer that the proportion of valid variance in the composite performance measures varies from a high of about 70% (for Recognition) to a low of about 43% (for Administrative effectiveness) and that the typical composite measure contains about 55% valid variance.

In contrast to the valid variance, which tends to accumulate when individual components are combined to form a new composite measure, error variance tends to cancel out. In the present case, this is as true for the correlated error variance as for the residual error variance, because the components come from different raters and their correlated error factors are statistically independent. Using the Bohrnstedt (1969) formula and the estimates of correlated error shown in Exhibit 14.2, we have estimated the impact of each separate correlated error effect on the composite measures. As shown in Exhibit 14.3, the SA + SB composite is estimated to reflect a .26 SA correlated error effect, and a .25 SB correlated effect. For the SA + SB + EV composite, the correlated error effects are estimated at .20 for SA., .19 for SB, and .33 for EV.

By squaring the above estimates, we can arrive at some summary statements about the estimated variance composition of the composite measures. We find that a typical SA + SB composite includes 55% valid variance, 7% SA correlated error variance, 6% SB correlated error variance, and 32% residual variance. Similarly, the typical SA + SB + EV measure contains 56% valid variance, 4% SA correlated error variance, 4% SB correlated error variance, 11% EV correlated error variance, and 25% residual variance.

Interrelationships among the aspects of performance

As a by-product of estimating the models discussed above, we also obtain information about the interrelationships among the true performance variables. These appear as the upper figure in each cell of the matrix shown in Exhibit 14.4.[9] For comparison, the exhibit also includes the correlations between the observed measures after combining the SA, SB, and EV data; these are the lower figures in each cell. In some cases, important differences appear between the two figures in each cell. These differences are attributable to removing the effects of correlated errors (which spuriously *raise* the associations among the observed measures) and random errors (which *lower* the associations among the observed measures).

Some of the most interesting differences involve the Applications effectiveness measure. The true version of this variable shows modest *negative* relationships to the true versions of Training effectiveness and Recognition, results that did not appear for the observed measures, and a more positive association with true R & D effectiveness than appeared for the observed measures. All three of these shifts seem in accord with our expectations, given what we know about the specializations of research units.

Certain other interesting shifts involve the General contribution measure. In its true version, it appears more strongly correlated with Recognition and with R & D effectiveness than was the case with the observed measures. Again, these shifts seem reasonable.

We might take special note of the relatively high coefficient,

Exhibit 14.4. Relationships among aspects of performance[a]

	General Contribution	Recognition	Social Value	Training effectiveness	Administrative effectiveness	R & D effectiveness
Recognition	.67					
	.55					
Social value	.39	−.01				
	.32	.09				
Training effectiveness	.26	.32	−.05			
	.30	.35	.09			
Administrative effectiveness	.29	.07	.10	.08		
	.25	.15	.19	.12		
R & D effectiveness	.83	.49	.30	.31	.30	
	.67	.44	.29	.33	.21	
Applications effectiveness	.03	−.22	.29	−.32	−.10	.43
	.12	−.06	.32	.33	.08	.33

[a]Upper figure: linkages among true variables (results from form 2 of the model). Lower figure: correlations among observed measures (SA, SB, and EV combined).

.83, estimated for the association between true General contribution and true R & D effectiveness. It has been suggested that the measures of these two concepts might actually tap just one underlying phenomenon, but show a less-than-perfect correlation because of measurement errors.[10] This chapter's analysis adjusts for those errors and finds that although the correlation is moderately high between R & D effectiveness and General contribution, it does not reach 1.00. (The parameter estimate of .83 suggests that 69% of the variance in one true variable overlaps with that of the other.) Thus, the analysis suggests that it is appropriate to distinguish between the two concepts.

5. Discussion

The results presented in this chapter lend themselves to a number of uses. One, of course, is the sheer descriptive information they provide about the estimated variance composition of the rated-effectiveness measures. Because these measures play central roles in other analyses, it is important to have some idea about how well they reflect what they are supposed to reflect (performance), and to what extent they reflect extraneous elements (bias/halo and residual errors).

The results can also be used to guide decisions about subsequent development and use of the survey approach for assessing research-unit performance. Some of the procedures adopted in the past (e.g., obtaining performance ratings from staff scientists as well as from unit heads) seem to have contributed substantially to the validity of the final measures, and these practices should probably be continued. On the other hand, data from the external evaluators was estimated to be rather low in validity and heavily saturated with bias/halo effects. Although combining these data with the ratings by unit heads and staff scientists does not seem to have detracted from the quality of the performance measures, it does not seem to have enhanced them much either.

The results presented here have a third use: They can significantly enlighten one's interpretation of other analyses. It is widely known that the relationship between a dependent variable and one or more independent variables is affected by the errors in one's measures, and with the estimates now available we can at least begin to determine just what these effects will be. Formulas provided by Cochran (1970) and Guilford[11] (1954) can be used for this purpose. From them one can determine, for example, that the explained variance in predicting a typical rated-effectiveness measure *cannot exceed* .57 unless the predictor variables share some of the same correlated errors as the performance measure. Thus, if one were fortunate enough to have *perfectly* valid predictor variables, and if these provided a *complete* explanation of, say, R & D effectiveness (which happens to have a typical validity), one would still observe a squared multiple correlation of only .57. Carrying the example still further, assume that we have a complete explanation of R & D effectiveness, but are trying to make the prediction using a set of independent variables that are no more valid than the performance measures and that do not have any errors in common with them. In this case, the observed *R*-square would be only .34 – despite the perfect prediction! It is very clear that one must interpret any observed relationship with respect to what is maximally obtainable, which depends on having knowledge of – or at least some estimates of – the composition of one's measures.[12]

We conclude with the question with which we started: How good are the performance measures? It is a question that cannot be answered in the most natural way, by comparing these measures to others, because the social science literature contains few estimates of construct validity and none that we know of regarding measures of research-unit performance. Techniques for deriving such estimates are too new for there to be a wide body of previous results with which comparisons can be made. In an absolute sense, the measures developed for the International Study are far from perfect. They have moderately high reliabilities (.72 to .82), but a significant part of the reliability is traceable to correlated measurement error rather than to true variance. We have estimated that only slightly more than half the total variance in a typical composite performance measure is valid variance. Although this is not very high, it nevertheless seems substantial enough to make possible an in-depth analysis of factors that relate to research-unit effectiveness. Given the subtlety of this concept, one should perhaps be pleased that it has been captured at all, and that the performance measures seem as sensitive to it as we estimate them to be.

Annex: a general structural model for the relationship between two measures

Exhibit 14.5 shows a general structural model that can be used to consider the relationship between two measures from the study on research units. The general structural equation for use with standardized variables is: a = cbd + ef + gh + ij.[13] Examples of ways in which this can be applied follow.

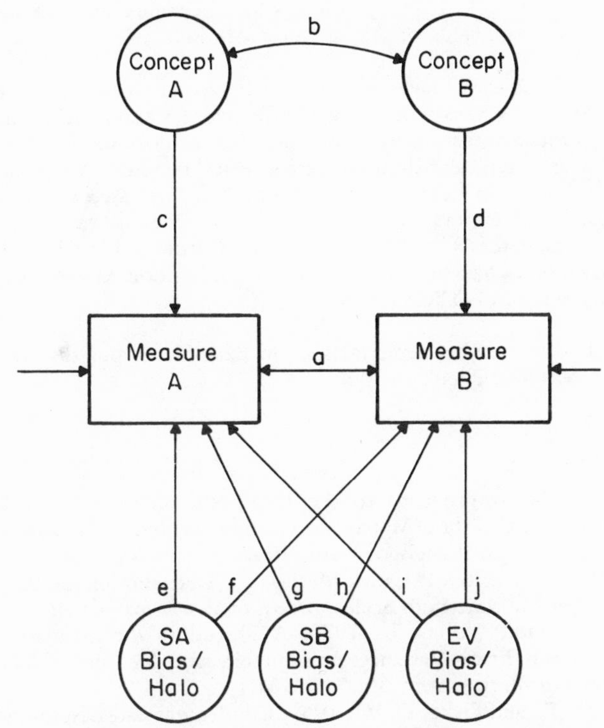

a = Observed relationship between Measure A and Measure B
b = Relationship between Concept A and Concept B
c = Validity of Measure A
d = Validity of Measure B
e = SA bias/halo effect on Measure A
f = SA bias/halo effect on Measure B
g = SB bias/halo effect on Measure A
h = SB bias/halo effect on Measure B
i = EV bias/halo effect on Measure A
j = EV bias/halo effect on Measure B

Exhibit 14.5. A general structural model for the relationship between two measures.

Example 1. If measure A is the SA + SB + EV version of R & D effectiveness and measure B is some other measure that has perfect validity and shares no common errors with measure A, what is the maximum relationship possible between measures A and B? Here we need to solve for a, given that $b = 1.00$ (the maximum possible relationship), $d = 1.00$ (from our specification of the problem), $c = .76$, e = .20, $g = .19$, $i = .33$ (all from Exhibit 14.3), $f = h = j = 0$ (from our specification of the problem). Then, $a = .76$ and $a^2 = .57$.

Example 2. Assume the same as in Example 1, except that the validity of measure B is the same as that of measure A. In this case, all parameters remain the same as in Example 1, except for *d*, which becomes .76. Solving the equation for *a* produces a value of .58 and an a^2 of .34.

Example 3. Assume we have an observed Pearson correlation of .40 between the SA + SB + EV version of R & D effectiveness and another measure that comes from the SB respondents and that we assume has the same variance composition as a typical SB-based performance measure. What can we infer about the relationship between the concepts? In this case, we must solve the equation for *b*. Parameters *c, e, f, g, i,* and *j* have the same values as they did in Example 1; parameters $d = .67$ and $h = .41$ (all from Exhibit 14.2, because we assume measure B has the same variance composition as a typical SB-based performance measure). Then $b = .63$.

Example 4. Assume the same facts as in Example 3, but that the observed relationship was .08. Then $b = .00$.

References

Alwin, D., 1974, Approaches to the Interpretation of Relationships in the Multitrait-multimethod Matrix. *In* Costner, H. (ed.), *Sociological Methodology 1973–74,* San Francisco, Jossey-Bass.

Bohrnstedt, G. W., 1969, A Quick Method for Determining the Reliability and Validity of Multiple-item Scales, *American Sociological Review,* 34: 542–548.

Boruch, R. F., and Wolins, L., 1970, A Procedure for Estimation of Trait, Method, and Error Variance Attributable to a Measure, *Educational and Psychological Measurement,* 30: 547–574.

Campbell, D. T., and Fiske, D. W., 1959, Convergent and Discriminant Validation by the Multitrait-multimethod Matrix, *Psychological Bulletin,* 56: 81–105.

Cochran, W. G., 1970, Some Effects of Errors of Measurement on Multiple Correlation, *Journal of the American Statistical Association,* 65: 22–34.

Costner, H. L., 1969, Theory, Deduction and Rules of Correspondence, *American Journal of Sociology,* 75: 245–263.

Cronbach, L. J., and Meehl, P. E., 1955, Construct Validity in Psychological Tests, *Psychological Bulletin,* 52: 281–302.

Duncan, O. D., 1966, Path Analysis: Sociological Examples, *American Journal of Sociology,* 72: 1–16.

Goldberger, A. S., 1972, Structural Equation Methods in the Social Sciences, *Econometrica,* 40: 970–1002.

Guilford, J. P., 1954, *Psychometric Methods* (2d ed.), New York, McGraw-Hill.

Heise, D. R., and Bohrnstedt, G. W., 1970, Validity, Invalidity, Reliability. In Borgatta, E. F. (ed.), *Sociological Methodology 1970,* San Francisco, Jossey-Bass.

Land, K. C., 1970, On the Estimation of Path Coefficients for Unmeasured Variables from Correlations among Observed Variables, *Social Forces,* 49: 506–510.

Joreskog, K. G., 1969, A General Approach to Confirmatory Maximum-Likelihood Factor Analysis, *Psychometrika,* 34: 183–202.

Joreskog, K. G., 1970, A General Method for the Analysis of Covariance Structures, *Biometrika,* 57: 239–251.

Joreskog, K. G., 1973, A General Method for Estimating a Linear Structural Equation System. *In* Goldberger, A. S., and Duncan, O. D. (eds.), *Structural Equation Models in the Social Sciences,* New York, Seminar Press.

Joreskog, K. G., and Van Thillo, M., 1972, Lisrel: A General Computer Program for Estimating a Linear Structural Equation System involving Multiple Indicators of Unmeasured Variables, unpublished research bulletin, RB-72-56, Princeton, N.J., Educational Testing Service.

Notes

1. It is assumed that readers of this chapter are familiar with the performance ratings obtained in this study and how individual questionnaire items have been clustered together to form certain performance measures. These matters are discussed in Chapter 2.

2. This model can be considered a restricted factor analysis model (Boruch and Wolins, 1970). Note that it contains certain factors that are allowed to relate to one another (the performance factors), as in an oblique factor solution, and also certain others that are constrained to be independent from all others (the bias/halo factors), as in an orthogonal solution. It is a *restricted* factor analysis model because many of the factor loadings are constrained in some way (e.g., to be zero). Goldberger (1972) has noted that factor analysis represents a special case of structural equation modeling.

3. In calculating these discrepancies (and also those cited below), all observed measures have been standardized. Thus, the co-variances are correlations, and one can interpret the average discrepancy figure as a difference between observed and fitted correlations of about .04.

4. An entirely different analysis, reported in Chapter 4, arrived at highly similar estimates for the impact of correlated errors on these performance measures (see Exhibits 4.8 and 4.9).

5. To obtain the percentage of variance attributable to a given source, one squares the parameter estimate.

6 The square root of 52% = .72.

7. If we were to assume that *individual* SB raters produced data with validity and reliability identical to what we have estimated for the SA raters, and if we were to combine the data from three such SB raters, the estimated validity of the composite would be .64 (derived by applying Formula 14.37 in Guilford, 1954). This theoretically derived .64 is highly consistent with the estimte of .67 from our measurement model and suggests that the higher construct validity of the SB measures is almost wholly attributable to the fact that they are based on a composite.

8. These estimates were derived under the assumption that the individual measures had been standardized to have identical variances before being combined into the respective composites. Actually, this standardization did not take place, but a separate estimate of validity that took account of the differing variances of the components of the Social-value aspect of performance (where the differences in variance are greatest) produced results identical to those shown in Exhibit 14.3. We infer that estimates in Exhibit 14.3 are applicable to the composite measures as they have actually been constructed.

9. We show results from form 2 of the model because it was this form that showed the best fit to the data. Estimates of these parameters from form 1 of the model were highly similar to those from form 2. Omitting the bias factors to produce form 3 of the model not only worsened the fit of the model to the

data, but also made all these parameters more strongly positive (or less strongly negative).

10. See, for example, Chapter 11.

11. The relevant formulas from Guilford are 14.35 and 14.36.

12. The annex to this chapter portrays a model that may be useful in helping to conceptualize these matters.

13. This formula derives from the general formula of path analysis (Duncan, 1966).

Appendix: questionnaire contents

This Appendix presents the contents of the five questionnaire forms used for collecting data in Round 1 of the International Comparative Study on the Organization of Research Units. Some of the questionnaire forms involve substantial overlaps with others, and consequently it is not necessary to reproduce here all forms in their entirety. However, given the material that does appear in this appendix, plus the following details about the content of each questionnaire form, the full information for all five forms is available.

The RU questionnaire. This questionnaire, directed to the administrator of the research unit, but completed by the unit head if there were no administrator, consists of questions 1 through 5 (plus certain additional unnumbered control items on the back cover of the questionnaire booklet). All parts of the RU questionnaire are reproduced in this Appendix (see pages 425–437).

The SA questionnaire. This questionnaire is addressed to the head of the research unit. It consists of the following questions: A–H, J–L, N, Q, and R–T, plus control information on the back cover (similar to the RU form). The SA questionnaire (except for the back-cover material) is also reproduced in its entirety in this Appendix (see pages 438–463).

The SB questionnaire. This questionnaire is addressed to staff scientists and includes many of the same questions that appear in the SA questionnaire. The questions are: A (except items A1b and A1c are omitted), B, C, D, J (with some changes, described below), K, L, Q, S, and T, plus the control information. In addition, the SB questionnaire includes questions M and P, which do not appear in the SA questionnaire. Within question J, the item J1c that appears in the SA questionnaire is omitted from the SB questionnaire, and several new items are added in questions J2 and J4. Reproduced in this Appendix are the pages from the SB questionnaire that present questions J2, J4, M, and P (see pages 464, 465, 466, and 467). Other pages in the SB questionnaire are identical to the relevant portions of the SA questionnaire.

The TS questionnaire. This questionnaire is addressed to the technical support staff of the unit and includes questions A, B, J, and M, plus control information. With the following exceptions, all questions are identical to those in the SB form: Question A has fewer items and some different wordings; question J3 includes three additional items (J3m, J3n, and J3p); question J4 is omitted. Two pages from the TS questionnaire are reproduced in this Appendix – those that present question A (on page 468) and the additional items in question J3 (on page 469).

The EV questionnaire. This questionnaire is addressed to external evaluators and consists of the items in question T (with the exception of items Tei and Teii), plus one additional item asking about the evaluator's acquaintance with the unit being rated. No pages from the EV questionnaire appear in this Appendix.

UNITED NATIONS EDUCATIONAL, SCIENTIFIC AND CULTURAL ORGANIZATION

Unesco/NS/ROU/295/RU
Paris, October 1973
Original: English

INTERNATIONAL COMPARATIVE STUDY ON THE ORGANIZATION OF RESEARCH UNITS

GENERAL INFORMATION RELEVANT TO THE RESEARCH UNITS

Form "**RU**"

EXPLANATORY NOTES

Thank you for your co-operation in the Unesco International Comparative Study on the Organization of Research Units.

This questionnaire is one of a series of instruments designed to provide relevant data for studying and evaluating the organization of research units. The administration of the set of questionnaires and the subsequent analysis of their contents constitutes the survey research project in which you have been asked to participate. The major premise guiding this work is that a better understanding of the organization of individual research units will facilitate improved management of research units in general and stimulate decisions which may improve their efficiency and effectiveness.

Your unit is one of 200-250 in your country asked to co-operate in this study. All of the units were chosen by the national scientific research team conducting the project, in conjunction with the national organization(s) sponsoring this work in your country. No effort has been made to single out your unit or the organization to which it belongs. Your selection is solely the result of a national sampling plan.

In addition to your country, this study is being conducted simultaneously in several other European countries. The person who gave you this questionnaire your interviewer, will be glad to tell you the names of the other participating countries.

In answering this questionnaire, it is most important that your responses be as complete and candid as possible. In addition to facts, many questions ask for your opinions and perceptions. Thus, the value of this work relies heavily upon how you complete each question.

Concerning the confidentiality of your replies, both Unesco and the national authority responsible for this project declare that all responses will be kept in strict confidence. Further, both declare that in subsequent analysis of data and presentation of results, no responses from either an individual or the unit to which he or she belongs will be identified.

Any feedback of results at the national or international level will come from your national scientific research team. Your interviewer will be glad to tell you about your country's plans for communicating results back to interested participants.

You may now begin to complete this questionnaire. Instructions for completing each question are given just before each question is asked. Please read them carefully before replying. If you have any questions, please ask your interviewer.

PLEASE WORK ALONE. DO NOT CONSULT WITH ANYONE ELSE IN MAKING YOUR REPLIES.

When you have finished, please return your completed questionnaire to your interviewer.

Once again, thank you for your help.

....

on behalf of the entire international research team of the Unesco International Comparative Study on the Organization of Research Units

<u>Organization</u>: The body containing the unit and whose activity (total or partial) can be considered as scientific or technological; it constitutes a legal person under the applicable national legislation.

For the purposes of this study a <u>research unit</u> is one which meets <u>all</u> of the following criteria :

(a) Has at least one leader who is a core member

(b) Has at least three core members, each of whom has been a unit member for at least half a year

(c) Has a total expected life-span of at least one year,

and where a <u>"core member"</u> is a person who devotes at least 8 hours per week to the work of the unit and who has communication (direct or indirect) with the unit leader(s) at least once each month.

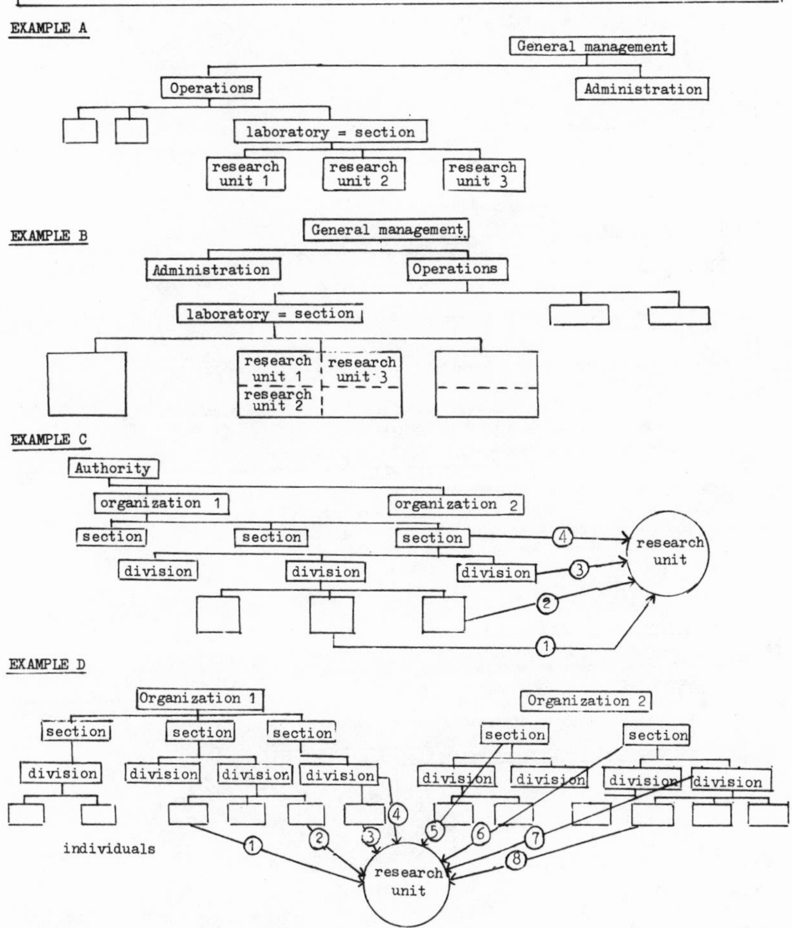

1. IDENTIFICATION OF THE RESEARCH UNIT AND SIZE OF THE ORGANIZATION TO WHICH THE UNIT BELONGS

- RU 3 -

1. Years of existence of the unit* and of the organization*

Please indicate

a. Year the unit first came into existence — . . . 1 / 37 - 38

b. Year the organization to which the unit belongs first came into existence — 39 41

2. Head(s) of the unit

Caution: do not mention head of the whole organization or section to which the unit belongs

Please select ONE number from the left and write it in the space provided

The unit has

1 = one head

2 = more than one head — . . 42

3. Status and place of the unit in relation to the administrative structure of the organization to which the unit belongs

Please select ONE number from the left and write it in the space provided

1 = The research unit corresponds to one administrative entity (as in example A on the left)

2 = The research unit constitutes a part of one administrative entity (as in example B on the left)

3 = The members of the research unit are drawn from more than one administrative entity within the organization (as in example C on the left) — . . 43

4 = The members of the research unit are drawn from more than one administrative entity from different organizations (as in example D on the left)

4. Total staff of the organization

a. The total number of persons on the payroll of the organization to which the unit belongs is

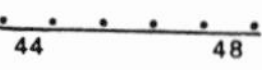

b. The total number of scientists and engineers on the payroll of the organization engaged in research and experimental development activities (R & D) is — 49 52

This question concerns exclusively premises and land used for research and experimental development (R & D) and other scientific activities (e.g. computing centres, museums, zoological and botanical gardens, scientific and technical libraries or documentation services, rooms for scientific meetings, experimental stations, etc.). Premises and land for other activities such as entertaining, restaurants and other similar accommodations should be excluded.

Library services: Include in principle all operations required to obtain scientific and technical information stored in one or other material support (books, periodicals, reprints, films, tapes, etc.).

Science information officer: A person employed by the unit or organization, whose professional function is to find and supply scientific or technical information in any form to scientists, engineers or technicians in response to particular user enquiries. Science information officers often interpret their responsibilities much more widely, e.g. by anticipating needs before these are formulated as specific enquiries. Librarians in the traditional sense are not to be included except where a professionally trained information officer is also carrying out the functions of a librarian.

2. FACILITIES AT THE DISPOSAL OF THE RESEARCH UNIT

1. Premises and land*

How many m^2 premises and/or land does the unit have for its use

a. m^2 premises

b. m^2 land

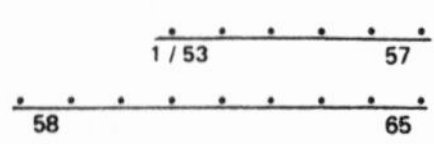

2. Need and availability of expensive equipment

If the work of the unit requires the use of expensive equipment, please write in the spaces provided for each of the four categories below, the needs and availability of expensive equipment

Caution: Avoid leaving blanks, by answering where necessary "NA" (not applicable) or "UN" (unable to reply):

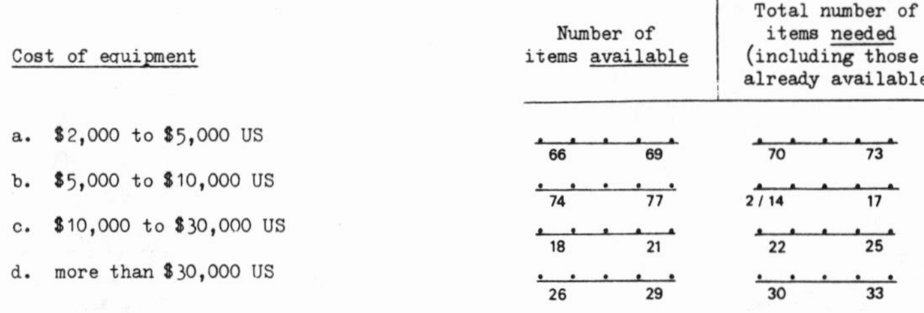

Cost of equipment	Number of items available	Total number of items needed (including those already available)
a. \$2,000 to \$5,000 US	66 69	70 73
b. \$5,000 to \$10,000 US	74 77	2 / 14 17
c. \$10,000 to \$30,000 US	18 21	22 25
d. more than \$30,000 US	26 29	30 33

3. Information

a. Is there an internal library service available to your unit

If yes, write "1"

If no, write "0" 34

b. Does your unit enjoy the services of a science information officer

If yes, write "1"

If no, write "0" 35

c. Does your unit provide all or some of its members with subscriptions to computerized retrieval information services

If yes, write "1"

If no, write "0" 36

Scientist and engineer: This group includes any person who has received scientific or technical training in the fields of exact and natural sciences, engineering, agricultural, medical or social sciences and humanities as specified below

(i) completed education at the third level leading to an academic degree
(ii) completed third level non-university education (or training) which does not lead to an academic degree but is nationally recognized as qualifying for a professional career. It is necessary for each country to establish criteria for distinguishing between scientists and engineers as defined on this basis and technicians who have received formal training
(iii) training and professional experience which is nationally recognized (e.g. membership in professional societies, professional certificate or licence) as being equivalent to the formal education indicated in (i) and (ii).

Technician: This group includes any person who has received specialized vocational or technical training in any branch of science or technology as specified below

(i) one to two years' training beyond completed education at the second level or three to four years' training beyond the first cycle of secondary education, whether or not leading to a degree or diploma
(ii) on-the-job training and professional experience which is nationally recognized as being equivalent to the level of education indicated in (i)

Laboratory assistants who meet the requirements (i) and (ii) are also classed as technicians.

Other personnel: The residual group includes skilled workers, such as machinists, sheet metal workers and other trade workers, operatives etc. as well as unskilled workers; all clerical, administrative and other supporting personnel. Exclude security, janitorial and maintenance personnel engaged in general house-keeping acitivities.

4. Computerized data processing

a. Please indicate the NEED and ACCESS your unit has to computerized data processing by selecting ONE number from the left and putting it in the space provided

1 = No need for computerized data processing

2 = Computerized data processing needs, but no access to it

3 = Use of computerized data processing through others outside the unit — 2/37

4 = Direct use of computerized data processing by members of the unit

b. How many members of the unit can use a computer programme to process the data they use or create — 38 - 39

3. TRAINING AND CAREER DEVELOPMENT FACILITIES IN THE RESEARCH UNIT

Please indicate whether the training and career development facilities listed below are used by the specified members of the unit

Select ONE number from below and write it in the space provided

Facilities Used By

Training and career development facilities	Scientists & engineers*	Technicians*& other personnel*	Both	
a. Formal courses (minimum 2 weeks)	1	2	3	40
b. Conferences or seminars	1	2	3	41
c. Training visits	1	2	3	42

<u>Administratively attached</u>: on the payroll of the organization as a member of this research unit

<u>Scientist and engineer</u>: see definition p. – RU 6 –

<u>Technician</u>: see definition p. – RU 6 –

<u>Core member</u>: see definition p. – RU 2 –

<u>Other personnel</u>: see definition p. – RU 6 –

<u>Levels</u>: A <u>first-level scientist or engineer</u> is one who is not responsible for guiding or supervising the work of other scientists or engineers

A <u>second-level scientist or engineer</u> is one responsible for guiding or supervising the work of other scientists or engineers

A <u>third-level scientist or engineer</u> is one responsible for guiding or supervising the work of second-level scientists or engineers

<u>Annual Expenditures</u>: funds actually spent during a given year on the unit's own personnel, activities, equipment, etc., <u>exclusive</u> of capital and overhead costs borne by the institution, <u>where</u>:

Personnel expenditures include wages, salaries and all related elements of labour of scientists, engineers, technicians and other personnel (see definition p.– RU 6 –)

Capital costs include expenditure or investment in land, buildings and major equipment

Overhead costs include repairs and maintenance costs; water, gas, electricity, steam, etc.

4. HUMAN AND FINANCIAL RESOURCES OF THE RESEARCH UNIT

1. Human resources : Growth of personnel

Please indicate for the specified members of the unit in the spaces provided:

- the present number administratively attached*
- the present number not administratively attached
- the initial number 36 months ago
- the numbers having joined and left during the last 36 months

	Number HERE NOW		Number HERE 36 months ago	Number having LEFT during last 36 months	Number having JOINED during last 36 months
	administratively attached	not administratively attached			
a. Scientists & engineers identified as core members*					
– 1st level	. . . 2/43-44	. . . 45-46	. . . 47-48	. . . 49-50	. . . 51-52
– 2nd level	. . . 53-54	. . . 55-56	. . . 57-58	. . . 59-60	. . . 61-62
– 3rd level	. . . 63-64	. . . 65-66	. . . 67-68	. . . 69-70	. . . 71-72
b. Technicians identified as core members*	. . . 73-74	. . . 75-76	. . . 77-78	. . . 79-80	. . . 3/14-15
c. Other personnel*	. . . 16-17	. . . 18-19	. . . 20-21	. . . 22-23	. . . 24-25

2. Finance

a. Sources of income

Please indicate the percentage distribution of last year's income of the unit according to sources of funds

i. National sources of funds

a. organization's own funds . . . .% 26 28

b. grants or contracts earmarked for the unit, originating from

1. research foundations, research councils and similar grant-giving bodies, both public and private . . . .% 29 31

2. industrial or commercial enterprises, both public and private . . . .% 32 34

3. other sources . . . .% 35 37

ii. Foreign sources of funds . . . .% 38 40

Total 1 0 0 %

b. Growth of annual expenditures

Please indicate in percentage the average growth of annual expenditures* of the unit taking 100 as a base index 3 years ago . . . .% 41 43

Training and career development facilities: see question p. - RU 7 -

Low-cost equipment: Office furniture (including typewriters and desk-top calculating machines) and minor laboratory equipment whose purchasing cost is less than US $500

Expensive equipment: Any piece of equipment required by scientific and technological activities whose purchasing cost exceeds US $500 (e.g. spectrographs, electronic computers, etc.)

5. DELAYS FOR SATISFACTION OF NEEDS

Please indicate, for each operation listed below – WITHIN THE ORGANIZATION AND ITS APPROVED BUDGET – HOW MUCH TIME is required between the request made by the unit and satisfaction of need. (Caution: exclude delays due to lack of funds.) Write the NUMBER corresponding to the approximate length of delay in weeks in each space provided.

Caution: Avoid leaving blanks, by answering where necessary "NA" (not applicable) or "UN" (unable to reply)

	Delay between initiation of request and approval decision in the organization	Delay between approval decision and satisfaction of need
a. Staffing		
i. Hiring personnel for a definite period	3/44 – 45	46 – 47
ii. Hiring personnel for an indeterminate period	48 – 49	50 – 51
iii. Termination of employment of personnel hired for a definite period	52 – 53	54 – 55
iv. Termination of employment of personnel hired for an indeterminate period	56 – 57	58 – 59
b. Equipment		
i. Hiring or buying low-cost equipment * (value up to US $500 per piece)	60 – 61	62 – 63
ii. Hiring or buying expensive equipment* (value greater than US $500 per piece)	64 – 65	66 – 67
c. Services		
i. Using training and career development facilities*	68 – 69	70 – 71
ii. Using external information services	72 – 73	74 – 75
iii. Obtaining a scientific or technical translation	76 – 77	78 – 79
d. Dissemination of results		
i. Submitting research results for publication	4/14 – 15	16 – 17
ii. Circulating research results outside the unit	18 – 19	20 – 21

Code numbers of the unit — type of org. (1); country (2 - 3); discipline (4 - 5); unit no. (6 - 9)

Interviewed person (I/P) code — 10 - 11

Date of reply to the questionnaire — day (14 - 15); month (16 - 17); year (18 - 19)

Response Reliability — 20

Interviewer's code — 21 - 22

Number of core members situated in locations other than the headquarters of the unit — 23-24

Number of core members who:	Scientists and engineers (including heads)	Technical and Service Staff
answered and returned the questionnaire	25-26	27-28
were unable to reply	29-30	31-32
refused to reply	33-34	35-36

SC/WS/400

EXPLANATORY NOTES

Thank you for your co-operation in the Unesco International Comparative Study on the Organization of Research Units.

This questionnaire is one of a series of instruments designed to provide relevant data for studying and evaluating the organization of research units. The administration of the set of questionnaires and the subsequent analysis of their contents constitutes the survey research project in which you have been asked to participate. The major premise guiding this work is that a better understanding of the organization of individual research units will facilitate improved management of research units in general and stimulate decisions which may improve their efficiency and effectiveness.

Your unit is one of 200-250 in your country asked to co-operate in this study. All of the units were chosen by the national scientific research team conducting the project, in conjunction with the national organization(s) sponsoring this work in your country. No effort has been made to single out your unit or the organization to which it belongs. Your selection is solely the result of a national sampling plan.

In addition to your country, this study is being conducted simultaneously in several other European countries. The person who gave you this questionnaire, your interviewer, will be glad to tell you the names of the other participating countries.

In answering this questionnaire, it is most important that your responses be as complete and candid as possible. In addition to facts, many questions ask for your opinions and perceptions. Thus, the value of this work relies heavily upon how you complete each question.

Concerning the confidentiality of your replies, both Unesco and the national authority responsible for this project declare that all responses will be kept in strict confidence. Further, both declare that in subsequent analysis of data and presentation of results, no responses from either an individual or the unit to which he or she belongs will be identified.

Any feedback of results at the national or international level will come from your national scientific research team. Your interviewer will be glad to tell you about your country's plans for communicating results back to interested participants.

You may now begin to complete this questionnaire. Instructions for completing each question are given just before each question is asked. Please read them carefully before replying. If you have any questions, please ask your interviewer.

PLEASE WORK ALONE. DO NOT CONSULT WITH ANYONE ELSE IN MAKING YOUR REPLIES.

When you have finished, please return your completed questionnaire to your interviewer.

Once again, thank you for your help.

....

on behalf of the entire international research team of the Unesco International Comparative Study on the Organization of Research Units

Code	Country
000	your unit's country
010	Abu Dhabi
014	Afghanistan
018	Albania
021	Algeria
029	Andorra
032	Angola
040	Argentina
044	Australia
047	Austria
052	Bahamas
054	Bahrain
056	Bangladesh
058	Barbados
064	Belgium
068	Bermuda
076	Bolivia
084	Botswana
089	Brazil
094	British Honduras (Belize)
106	Brunei
109	Bulgaria
113	Burma
116	Burundi
125	Cameroon
131	Canada
144	Central African Republic
149	Sri Lanka
153	Chad
156	Chile
158	People's Republic of China
160	Republic of China
170	Columbia
178	Congo
180	Zaïre
186	Costa Rica
189	Cuba
192	Cyprus
194	Czechoslovakia
198	Dahomey
202	Denmark
208	Dominican Republic
219	Ecuador
226	El Salvador
230	Equatorial Guinea
236	Ethiopia
252	Fiji (Islands)
256	Finland
260	France
262	French Guinea
276	Gabon
280	Gambia
290	Federal Republic of Germany
292	German Democratic Republic
300	Ghana
308	Greece
318	Guadeloupe
320	Guam
322	Guatemala
326	Guinea
330	Guyana
334	Haiti
342	Honduras
344	Hong Kong
348	Hungary
352	Iceland
360	India
364	Indonesia
370	Iran
372	Iraq
376	Ireland
380	Israel
384	Italy
388	Ivory Coast
392	Jamaica
394	Japan
400	Jordan
404	Kenya
406	Khmer Republic
408	Democratic People's Republic of Korea
410	Republic of Korea
414	Kuwait
418	Laos
422	Lebanon
430	Lesotho
434	Liberia
438	Libyan Arab Republic
446	Luxembourg
450	Macao
454	Madagascar
456	Malawi
458	Malaysia
474	Maldive Islands
478	Mali
480	Malta
484	Martinique
488	Mauritania
490	Mauritius
496	Mexico
504	Monaco
508	Mongolia
516	Morocco
524	Mozambique
540	Nepal
544	Netherlands
556	New Caledonia
564	New Hebrides
568	New Zealand
572	Nicaragua
576	Niger
580	Nigeria
600	Norway
612	Pakistan
614	Panama
624	Paraguay
628	Peru
632	Philippines
638	Poland
642	Portugal
656	Puerto Rico
660	Qatar
670	Rumania
674	Rwanda
680	St. Helena
688	St. Kitts
690	St. Lucia
708	Saudi Arabia
712	Senegal
716	Seychelles
720	Sierra Leone
726	Singapore
730	Somali
736	South Africa
740	Rhodesia
742	People's Democratic Republic of Yemen
756	Spain
778	Sudan
782	Surinam
786	Swaziland
788	Sweden
790	Switzerland
792	Syrian Arab Republic
798	Thailand
802	Togo
806	Tonga
810	Trinidad & Tobago
814	Tunisia
818	Turkey
827	Uganda
840	USSR
843	Byelorussian SSR
844	Ukraine SSR
860	United Arab Emirates
868	Arab Republic of Egypt
870	United Kingdom
882	Tanzania
890	United States of America
906	Upper Volta
910	Uruguay
914	Venezuela
918	Democratic Republic of Viet Nam
920	Republic of Viet Nam
928	Western Samoa
936	Yemen Arab Republic
942	Yugoslavia
946	Zambia

A. INDIVIDUAL PROFILE

1. Your present position in the unit

   a. Insert the number of year(s) you have been a member of your present unit — . . . 1 / 23 - 24

   b. Please indicate,

      i. how many scientists and engineers you directly supervise in the unit — . . . 25 - 26

      ii. how many technicians you directly supervise in the unit — . . . 27 - 28

   c. Write the last two digits of the year of your appointment as head of the unit — . . . 29 - 30

2. Personal information, formal education and research and experimental development (R&D) experience

   a. Year of birth — . . . 31 - 32

   b. Sex 1 = male
      2 = female — . . 33

   C. Number of years full-time equivalent education/training (since first year primary school including post-graduate studies and research leading to a Doctor's degree (Ph.D.)) — . . . 34 - 35

   d. Number of year(s) of R&D experience — . . . 36 - 37

   e. Fields of specialization acquired in your R&D work

   Please list below in CAPITAL LETTERS and WITH THEIR 6 DIGIT CODE NUMBERS up to three items taken from the attached list "International Standard Nomenclature for fields of science or technology". Specify the countries where you primarily acquired your specializations, using the country codes supplied on the opposite page.

   Caution: IF you acquired your fields of specialization in your unit's country WRITE "OOO", otherwise write the country code of the appropriate country.

Fields of specialization	Code number	Country
1.__________	38 43	44 . . . 46
2.__________	47 52	53 . . . 55
3.__________	56 61	62 . . . 64

3. Contribution to products of the unit

Please indicate the NUMBER of different types of products issued during the PAST THREE YEARS and resulting from YOUR WORK in the unit

Caution: Please fill in ALL SPACES
either with a number, including "0" if none
or with "NA" if not applicable
with "UN" if unable to reply

		Number of products
a.	Books (including editorship)	. . . 1/65-66
b.	Original scientific or technical articles published in the open literature	. . . 67 68
c.	Patents or patent applications	. . . 69-70
d.	Algorithms, blueprints, flowcharts, drawings, etc.	. . . 71-72
e.	Reviews and bibliographies published in the open literature	. . . 73-74
f.	Internal reports on original R&D work within your organization	. . . 75-76
g.	Routine internal reports	. . . 77-78
h.	Other (please specify)	. . . 79-80

____

____

B. REMUNERATION AND ADVANCEMENT

Please indicate your views towards your remuneration, your advancement and the actual advancement system for each of the following pairs of statements below by selecting ONE number for each and writing it in the space provided

Caution: Please avoid leaving blanks by writing in the space provided "NA" if not applicable, or "UN" if unable to reply

1. Remuneration

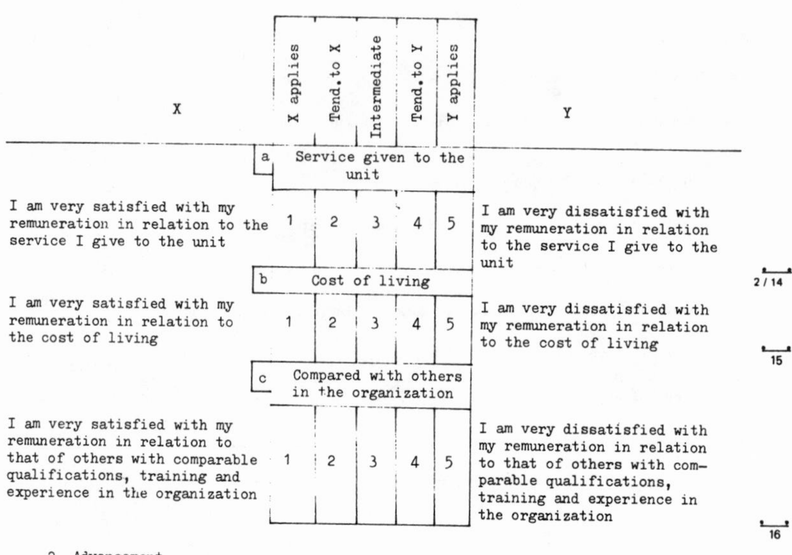

X	X applies	Tend. to X	Intermediate	Tend. to Y	Y applies	Y	
	a Service given to the unit						
I am very satisfied with my remuneration in relation to the service I give to the unit	1	2	3	4	5	I am very dissatisfied with my remuneration in relation to the service I give to the unit	2/14
	b Cost of living						
I am very satisfied with my remuneration in relation to the cost of living	1	2	3	4	5	I am very dissatisfied with my remuneration in relation to the cost of living	15
	c Compared with others in the organization						
I am very satisfied with my remuneration in relation to that of others with comparable qualifications, training and experience in the organization	1	2	3	4	5	I am very dissatisfied with my remuneration in relation to that of others with comparable qualifications, training and experience in the organization	16

2. Advancement

X						Y	
	a Advancement						
My advancement opportunities seem to be essentially dependent upon my performance in my work	1	2	3	4	5	My advancement opportunities seem to be essentially independent of my performance in my work	17
	b Advancement prospects						
I am very satisfied with my advancement opportunities in relation to those of others with comparable qualifications, training and experience	1	2	3	4	5	I am very dissatisfied with my advancement opportunities in relation to those of others with comparable qualifications, training and experience	18

C. ACTIVITIES AND TASKS PERFORMED

Caution: Please read all this page carefully before answering the questions

> Design and engineering studies: Consist of the preparation of (original) blueprints and other supporting material such as cost/effectiveness calculations, which combine existing products and processes with a view to manufacturing goods or delivery services.
>
> Extension work: Consists of helping to carry original research and experimental development results into effective practical application.
>
> Scientific observation and/or monitoring work: Cover repetitive scientific work performed through established practices with existing instrumentation and aimed at collecting quantitative or qualitative data on natural phenomena. Monitoring work includes an element of compulsory periodicity.
>
> Scientific surveys: Consist of the systematic probing into the characteristics and dynamics of observable sites or phenomena.

1. Activities performed

Please indicate below IN PERCENTAGES how much of your total work time (= 100%) you have spent THIS year ON

a. Research and experimental development

i.	Inside the unit	. . . .% (2/19 21)
ii.	Outside the unit	. . . .% (22 24)

b. Other scientific and technical functions (inside or outside the unit)

i.	Administration	. . . .% (25 27)
ii.	Teaching, including the preparation of pedagogic material and popularization of science	. . . .% (28 30)
iii.	Consulting work (including medical), extension work,* standardization work	. . . .% (31 33)
iv.	Scientific information and/or documentation not directly relevant to your research	. . . .% (34 36)
v.	Routine and control analysis or measurements, scientific observations and/or monitoring work,* scientific surveys*	. . . .% (37 39)
vi.	Design and engineering studies,* feasibility studies	. . . .% (40 42)
vii.	Other professional functions	. . . .% (43 45)
	TOTAL (a) and (b)	1 0 0 %

2. Number of on-going research projects*

> Research project: A group of interrelated research and experimental development activities aimed at obtaining original results by creating new theories and methods, improving the understanding of nature, inventing and developing new products or processes, discovering new fields of investigation, etc. The progress achieved on a research project is usually reported upon separately as one whole to higher hierarchical levels or sponsoring authorities of the unit. The work performed may - or may not - be directed towards a specific practical aim.

If you have been directly INVOLVED during the last three years inside or outside the unit, either as EXECUTOR OR PROJECT OFFICER in the carrying out of ONE or MORE R & D projects, please indicate how many

a. Inside the unit . . . 2/46-47

b. Outside the unit . . . 48-49

3. Areas of activity in research and experimental development (R & D)

You are given below a list of main areas of research and experimental development activities (R & D) usually performed by a research unit. Please WRITE the number in the space provided corresponding to your PERSONAL INVOLVEMENT in EACH AREA

Caution: Please avoid leaving blanks, by writing in the space provided "NA" if not applicable or "UN" if unable to reply

My personal involvement is: Areas	Very High	High	Medium	Low	Very Low	
a. Perception and identification of an area of interest	1	2	3	4	5	. . 50
b. Literature review	1	2	3	4	5	. . 51
c. Problem precision: conceptualization, formulation, analysis	1	2	3	4	5	. . 52
d. Orientation and perception of methods and techniques, apparatus, etc.	1	2	3	4	5	. . 53
e. Time-table, administration, organization and economic considerations	1	2	3	4	5	. . 54
f. Formulation and statement of hypotheses	1	2	3	4	5	. . 55
g. Research design: planning, strategies and experimental outlay	1	2	3	4	5	. . 56
h. Collection and production of data, including experimental work	1	2	3	4	5	. . 57
j. Results: detailed analysis, interpretation and conclusions	1	2	3	4	5	. . 58
k. Report writing, e.g. for publication, dissertation, etc.	1	2	3	4	5	. . 59

D. METHODS USED IN THE RESEARCH WORK

1. Please indicate below how, in your opinion, the following methods are significant in your research work, by rating each of them in the following way

   1 = insignificant

   2 = tending to be insignificant

   3 = tending to be essential

   4 = essential

   Caution: Please avoid leaving blanks by writing in the space provided, "NA" if not applicable or "UN" if unable to reply

   a. Systematic use of a hypothesis followed by experiments or observation to verify the hypothesis — 2/60

   b. Formulation of axioms or postulates from which theorems are deduced through applications of formalized logic — 61

   c. Factorial analysis, multivariate analysis, probabilistic models, dimensional analysis models, etc. — 62

   d. Operational models, morphological models, inductive models, predictive models, matrices of discovery, system analysis, etc. — 63

   e. Brainstorming, forecasting, synectics, etc. — 64

2. Interdisciplinary orientation

   a. In carrying out your research projects, do you borrow some methods, theories or other specific elements developed in other fields, not normally used in your research

      If No, write "0", and move to Part E of the Questionnaire

      If Yes, write "1" and continue — 65

   b. Using the "International standard nomenclature for fields of science or technology", write the names of these other fields and their TWO-DIGIT major category codes

Name	Code
________________	66-67
________________	68-69
________________	70-71

E. SCIENTIFIC FIELDS AND RESEARCH PROJECTS OF THE RESEARCH UNIT

> Scientific fields: A list of scientific fields and disciplines is provided with this questionnaire
>
> **Research project: See p. – SA 6 –

1. Scientific fields in which the research unit is actively engaged

   Please CHECK in the attached "International standard nomenclature for fields of science or technology" SIX ITEMS which correspond to the SCIENTIFIC FIELDS * in which your unit has been actively engaged during the last three years and LIST THEM BELOW in CAPITAL LETTERS AND WITH THEIR SIX-DIGIT CODE NUMBER

a. ______________________ 2/72 77

b. ______________________ 3/14 19

c. ______________________ 20 25

d. ______________________ 26 31

e. ______________________ 32 37

f. ______________________ 38 43

2. NUMBER of research projects * carried out inside the unit at the PRESENT TIME 44-45

3. Approximate duration from now on of the MOST IMPORTANT – in terms of volume of work and/or scientific significance – research projects going on in the unit (up to six)

   Please indicate below, FOR EACH OF THESE RESEARCH PROJECTS

   i. the number of years the project has been going on

   ii. the number of years it is expected to continue

   DO NOT LEAVE BLANKS for any research project

   Caution: Avoid blanks by answering where necessary "NA" if not applicable or "UN" if unable to reply

	Number years project going on	Number years expected to continue
Project 1	46-47	48-49
Project 2	50-51	52-53
Project 3	54-55	56-57
Project 4	58-59	60-61
Project 5	62-63	64-65
Project 6	66-67	68-69

F. SCIENTIFIC EXCHANGES OF THE RESEARCH UNIT

1. Visiting scientists and engineers during the past year

   a. Please indicate the total number of visiting scientists and engineers that your unit has received during the past year for at least 5 working days

      i. From your country 3/70 72

      ii. From abroad 73 75

   b. Please indicate for each of the following pairs of extreme statements, the column which most accurately describes your views about the qualification of the units from which you have received visitors during the past year by selecting ONE number for each pair of statements below and writing it in the space provided

      Caution: Please avoid leaving blanks by writing in the space provided "NA" if not applicable or "UN" if unable to reply

X		X applies	Tend. to X	Intermediate	Tend. to Y	Y applies	Y	
These scientists and engineers who have visited your unit, generally represent more scientifically and technically advanced units than your own	i	from your country					These scientists and engineers who have visited your unit, generally represent less scientifically and technically advanced units than your own	
		1	2	3	4	5		76
	ii	from abroad						
		1	2	3	4	5		77

2. Scientists and engineers of your unit sent out during the past year

   a. Please indicate the number of visits to other units made by scientists and engineers of your unit for scientific or technical purposes during the past year for at least 5 working days

      i. To other units in your country 78 80

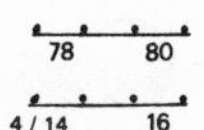

      ii. To units abroad 4/14 16

b. Please indicate, for the following pair of extreme statements, the column which most accurately describes your views about the qualification of the units abroad which have been visited by scientists and engineers of your unit during the past year by selecting ONE number for the pair of statements below and writing it in the space provided

Caution: Please avoid leaving blanks by writing in the space provided, "NA" if not applicable or "UN" if unable to reply

X		X applies	Tend. to X	Intermediate	Tend. to Y	Y applies	Y	
The units visited by the scientists and engineers of your unit generally represent more scientifically and technically advanced units than your own	i	in your country					The units visited by the scientists and engineers of your unit generally represent less scientifically and technically advanced units than your own	
		1	2	3	4	5		4/17
	ii	abroad						
		1	2	3	4	5		18

3. Information and material flows

a. Please indicate for the last year approximately how many of the forms of research results specified below your unit has sent to (no matter who takes the initiative of sending) or received from other individuals or organizations working in the same field

Caution: Please avoid leaving blanks by writing "0" if none, "NA" if not applicable or "UN" if unable to reply

	Sent to	Received from
i. unpublished documents	19-20	21-22
ii. publications	23-24	25-26
iii. materials (e.g. tapes, films, substrates, samples, etc.)	27-28	29-30

4. Sharing and/or joint management of the research work

   a. How many projects has YOUR UNIT conducted during the past year involving sharing of work and/or joint management with other unit(s) in the country or abroad

      Please indicate the NUMBER (including "0" if none) . . . 4/31 - 32

   b. What is the percentage of the unit's research and experimental development activities (R&D) involving sharing of the work and/or joint management . . . .% 33 35

5. Scientific and technical meetings

   How many open national or international meetings with external participation has your unit either organized or been represented at during the past year (conferences, symposia, seminars, etc.)

   Please indicate the NUMBER (or "0", if none) in the appropriate spaces below

	Scientific/technical meetings with external participation
a. Number of scientific/technical meetings organized by the unit itself	. . . 36 - 37
b. Number of scientific/technical meetings attended by members of the unit	. . . 38 - 39

G. EVALUATING THE WORK OF THE RESEARCH UNIT

1. How frequently is a systematic evaluation of the work of the unit (i.e. an evaluation repeated at regular intervals) done
   Select ONE number below and write it in the space provided

   1 = one or more times each month

   2 = several times a year

   3 = once each year . . 40

   4 = every few years

   5 = never

   If NEVER go to Question H , page SA 10

2. Who is responsible for carrying out the systematic evaluation
   CHECK ALL THAT APPLY by writing "1" if YES or "0" if NO

   a. scientists and engineers of the unit . . 41

   b. the head(s) of the unit . . 42

   c. persons higher up in the hierarchy of the organization . . 43

   d. persons outside the organization . . 44

H. CHOICE OF RESEARCH THEMES OF THE RESEARCH UNIT

1. Write in percentages how much each of the following factors influences the choice of research themes of your unit by writing the numbers in the spaces provided

   i. Guidelines and/or instructions from national science policy-making bodies (ministries for science, academies of science, research councils etc.) . . . .% 4/45 47

   ii. Guidelines coming from the authority or industrial enterprise(s) controlling the organization to which your unit belongs . . . .% 48 50

   iii. Guidelines from the governing organ(s) of the organization to which your unit belongs . . . .% 51 53

   iv. Practical needs identified by your unit . . . .% 54 56

   v. The scientific significance and promise of the research . . . .% 57 59

   vi. Other (please specify) . . . .% 60 62

   ____

   ____

   TOTAL 1 0 0 %

2. Attitude of governing board towards research

   How strongly research-minded is the governing board of the organization to which your unit belongs

   Please select ONE number from below and write it in the space provided

   1 = very research-minded (X)
   2 = tendency to (X) above
   3 = "average" as regards extremes (X) and (Y) . . 63
   4 = tendency to (Y) below
   5 = not very research-minded (Y)

3. Influence of the financing sources

   How dependent is your unit on the sources which finance it in the choice of its research themes

   Please select ONE number from below and write in the space provided

   1 = dependent (X)
   2 = tendency to (X) above
   3 = "average" as regards extremes (X) and (Y) . . 64
   4 = tendency to (Y) below
   5 = independent (X)

J. WORKING CLIMATE IN THE RESEARCH UNIT

This question aims to obtain your views on the climate of the unit, such as attitudes on technical and non-technical matters, personal attitudes and perceptions, personal involvement in the work, and atmosphere of the unit, etc.

Please indicate, for each of the following pairs of extreme statements, the column which most accurately describes your views by selecting ONE number for each pair below and writing it in the space provided

Caution: Please avoid leaving blanks by writing in the space provided "NA" if not applicable or "UN" if unable to reply

1. Arguments

X	X applies	Tend. to X	Intermediate	Tend. to Y	Y applies	Y	
I am rarely involved in unconstructive arguments over technical matters						I am often involved in unconstructive arguments over technical matters	
a With others in the unit	1	2	3	4	5		4 / 65
b With the administrators of the organization	1	2	3	4	5		66
c With leadership in the organization	1	2	3	4	5		67
d Non-technical arguments							
I am rarely involved in unpleasant arguments over non-technical matters (politics, religion, race, colour, personal matters) with others in the organization	1	2	3	4	5	I am often involved in unpleasant arguments over non-technical matters (politics, religion, race, colour, personal matters) with others in the organization	68

2. Individual attitudes and perceptions

X		X applies	Tend. to X	Intermediate	Tend. to Y	Y applies	Y	
	a	Feeling of job security in my work						
I have a feeling of high job security in my work		1	2	3	4	5	I have a feeling of low job security in my work	4 / 69
	b	Thinking of leaving the unit						
I rarely if ever consider leaving the unit		1	2	3	4	5	I would leave the unit if I had a suitable opportunity to do so	70
	c	Other employment opportunities						
I anticipate few difficulties in finding a similar or better position should I leave the unit		1	2	3	4	5	I see little chance of finding a similar or better position should I leave the unit	71
	d	Voluntary overtime						
I do a great deal of voluntary overtime		1	2	3	4	5	I do no voluntary overtime	72
	e	Optimal time pressure						
I work under much less time pressure than I think is optimal for me		1	2	3	4	5	I work under much more time pressure than I think is optimal for me	73
	f	Knowledge of assessment of my performance						
I am very well informed of the assessment of my performance		1	2	3	4	5	I am very poorly informed of the assessment of my performance	74
	g	Satisfaction with training and career development facilities						
I am very satisfied with the training and career development facilities available		1	2	3	4	5	I am very dissatisfied with the training and career development facilities available	75
	h	Manpower recruitment system						
I am very satisfied with the manpower recruitment system of the unit		1	2	3	4	5	I am very dissatisfied with the manpower recruitment system of the unit	76

3. <u>General atmosphere of the unit</u>

X	X applies	Tend. to X	Intermediate	Tend. to Y	Y applies	Y	
	a	Innovation and pioneering					
There is generally a very innovative spirit and sense of pioneering in the unit	1	2	3	4	5	There is a very traditional spirit and stultifying atmosphere in the unit	4/77
	b	Dedication to the work					
There is an atmosphere of great dedication to work in the unit	1	2	3	4	5	There is the feeling that everyone in the unit only works to make a living	78
	c	Consideration towards new ideas in R&D or other technical matters					
Nearly all new ideas for research or other technical matters are given adequate consideration	1	2	3	4	5	Very few new ideas for research or other technical matters are given adequate consideration	79
	d	Consideration towards new ideas in non-technical matters					
New ideas for improvement in non-technical matters are given serious consideration	1	2	3	4	5	New ideas on non-technical matters are ignored and existing practices are generally maintained	80
	e	Acceptance of ideas coming from junior staff or technicians of the unit					
New ideas on all matters from junior staff or technicians are as readily considered as if they originate from the senior staff	1	2	3	4	5	Any new ideas considered at all are only taken seriously if they come from senior staff	5/14
	f	Co-operation among scientists & engineers in the unit					
There is a very high degree of co-operation among the scientists and engineers of the unit	1	2	3	4	5	There is very little or no co-operation among the scientists and engineers of the unit	15
	g	Scientific/technical staff meetings in the unit					
Scientific/technical staff meetings are convened very frequently	1	2	3	4	5	Scientific/technical staff meetings are very rare in the unit	16
	h	Participation of the technical/service staff in meetings					
The technical/service staff are very often invited to participate in scientific/technical staff meetings	1	2	3	4	5	The technical/service staff are very rarely or never invited to participate in scientific/technical staff meetings	17

X	X applies	Tend. to X	Intermediate	Tend. to Y	Y applies	Y	
	j Administrative restrictions on scientists & engineers of the unit						
The restrictions imposed on the scientists and engineers of the unit by administrative regulations are minimal	1	2	3	4	5	The restrictions imposed on the scientists and engineers by administrative regulations are excessive	5 / 18
	k Distractions						
There are few if any distractions (noise, phone calls, unforeseen visits, etc.) to interrupt the work in the unit	1	2	3	4	5	There are so many distractions that work is practically impossible	19

4. Types of assistance received from other members of the research unit

Questions in this section inquire about types of assistance which you may in general receive from other members of the research unit

In answering, please consider all members of the unit, professional and non-professional

Caution: Please avoid leaving blanks by writing in the space provided, "O" if none, "NA" if not applicable, "UN" if unable to reply

a. HOW MANY people in the unit are particularly useful TO YOU for giving technical information — 20-21

b. HOW MANY people in the unit are particularly useful TO YOU for providing original ideas — 22-23

c. HOW MANY people in the unit are particularly useful TO YOU for providing administrative help (e.g. in getting needed resources and facilities, information about administrative developments, etc.) — 24-25

d. What is the TOTAL number of SEPARATE people referred to in your responses to (a), (b) and (c) above — 26-27

K. BUDGET, FACILITIES AND SERVICES AVAILABLE TO THE RESEARCH UNIT

Please indicate, for each of the following pairs of extreme statements, the column which most accurately describes your views with regard to facilities and services available to the unit by selecting ONE number for each pair of statements below and writing it in the space provided

Caution: Please avoid leaving blanks, by writing in the space provided "NA" if not applicable or "UN" if unable to reply

X		X applies	Tend. to X	Intermediate	Tend. to Y	Y applies	Y	
	a	Working space						
The space required for the work of the unit is highly adequate		1	2	3	4	5	The space required for the work of the unit is highly inadequate	5 / 28
	b	Scientific equipment						
The unit is well equipped scientifically		1	2	3	4	5	The unit is poorly equipped scientifically	29
	c	Office equipment						
The unit has excellent office equipment		1	2	3	4	5	The unit has very poor office equipment	30
	d	Sharing of equipment						
The way in which equipment is shared in the unit is very satisfactory		1	2	3	4	5	The way in which equipment is shared in the unit is very unsatisfactory	31
	e	Administrative and secretarial assistance						
The administrative and secretarial assistance the unit receives is very satisfactory		1	2	3	4	5	The administrative and secretarial assistance the unit receives is very unsatisfactory	32
	f	Technical assistance						
The technical assistance and services the unit receives are very satisfactory		1	2	3	4	5	The technical assistance and services the unit receives are very unsatisfactory	33
	g	Library facilities						
The library facilities available to the unit are highly satisfactory		1	2	3	4	5	The library facilities available to the unit are highly unsatisfactory	34
	h	Information services						
The information services available to the unit are very satisfactory		1	2	3	4	5	The information services available to the unit are very unsatisfactory	35
	j	Adequacy of the budget						
The current budget of the unit is adequate to allow successful completion of the unit's current research and/or scientific tasks		1	2	3	4	5	The current budget of the unit is not adequate to allow successful completion of the unit's current research and/or scientific tasks	36
	k	Human resources						
I am very satisfied with the human resources available to the unit, as compared with its current research project(s) and/or scientific task(s)		1	2	3	4	5	I am very dissatisfied with the human resources available to the unit, as compared with its current research project(s) and/or scientific task(s)	37

L. PATTERNS OF INFLUENCE

Please indicate how much influence each of the following has on the research and management decisions relevant to the unit by selecting ONE number from below and writing it in the space provided according to the amount of influence

1 = high influence (X)
2 = tendency to (X) above
3 = "intermediate" as regards extremes (X) and (Y)
4 = tendency to (Y) below
5 = low influence (Y)

	Unit head(s)	Other scientists & engineers inside unit	Leadership outside unit but inside organization	Authorities or customers outside organization
a. Influence in Research Work				
i. Choice of specific research tasks	5 / 38	39	40	41
ii. Choice of methods used	42	43	44	45
iii. Publication and circulation of research results	46	47	48	49
b. Influence on management decisions				
i. Allocation of work within the unit	50	51	52	53
ii. Co-ordination and/or co-operation with other units	54	55	56	57
iii. Use of training and career development facilities	58	59	60	61
iv. Hiring personnel for a definite period	62	63	64	65
v. Termination of employment of personnel	66	67	68	69
vi. Hiring or buying low-cost equipment (value up to $500 US per piece)	70	71	72	73

N. ORGANIZATION AND PLANNING OF THE RESEARCH WORK IN THE RESEARCH UNIT

1. Please characterize the organization and planning of the research work in the unit by selecting for each item ONE number from below and writing it in the space provided

Caution: Please avoid leaving blanks by writing in the space provided "NA" if not applicable or "UN" if unable to reply

X	X applies	Tend. to X	Intermediate	Tend. to Y	Y applies	Y	
	a Scientific/technological objectives						
The scientific/technological objectives of the research work performed by the unit are closely related	1	2	3	4	5	The scientific/technological objectives of the research work performed by the unit are loosely connected	5/74
	b Nature of research work						
The nature of research work in the unit involves extensive co-operation among its members	1	2	3	4	5	The nature of research work in the unit is organized mainly on an individual basis	75
	c Budget of the unit						
The budget of the unit is established as a whole, without any indication of the share allotted to each of its research workers	1	2	3	4	5	The budget of the unit is established as a collection of the budgetary allotment earmarked for each of its research workers	76

2. Research planning in the unit

Please indicate the extent to which formal planning methods are used in the research by selecting for each item ONE number from below and writing it in the space provided

1 = usually
2 = often
3 = sometimes
4 = seldom
5 = very rarely

Caution: Please avoid leaving blanks by writing in the space provided "NA" if not applicable or "UN" if unable to reply

a. Formal planning of the research (e.g. by means of opportunity and constraint analysis, environmental analysis, intuitive forecasting methods, dynamic system modelling, relevance matrix methods, risk analysis, probability methods, etc. 77

b. Scheduling the research(e.g. PPBS - Programme Planning and Budget System, PERT - Programme Evaluation and Review Technique, RPD - Research Planning Diagrams, etc.) 78

Q. CONTACTS WITH OTHER UNITS

Questions in these sections inquire about the nature and frequency of contacts both inside and outside the organization to which your unit belongs, and seek your views about their quality and their influence on the efficiency of the research work of the unit

Please write ONE number below in each of the spaces provided

Caution: Please avoid leaving blanks by writing in the space provided "NA" if not applicable or "UN" if unable to reply

1. Is there within easy access AND active in the same or similar field(s)

   a. One or more institutions of higher education

      If yes, write how many
      If no, write "0" 6/14 - 15

   b. One or more research units belonging to your organization

      If yes, write how many
      If no, write "0" 16 - 17

   c. One or more research units outside your organization

      If yes, write how many
      If no, write "0" 18 - 19

2. Frequency of contacts

   1 = very rarely
   2 = annually
   3 = quarterly
   4 = monthly
   5 = weekly
   6 = daily

   a. How often do you discuss your work with members of other research units within your organization 20

   b. How often do you visit (or are you visited by) colleagues from other organizations working in the same field either in your own country or abroad 21

3. Satisfaction about contacts

   1 = very satisfied (X)
   2 = tendency to (X) above
   3 = "intermediate" as regards extremes (X) and (Y)
   4 = tendency to (Y) below
   5 = very dissatisfied (Y)

   a. How satisfied are you with the opportunities you have to discuss your work with members of other research units within your organization 22

   b. How satisfied are you with the opportunities you have to visit colleagues in other organizations working in the same field 23

4. Effect of contacts

X	X applies	Tend. to X	Intermediate	Tend. to Y	Y applies	Y
	Effect on scientific or technical performance					
There is a highly beneficial effect on my scientific or technical performance arising from contacts with other units	1	2	3	4	5	There is almost no discernible effect on my scientific or technical performance arising from contacts with other units . . 6/24

5. Research teams in the same field

Please list below names of up to five people who work in your speciality, or in the closest possible specialities to your own, either in your country or abroad

Caution: Please (i) PRINT their names and initial(s) of first name(s) in CAPITAL LETTERS

(ii) INDICATE their MAILING ADDRESS as completely as possible (that is: name of their institution; country; state, county or province; street and no.), also in CAPITAL LETTERS

1 ____

2 ____

3 ____

4 ____

5 ____

R. PRODUCTS OF THE RESEARCH UNIT

Please indicate the NUMBER of DIFFERENT TYPES of written products and/or prototypes issued during the PAST THREE YEARS and resulting from WORK done by members of YOUR UNIT

Caution: Please fill in ALL SPACES

either with a number, including "0" if appropriate

or with "NA" if not applicable
with "UN" if unable to reply

	Number of products produced by the unit
1. Written Products	
a. Books (including editorship)	. . . 6 / 25 - 26
b. Original scientific or technical articles published in the open literature	
i. in the unit's country	. . . 27 - 28
ii. abroad	. . . 29 30
c. Patents or patent applications	
i. in the unit's country	. . . 31 - 32
ii. abroad (with government guarantee)	. . . 33 - 34
d. Algorithms, blueprints, flowcharts, drawings, etc.	. . . 35 - 36
e. Reviews and bibliographies published in the open literature	. . . 37 - 38
f. Internal reports on original R & D work within your organization	. . . 39 - 40
g. Routine internal reports	. . . 41 - 42
h. Other written products (please specify) ____________________ ____________________	. . . 43 - 44
2. Prototypes and other Undocumented Products	
a. Experimental prototypes of devices, instruments and apparatus, components of devices, etc.	. . . 45 - 46
b. Experimental materials such as fibres, plastics, glass, metals, alloys, substrates, chemicals, drugs, plants, etc.	. . . 47 - 48
c. Prototype computer programmes	. . . 49 - 50
d. Audio-visual materials	. . . 51 - 52
e. Other undocumented products (please specify) ____________________ ____________________	. . . 53 - 54

S. APPLICATION OF THE RESULTS OBTAINED BY THE RESEARCH UNIT

Please indicate, for each of the following pairs of extreme statements, the column which most accurately describes your views on the practical application of the research results of your unit during the LAST THREE YEARS by selecting ONE number for each pair of statements below and writing it in the space provided

<u>Caution:</u> Please avoid leaving blanks, by writing in the space provided "NA" if not applicable or "UN" if unable to reply

	X	X applies	Tend. to X	Intermediate	Tend. to Y	Y applies	Y	
a	Most of the unit's research results find follow-up or practical application	1	2	3	4	5	None of the unit's research results find any follow-up or practical application	. . 6 / 55
b	Most of the unit's experimental development activities are made use of	1	2	3	4	5	None of the unit's experimental development activities are made use of	. . 56
c	There is strong pressure from <u>outside</u> the unit to ensure that its results find follow-up or practical application	1	2	3	4	5	There is no pressure from <u>outside</u> the unit to ensure that its results find follow-up in practical application	. . 57
d	The unit maintains close contacts with those ensuring the follow-up or practical application of its results	1	2	3	4	5	The unit does not maintain any contacts with those ensuring the follow-up or practical application of its results	. . 58

T. VALUE OF THE WORK OF THE RESEARCH UNIT

Please indicate, for each of the following pairs of extreme statements, the column which most accurately describes your views about the value of the work of the research unit covering the LAST THREE YEARS by selecting ONE number for each pair of statements below and writing it in the space provided. Since this questionnaire is used in a variety of organizational settings, some questions may be irrelevant to certain individual units

Caution: Please avoid leaving blanks by writing in the space provided "NA" if not applicable or "UN" if unable to reply

X		X applies	Tend. to X	Intermediate	Tend. to Y	Y applies	Y	
	a	Productiveness						
The unit has been highly productive in the sense of adding knowledge, methods or inventions in its field of work work		1	2	3	4	5	The unit's productivity has been very low in the sense defined	6/59
	b	Innovativeness						
The unit has been highly innovative in generating useful new ideas, approaches, methods, inventions or applications in its field of work		1	2	3	4	5	The unit has been very uninnovative in the sense described	60
	c	Effectiveness						
The work of the unit has been extremely useful in helping the organization to which it belongs to carry out its responsibilities with regard to:							The work of the unit has been largely ineffective in furthering the objectives of the organization to which it belongs with regard to:	
	i	Research and experimental development (R&D)						
		1	2	3	4	5		61
	ii	Training of scientists and engineers						
		1	2	3	4	5		62
	d	Scientific/technical objectives other than R&D						
The work of the unit has been extremely useful to its Organization regarding its scientific/technical objectives other than R&D and training (e.g. consulting work, routine and control analysis and studies, scientific information and/or documentation)		1	2	3	4	5	The work of the unit has been largely ineffective for its Organization regarding its scientific/technical objectives other than R&D and training	63

	X	X applies	Tend. to X	Intermediate	Tend. to Y	Y applies	Y	
e		Response from the scientific communities						
i	The unit has a high international reputation	1	2	3	4	5	The unit is virtually unknown abroad	6/64
ii	The publications of the unit are in high demand and often cited in literature	1	2	3	4	5	The publications of the unit are largely ignored	65
f		Social value						
	The social value of applications given (or which may be given) to the results of the unit's work are highly positive	1	2	3	4	5	The social value of applications given (or which may be given) to the results of the unit's work are highly negative	66
g		Usefulness						
	The work of the unit has been extremely useful in helping to solve some current problems facing society	1	2	3	4	5	The work of the unit has been largely ineffective in helping to solve some current problems facing society	67
h		Quality of the work of the unit						
	The unit has been very successful in meeting the quality requirements associated with its work (e.g. design, product performance, validity of results, consumer reception, presentation of findings)	1	2	3	4	5	The unit has been very unsuccessful in meeting the quality requirements associated with its work	68
j		Administrative effectiveness						
	The unit has been very successful with regard to:						The unit has been very unsuccessful with regard to:	
i		Meeting its schedules						
		1	2	3	4	5		69
ii		Staying within its operating budget						
		1	2	3	4	5		70
k		General contribution to science or technology						
	The unit has made an outstanding contribution to scientific or technical development in its field	1	2	3	4	5	The unit has made little or no contribution to scientific or technical development in its field	71

Question J.2 in the SB Questionnaire

2. Individual attitudes and perception

	Item	X	X applies	Tend. to X	Intermediate	Tend. to Y	Y applies	Y	
a	Feeling of job security in my work	I have a feeling of high job security in my work	1	2	3	4	5	I have a feeling of low job security in my work	2/70
b	Thinking of leaving the unit	I rarely if ever consider leaving the unit	1	2	3	4	5	I would leave the unit if I had a suitable opportunity to do so	71
c	Interest of the work	The work I do is very interesting	1	2	3	4	5	The work I do is not very interesting	72
d	Adaptation to the work	My tasks in the unit are in excess of my capabilities	1	2	3	4	5	My tasks in the unit are far below my capabilities	73
e	Other employment opportunities	I anticipate few difficulties in finding a similar or better position should I leave the unit	1	2	3	4	5	I see little chance of finding a similar or better position should I leave the unit	74
f	Voluntary overtime	I do a great deal of voluntary overtime	1	2	3	4	5	I do no voluntary overtime	75
g	Optimal time pressure	I work under much less time pressure than I think is optimal for me	1	2	3	4	5	I work under much more time pressure than I think is optimal for me	76
h	Knowledge of assessment of my performance	I am very well informed of the assessment of my performance	1	2	3	4	5	I am very poorly informed of the assessment of my performance	77
j	Responsibilities desired	I would like to have more responsibilities in the unit	1	2	3	4	5	I would like to have less responsibilities in the unit	78
k	Satisfaction with training and career development facilities	I am very satisfied with the training and career development facilities available	1	2	3	4	5	I am very dissatisfied with the training and career development facilities available	79
m	Manpower recruitment system	I am very satisfied with the manpower recruitment system of the unit	1	2	3	4	5	I am very dissatisfied with the manpower recruitment system of the unit	80

Question J.4 in the SB Questionnaire

X		X applies	Tend. to X	Intermediate	Tend. to Y	Y applies	Y	
	k	Distractions						
There are few if any distractions (noise, phone calls, unforeseen visits, etc.) to interrupt the work in the unit		1	2	3	4	5	There are so many distractions that work is practically impossible	3/23

4. Types of assistance received from other members of the research unit

Questions in this section inquire about types of assistance which you may in general receive from other members of the research unit

In answering, please consider all members of the unit, professional and non-professional

Caution: Please avoid leaving blanks by writing in the space provided, "O" if none, "NA" if not applicable, "UN" if unable to reply

a. HOW MANY people in the unit are particularly useful TO YOU for giving technical information 24-25

b. HOW MANY people in the unit are particularly useful TO YOU for providing original ideas 26-27

c. HOW MANY people in the unit are particularly useful TO YOU for providing administrative help (e.g. in getting needed resources and facilities, information about administrative developments, etc.) 28-29

d. What is the TOTAL number of SEPARATE people referred to in your responses to (a), (b), and (c) above 30-31

e. Please indicate for each of the 3 given situations ONE number from below, by putting it in the space provided

1 = Head of the unit

2 = Scientists or engineers

3 = Other personnel

THE member of the unit MOST useful to you for:

i. giving technical information 32

ii. providing original ideas 33

iii. providing administrative help 34

M. IMMEDIATE SUPERVISOR

Please indicate, for each of the following pairs of extreme statements the column which most accurately describes your contacts with and satisfaction towards your immediate supervisor by selecting ONE number for each pair of statements below and writing it in the space provided

Caution: Please avoid leaving blanks by writing in the space provided "NA" if not applicable or "UN" if unable to reply

X		X applies	Tend. to X	Intermediate	Tend. to Y	Y applies	Y	
	1	Contacts with immediate supervisor						
I have daily working contacts with my immediate supervisor	a	1	2	3	4	5	I rarely have working contacts with my immediate supervisor	4/14
There is a highly beneficial effect on my scientific or technical performance arising from contacts with my immediate supervisor	b	1	2	3	4	5	There is almost no discernible effect on my scientific or technical performance arising from contacts with my immediate supervisor	15
	2	Satisfaction with immediate supervisor						
I am very satisfied with my immediate supervisor as regards his:							I am very dissatisfied with my immediate supervisor as regards his:	
	a	professional ability						
		1	2	3	4	5		16
	b	personality and character						
		1	2	3	4	5		17
	c	leadership qualities						
		1	2	3	4	5		18
	d	knowledge of the fields in which the unit is active						
		1	2	3	4	5		19
	e	the amount of work <u>he</u> does						
		1	2	3	4	5		20
	f	support of my work						
		1	2	3	4	5		21

P. RESEARCH PLANNING IN THE RESEARCH UNIT

Please indicate, for each of the following pairs of extreme statements, the column which most accurately describes your views and/or degree of satisfaction about the research planning and the execution of the work in the unit by selecting ONE number for each pair of statements below and writing it in the space provided

Caution: Please avoid leaving blanks by writing in the space provided "NA" if not applicable or "UN" if unable to reply

1. Planning of the research work

X		X applies	Tend. to X	Intermediate	Tend. to Y	Y applies	Y	
	a	Adequacy of the research planning						
The research planning is very well conceived		1	2	3	4	5	The planning tends to be poorly conceived	4/22
	b	Interest of the research activities						
The research activities of the unit are very interesting and conceptually exciting		1	2	3	4	5	The reseach activities tend to be uninteresting and unimaginative	23
	c	Coherence of the research programme						
The research programme of the unit is highly coherent		1	2	3	4	5	The research programme is utterly fragmented	24

2. Information on research and planning

X							Y	
	a	Information on the on-going research						
I am kept very well informed of all aspects of the research carried out by the unit		1	2	3	4	5	I am kept in ignorance of most aspects of the on-going research	25
	b	Information on research planning						
I am kept very well informed of all aspects of the research planning of the unit		1	2	3	4	5	I am kept in ignorance of most aspects of the research planning in the unit	26
	c	Participation in research planning						
I participate at every stage in the planning of the research		1	2	3	4	5	I am kept right out of the planning of the research	27

A. INDIVIDUAL PROFILE

1. Please characterize your <u>present position</u> in the unit

   a. Insert the number of year(s) you have been a member of your present unit — . . . 1/23 - 24

   b. Characterize your position in the unit by selecting ONE number from below and writing it in the space provided

      1 = technician, designer, draftsman, etc.

      2 = laboratory assistant

      3 = secretarial assistant — . . 25

      4 = administrative assistant

      5 = other specialized worker

         (Please specify)________________________

2. Please characterize your <u>formal education and work experience</u>

   a. Year of birth — . . . 26 - 27

   b. Sex — 1 = male; 2 = female — . . 28

   c. Number of years of full-time education (since first year primary school) — . . . 29 - 30

   d. Number of year(s) of work experience — . . . 31 - 32

Portion of Question J.3 in the TS Questionnaire (items j–p only)

	X	X applies	Tend. to X	Intermediate	Tend. to Y	Y applies	Y	
j		Administrative restrictions on scientists & engineers of the unit						
	The restrictions imposed on the scientists and engineers of the unit by administrative regulations are minimal	1	2	3	4	5	The restrictions imposed on the scientists and engineers by administrative regulations are excessive	1/60
k		Distractions						
	There are few if any distractions (noise, phone calls, unforeseen visits, etc.) to interrupt the work in the unit	1	2	3	4	5	There are so many distractions that work is practically impossible	61
m		Knowledge of the activities of the unit						
	I am kept very well informed of the affairs of the unit	1	2	3	4	5	I am not kept informed of the affairs of the unit	62
n		Equipment						
	I am very satisfied with the equipment available for my work	1	2	3	4	5	I am very dissatisfied with the equipment available for my work	63
p		Services						
	I am very satisfied with the services available for my work	1	2	3	4	5	I am very dissatisfied with the services available for my work	64